CANADIAN FOREIGN POLICY AND
INTERNATIONAL ECONOMIC REGIMES

As the world economy becomes increasingly interdependent, and
Canada broadens its position as a trading nation, the country's political
and economic welfare will directly depend on its response and reaction
to a wide range of economic regimes which govern the international
economy. This book is an important and timely analysis of past and
current Canadian foreign policy towards both the formal and less
formal regimes which regulate such areas as international trade and
financial transactions, international service industries, resources, and
the environment. Written from a broad range of perspectives and
including chapters by political scientists, economists, lawyers, and
business and policy analysts, this book makes clearer the fascinating
complexity of Canadian foreign economic policy.

A. CLAIRE CUTLER is an assistant professor in the Department of Political
Science at Simon Fraser University and a research associate at the
Institute of International Relations at the University of British Colum-
bia.

MARK W. ZACHER is Director of the Institute of International Relations
and a professor in the Department of Political Science at the University
of British Columbia.

EDITED BY A. CLAIRE CUTLER
AND MARK W. ZACHER

Canadian Foreign Policy and International Economic Regimes

UBCPress
Vancouver

© UBC Press 1992
Printed in Canada on acid-free paper ∞

ISBN 0-7748-0404-1 (hardcover)
ISBN 0-7748-0417-3 (paperback)

Canadian Cataloguing in Publication Data

Main entry under title:
Canadian foreign policy and international economic regimes

(Canada and international relations, ISSN 0847-0510 ; v. 5)
Based on papers presented at the Conference on Canada and
International Economic Regimes, held at the University of
British Columbia on May 30 and 31, 1990.

Includes bibliographical references and index.
ISBN 0-7748-0404-1 (bound). – ISBN 0-7748-0417-3 (pbk.)

1. Canada – Foreign economic relations – Congresses.
2. Canada – Foreign relations – Congresses. 3. International
economic relations – Congresses. I. Cutler, A. Claire.
II. Zacher, Mark W., 1938- III. Conferences on Canada and
International Economic Regimes (1990 : University of British
Columbia). IV. Series.

HF1479. C35 1992   337.71   C92-091137-4

Index: Laura Houle

This book has been published with the help of a grant from
the Institute of International Relations, University of
British Columbia.

UBC Press
University of British Columbia
6344 Memorial Rd
Vancouver, BC V6T 1Z2
(604) 822-3259
Fax: (604) 822-6083

Contents

Acknowledgments

All but one selection in this volume were presented at the Conference on Canada and International Economic Regimes, held at the University of British Columbia, Vancouver, BC, on 30 and 31 May 1990, under the auspices of the Institute for International Relations. We would like to thank the Institute staff for all their assistance in preparing for the conference and in facilitating publication of this book.

In addition, the project was made possible by a generous grant from the Donner Canadian Foundation, for which we are very grateful.

Canadian Foreign Policy and
International Economic Regimes

Introduction

A. Claire Cutler and Mark W. Zacher

This volume was inspired by the belief that Canada, like other states, has become increasingly concerned with the character of international economic regimes, and that the nature of these regimes is now significant to many important foreign policies. This is an inevitable product of the multiple and growing interdependencies among states which create conditions and problems that require co-operative responses and solutions.

The belief that co-operation in multilateral forums enhances Canadian influence as a small- or medium-sized power is often cited as the central rationale for a strong commitment to multilateral regimes. Other arguments in favour of such a commitment are that multilateralism enhances economic welfare and peace in our interdependent world and that it assists in mitigating the overwhelming influence of the United States on Canada. It is also argued that Canada derives many important benefits from regimes that promote economic liberalization. Openness or liberalization is thought to contribute to welfare and the probability of peace. Indeed, Canadian foreign policy officials stress that Canada has a strong interest in multilateralism and economic liberalization because this enhances economic welfare and Canadian influence in international affairs. Several of these factors were emphasized in a recent speech delivered by the then minister of external affairs, Joe Clark:

> There are foreign policy choices open to some countries which have never been open to Canada. We could never aspire to be a great power. Our population and our economy are too small. The choices of conquest, or of

empire have never been open to Canada. Nor has it ever been open to us to act unilaterally or alone. On all important issues, success for Canada has meant cooperation with others. Look at economics. We are a country of traders. We depend on the international economy as do few others. We need clear rules, open access, stable markets. That means we must pursue our economic interests with others. So we have pursued a policy of more open trade through cooperation with other traders. [1]

The various chapters in this volume explore Canadian policies regarding international economic regimes in a variety of sectors and issue areas. A broad range of issues are embraced, including the regulation of international trade and financial transactions, international service industries (shipping, air transport, and telecommunications), resources, and the environment. The chapters reveal that the Canadian commitment to multilateralism and liberalization is an exaggerated and, in some cases, an inaccurate portrayal of Canadian foreign policy. Canada has often resisted the creation of multilateral regimes and has adopted unilateral responses or sought bilateral agreements with the United States to address many problems. Like most states, Canada has exhibited a wide variety and a high degree of variation in foreign policy responses, some of which exhibit anti-multilateral and anti-liberal tendencies. Furthermore, in some areas, Canadian policy might aptly be described as mercantilist-multilateralism, as multilateral forums are used to promote rather protectionist policies. While the importance of international economic regimes for the conduct of Canadian foreign economic policies is emphasized in the chapters, an uneven commitment to the principles of multilateralism and liberalism is revealed. Insights are also provided into broader issues concerning the factors that influence the formulation of international regimes in general.

International regimes have been 'broadly defined as governing arrangements constructed by states to co-ordinate their expectations and organize aspects of international behaviour in various issue-areas.'[2] More specifically, international regimes may be defined as 'sets of implicit or explicit principles, norms, rules, and decision-making procedures around which actors' expectations converge in a given area of international relations.'[3] This definition usefully highlights the importance of both formal and informal means of governing and regulating international relations. In addition, it emphasizes the role of convergent expectations in generating acceptable standards of conduct that guide states in the formulation of foreign policies and that often limit the foreign policy options available to them. While students of Canadian foreign economic policy are generally familiar with the more formally institutionalized regimes governing international trade and investment, international air transport, telecommunications, and fisheries, insufficient consideration has been given to more informal arrangements and practices. The system of international shipping conferences, the international co-ordination of monetary policy, the regulation of private commercial transactions, and bilateral environmental relations involve less formalized customs and practices that impinge upon the formulation of Canadian foreign economic policies.

In exploring the development of both formal and informal arrangements governing foreign economic policy, this volume also generates insights into the factors and conditions that influence states' policies towards international regimes. Theories of international regimes posit that states will participate in and enforce regime standards and injunctions in response to problems of co-ordination and in situations where unilateral action will not produce the desired or optimal result. Collective goods problems, prisoners' dilemma situations, the tragedy of the commons, and the minimization of transaction and information costs are regarded as the types of problems that generate mutual interests and the need for co-operative policy responses.[4] In a related vein, others suggest that states will participate in international regimes to enhance economic welfare and autonomy.[5] Still others suggest that the determining factor is a state's capabilities relative to other states, positing that the most powerful or hegemonic state will exercise leadership in establishing international regimes created by multilateral organizations.[6]

Canadian policies towards international economic regimes have been influenced by many of these factors. The themes of the political and economic benefits of participating in multilateral regimes that promote economic liberalization appear throughout the selections in this volume. However, so do the goals of enhancing economic welfare and autonomy through the support of rather protectionist or mercantilist regimes. Furthermore, in many sectors, Canada emerges as a small- or medium-sized power constrained in its ability to influence the nature of international regimes in the face of more powerful states. Canada's inability to fashion regime standards in a manner suitable to national policy concerns has, in some cases, resulted in the adoption of unilateral and bilateral, rather than multilateral, policy responses. Moreover, the overwhelming importance to Canada of the policies adopted by the United States towards international economic regimes further emphasizes the position of Canada as a medium-sized and, in come cases, a dependent economic power. Yet another theme that appears throughout much of this volume is the important influence of Canadian domestic political factors. Domestic considerations have constrained Canadian participation in and support for some regimes while facilitating support for others. Such insights should shed some light on the role of domestic political processes in regime formation, an area generally regarded as neglected by many regime analysts. All of these themes are considered in detail in the four major parts of this volume. While some of the chapters address issues raised by regimes analysis more directly than do others, reflecting the interdisciplinary nature of the volume's contributors, they all provide important insights into the factors influencing Canada's foreign economic policies.

Part One focuses on the regulation of international trade. Finlayson and Bertasi review the evolution of Canada's postwar international trade policy. They outline the fundamental principles underlying the General Agreement on Tariffs and Trade (GATT) regime: nondiscrimination, national treatment, liberalization, reciprocity, transparency, and multilateral surveillance. Noting that 'the Canadian government's postwar commitment to multilateralism and nondiscrimination in international trade was never absolute,' they address the tensions between multilateral and bilateral policy responses and between liberalism and protectionism. The authors consider the changing nature of Canadian trade interests and policy approaches and the positions adopted by Canada in the GATT negotiations. The Canada-U.S. Free Trade Agreement (FTA) is regarded as an attempt tc fashion an institutional and legal framework that better reflects the nature and patterns of Canadian trade. It also reflects a further shift towards bilateralism and is consistent with what the authors describe as a growing trend towards regionalism in the management of international trade and underlines the overwhelming importance of Canadian trade relations with the United States. In reviewing the issues on the agenda at the Uruguay Round negotiations, Canadian negotiating positions, the possibility of the failure of the negotiations, and further fragmentation of the GATT regime, the authors argue that Canada faces an additional challenge. The development of 'domestic policies and structures that better enable Canadian industries and workers to adapt to ever intensifying international competition is almost certain to be the most urgent "trade policy" challenge facing the country in the decade ahead.'

Thomas further analyzes the issue of Canadian bilateralism in his discussion of the Canada-U.S. Free Trade Agreement. He reviews the nature of Canadian and American interests in a bilateral accord, noting that the negotiations were undertaken 'in an atmosphere of declining confidence in the GATT system and questions about other trading partners' commitment to GATT discipline.' The importance of securing access to U.S. markets in the face of growing protectionism in American trade policy figured prominently in the decision to pursue a bilateral accord and attests to the overwhelming influence of the United States on Canadian trade policy. Thomas reviews the domestic Canadian debate between 'multilateralists' and 'bilateralists' and argues that while the agreement does constitute a bilateral accord, the GATT is 'deeply embedded' in the FTA. 'The conceptual basis of the GATT formed the basis for the free trade negotiations and the resulting agreement. GATT pervades the FTA; one cannot understand the effect of FTA obligations without referring to the General Agreement.' The recourse to bilateral arrangements in the face of the failure of the GATT regime to address Canadian trade interests provides important insights into the link between bilateral and multilateral policy responses. However, the author does note that there are limits to the bilateral approach as well. Some issues simply could not be dealt with effectively in bilateral negotiations – their resolution has been left for the multilateral negotiations. The possibility of achieving outcomes, through a bilateral process, that are essentially consistent with the principles underlying the broader trade regime suggest that bilateral arrangements need not necessarily undermine the multilateral regime. Indeed, Thomas observes that the agenda for the Uruguay Round bears 'a striking resemblance to the bilateral negotiating agenda.' The author, who participated in the negotiations as a policy advisor to the federal minister of international trade, closes with some interesting insights regarding negotiations between unequals, arguing that the outcome of these negotiations demonstrates that there is a converse to the principle that a smaller power does not fare as well as does a larger country in bilateral negotiations.

Cohn focuses on Canadian agricultural trade policies and shows the critical role that domestic interests can play in influencing national support for international regimes. In addition, his analysis discloses important limitations to the effectiveness of unilateral policy responses and the need for co-operative approaches to achieving Canadian agricultural trade objectives. Agricultural trade is 'a specific regime nested within the relatively more diffuse international trade regime' and, as such, is informed by the principles governing the international regime. Cohn notes, however, that while Canada supports the liberalization of agricultural trade, rather protectionist positions have been adopted at the Uruguay Round of GATT negotiations. He observes that there has been a 'persistent tension' between the regime principles of 'liberalism' and 'exemptionalism,' whereby states or trade areas are released or exempted, permanently or temporarily, from GATT obligations. This tension is evident in the conflict between the more liberal export interests, like grain traders, and the more illiberal producers, who rely on domestic markets and are concerned with supply management (for example, dairy and poultry producers). The author reviews domestic political and economic impediments to submitting agricultural trade to GATT discipline and the adoption of bilateral and plurilateral policies in response to the ineffectiveness of GATT in regulating agricultural trade. He shows that while Canada has 'a major stake' in agricultural liberalization, rather inconsistent policies have been adopted. The various trade management strategies open to Canada (unilateral, bilateral, plurilateral, and multilateral) are discussed and evaluated. The author concludes that 'Canada is certainly not alone in following contradictory policies, and all major trading nations share the dilemma of balancing domestic against global political realities.' Furthermore, while Canada has real interests in the establishment of a strong agricultural regime, Cohn argues that unilateral, bilateral, and plurilateral strategies adopted to promote liberalization can complement the multilateral approach.

Cutler addresses the international regulation of private trade relations. The regime governing private international trade complements the GATT regime in that it reflects similar assumptions regarding the positive economic benefits that flow from reducing impediments to trade and enhancing visibility, transparency, and certainty in commercial transactions. However, until recently Canada was not terribly interested or actively involved in the regime. This is notable because the unification of commercial law is a process that produces tangible benefits in terms of reducing transaction costs and promoting certainty in commercial transactions. The late awakening of Canada to the benefits generated by international regulatory arrangements that harmonize and unify trade laws is discussed, and various explanations regarding the shift in Canadian policies and attitudes are considered. The author shows the importance of the link between domestic political/legal considerations and support for international regimes. Domestic constitutional problems deriving from limitations on the federal treatymaking power have placed obstacles to Canadian support for the regime. However, these obstacles are not insurmountable and have been overcome in some areas through federal-provincial co-operation. The possibility of further participation in the regime through similar federal-provincial co-operation is argued to be a preferable strategy to unilateral federal action. In addition, the analysis discloses the importance that the policies adopted towards the regime by Canada's major trading partners have had on the formulation of Canadian policies. In particular, Canada has watched the United States closely, following its lead in a number of areas. Canada's dependence on international trade and the increasing adoption of regime conventions and standards by Canadian trading partners suggest that Canada will have little choice but to participate in the regime in the future.

Part Two focuses on the regulation of international financial trans-actions. The first two chapters deal with Canadian policies towards foreign investment. Brander addresses the domestic dimension of Canadian foreign investment policy, while Paterson focuses more on the international dimension.

In addressing the domestic aspects of Canadian foreign investment policy, Brander explores the link between domestic policy concerns and foreign economic policy. He evaluates the validity of arguments advanced to justify national restrictions on foreign direct investment, reviewing concerns regarding the loss of economic welfare, economic and political sovereignty, and the compromise of Canadian social and cultural objectives. The author argues that the open investment policy followed by Canada through most of its history 'has played no small part in Canada's economic success as a nation.' Brander reviews the history of Canadian policy towards foreign investment and shows that, apart from the brief anti-investment interlude of the 1970s, which he argues was misguided, Canada has been relatively open to foreign investment. The positive economic benefits of an open investment policy are further considered in reference to the economic growth rates and investment policies of other countries. Brander considers Canada's 'possible debt crisis' and makes the case for a tax on foreign investment in fixed assets. He concludes that as part of an 'integrated international investment community,' where financial integration has moved ahead of international regulatory measures, the 'need at this stage is not for unilateral investment restrictions but for a broadly based international framework for investment regulation.'

Paterson develops this theme, reviewing the various international accords and bilateral arrangements governing foreign investment and trade in services. He observes that much of the domestic debate 'has been driven by long-standing Canadian concerns about our cultural and economic relationship with the United States.' However, concerns expressed domestically 'do not appear to have been advanced by Canada with the same degree of concern at the multilateral level,' which, in part, reflects a structural separation of policy formulation at the domestic and international levels. Canada's international orienta-tion 'appears to consist of passive support for continuing liberalization of existing restrictive measures as well as restrictions on the introduc-tion of new measures.' Arguing that this passive approach may ulti-mately undermine the international legitimacy of domestic investment restrictions, the author proposes that a more active role is required. Furthermore, though he notes that by the 1980s there was a shift towards greater support for liberalization of investment restrictions, he observes that there is no 'clearly articulated Canadian policy' on investment controls. This raises the possibility that Canadian policy will be perceived internationally as being 'no different from that of the United States,' or that shifts in Canadian policies in the 1980s will go unnoticed 'except in relation to the privileges granted American investors under the FTA.' However, Paterson concludes that Canada's entry into international agreements that are 'liberal in character' and that 'represent structural changes' will limit the ability of the government to adopt protectionist investment policies in the future, even if there are domestic pressures to do so. This raises the interesting possibility that states, once committed to an international regime, are constrained in their ability to tailor policy responses to meet domestic demands.

In the next chapter Webb reviews Canadian policies regarding the international monetary regime since 1945. The international monetary regime is defined as 'the set of principles, norms, rules, and decisionmaking procedures relevant to the issue of how governments reconcile national macroeconomic objectives with international constraints.' This is an area where the achievement of national policy goals should dictate international co-operative responses. However, domestic political constraints have prevented the development of a strong regime. The regime is 'rather loosely defined, as few governments have been willing to accept formal international constraints on their freedom to select policies that serve their domestic political interests.' Webb challenges the view that small- or medium-sized powers can utilize multilateral arenas to enhance their influence. Indeed, Canada has turned to bilateral arrangements with the United States due to its inability to influence the global regime norms. He challenges the belief that Canada is a 'principal power' in the international system. Canada's weakness is evident in its inability to influence regime norms and its ability 'to evade regime norms without facing severe diplomatic repercussions and without undermining the strength of the norms themselves.' Webb shows that while Canada has consistently expressed support for regime norms, it has not conformed to injunctions that interfere with domestic macroeconomic objectives. 'Canada has been no more supportive of the international regime than have other countries' and has even violated regime norms in response to domestic policy objectives. Furthermore, 'Canadian leaders have found that multilateral institutions are not very responsive to specifically Canadian concerns.' Consequently, Canada has turned to bilateral negotiations with the United States when vital interests are at stake. Webb paints a rather different picture than that of the Canadian foreign policy literature, where Canada is depicted as a 'strong and active supporter of multilateral institutions' and as a 'principal power' in the international system. He shows that while Canada has expressed strong rhetorical support for multilateralism, the actual formulation of monetary and fiscal policies exhibits bilateral and unilateral decisionmaking. He concludes that 'macroeconomic policymaking in Ottawa is dominated by parochial domestic considerations.'

Part Three deals with Canadian policies towards the international regulation of air transport, shipping, and telecommunications services. In all three areas, Canada for many years supported multilateral but very illiberal, even mercantilist, regimes and has recently moved towards economic liberalism at the cost of weakening multilateralism. Each area underlines the importance of domestic interests in the formulation of foreign economic policy responses. In addition, in some cases, Canada has been unable to significantly shape the nature of the international regimes, reflecting its status as a small- or medium-sized power. Furthermore, the importance of Canada-U.S. bilateral relations is particularly evident in Canadian policies towards the regulation of international air transport and telecommunications.

Dresner and Tretheway focus on the changing regime in international air transport. They show that from the end of the Second World War until the early 1970s international air transport was regulated by an international cartel, centred largely on the International Air Transport Association (IATA). The IATA set prices and divided the market by allocating routes and capacities. Bilaterally negotiated aviation treaties embodied IATA restrictions. In the early 1970s, IATA's regulatory role was undermined by a number of developments. This resulted in the emergence of a new regime, in which 'cartel price-setting by IATA has been replaced by competitive forces.' Of significant influence was the adoption by the United States of a 'pro-competitive international policy' and the negotiation of a series of 'liberal' bilateral agreements. While domestic air transport was largely deregulated in Canada in the 1980s, Canada did not liberalize international air transport. The authors argue that 'international air transport policy is still largely tuned to the old postwar regime. A new look and new policies are required.' They note as well that Canada has not played a 'leadership role in shaping the international transport regime.' Canadian air carriers are 'relatively small participants in world air transport,' particularly when compared with American carriers: 'Canadian negotiators do not have the bargaining power necessary to force regime changes to Canada's benefit.' In addition, Canadian bilateral negotiations have been largely 'airline-driven,' and, while the authors consider the possibility that consumer interests might come to play a more significant role, they are guarded in their prognosis. This suggests that there will have to be a significant readjustment of domestic influences for Canada to embrace a more liberal policy towards international air transport.

Heaver focuses on Canadian policy regarding international shipping conferences, which are 'voluntary associations (cartels) of liner
firms...designed to constrain competition among the member lines
and to reduce the effects of competition from "outsiders."' The benefits
said to flow from these arrangements would include the stabilization
of rates and services desired by shipping lines and shippers. These
conferences have regulated liner shipping routes since the latter part of
the nineteenth century. The author describes the development, structure, and practices of liner conferences, showing how technological
changes in transportation have created new market conditions and the
need for different regulatory arrangements. Governments have
adopted a variety of approaches to liner conferences. U.S. moves to
deregulate the industry and thereby create a more competitive environment occasioned a rethinking of Canadian policy, which till then
exhibited at least implicit support for liner conferences. Canadian
legislative changes reflect guarded moves towards liberalization.
However, the author observes that there is 'no definitive answer' to the
question of the continuing utility of the conferences. While there appears to be a change in the attitudes of many shippers, at home and
abroad, favouring a more 'market-oriented' philosophy, 'Canadian
shippers have not really debated elimination of conferences as a practical possibility.' In any case, he argues that Canada is constrained by
the policy approaches of other governments: 'The political costs of
independent action would likely be high, as Canada would be acting
against the preference of other countries for a multilateral approach as
well as against their policies on conferences.' He concludes that while
Canada has largely 'borrowed' policies on liner conferences in the past,
there is an opportunity to play a 'stronger proactive role' in the development of liner shipping policy.

From the mid-nineteenth century until very recently, an international cartel of national telecommunications administrations regulated
telecommunications by dividing the international market, regulating
the division of revenues from international telecommunications and, to
a degree, controlling prices. Globerman, Janisch, Schultz, and Stanbury
review Canadian policy towards the regulation of telecommunications. They identify the companies and institutions that are the 'major
players' and consider significant technological changes and economic
incentives that are creating pressures to integrate and liberalize telecommunication services. Noting that Canada participates in two sets of
regulatory arrangements, the traditional international regime centred
around the International Telecommunications Union (ITU) and the
bilateral Canada-U.S. regime, they compare and contrast the two arrangements and consider the impact of the Canada-U.S. Free Trade

Agreement upon the latter. In describing the international, ITU-based regime, they note the existence of considerable strain. Of significance are moves by a number of states to introduce competition among and between international carriers. Canada has adopted a 'rather middle-of-the-road, albeit with a slight tilt towards the pro-competitive position' in recent negotiations. The Canadian position reflects a conflict between telecommunications carriers and business users, the latter adopting a more pro-competitive position. The authors argue that states in favour of changing the ITU regime, like the United States, are utilizing the GATT negotiations as a means of replacing the traditional regime. The goal is to replace the traditional regime, premised upon the principles of co-operation, closure to foreign carriers, and national control, with a regime premised upon 'diametrically opposite principles,' including competition, access by foreign carriers, and a dilution of national control. In the United States the challenge is supported by 'a powerful broad-based telecommunications industry coalition that includes both consumer and producer interests.' However, a 'strong user and/or service coalition has not yet become a presence in the Canadian domestic process.' The authors conclude that 'the traditional international telecommunications regulatory regime is about to be transformed. The traditional regime, built on domestically closed and internationally co-ordinated telecommunications systems, will be transformed into one based on domestically fused and integrated systems subject to the forces of competition.' The authors observe that Canada must 'grapple with the fusion of domestic telecommunications systems and the decline in national regulatory control.'

Part Four includes chapters on the international regulation of fisheries resources and the environment. Both papers highlight the significance of bilateral Canada-U.S. regulatory arrangements. In addition, both areas involve formal and informal regulatory arrangements.

Munro focuses on the international dimensions of Canadian fisheries management issues. While noting that Canada supported multilateralism at the Third United Nations Conference on the Law of the Sea (UNCLOS III), he shows that bilateral agreements have also been sought to deal with other problems. In addition, certain Canadian policies exhibit considerable protectionism. The author argues that, though the Extended Fisheries Jurisdiction negotiated at UNCLOS III, which Canada strongly supported, has resulted in a transfer of considerable fisheries resources to Canada, particularly off the Atlantic coast, the transfer has given rise to management problems. The problem of over-exploitation in offshore fisheries has re-emerged, while problems of managing shared and straddling stocks must be dealt with. With regard to shared stocks, Canada and the United States have entered into bilateral arrangements, with considerably greater success off the Pacific coast than off the Atlantic coast. With regard to the issue of straddling stocks, which concerns the management of stocks that cross the Exclusive Economic Zone (EEZ) into the high seas and thus raises issues concerning Canada's relations with distant water fishing nations, the author notes how Canada, like the United States, has practised considerable protectionism. Munro evaluates the validity of the infant industry and the employment arguments commonly provided to support protection and notes that Canadian policy, like that of the United States, has been autarkic. 'Since the mid-1980s, the adherence to what is essentially autarkic policy has not been weakened. If anything, it has become more determined.' As a result, 'Canada, like the U.S., has, by reducing distant water fishing nation activity in its EEZ to the minimum, sharply reduced its leverage over these nations.' The author concludes that there are no clear solutions to this problem but notes that some problems have been managed successfully.

Munton and Castle focus on the growth of the Canada-U.S. environmental regime governing transboundary pollution. They address the issues of water quality in the Great Lakes as well as air quality and observe that in 'both cases, the history of Canada-U.S. co-operation and conflict goes back several decades.' However, the agreements reached have largely operated at the level of rhetoric, as governments have ignored their commitments and 'have refused to follow up the rhetoric with action, to set and implement pollution control laws, to provide the funding often required by abatement programs, and to take action if necessary against polluters.' While the regulation of air quality, in comparison with that of the water quality of the Great Lakes, is only in its infancy, the authors note two striking similarities. The first is that in both cases, the United States produces more pollutants. The second is that in both instances, Canada has been the 'demandeur.' 'Most, but not all, of the pollutants dumped into the Great Lakes originate on the U.S. side. The sulphur and nitrogen oxides that lead to most of the acid rain in North America as well as to most of that in Canada originate in the United States. The transboundary flow of acid rain means in both cases that unilateral Canadian action to deal with the problem would be ineffective.' Yet, they argue that the high costs and limited benefits accruing to the United States, in comparison with those accruing to Canada, have rendered a bilateral agreement less attractive to the United States. This asymmetry is characterized as 'environmental dependence.' Furthermore, the 'Great Lakes regime and the emerging air quality regime are, in substantive regulatory terms, no more than ratifications of predetermined American policies.' Canada, as a smaller, weaker, and environmentally-dependent state, has sought the creation of comprehensive environmental regimes but has had limited success in this endeavour. The lack of success is due in part to domestic constraints in both countries and the reluctance of both countries to surrender significant autonomy in the formulation of environmental policies. However, the authors conclude that though both governments retain control over their environmental policies, 'the problems with which they grapple are increasingly transboundary in nature and the structures within which they operate are increasingly artifices of the emerging bilateral regimes.'

In the Closing Perspective, Ostry reflects on the challenge of fashioning institutional responses to the 'most momentous political and economic transformation of the century.' She suggests that middle-sized powers, like Canada, may have greater opportunity to exert influence through coalition formation in a multipolar world than under conditions of hegemony. Ostry argues that Canada is unique among the middle-sized powers who have a stake in multilateralism. As 'the smallest of the large and the north of the south' Canada 'is in a position to exert a leadership role via the power-leveraging route of coalitions.' The author illustrates this special role with Canadian initiatives to build a World Trade Organization and the potential for exercising leadership in proposing new responsibilities for the Organization for Economic Cooperation and Development (OECD). Her discussion provides an interesting contrast to many of the chapters, which stress Canada's limited ability to shape international economic regimes.

The picture of Canadian policies towards international economic regimes portrayed in many of the chapters is not that of a country that is particularly unique or irresponsible. Rather it is a picture of a country that is quite pragmatic and, hence, inconsistent in its adoption of certain policies. More specifically, Canada has not wholeheartedly embraced multilateralism and economic liberalism as many would suggest. On various issues Canada has supported and opposed these principles in varying degrees at different times. Canada has been a very normal country that has not been above the fray of international politics.

In the area of economic liberalization, Canada has opposed liberalizing arrangements when it has seen competitive markets undermining its efficiency or its control of industries that are perceived to be crucial to the promotion of domestic goals and national autonomy. Canadian policies towards the international service industries over most of the postwar period provide excellent examples of these tendencies. In addition, the desire to protect domestic interests and producers has led to periodic rejections of open competition in the GATT trade barriers regime, in international air transport and telecommunications industries, in the management of some fisheries issues, and, at certain times, in foreign investment policies.

Nor has Canada been the paragon of multilateralism. The desire to maintain a wide latitude of discretion in certain domestic policy areas, as in the case of monetary and fiscal policies, has inhibited a strong commitment to multilateralism. In addition, one factor that has been evident in almost all of the chapters is the overriding importance of the United States to Canada's international economic relations. Canada seems almost always to be confronting the issues of striking a deal with the United States or responding to American policies, because most transactions are with that country. This is evident in Canadian policies towards the regulation of private trade relations and in the bilateral trade and environmental regimes. Furthermore, in a world of increasingly more cohesive economic blocs, the temptation for Canada to continue in this approach will increase. Canada seems to be caught between the Scylla of multilateralism, diversification of ties, and greater interdependence on the one hand and the Charybdis of bilateralism and greater dependence on the United States on the other. It remains to be seen whether or not Canadian policymakers will be able to carve out an international leadership role in building international regimes. One thing, however, is certain. Such leadership will require greater consistency in policy approaches than has hitherto been apparent.

PART ONE

Regulation of International Trade

CHAPTER ONE

Evolution of Canadian Postwar International Trade Policy

Jock A. Finlayson with Stefano Bertasi

INTRODUCTION

Since the Second World War, Canada's trade and broader foreign economic policies have been shaped by an evolving international economic system whose basic legal and institutional features were laid down by a small group of states in the last half of the 1940s. The United States and Britain were the most influential participants in the discussions aimed at fashioning a postwar economic order.[1] The international economic institutions founded during this period – notably the International Monetary Fund (IMF) and the General Agreement on Tariffs and Trade (GATT) – were dedicated to the promotion of a liberal multilateral economic order. 'They assumed the economic theory of comparative advantage, and the premise that the competitive forces at work in international economics and the effective operation of the price system would benefit the world economy and the economies of individual countries.'[2]

In the sphere of international trade, adherence to liberal principles meant reducing barriers to the free flow of goods across national borders, developing a set of international rules which national governments would apply in setting their trade policies and import regulations, and relying on multilateral means to settle disputes. The GATT provided a legal and institutional framework for the postwar trade regime. Both an international organization based in Geneva and a treaty or 'code of conduct' that sets forth rules concerning the use of trade barriers by member states, for more than four decades the GATT – together with various subsidiary accords and agreements negotiated under its auspices – has been the central international instrument governing world trade. Originally limited to 23 signatories, by 1991 some 102 countries were full-fledged GATT members ('Contracting Parties' in GATT lexicon), while another 30 applied the agreement on a de facto basis. Member countries account for more than four-fifths of world trade.

It is not possible to review here in any detail the structure or history of the GATT. But attention must be drawn to the handful of fundamental principles that underlie the GATT trade regime:[3]

- *Nondiscrimination.* At the heart of the GATT is the most-favoured-nation (MFN) or 'nondiscrimination' principle, according to which all member states are to apply tariff duties and other trade barriers equally to imports from all other GATT members. The main exception to the MFN principle is the acceptance of regional trade agreements in Article 24 of the General Agreement. Such schemes have proliferated in the past thirty years, with the result that the proportion of global trade conducted on an MFN basis has declined since the 1950s while that conducted within regional trade arrangements (e.g., the European Community) has increased. A second important departure from the MFN principle has been the adoption, by virtually all developed countries, of preferential tariff schemes which impose lower tariff rates on selected imports from developing countries. Although they violate the MFN principle, such schemes have been given explicit legal sanction within the GATT.
- *National Treatment.* Closely related to the principle of nondiscrimination is that of national treatment, which holds that domestic products and imports should be treated equally under domestic laws and regulations once tariffs and other allowable border measures have been applied to the imported goods.
- *Liberalization.* A basic normative underpinning of the GATT regime is the commitment to achieving progressively freer trade. In practice, trade liberalization under the GATT has mainly involved periodic negotiations to lower tariffs. Only modest progress has been made in dismantling non-tariff trade distortions such as subsidies, discriminatory government procurement policies, or protectionist trade remedy laws. Reducing non-tariff barriers through multilateral negotiations tends to be much more difficult than agreeing to lower tariffs. Tariffs on goods have fallen and world trade has expanded dramatically since the GATT was established. However, a high degree of protection has persisted in some sectors (notably agriculture), and there has also been a trend towards 'managed trade' in certain industries (e.g., textiles and clothing, steel, automobiles, and semi-conductors). Moreover, to date the GATT has not provided a framework for regulating or liberalizing direct foreign

investment flows or trade in services – both of which are assuming more importance in the global economy.

– *Reciprocity*. International trade theory emphasizes that most countries can improve their economic welfare when they unilaterally reduce their own trade barriers – whether or not their trading partners follow the same course. In the real world of international commercial diplomacy, however, the economists' advice is rarely followed. During multilateral negotiations to reduce trade barriers, GATT members have generally followed an approach that has been aptly characterized as 'mercantilist bargaining.'[4] States engaged in GATT negotiations seek to achieve a reciprocal balance of advantages and concessions vis-à-vis their trading partners; they generally avoid unilateral actions to lower their own barriers, since this would amount to throwing away their 'bargaining chips.' Countries that grant trade concessions – for example, lower tariffs – expect their trading partners to reciprocate by offering concessions of their own.

– *Transparency and Multilateral Surveillance*. An important feature of the GATT is that trade restrictions, and member countries' trade policies more generally, are subject to scrutiny and evaluation in a multilateral forum. Improving the quality, quantity, and visibility of information bearing on international commerce and national trade policies is an essential prerequisite to multilateral trade liberalization.[5] From this follows the GATT principle that when countries restrict trade, they should rely on border measures, such as tariffs, rather than non-tariff barriers and domestic policy instruments that are less transparent and more conducive to discriminatory application. In practice, as tariffs have been gradually reduced, countries have come to rely more heavily on less visible forms of protection.

The remainder of this chapter is concerned with the evolution of postwar Canadian trade policy. Both Canadian participation in the multilateral trading system and salient developments in bilateral Canada-United States trade relations are considered. The chapter is organized along chronological lines. The following section covers the period from the late 1940s through the 1970s. The next section, the longest, focuses on the 1980s. It first describes the pattern of Canadian trade in the 1980s, then moves on to analyze the factors behind Canada's decision to pursue free trade with the United States, and concludes with a brief review of the main elements of the ongoing GATT Uruguay Round negotiations from Canada's perspective. A few speculative observations on Canada's future role in a multilateral trading system in the light of current trends in the wider global economy close the chapter.

TRADE POLICY THROUGH THE 1970s

The Early Postwar Period

Canada was deeply involved in the deliberations that led to the creation of the GATT in 1947 and supplied the organization's first executive director, Mr. Dana Wilgress. Since 1947, the GATT has been at the centre of Canadian trade policy. It has influenced the content of Canada's trade laws and import regulations and has served as the principal instrument governing Canada's trade with the United States (until 1989), Japan, and most other trading partners.

The MFN principle enshrined in the GATT was viewed favourably by Canadian policymakers, who were anxious to expand world trade on a nondiscriminatory basis, forestall the emergence of trade blocs, and diversify Canada's own external economic ties. Canada's strong commitment to multilateralism in postwar economic diplomacy was closely intertwined with its participation in and support for the GATT. But while a strong, rules-based multilateral trade system has been a long-standing Canadian objective, the Canadian government's postwar commitment to multilateralism and nondiscrimination in international trade was never absolute. Canada's membership in the GATT did not mean that Canada would henceforth eschew bilateral commercial agreements of all kinds. Before the war, the two most important of Canada's bilateral/plurilateral trade arrangements were with the United Kingdom/Commonwealth and the United States. In 1932, the Canadian government had taken the lead in organizing a conference that led to the so-called 'Ottawa Agreements,' which consolidated and extended the system of preferential tariffs among members of the British Commonwealth. Then, in 1935 and again in 1938, Canada negotiated tariff reductions with the United States. These Canada-U.S. trade agreements, coupled with the subsequent wartime economic experience, presaged a long-term shift in Canada's trade orientation – away from Britain and towards the United States.

With the establishment of the GATT, the bilateral Canada-U.S. agreements were in effect superseded by the most-favoured-nation tariff reductions and tariff 'bindings' agreed to by both countries, and the GATT became the legal framework governing Canada-U.S. trade. However, that Canada remained at least somewhat receptive to bilateral approaches to promoting its commercial interests is suggested by the fact that it engaged in negotiations with the United States in 1947–8 that very nearly resulted in the adoption of a wide-ranging bilateral trade agreement; and then, a decade later, it negotiated the Canada-U.S.

Defence Production Sharing Agreement, which gave Canadian industry preferential access to the u.s. defence market.[6] In addition, in the years after 1947, Canada continued to apply (generally) lower British Preferential tariff rates to imports from Commonwealth countries, and its exports continued to benefit from the similarly favourable rates in place in these countries. Thus, Canada's vigorous advocacy of multilateralism and nondiscrimination as guiding principles of international trade policy was tempered by the desire to safeguard existing trade preferences as well as by a belief in the potential efficacy of bilateral approaches to achieving improved access to external markets.

Although Canada was a leading participant in the early GATT negotiations, it entered the postwar period with a set of highly protectionist trade policies in place, in part a legacy of the high tariff policy that was at the core of the original National Policy of 1878-9. From the late 1940s through the 1960s, Canadian policymakers and much of the business community (especially manufacturing interests) remained steadfastly opposed to deep cuts in Canada's high tariffs. During the original GATT negotiations in 1947, and in the subsequent rounds of 1949 and 1951, Canada agreed to only a modest scaling back of its tariffs (in exchange for the generally larger reductions agreed to by the United States and several European countries). The average Canadian tariff on dutiable imports, for example, fell from 22 per cent in 1941 to just over 16 per cent by the end of the 1950s.[7] Canadian tariff rates remained significantly higher than those of most other industrial countries, and in many product categories tariffs were still prohibitive.

Canadian trade with the United States continued to grow in absolute terms and as a percentage of the country's total external trade during the 1950s. By 1955, 60 per cent of Canadian exports were sold to the United States, and more than 70 per cent of imports came from the u.s. The u.s. was also the source of three quarters of the foreign capital flowing into Canada.[8] Increasing economic dependence on the United States began to alarm some policymakers and academics. Shortly after his victory at the polls in 1957, Prime Minister John Diefenbaker promised to shift 15 per cent of Canada's trade from the United States to Britain. Exactly how this was to be accomplished in a market-based economy in which decisions to invest, produce, and sell were largely in the hands of private business was not made clear. (The same question arose in connection with Prime Minister Trudeau's 'Third Option,' unveiled in 1972; see below.) In any case, Diefenbaker's pledge had no discernible impact on Canadian trade flows. And the development of regional trade and economic agreements in Europe – first the European Common Market followed shortly thereafter by the European Free

Trade Association – combined with Britain's growing economic links to Europe, promised to render ever more difficult Canada's halting efforts to reduce dependence on the American market.

Developments in the 1960s

After more than fifteen years of slow, incremental progress towards trade liberalization in the GATT, a dramatic step forward was taken during the 'Kennedy Round' negotiations (1963-7).[9] Sixteen industrial countries agreed to slash their tariffs on dutiable manufactured products by an average of 40 per cent and those on agricultural imports by a smaller but still substantial amount.[10] Canada, however, was not among the countries prepared to accept big reductions in its existing tariffs. Rather than the 'linear' or across-the-board tariff cuts favoured by most other industrial countries, Canada's goal was to achieve freer trade selectively on a sector-by-sector basis. Canadian negotiators contended that bargaining should focus on reducing both tariffs and non-tariff barriers in sectors such as pulp and paper, aluminium, steel, and chemicals – all industries in which Canada had competitive advantages because of its rich resource base and in which foreign 'tariff escalation' militated against increased processing within Canada of resource-based products prior to export.[11] However, it turned out that the major economic powers – the U.S., Japan, Britain, and the European Community – were not interested in negotiating by sector; they preferred to devote their energies to finding a formula that would produce deep cuts in tariffs across all industrial products. Canada's dependence on natural resources, coupled with the fact that Canadian manufacturing was smaller-scale and less competitive than were U.S. and European industry, led Canadian policymakers to conclude that Canada could not agree to make substantial cuts in its tariffs. (Australia and New Zealand took the same position.) But thanks to GATT's most-favoured-nation principle, all three countries benefited from the tariff reductions agreed to by the major economies during the Kennedy Round. Canada did join most other industrial countries in signing the Anti-Dumping Code negotiated in the latter stages of the Kennedy Round. Although never fully implemented, the code represented the first effort to update and clarify the GATT's rules governing the use of non-tariff barriers, a task that was to become the principal focus of negotiations during the 1970s.

In addition to new initiatives to liberalize global trade through the GATT, the 1960s brought important developments in Canada-U.S. trade relations. Dependence on the American market continued to grow, with the share of Canada's exports destined for the U.S. jumping from

60 per cent in 1961 to almost 70 per cent in 1969. And this was occurring at a time when the Canadian economy was becoming more exposed generally to the international economy: merchandise exports accounted for 15 per cent of Canada's gross domestic product in 1964 but for almost 20 per cent five years later.[12] On a selective basis, Canadian government and private sector decisionmakers were becoming more interested in bilateral trade 'deals' with the United States. Interest in liberalized Canada-U.S. trade was growing despite a continuing attachment to multilateralism as the key principle underlying Canadian trade policy.

Following a U.S. threat to impose stiff countervailing duties on exports to the U.S. of automobiles manufactured in Canada with the benefit of generous duty rebates on imported transmissions, engines, and parts, the two countries commenced negotiations which resulted in the Auto Pact of January 1965. The Auto Pact established conditions approximating free trade in cars, trucks, buses, parts, and accessories. (Certain safeguards, however, were built in to the agreement to encourage the major auto producers to undertake manufacturing in Canada.) It paved the way for rationalization, increased specialization, and higher productivity within the North American auto industry. The agreement was of considerable benefit to the North American auto producers and to Canada, whose share of North American automobile production jumped from 6.7 per cent in 1964 to more than 13 per cent by the early 1970s.[13] It also had a dramatic effect on the composition of Canadian exports. As a proportion of total Canadian merchandise exports, manufactured goods increased from 15 per cent in 1965 to well over 30 per cent by 1970, largely because of rising Canadian exports to the United States of automobiles and parts.

Changing Trade Interests

The decade of the 1970s saw an impressive expansion of Canada's trade, primarily in the form of simultaneous increases in exports and imports of manufactured goods. This paralleled the evolving pattern of trade among the industrialized countries as a group. By the late 1960s, the vast majority of intra-OECD trade was accounted for by exchanges of manufactured products, and individual countries had become significant exporters and importers of increasingly differentiated products and components falling within the same broad industrial categories (e.g., automobiles in the case of Canada). This pattern of 'intra-industry' exchange did not fit the predictions flowing from traditional neoclassical trade theory, which held that with tariff liberalization, trade among countries would mainly take the form of 'inter-industry' trade. According to traditional theory, as tariffs were lowered, a given country would become an exporter of products falling within a particular industrial category (say chemicals) in which it had an international comparative advantage, and an importer of other products (say machinery products) in which its trading partners had developed a comparative advantage. At the same time, the domestic industries in which it did not have a comparative advantage would shrink and perhaps even disappear as trade liberalization proceeded.

The traditional theory of international trade rested on some key assumptions – for example, that capital is immobile internationally, that all countries have equal access to technology, that international markets approximate the conditions of 'perfect competition' presumed in standard economics textbooks, and that returns to scale in manufacturing production are constant. These assumptions are at variance with the nature of contemporary international production structures and trade flows. In the modern global economy, capital is highly mobile (and becoming more so); countries – and firms – do not have equal access to technology, and, indeed, technology now constitutes a critical dimension of competition among firms and countries; and transnational enterprises dominate world markets and trade in many industrial sectors.

By the early 1970s, most trade in manufactured products among developed economies was occurring within a limited number of broad industrial sectors, notably, transport equipment, chemicals, electronic products and components, and machinery. Such intra-industry trade tends to facilitate further trade liberalization because it imposes fewer and smaller adjustment costs than does inter-industry trade. The growing internationalization of production in manufacturing industries in the 1960s and 1970s was accompanied by a dramatic rise in the importance of non-arms length transactions in goods and services within and among related companies. According to some estimates, by the mid-1970s, 40 per cent of intra-OECD trade consisted of transfers of products, components, and services within transnational enterprises. (In the case of Canada-U.S. trade, it has been estimated that 35-40 per cent is intra-firm, while close to 70 per cent is conducted on a non-arms length basis.) [14] The trend towards intra-industry trade, and the expanding role of transnational enterprises in structuring markets and international transactions, had a major impact on the character of Canadian trade by the 1970s.

Between 1971 and 1981, the volume of Canada's exports of manufactured products nearly doubled. Due largely to increased shipments to the U.S. of automobiles and other manufactures, the commodity composition of Canadian trade was becoming more diversified. Nonetheless, resource-based products still figured more prominently – and manufactured goods were relatively less important – in Canada's export profile than in those of most other industrial countries. Meanwhile, the destination of trade continued gradually to shift towards the United States. The diminishing importance of Commonwealth tariff preferences, the negative effect on Canada's exports of Britain's accession to the European Community in 1973, and the gradual development of a larger West European free trade zone all served to reinforce the trend towards closer north-south economic linkages.

The 'Third Option'

In 1970, the Liberal government led by Prime Minister Pierre Elliot Trudeau published a review of Canadian foreign policy entitled *Foreign Policy for Canadians*. An underlying theme of this series of documents was concern over Canada's economic dependence on the United States – and especially the threat posed by greater North American economic integration to Canada's ability to preserve sovereignty and political independence. Referring to the 'constant danger that sovereignty, independence, and cultural identity may be impaired,' the foreign policy review called for 'a conscious effort on Canada's part to keep the whole situation under control. Active pursuit of trade diversification and technological cooperation with European and other developed countries will be needed to provide countervailing factors.'[15] As if to justify these worries about dependence on the United States, in 1971 U.S. President Nixon shocked Canada – and other U.S. trading partners – by imposing a range of punitive measures to correct the deteriorating American balance of payments situation. Included among these measures was a 10 per cent tariff surcharge on all U.S. dutiable imports. In the 1960s, Canada had succeeded in winning exemptions from similar – though milder – U.S. actions designed to address its balance of payments problems. This time, however, there was to be no special treatment for Canada; indeed, Canada was explicitly identified as one of the targets of the American actions because of its persistent merchandise trade surplus with the United States. Within Canada, media reports suggested that up to 100,000 jobs could be lost because of the U.S. tariff surcharge. Canadian cabinet ministers and senior officials quickly flew to Washington in an effort to persuade the Nixon administration that Canada's merchandise trade surplus was essential to enabling the country to finance its large deficit on trade in services. Although no exemption from the tariff surcharge – which turned out be short-lived in any case – was secured, the Americans did abandon the idea of pressuring Canada to revalue its currency.[16]

The unilateral u.s. tariff surcharge, coupled with the impetus provided by mounting criticism of American foreign and defence policies (including the prosecution of war in Vietnam), created a propitious domestic political environment for the Trudeau government's decision to enunciate a new approach for dealing with the United States in the early 1970s. The new vision was outlined in a now famous article published in the fall of 1972. Authored by then secretary of state for external affairs Mitchell Sharp, the article suggested that three broad options were available to Canada in structuring its relations with the United States. The first amounted to the status quo, whereby Canada would seek 'to maintain more or less its present relationship with the United States with a minimum of policy adjustments.' The second option would see Canada 'move deliberately toward closer integration with the United States.' The third and preferred option, according to Sharp, was for Canada to 'pursue a comprehensive long-term strategy to develop and strengthen the Canadian economy and other aspects of its national life, and in the process to reduce the present Canadian vulnerability.' [17]

Reducing Canada's economic dependence on the United States was the overriding goal of the 'Third Option.' Several steps were taken in the 1970s in a bid to increase national control over the economy and spur secondary manufacturing. The Trudeau government created the Foreign Investment Review Agency in 1973 and gave the new agency extensive powers to screen all foreign takeovers and expansions of existing foreign-owned businesses in Canada. The thinking behind the Third Option strengthened the government's determination to 'Canadianize' and exercise more state control over the energy sector following the 1973-4 (and later the 1980-1) oil price shocks and also gave sustenance to its inclination to establish more government-owned corporations to serve as vehicles for influencing Canadian industrial development. Ironically, however, the Third Option left virtually no imprint on Canada's trade policy or trade relations with other countries – even though its putative purpose was to diversify Canada's foreign economic linkages away from the United States. It is true that after 1972 various efforts were made to strengthen and upgrade Canada's diplomatic relations with China, the Soviet Union, and other countries that might prove to be 'counterweights' to the u.s.; that Canadian cabinet ministers and officials travelled the globe to sell Canadian goods to other countries; and that a vague 'Contractual Link' was negotiated with the European Community in 1976. But these and other initiatives taken in the wake of the Third Option were not accompanied by sustained government efforts and concrete programs, were generally viewed by the business community as having only marginal relevance to their commercial interests, and in any case were patently inadequate to counter the powerful economic and commercial pull exerted by the huge and proximate American market. Not surprisingly, the Third Option failed utterly to diversify Canadian trade or to retard in any way the longer term process of North American economic integration.[18]

GATT Negotiations in the 1970s

The seventh round of GATT negotiations, the so-called 'Tokyo Round,' began in 1973. This was, to say the least, an inauspicious time to be embarking on a bold multilateral initiative to liberalize international trade. The ministerial declaration officially launching the round was issued shortly before the quadrupling of oil prices in 1973-4, and initial efforts to get the talks under way were undermined by the subsequent onset of recession among the major industrial countries. The Tokyo Round was launched in the teeth of intensifying protectionist pressures worldwide. Growing exports of textiles, clothing, footwear, and many other consumer goods from newly industrializing countries had prompted most developed countries to impose quantitative restraints on imports of such products (particularly from LDC's). Canada, for example, applied new global quotas on imports of clothing in 1976. In the past, as far back as the late 1950s, it had limited imports of textile products from Japan and other 'low-cost' suppliers, but it had not previously applied such measures to clothing imports. Later in the decade, Canada abandoned the global quota and instead negotiated a series of bilateral restraint agreements with individual Third World exporting countries under the framework provided by the GATT Multifibre Arrangement.[19] Also in the 1970s, the United States and other countries moved to restrict imports of automobiles and certain other manufactured products from Japan as the latter continued to strengthen its competitive position and improve its technogical sophistication across a range of manufacturing industries.

Protectionism in the 1970s increasingly took the form of direct limitations on trade through the use of so-called 'voluntary' export restraints (VER's) or 'orderly marketing agreements' (OMA's). The purpose of these measures was to limit the growth of trade – and in some cases to reduce existing levels of trade – in sensitive industrial sectors in an often-futile bid to save domestic jobs. Typically, they emerged following negotiations between exporting and importing countries – negotiations that usually took place without reference to the rules or procedures of the GATT. The proliferation of bilateral arrangements to restrict trade, of various forms of administered protection based on the operation of domestic trade remedy laws (most notably in the United

States), and of a host of other non-tariff distortions to trade throughout the 1970s – a trend referred to by the end of the decade as the 'new protectionism'[20] – raised the proportion of total world trade that was 'managed' by governments. The instruments of the 'new protectionism' were inconsistent with international rules and principles, and the result was a gradual erosion of the GATT's authority throughout the 1970s.[21] Reversing the trend to managed trade, updating the GATT's rules relating to non-tariff measures (NTM's), and restoring the GATT's perceived relevance and effectiveness were therefore the principal challenges confronting the Tokyo Round negotiators.

The GATT Tokyo Round (1973-9) marked the first time since 1947 that trade negotiators focused mainly on non-tariff measures rather than on tariffs. Canada participated more actively in these negotiations than it had in the earlier Kennedy Round. Canadian representatives again raised the possibility of negotiating improved market access on a sector basis, but this suggestion was brushed aside by the major economic powers who were intent on developing an ambitious tariff-cutting formula to be applied to all industrial trade. This time around Canada agreed to be part of the 'linear' tariff negotiations involving all developed countries. As a result, Canada – along with other OECD countries – committed itself at the close of the round to slashing its non-agricultural tariffs by an average of 40 per cent between 1979 and 1987. After the full phasing in of these cuts, Canada's weighted average tariff rate on dutiable industrial products fell from 15 per cent to about 9 per cent – a steep decline in the average level of protection afforded to Canadian manufacturing. [22].

More important than the tariff-cutting package produced during the Tokyo Round were the six new NTM 'codes' that were accepted by Canada, all of the other developed countries, and a handful of LDC's. These updated, elaborated, and, in a few instances, liberalized the GATT's existing rules in a variety of areas relevant to market access. Several areas of Canadian trade law and policy were affected.[23] For example, as a signatory to the 1979 GATT Code on Customs Valuation, Canada was obliged to adopt an entirely new method for assessing the value of imports for purposes of levying customs duties.[24] As a participant in the Code on Government Procurement, Canada was required to open up limited areas of domestic government procurement to greater foreign competition; at the same time, Canadian industry gained modestly improved access to government procurement markets in other signatory countries. Following the negotiation of codes dealing with dumping and subsidies/countervailing duties in the Tokyo Round, Canada passed legislation – the Special Import Measures Act (SIMA) – establishing a new system for dealing with trade remedy cases involving imports into Canada of foreign products alleged to be dumped or subsidized.[25]

The Tokyo Round represented a step forward for multilateral trade liberalization because of the large tariff cuts agreed to and the progress made in tackling a number of important NTM's. But it did not signal a decisive reversal of the rise in protectionism and managed trade evident during the 1970s. The round failed to achieve meaningful liberalization of agricultural trade; did not produce a new 'safeguards' code to stem the tide of managed trade arrangements and the proliferation of trade-restricting measures adopted outside the purview of the GATT; was unable to reach agreement on major new disciplines on the use of government subsidies; and did not result in a significant overall decline in either the number or the trade-distorting impact of the wide array of non-tariff measures maintained by industrial countries. A noteworthy consequence of the Tokyo Round has been the growing complexity and fragmentation of the trade regime. The formal acceptance by the GATT of the principle of 'special and differential treatment' for developing countries, the proliferation of new codes and code committees in which only a sub-set of the entire GATT membership participates, and the related emergence of the concept of 'conditional MFN treatment'[26] – these legacies of the Tokyo Round served not only to complicate and differentiate countries' participation within the regime but also to reinforce divisions among the very diverse group of states comprising the organization's membership.

THE RETHINKING OF CANADIAN POLICY IN THE 1980s: BILATERALISM AND THE EXPANDING MULTILATERAL AGENDA

Throughout much of the postwar period trade policy was a subject of little interest among Canadian political scientists and students of international relations,[27] and trade issues generally had a low political salience within the Canadian policymaking process. The 1980s saw a marked change in this situation. During this turbulent decade, Canadian industries and workers were forced to contend with much tougher international competition and intensifying adjustment pressures; Canada joined more than 100 other countries in launching a new round of GATT negotiations that focused on an agenda of trade issues unprecedented in both scope and complexity; and – following a hotly-contested national election that largely turned on the issue – Canada took a turn towards bilateralism and continentalism by implementing a comprehensive free trade agreement with the United States. Before addressing the highlights of Canada's trade policy in the decade just past, it will be useful to review briefly the structure of Canadian external trade as of the late 1980s.

Trade Structure

According to data collected by the GATT Secretariat, Canada ranked as the eighth largest world exporter in 1990, accounting for 3.8 per cent of the value of global merchandise exports. It was the ninth largest importer, accounting for 3.3 per cent of global imports in the same year.[28] Canada's relative global ranking as an exporter and importer has fallen slightly since the 1970s.[29]

The United States became even more predominant among Canada's trading partners in the 1980s. This reflected robust U.S. economic growth during much of the decade (a development which always exerts a positive impact on Canada's exports), increasingly close cross-border commercial ties, and the relative inaccessibility of most overseas markets to Canadian manufacturing industries. By 1989, fully 75 per cent of Canada's merchandise exports were shipped to the United States, and 70 per cent of imports originated there. Japan accounted for 6 per cent of exports and the same proportion of imports; the 12 member states of the European Community bought 8 per cent of Canada's exports and supplied 11 per cent of its imports; and trade with all other countries combined represented only 11 per cent of Canada's exports and 14 per cent of its imports. [30]

Traditionally, Canada has run a healthy merchandise trade surplus, which partly offsets a large deficit on international services transactions (attributable to deficits in such categories as travel, insurance, and freight as well as to substantial net outflows of profits, dividends, and interest). In the 1982-5 period, Canada's merchandise trade surplus ranged between $11 and $13 billion annually. It remained high until 1986, when slumping world energy prices and slower U.S. economic growth shaved several billion dollars from Canada's export total. Brisk import growth – partially due to a major investment boom over 1987-9 which sucked in large volumes of machinery and equipment imports – and the appreciation of the Canadian dollar after 1986 helped to reduce the annual trade surplus to the $4-$5 billion range by the latter years of the decade. [31]

Examination of the composition of Canada's exports and imports reveals that as a proportion of total merchandise, exports manufactured goods jumped from 30.6 per cent to 42.5 per cent over the 1980s, an increase of about 40 per cent (Table 1). The share of manufactures in Canadian imports moved up in tandem, with end products comprising more than two-thirds of total imports in 1988. Table 2 shows that the manufacturing

TABLE 1

Evolution of the composition of Canadian imports and exports,
1980-8 (% of total merchandise exports and imports)

	1980	1988
Exports		
Food/agriculture	10.9	8.4
Raw materials*	19.4	12.8
Fabricated materials*	38.8	35.7
End products*	30.6	42.5
Special transactions	0.3	0.6
Total	100.0	100.0
Imports		
Food/agriculture	7.0	5.4
Raw materials*	16.4	5.7
Fabricated materials*	18.4	18.8
End products*	57.1	68.0
Special transactions	1.1	2.1
Total	100.0	100.0

SOURCE: Statistics Canada, *Summary of Canadian International Trade*
NOTES: *Inedible

sector has become more export oriented and has experienced increasing import penetration over the same time period – a pattern that is consistent with theories of intra-industry and intra-firm trade as well as with evidence from other industrial countries. The data in Table 2 point to a Canadian economy whose goods-producing sector has become increasingly linked to the wider global economy. Rising support for freer trade within Canada's manufacturing industries in the 1980s

TABLE 2

Import penetration and export orientation of
Canadian manufacturing, 1981-7

	1981	1984	1987
Exports as % of shipments	29.9	35.4	35.9
Imports as % of Canadian market	31.8	35.4	37.0

SOURCE: Canadian Labour Market and Productivity Centre, 'Restructuring in Canadian Manufacturing in the 1980s, May 1989

had much to do with the greater outward-orientation of this traditionally protected sector (see below). Table 3 provides a more detailed look
at the commodity composition of Canadian trade as of the late 1980s.
The importance of the transportation equipment sector – principally
motor vehicles and parts – in both exports and imports is readily
apparent. Particularly striking is the fact that automobiles and other
transportation equipment accounted for more than two-thirds of the
value of all Canadian end-product exports; all other end products
together represented just 13 per cent of total merchandise exports. On
the import side, Canada imported large volumes of machinery and
other equipment/tools in addition to transportation equipment. End
products other than transportation equipment amounted to more than
37 per cent of Canada's merchandise imports – almost three times
higher than in the case of exports.

These data underline the unbalanced character of Canada's trade in
manufactures. Canada is heavily dependent on the broad motor vehi-
cle/transportation equipment sector to generate export earnings, and

TABLE 3

Main categories of Canada's merchandise trade, 1988
(% of total imports and exports)

	Exports	Imports
Food/agricultural products	8.4	5.4
Raw materials	12.8	5.7
Fabricated materials	35.7	18.8
wood & paper	16.2	1.7
textiles	0.4	1.6
chemicals	5.8	5.5
iron & steel	1.8	2.3
non-ferrous metals	6.7	2.2
other	4.8	5.5
End products	42.5	68.0
all types of machinery	3.3	6.3
transportation equipment	29.3	30.7
other equipment/tools	4.6	17.5
other end products	5.3	13.5
Special transactions	0.6	2.1
Total	100.0	100.0

SOURCE: Statistics Canada, *Summary of Canadian International Trade*

virtually all exports in these categories are destined for a s⁺
– the United States. Other than automobiles and parts, u.
relies on a relatively limited number of manufactured exports –
though the range of manufactured products sold abroad has expanded
quite impressively in recent years. Table 4 points to Canada's weak
competitive position in many international markets for manufactured
goods. It summarizes Canada's trade in what Statistics Canada defines as 'R&D-intensive' products. International trade in these product
categories has expanded very rapidly in recent decades and is expected
to continue growing at an above-average rate in the future. As noted in
the table, only in the case of a single high-technology product category
– aerospace – did Canada record a positive trade balance in 1988
(telecommunications was almost in balance).[32]

A host of factors have been cited to explain Canada's limited success

TABLE 4
Canada's trade in 'R&D-intensive' products, 1987
(millions of current dollars)

	Exports	Imports	Balance
Aerospace	3,044	2,634	+410
Computers & related equipment	2,488	5,168	-2,680
Electronic equipment	925	2,040	-1,115
Telecommunications equipment	1,806	1,842	-36
Scientific instruments	962	2,355	-1,393
Electronic machinery	466	1,135	-669
Non-electrical machinery	2,174	3,642	-1,468
Chemicals (including drugs)	1,699	1,940	-261
Total	13,564	20,756	-7,192

SOURCE: Statistics Canada, *Science Statistics*, May 1988

in global markets for manufactured products and its limited penetration of foreign markets outside of North America. Among the most
prominent in the literature have been Canada's high levels of inbound
foreign direct investment/ownership, coupled with the historically
low propensity to export of most foreign-owned branch-plant firms
whose primary raison d'etre has been to serve the domestic market; the
small scale and inadequate size of most Canadian manufacturing
industries; the effect of Canada's own high tariffs in retarding innovation and the development of internationally competitive secondary
industries; and a lack of outward orientation on the part of most

Canadian entrepreneurs and business managers.[33] Several of these
traditional characteristics of Canada's industrial structure are changing
because of the globalization of business activity, the effects of the
Canada-U.S. Free Trade Agreement, falling Canadian tariffs, the restructuring of many Canadian manufacturing industries (and the concomitant impact on the role of foreign-owned manufacturing subsidiaries),
and the increasing importance of direct foreign investment and new
types of strategic alliances such as joint ventures and licensing agreements within the international trading system.[34] Most Canadian economists believe that these trends will have a positive influence on
Canada's economic performance in the 1990s by raising manufacturing
productivity, forcing Canadian industries to become more internationally competitive, creating new export and investment opportunities for
Canadian firms, and fostering a more outward-looking Canadian business community.

Canada-U.S. Free Trade

Although the decision to negotiate the Canada-United States Free
Trade Agreement (FTA) did not signal the abandonment of the multilateral trade system by either Canada or the U.S., it did mark a turning
point for both countries. Hitherto, they had been content, for the most
part, to manage their extensive trade relationship – two-way trade
approaches $200 billion per year – through the multilateral legal,
institutional, and negotiating framework provided by the GATT. With
the FTA in place, there is now a separate bilateral instrument to govern
and further evolve this trade relationship – although it must be stressed
that the FTA is complementary to rather than inconsistent with the
principles and rules of the GATT.[35] The FTA is analyzed in more detail
elsewhere in this volume, and no attempt will be made here either to
describe its provisions or to assess the political controversy that arose
in Canada with respect to its negotiation and implementation.[36] Instead, the focus of this brief discussion will be on the factors which led
Canadian policymakers and the bulk of the country's business community to support bilateral free trade in the last half of the 1980s.

The road to the FTA was paved with academic research studies and
government reports. As far back as the 1960s, prominent Canadian
economists were advocating the establishment of a Canada-U.S. free
trade area, but these early studies initially had little impact on official
thinking.[37] A more important development was the 1982 report of the
Senate Standing Committee on Foreign Affairs. Following lengthy
hearings, the Liberal-dominated committee recommended that Canada pursue a bilateral free trade treaty with the United States while also

remaining an active participant in the GATT. The senators rejected the contention that this would undermine Canada's trade prospects outside North America or lead inevitably to economic or political union with the United States.[38] More influential still in shaping élite thinking about the future of Canadian trade policy in the 1980s was the work of the Macdonald Royal Commission – so named for its chairman, Donald Macdonald, a prominent former cabinet minister in the Trudeau government.[39] Negotiation of a comprehensive free trade agreement with the U.S. was the centrepiece of the commission's myriad recommendations. This controversial proposal was given strong support by several drawers full of research studies (most written by economists) produced for the commission.[40] Publication of the Macdonald Commission Report in 1985 buttressed what was by now already fairly widespread support within the Canadian business community for bilateral free trade. Shortly after the appearance of the commission's report, the Mulroney government decided to make a formal overture to the Americans. Negotiations commenced in May 1986, and the FTA was concluded in October of the following year.

Behind this growing sentiment in favour of a Canada-U.S. trade agreement in the 1980s lay a number of factors.[41] First, Canada not only continued to rely disproportionately on the U.S. as an export market but actually saw its dependence rise over the first few years of the decade. By 1986, exports of goods and services amounted to close to 30 per cent of Canada's GDP, with upwards of three-quarters of this destined for the U.S. market – meaning that exports to the United States represented more than one-fifth of Canada's GDP. For many goods-producing industries – for example, automobiles, aerospace, pulp and paper, and lumber – the U.S. market absorbed the lion's share of their output. Second, the United States was by far the most attractive and accessible foreign market for export-oriented Canadian manufacturers. Despite successive rounds of multilateral tariff cuts under the GATT, Canada has had only modest success selling finished goods to the Europeans and Japanese, who remain overwhelmingly buyers of Canadian resources and semi-processed commodities. In contrast, the American market has been more open to Canadian manufacturers, partly because of geographic proximity and long-standing cross-border commercial ties but partly, too, because the European and Japanese markets tend to be more inward-looking and difficult for offshore manufacturers to penetrate. Third, by the early 1980s it had become abundantly clear that Canada's once-high tariffs were no longer sufficient to shield Canadian industry from international competition in the domestic market. Falling Canadian tariffs following the conclusion of the GATT Tokyo Round in 1979 further eroded the competitive advantages enjoyed by Canadian manufacturers in their home market. As a consequence, more manufacturers – including some foreign-owned 'branch plants' originally established solely to serve the Canadian market – came to view exporting as essential to their long term viability in a more competitive global economy. However, virtually alone among the advanced industrial countries, Canada was unable to offer its exporting industries free access to a large market of at least 100 million consumers.

A fourth consideration which prompted many policymakers and most of the Canadian business community to look favourably towards the prospect of a bilateral trade pact was frustration with the very real limitations of the cumbersome process of multilateral trade bargaining in the GATT. With upwards of 100 member countries, it is perhaps not surprising that the GATT has experienced mounting difficulty fashioning consensus and taking effective action on major trade policy issues since the 1960s. During much of the 1980s, evidence of the near-breakdown of the multilateral trade system was not difficult to find – whether in the continued proliferation of managed trade and GATT-illegal trade restraints, in the GATT's patent inability to address the most crucial trade disputes among the major economic powers (the U.S., Japan, and the EC) or to prevent these powers from taking unilateral actions, or in the failure, within the GATT, to grapple with such issues as investment or the impact of national industrial and technology policies on trade and market access. In addition, in the eyes of many Canadian officials and business leaders the GATT had not proven to be an effective vehicle for lowering foreign (especially U.S.) non-tariff barriers, which, moreso than foreign tariffs, were now the principal obstacles to the modernization and restructuring required to make Canadian industry more globally competitive.

Yet another factor lending support to arguments in favour of a bilateral trade agreement was the growing popularity of regional trade arrangements worldwide. Most important in this context was the renewed momentum towards European integration in the 1980s, following a decade in which the European Community (EC) had languished. The groundwork for the European Community's 1992 Single Market Program was laid by 1985 with the publication of a White Paper entitled *Completing the Internal Market*. Ratification by the EC member governments of the Single European Act in February 1986 paved the way for the implementation of the many liberalizing provisions outlined in the White Paper.[42] Closer economic ties were also being forged between the member countries of the European Free Trade Association and the EC, as well as between Japan and the fast-growing economies of East Asia, during this period. All of this imparted strength and credibility to the argument that Canada and the United States should move to liberalize their bilateral trade and develop a specific instrument to govern Canada-U.S. trade relations.

Finally, the reality and spectre of U.S. protectionism was also pivotal in generating support among Canadian policymakers and the business community for bilateral free trade. Fuelled by ballooning U.S. trade and current account deficits, the first half of the 1980s witnessed increasingly protectionist policies in the United States. This took several forms: changes to the trade laws in 1979 and 1984 which made it easier for U.S. industries to harass and restrict imports; more frequent use of dumping and countervail trade remedy laws by American industries seeking relief from import competition (over the period 1979-88, no fewer than 427 antidumping actions and 371 countervail petitions were launched by U.S. industries); and more unilateral U.S. actions to directly 'punish' trading partners deemed to be behaving 'unfairly.'[43] Proponents of Canada-U.S. free trade believed that Canada's best chance to curb – or at least impose some fetters on – the potpourri of policies and practices that define contemporary American protectionism was through a bilateral agreement endowed with provisions concerning dispute settlement, trade remedy laws, and non-tariff barriers as well as the more 'traditional' issues of tariffs, rules of origin, and quotas. Their hope was that by winning more secure access to the huge American market, Canada could instill confidence in its industries and attract the investment capital that would enable them to modernize and restructure in order to compete globally.

The resulting FTA is a far-reaching agreement that goes a long way towards meeting Canada's objectives. Most economic analyses of the impact of the FTA predicted that it would produce gains for Canada in the form of higher productivity, increased business investment, and higher national incomes over the 1990s – although the combined impact of the 1990-1 recession, high real interest rates, and an overvalued Canadian dollar since 1988 has been to delay if not lessen the economic benefits expected to flow from the agreement.[44] By phasing out tariffs, by reducing other trade barriers, and by putting in place a set of rules and principles that addresses a wide range of trade-related issues – including trade in services and investment – the FTA goes beyond either the current GATT rules or, indeed, the modernized GATT regime that may emerge at the conclusion of the ongoing Uruguay Round (see below). As noted by some of its critics, the FTA did not satisfy all of Canada's goals. Undoubtedly its greatest deficiency from a Canadian standpoint was the failure to reach agreement on a new system of rules to govern the use of trade remedies and government subsidies – although these contentious issues, on which only limited progress has been made in the GATT, will be the subject of ongoing discussion between the two countries through the mid-1990s. Viewed in a longer term context, the FTA is perhaps best seen as a belated attempt by governments to catch up to the economic and business realities arising from growing North American economic integration through devising an institutional and legal framework commensurate with the rapidly evolving and exceptionally dense trade and investment relationship that has developed across the 49th parallel.

The Uruguay Round

The eighth round of multilateral GATT negotiations, known as the Uruguay Round, began in September 1986 in Punta del Este, Uruguay, and was initially scheduled to conclude by the end of 1990. A stalemate over agriculture and a few other issues caused the talks to collapse at the December 1990 ministerial meeting. Tentative steps to restart the round were taken in the early months of 1991. The negotiations could not be formally re-launched until the u.s. Congress had agreed to extend 'fast-track' legislative authority enabling the u.s. government to participate in GATT negotiations beyond June 1991. At the time of writing (May 1991), it appeared that the Bush administration would win an extension of the 'fast-track,' and that the stage would thus be set for the Uruguay Round negotiations to continue, in the hope of reaching a comprehensive set of accords within a year or so.

The Uruguay Round represents a crucial test of the strength and adaptability of the GATT regime.[45] The range of issues under discussion in the round is ambitious and exceptionally complex. At the same time, the many weaknesses afflicting the GATT as the main instrument governing world trade are becoming more apparent. Priority goals identified by the GATT contracting parties at the start of the round included achieving further cuts in tariffs; reversing the growth of non-tariff measures and managed trade arrangements; defining new rules to circumscribe the use of trade-distorting subsidies and countervailing duties; bringing world trade in agriculture more firmly under GATT discipline; reaching agreement on new rights and obligations with respect to the so-called 'new issues' – trade in services, trade-related investment measures, and protection of intellectual property rights; and improving the functioning of the overall GATT system, including the participation of developing countries and dispute settlement mechanisms. Fifteen separate negotiating groups were struck to tackle these issues.[46]

In broad terms, the Uruguay Round poses two overriding challenges to Canada and other GATT members. The first is to update and expand the GATT's structure of principles and rules in order to capture a bigger share of global economic transactions. This requires that significant progress be made in reducing trade-distorting NTM's and in developing regulatory frameworks to cover the 'new issues' – services, investment, and intellectual property. A second – and equally important – challenge is to halt the proliferation of GATT-illegal trade restrictions and managed trade arrangements, and to bring a significant proportion of those currently in place under GATT scrutiny and discipline. (The World Bank estimates that close to 20 per cent of industrial countries' imports are now covered by voluntary export restraint arrangements and other quantitative restrictions; other estimates are even higher.[47]) This requires, inter alia, the adoption of a new safeguards agreement as part of the Uruguay Round package, the liberalization of textile and apparel trade under the GATT Multifibre Arrangement, and meaningful progress in liberalizing market access for agricultural products and curtailing trade-distorting agricultural support programs. These priority areas are related. If a rising proportion of international merchandise trade continues to escape effective multilateral supervision and discipline, it is unlikely that new GATT rules on trade in services, investment, or intellectual property protection will gain wide acceptance. In addition, many LDC's will lose faith in the GATT at a time when liberalization and market-oriented economic reforms are sweeping much of the developing world.

Canada is an active participant in the Uruguay Round bargaining. With the FTA in place, Canada's traditional preoccupation with the U.S. during previous GATT rounds has been replaced by renewed efforts to improve access to other foreign markets – the EC, Japan, the non-EC West European countries, Australia, and a few key developing countries (among them South Korea, Mexico, Brazil, and Thailand). Because its tariffs are, on average, higher than are those of most other developed countries, Canada is sensitive to the adjustment pressures that could arise if the Uruguay Round adopts an overall tariff-cutting formula designed to achieve both deep cuts and greater 'harmonization' of inter-country tariff levels. Accordingly, Canadian negotiators have voiced support for a phased cut in average dutiable tariffs in the range of one-third. Canada has attached a higher priority to reducing non-tariff measures that impede its exporters' access to offshore markets in Europe, Japan, and newly industrializing countries. Improving market access by limiting the trade-distorting effects of NTM's will mainly involve building upon and extending the existing GATT Codes in such areas as dumping, subsidies/countervail, and government procurement. In the case of agriculture, Canada's position can only be characterized as awkward. As a founding member of the 'Cairns Group' of agricultural exporting nations intent on bringing an end to the disastrous global agricultural subsidy war in which the U.S. and the EC are the leading protagonists, Canada has advocated deep reductions in export and production subsidies for temperate agricultural products.[48] However, as a country that confers not inconsiderable agricultural subsidies of its own and that strictly limits imports of certain farm products (notably dairy, eggs, and poultry), Canada has also tried to protect the interests of its less competitive domestic producers by defending vigorously its right to maintain supply management systems for various commodities. Straddling both sides of the issue in this way has undermined Canada's credibility and clout in the Uruguay Round bargaining on agriculture.

Like most other developed countries, Canada is anxious to extend the GATT's regulatory reach to encompass trade in services, trade-related aspects of investment, and intellectual property rights. Canadian policymakers recognize that the future effectiveness and relevance of the GATT will depend critically on finding a way to incorporate these areas into the broader GATT regime. In the case of services, Canada favours the development of a new General Agreement on Trade in Services (GATS) to regulate world trade in services – a fast-growing activity that now exceeds U.S. $600 billion per year and accounts for some 30 per cent of total world trade. Canada has taken the position that such an accord should be based on the core GATT principles of non-discrimination and national treatment, and that it should cover most categories of tradeable services. Canada has also promoted the idea of establishing a new, more comprehensive World Trade Organization (WTO). Such a body presumably would absorb existing GATT structures and provide a more solid institutional basis for implementing and administering new agreements reached during the Uruguay Round in areas such as as textiles, subsidies, trade in services, and intellectual property.[49] Establishment of a new WTO must await the completion of the Uruguay Round. The question of the GATT's future institutional structure cannot really be addressed until the substantive matters that have proven so contentious and caused the talks to progress at such a slow pace are settled.

CANADA AND THE INTERNATIONAL TRADE REGIME IN THE 1990s

At the time of writing (May 1991), it was unclear whether the 108 countries participating in the Uruguay Round talks would succeed in fashioning an overall agreement. A severe deadlock had developed on the key issue of agriculture, in large part because of the EC's unwillingness to accept the need for substantial cuts in the huge production and export subsidies for Community farmers provided under its Common Agricultural Policy (CAP) and the insistence of the United States, Canada, and other countries that meaningful cuts in these subsidies had to be part of the Uruguay Round grand bargain. Important issues surrounding trade in services, foreign investment, protection of intellectual property rights, a new safeguards code, subsidy definition, and textile and clothing trade rules also remained to be resolved when the round's original four-year negotiating timetable expired in late 1990.

The outcome of the Uruguay Round will determine whether the GATT remains central to the evolution of the postwar international trading system. It will not, however, determine whether international trade and economic interdependence continue to increase. The GATT regime is perhaps best understood as an example of what Susan Strange calls a 'secondary global power structure.'[50] These structures, she contends, are less important in shaping the course of international economic activity than are the 'primary global power structures' found in the areas of production, finance, knowledge, and international security. According to this view, it is developments in these primary structures that basically drive the evolution of the global economy. Thus, it can be argued that international exchanges of goods and services are destined to expand regardless of the fate of the Uruguay Round because of deeper structural trends – the globalization of business activity, the ever-increasing influence of transnational enterprises, declining communication costs, the integration of capital markets, and the rapid diffusion of technology and knowledge. From this follows the expectation that the internationalization of Canada's (and other Western economies') goods-producing industries – and of many service industries as well – will continue through the 1990s. This is not to deny that the effectiveness of the multilateral trade order has an impact on the growth or composition of international exchange; rather, it simply acknowledges that the forces propelling the international economy in the direction of integration and interdependence are sufficiently strong to overcome the difficulties that would be posed by the decline of global regulatory arrangements such as the GATT.

Nonetheless, the Uruguay Round does constitute a turning point for the postwar trade system. Achieving real progress on non-tariff barriers and the 'new issues' that now dominate the multilateral trade agenda is difficult, because these factors cut so much closer to the heart of national sovereignty than do the traditional issues of tariffs and quantitative restrictions. As seen in the Uruguay Round, the contemporary international trade agenda is interlaced with what were once basically matters of domestic policy – the regulation of service industries, protection of intellectual property, and government policies to support industry and promote science and technology. It is far from certain that GATT members will be prepared to make the adjustments in domestic policies upon which further progress down the path of trade liberalization will increasingly depend. The emerging agenda of international trade liberalization envisages a world in which governments' policies and standards concerning matters touching on international commerce will tend to converge. Indeed, to reduce *international* friction, it is becoming essential to promote convergence and harmonization of *domestic* policies.[51] While some signs of policy convergence are evident in the global economy of the early 1990s (notably the EC 1992 Single Market Program and, to a lesser extent, the Canada-U.S. FTA), the integration of global production and finance has proceeded much farther and faster. Thus, a significant gap exists between, on the one hand, the 'economic reality' of increasing interdependence, the global strategies being adopted by business enterprises, and the growing international flow of goods, services and investment, and, on the other, the generally piecemeal and halting policy and regulatory responses of governments and international institutions.

The possibility of further fragmentation or even an unravelling of the GATT regime in the 1990s cannot be discounted, particularly if the Uruguay Round is seen as a failure by any or all of the major economic powers. One likely consequence of such an outcome is an acceleration of moves towards regionalism in trade policy. The emergence of the 'triad' – Canada-U.S., the EC, and an Asian-Pacific bloc with Japan at its core – and the implementation of regional economic agreements of various kinds attest to the popularity of regional approaches to trade liberalization. For the many countries that trade mainly with other states in their own region, such arrangements are attractive: they offer most of the economic advantages of broader multilateral accords but typically are easier to negotiate, less complex to administer, and may entail fewer adjustment costs. Moreover, as Sylvia Ostry has recently pointed out, transnational enterprises are increasingly demonstrating a preference for regionalism and bilateralism for reasons of practicality, and because they view the cumbersome GATT process as decreasingly relevant to their global strategies and operations.[52] However, while they spur trade and have positive impacts on the countries involved, regional trade blocs are inherently discriminatory vis-à-vis non-participating countries; they are also demonstrably inferior – compared to true multilateral liberalization – on global economic efficiency and welfare grounds.[53] Yet in a world where the menu of policy choice is limited and always has far more second- or third-best solutions than ideal ones, the appeal of regional approaches to liberalization comes as no surprise.

Mexico's recent decision to pursue a free trade agreement with the United States and Canada is only the latest example of what has proven to be an enduring trend.[54] For Canada, already contending with the adjustment pressures of the FTA and the continuing powerful pull of north-south economic forces, the prospect of a wider North American free trade area poses both opportunities and risks. Undoubtedly there are advantages – including improving the efficiency of Canadian industries, winning better access to the fast-growing Mexican market, and preventing the United States from gaining a 'hub' position as the preferred North American investment location – to be reaped from including Mexico within a larger continental free trade zone. The major 'cost' of a trilateral North American agreement from Canada's perspective would be the diversion of trade from Canadian to Mexican exporters in the U.S. market. But it is essential to understand that any loss of preferential access to the U.S. market enjoyed by Canadian firms would occur even if Canada were not part of a three-way trade pact. There is a danger that regional trading blocs could fuel inter-bloc protectionism and reinforce Canadian industry's traditional preoccupation with the U.S. market. And because of the discriminatory features that attach to such schemes, a global trading system organized into regional blocs could put Canadian exporters at a competitive disadvantage when selling outside North America. Still, with Europe moving inexorably towards a strengthened trading bloc, and with the United States and Mexico apparently determined to strike a bargain, on balance it is in Canada's interest to be part of a North American agreement rather than to sit on the sidelines. The prospect of a trilateral continental agreement will signal a further strengthening of the tendency to look to bilateral and regional approaches to trade liberalization not just on the part of Canada and the United States but more broadly.

As a possible antidote to a more regionalized global economy based on the 'triad,' some leading U.S. trade policy analysts advocate the creation of a new 'super-GATT' – essentially, a free trade and investment zone among the twenty-four members of the OECD.[55] These countries have broadly similar commercial policy interests, trade mainly with each other, and together account for more than 60 per cent of global trade. Moreover, most of the signatories to a number of existing GATT codes and sub-agreements are OECD countries; the same is likely to be true of many of the agreements that may be reached in the Uruguay Round. The proposed 'super-GATT' would in effect replace the current GATT as the principal international instrument governing intra-developed country trade. An OECD free trade and investment zone would not be viewed favourably by 'outsiders' – such as developing countries – although in practice many LDC's protect their interests through existing trade and market access arrangements with the particular developed countries of greatest commercial interest to them, and these arrangements presumably would continue in place.[56] It is conceivable that some of the more advanced LDC's could be invited to participate in a future developed countries' trade 'club.' In any case, if the major developed countries judge the Uruguay Round results inadequate and/or conclude that progress in addressing the trade-related issues that are becoming priorities for the North (including competition policy, R&D, and science and technology policy) can no longer be made within the GATT context, they may begin to focus on fashioning a multilateral trade and investment regime within the framework of the OECD over the next decade.

Whether Canada can adapt to a world of globalizing industries, increasing competition, and accelerating technological change without incurring significant domestic adjustment costs is uncertain. Lack of federal-provincial policy co-ordination, a tradition of very weak institutional connections between industry and government (and also between business and organized labour), a highly dispersed and regionally differentiated national economy, a business community noted for its lack of outward-orientation, and a recent history of excessive reliance on the blunt instrument of monetary policy to regulate the macroeconomy – these features of the Canadian political economy suggest that Canada is far from optimally equipped to respond to the globalization of business activity in ways that maximize the resulting opportunites and minimize the adjustment costs. Whether or not Canadian trade policy continues to move in the direction of bilateralism/regionalism, and notwithstanding whatever happens to multilateralism as a principle and the GATT as an institution and legal agreement, developing domestic policies and structures that better enable Canadian industries and workers to adapt to ever-intensifying international competition is almost certain to be the most urgent 'trade policy' challenge facing the country in the decade ahead.

Reflections on the Canada-U.S. Free Trade Agreement in the Context of the Multilateral Trading System

Christopher Thomas

INTRODUCTION

This chapter provides a general overview of the Canada-United States Free Trade Agreement (FTA) and examines the FTA's origins, the negotiations, the agreement's relationship to the basic elements of the General Agreement on Tariffs and Trade (GATT), and the two countries' experience under free trade. It is written from the perspective of one who was involved in the negotiations (and thus has some appreciation of the Canadian government's negotiating objectives),[1] who has had some experience in both FTA and GATT dispute settlement, and who is also a student and practitioner of international trade law.

The fall of 1990 is a particularly interesting time to review the FTA. Some two years into free trade, Canada and the United States and most of the trading nations of the world are engaged in the final throes of a multilateral trade negotiation of unprecedented complexity under the auspices of the GATT, a negotiation the scope of which is reminiscent of the negotiations that sought to establish the International Trade Organization (ITO) in the aftermath of the Second World War. The ITO was stillborn by the rapid cooling of enthusiasm for multilateral diplomacy as a result of the Cold War.[2] Now, some forty years later, in the context of the Uruguay Round, Canada has launched an initiative to create a multilateral trade organization not unlike the ITO, with a stature equal to that of the International Monetary Fund and the World Bank. Canada's proposal has been received with varying degrees of enthusiasm, and, while an organization is unlikely to emerge in final form from the Uruguay Round, a work plan aimed at its creation could be one of the round's accomplishments.

WHY NEGOTIATE A FREE TRADE AGREEMENT?

The reasons for the decision to commence bilateral trade negotiations with the United States were many and varied. With the contracting parties of GATT now entering the final stages of the Uruguay Round, it is easy to forget that in the early 1980s there were even greater doubts than at present about the continued vitality of the GATT system. In fact, even as the Tokyo Round concluded in 1979, there were calls for the immediate launch of another round to deal with the unresolved issues of the Tokyo Round. To some observers, the Tokyo Round was not the triumph in trade liberalization that its supporters claimed it to be. Some considered it to be a step backward rather than forward. In spite of these criticisms, there was little interest among the contracting parties to resume multilateral negotiations quickly.[3]

In 1982, Canada chaired a GATT ministerial meeting which some hoped would lead to a new round. However, the meeting failed to find sufficient consensus and, notwithstanding the adoption of some modest reforms in dispute settlement, was considered to be a failure.[4] The sense of ennui and drift in the GATT continued. In 1985, a group of Eminent Persons published a report under the auspices of the GATT Secretariat outlining the problems of the GATT system and the many irritants that plagued the international trading system. The report, *Trade Policies for a Better Future*, called for the launch of a new round before it was too late.[5]

Although a launch was finally obtained in September of 1986, even now, at the time of this writing, the round's success and GATT's future is not assured. At the 26 July 1990 meeting of the Trade Negotiations Committee, GATT director General Arthur Dunkel expressed his deep sense of concern over the state of the negotiations. After reviewing the progress (or lack thereof) achieved in the fifteen negotiating groups, he observed that the pressure of time was greater than many would have thought. Clearly, the unspoken question was whether there was sufficient political will in national capitals to face the issues that must be addressed for the multilateral undertaking to be a success.[6]

It was in an atmosphere of declining confidence in the GATT system and questions about other trading partners' commitment to GATT discipline that the policy work leading to the decision to commence bilateral trade negotiations was undertaken, primarily in Ottawa but also in Washington. Interestingly, Canada was the demandeur in the negotiation.[7] The United States' interest in bilateral negotiations was motivated by issues that did not hold the same salience for Canada. For most of the postwar period the undisputed hegemonic economic power, in the 1970s and '80s, the United States began to confront the unfamiliar role of embattled competitor. Not only did it now face a revitalized Europe, but the era of Japanese ascendency was dawning. Even countries without fully developed economies were spawning industries that threatened long established U.S. industries such as steel-making, textiles, apparel, footwear, consumer electronics, office equipment, and automobiles. While Canada faced the same rapidly evolving international economy, its less fully developed economy did not face the kind of overall adjustment pressures encountered by its southern neighbour.[8]

The pressures of adjusting to declining competitiveness led many U.S. constituencies to call for protectionist action. Increasingly strident complaints about foreign market access problems and unfair foreign trade practices fell on receptive ears in Congress. Allegations of unfair trade practices, ranging from industrial targeting to subsidies, and lax foreign labour and environmental regulations led to pressures to amend U.S. trade remedy law and the enactment of sector-specific legislative restraints on imports.[9]

Reagan administration officials committed to the maintenance of the existing international trading system believed that a round of GATT negotiations that was responsive to the new trade issues of interest to the United States was imperative in order to stave off undesirable congressional action. (Interestingly, notwithstanding its trade liberalization rhetoric, the administration was driven to taking some of the most trade-restrictive actions in postwar history.) To attract sufficient congressional support to sustain a new round of multilateral negotiations and to rebuff the most dangerous congressional initiatives, the administration set an agenda which reflected new priorities and sought support for liberalization from new areas of growth in the domestic economy.[10]

The transition of the U.S. economy from a manufactures-based economy to one which was dominated by services, the concern that U.S. intellectual property was being misappropriated and used against American firms, and other private sector concerns were reflected in the Reagan administration's multilateral trade negotiations (MTN) agenda.[11] This is not to say that traditional concerns about international trade in goods were not still relevant. For example, the subsidy practices of other agricultural producers, particularly those of the Community, infuriated U.S. farmers and their congressional supporters. Thus, agricultural trade issues assumed an unprecedented centrality in the U.S. negotiating agenda. The emergence of new issues, however, ensured that the U.S. view of an appropriate MTN negotiating agenda was considerably broader than was that of the Tokyo Round.

For the United States, therefore, the bilateral negotiation with Canada actually fell within a broad strategy of prodding other trading partners into a new round of multilateral negotiations.[7] The United States employed a 'carrot and stick' approach, threatening to engage in more bilateral initiatives if other GATT members refused to agree to launch a new MTN.[12]

This is not to say that from the U.S. perspective a bilateral negotiation with Canada was not desirable on its merits. As the United States' largest export market as well as a major recipient of U.S. direct foreign investment, Canada was an important economic partner. As would be expected in a trading relationship of such size and complexity, there were irritants. Moreover, due to the peculiar dynamics of multilateral tariff negotiations and the mercantilist instincts of Canadian negotiators, through seven rounds of GATT negotiations Canada had managed to maintain one of the highest levels of tariff protection in the industrialized world. The United States had an interest, therefore, in resolving irritants and obtaining preferential access to the Canadian market.[13] Assuming Canada continued to maintain its traditional rather stinting negotiating attitude in multilateral tariff negotiations, the establishment of duty-free access to the Canadian market under a bilateral free trade agreement would provide U.S. industry with a significant competitive advantage over other foreign suppliers to the Canadian market.

Canada shared the concerns of its southern neighbour about rapid shifts in international competitiveness. At the same time, the increasing competitive pressure that the U.S. felt and the legislative and policy responses that it engendered had to be factored into Canadian decisionmaking. With an enormous and growing percentage of Canadian exports going into the United States market, Canadian policymakers felt it would be irresponsible to ignore the rise of protectionism in the United States. Observers such as the then-ambassador to the United States, Allan Gotlieb, viewed the new protectionism as a fundamental and virtually permanent feature of the U.S. political landscape, a view that began to gain widespread acceptance. Thus, to some Canadian policymakers, the negotiation of a free trade agreement with the United States had a prophylactic appeal in that it was thought that such an agreement would provide protection against U.S. protectionism.[14]

This is not to suggest that there was a clear consensus among the Canadian government's trade policymakers that a bilateral negotiation was appropriate. Quite to the contrary, there was a split between the bilateralists and the multilateralists that foreshadowed the vitriolic national debate in the 1988 federal election.

The multilateralists believed that the multilateral forum was the one that best protected Canada's interests. In the GATT, Canada could form strategic alliances on particular issues; the European Economic Community, Japan, and other countries might be enlisted to assist in issues vis-à-vis the United States. This opportunity for coalition building would be absent from a purely bilateral negotiation. Some feared that the United States could bring a power and depth to bear in a bilateral negotiation that might overwhelm Canada.[15]

The bilateralists pointed to the fact that many other states had concluded regional trading arrangements. They pointed to Canada's growing dependence on one market, a market which increasingly struggled with adjustment and dislocation due to rising international competition. The terms 'market access' and 'security of access' became identified with a bilateral negotiation.[16] GATT was said to be in grave condition, if not actually moribund, and the possibility for building coalitions to deal with the U.S. was argued to be more theoretical than real. Finally, preparation, not power, was believed to be the key to a successful trade negotiation.

Both sides could point to evidence that supported their positions. There was truth in much of what was said. What, then, tipped the balance in favour of a bilateral negotiation? The prophylactic appeal has already been mentioned. Equally important was the fact that the world had evolved in a way quite unanticipated by GATT's drafters in 1947. GATT's drafting history suggests that in 1947 few negotiators expected that Article 24 (which permits the negotiation of free-trade areas and customs unions as exceptions to GATT's non-discrimination rule) would be invoked very frequently. In 1947, it was thought that an essentially non-discriminatory trading system based on the most-favoured-nation principle was being created.[17]

Yet the GATT system (which, even at its inception, was unable to completely rid itself of preferences) did not remain non-discriminatory for long. Most importantly, the restoration of Europe and the desire to rid it of the threat of war led to the creation of the European Economic Community, a customs union, and, therefore, a major exception to GATT's non-discrimination rule. The U.S. and other contracting parties supported the creation of the EEC primarily for geopolitical reasons. In fact, a review of the GATT's deliberations on the Treaty of Rome's consistency with GATT Article 24 shows little concern that what might be emerging could constitute a massive derogation in fact (though not in law) from the non-discriminatory system envisaged by the drafters of the General Agreement.[18]

By the early 1980s, the countries of northern and western Europe had evolved into a complex trading area. At the core stood an expanding Community. On its periphery were the six member states of the European Free Trade Association (EFTA). In the early 1970s each EFTA member state negotiated a bilateral free trade agreement with the Community.

The Community also had an array of preferential agreements with former European colonial possessions (the Lomé Conventions). By design, this web of preferential agreements had trade diverting effects. With significant export interests in Europe, Canada and the United States began to appreciate the merits of a preferential bloc at a time when most-favoured-nation treatment no longer meant the best treatment accorded to a state's trading partners.[19]

It would be incomplete to overlook two other sources of pressure for the FTA. First, whereas in 1911, when the manufacturers of central Canada rallied to oppose free trade with the U.S., by the 1980s, the Canadian business community was generally supportive of a bilateral agreement.[20] The U.S. business community, to the extent that it was even aware of the free trade initiative, was also generally supportive, although agricultural and resource producers were as wary as were their Canadian counterparts.[21] Second, the early 1980s witnessed the election of conservative parties in both countries (although the northern one was in relative terms only nominally conservative). The Canadian party pledged to reduce government intervention in the economy, to place greater reliance on market forces, and to open Canada to new foreign investment. This was music to the Reagan administration's ears and a warm personal relationship developed between the leaders. The importance of this relationship should not be overlooked. Ultimately, as the efforts of ambassadors Reisman and Murphy ground to a halt, it was the exercise of political will at the highest levels that resuscitated a negotiation on the verge of expiring.[22]

THE NEGOTIATIONS

The negotiations were the subject of intense public and press interest in Canada. They were largely ignored in the United States. A number of observations can be made with respect to the process and the importance attached to them by the parties. Given the relative disparity and size of the two countries, it is not surprising that Canada approached the negotiations with a greater seriousness of purpose than did the United States. There was a very high level of commitment on Canada's side.[23] A former senior civil servant with trade policy experience was selected to head the negotiating team. Ambassador Simon Reisman immediately moved to establish a separate office outside the normal structure of the federal government.

This office, the Trade Negotiations Office (TNO), brought together over 100 trade policy and law specialists from various federal government departments. While much analytical work was done by the departments from which these professionals were seconded, the TNO was the focal point for the development of Canada's negotiating position.[24] Many of the key external affairs officials, for example, who were instrumental in laying the foundation for the free trade initiative, were assigned to the TNO.

Ambassador Reisman's negotiating mandate was set by the cabinet. Consistent with the parliamentary tradition, a special subcommittee of the Priorities & Planning Committee of Cabinet (the Subcommittee on Trade) was established.[25] It met on a regular basis to review progress and determine Ambassador Reisman's negotiating mandate.

A great deal of research was performed both within the TNO and in various federal government departments. The impact of free trade on different sectors of the Canadian economy was analyzed. Work was done on institutional arrangements that should be established under the agreement. The relationship between the FTA and Canada's obligations under the General Agreement was examined. It is fair to say that there is no trade negotiation in the history of Canada that examined so carefully the implications of the concessions that would be made.[26]

In addition, the government established an extensive private sector consulting framework known as the ITAC-SAGIT system (ITAC stands for International Trade Advisory Committee; SAGIT stands for Sectoral Advisory Group on International Trade). ITAC was composed of senior business people, academics, and others selected to represent the broad interests of the Canadian private sector. The fifteen SAGIT's were established to represent the entire spectrum of the Canadian economy and representatives from both business and labour were called upon to provide sectoral advice to the negotiators.

In contrast to this impressive display of resources and organization, in the United States, a beleaguered Office of the United States Trade Representative (USTR) had scarcely more people than did the TNO charged with the maintenance of the United States' trading relationships with the entire world. During the free trade negotiations, the USTR was obliged to deal with the launch of the Uruguay Round, the expansion of the European Community to include Spain and Portugal, China's proposed accession to the General Agreement, the enduring irritants in the U.S.-Japan relationship, and other important trade issues in addition to free trade with Canada. Thus, for a considerable time during the negotiations the United States was under-represented.[27] It was only when the negotiations entered into their final phase that the United States began to bring together the formidable resources of its government.[28]

This relatively skeletal U.S. negotiating team was headed by Ambassador Peter Murphy. Murphy, a former textiles negotiator and GATT negotiator, was a relative unknown to the Canadian side. Softspoken and closed-mouthed, he was temperamentally different from the ebullient, aggressive, charming, and abrasive Simon Reisman.[29] Murphy was a very careful and cautious negotiator. Thus, ironically, the smaller trading partner came to the negotiating table led by a man with a 'grand vision' of a North American partnership. The larger partner approached the table led by a man of significantly less seniority and access to the highest political offices, and who viewed the negotiations as an 'irritants-plus' negotiation. (Murphy took the position that the existing irritants between Canada and the United States had to be resolved before the essentials of a free trade agreement could be addressed.)

In the Canadian view, this approach to the negotiations seemed to be driven by short term political imperatives. It appeared that Murphy was primarily intent on ensuring that his positions were not assailed by the vocal minority of members of Congress who were concerned with the bilateral negotiations. It was felt that Murphy did not have a sufficient appreciation of just how far Canada was prepared to go to disavow some of its past policies.[30]

There is another school of thought. Those who had dealt with Murphy at the GATT in Geneva had come to appreciate his skill as a negotiator. Some believed that Murphy decided early in the negotiations that he personally did not have sufficient clout in the halls of Congress to ensure that an agreement would pass.[31] Moreover, some thought that Murphy believed that Canada would not hesitate to politicize the negotiations by raising them to the highest political level in order to achieve its objectives. According to this theory, Murphy delayed making significant commitments at the negotiating table, recognizing that ultimately the negotiations would be taken out of his hands and put into those of a more senior administration official with sufficient intra-agency clout to make the necessary commitments and deal with any controversial elements of the package vis-à-vis Congress. If, indeed, this was Murphy's belief and strategy, he turned out to be prescient.

The authority for the negotiations was granted in April of 1986. From that time until the end of August 1987, many meetings were held at the ambassadorial level and at the technical working group level. During this period the groups wrestled with definitional issues and attempted to make some progress. However, overall, the progress was unimpressive, and, by the beginning of September 1987, the Canadian side strongly believed that there was an absence of political will on the U.S. side to conclude an agreement.[32] Finally, Canada suspended the negotiations.

The Canadian position was genuinely held: relations between the

two countries' top negotiators had deteriorated. The absence of progress irritated Canadian officials. Although the necessary technical work
had been done, it was not thought possible to conclude the negotiations
given the rapidly approaching end to the president's negotiating mandate from Congress (due to expire on 4 October 1987). Canadian
officials believed that the essential bargains could not be struck by that
time.[33]

By all accounts Canada's decision to suspend the negotiations took
the American side by surprise. Some u.s. officials viewed it as
'grandstanding.' Others believed that it stemmed from a lack of appreciation on the Canadian side as to how matters were handled in
Washington. (The Americans thought that Canada had an insufficient
appreciation of the complicated nature of u.s. federal public policy.[34]
Canada did not appreciate that the bilateral negotiation could not
dominate the American trade negotiating agenda, let alone its economic agenda.) As is generally the case with most issues in Washington, DC, there would be a short period of time of only one or two weeks,
where the FTA would become an important policy issue that had to be
addressed by the administration.

Still others in the administration had believed Canada was so desir-
ous of a bilateral agreement for domestic political purposes that it
would be prepared to sign virtually anything, however modest, and
declare victory. It came as a surprise to them that there were certain
issues which were either non-negotiable or in which particular results
had to be obtained in order for the Canadian federal government to be
prepared to take the agreement to Parliament and to the Canadian
people.

As a result of Canada's decision to suspend the negotiations, the
president designated the Secretary of the Treasury, James Baker III, as
the senior American official charged with ensuring the conclusion of a
successful negotiation.[35] Responsibility for the negotiations was taken
away from Murphy, although he continued to participate in the u.s.
deliberations along with his senior official, u.s. Trade Representative
Clayton Yeutter. Thus, the decisionmaking power moved from the
executive branch of the White House to the powerful Treasury Department.

On the Canadian side, the prime minister's chief of staff, Derek
Burney (a career diplomat from the Department of External Affairs
seconded to the Prime Minister's Office), was designated to be the
senior Canadian official on the file.[36] Burney was assisted in this regard
by a troika comprised of International Trade Minister Pat Carney,
Finance Minister Michael Wilson, and Ambassador Reisman.

The next two weeks involved considerable shuttle diplomacy between the two capitals, culminating in an intensive three-day negotiation in Washington during the first week of October. With the president required to give notice of his intention to conclude a trade agreement with Canada by midnight October 3rd, even in the dying moments of that night, it appeared that an agreement could not be reached. The negotiations were foundering on the question of dispute settlement.[37] A variety of different models had been tabled by both sides. Finally, the one which ultimately ended up in the Free Trade Agreement took judicial review of administrative decisions in anti-dumping and countervailing duty cases out of the courts of the two countries and assigned it to a binational panel process which would be binding on the parties and governments of the two sides.[38] This was the essential bargain that permitted the FTA to be concluded.

EVENTS SINCE 1987

Since the launch and completion of the bilateral trade negotiations in 1986-7, much has happened in the GATT. The Uruguay Round was launched in September 1986. The round's agenda, as reflected in the Ministerial Declaration, was the most extensive in the history of the General Agreement. The negotiators were mandated to address institutional issues such as dispute settlement and the functioning of the GATT system. Negotiators were instructed to review existing GATT articles and related MTN agreements. With respect to sectoral issues, the negotiators were to address the traditionally virtually intractable issues of agriculture and trade in textiles and apparel. Certain MTN agreements (particularly the Anti-dumping and Subsidies Codes) were to be renegotiated. Negotiators were instructed to examine the possibility of negotiating GATT disciplines in the so-called 'new areas' of trade- related investment measures, trade-related intellectual property rights, and services.[39] In addition, during the round the GATT secretariat began to review the trade policies of individual contracting parties pursuant to a trade policy review mechanism.

Interestingly, when it was finally established, the MTN's negotiating agenda bore a striking resemblance to the bilateral negotiating agenda (leaving aside the multilateral institutional and surveillance issues). Indeed, as the essential bargains begin to take shape in the final phase of the multilateral negotiations, many of the concepts and negotiating objectives resemble chapters of the Free Trade Agreement. What is not yet clear is whether the over one hundred countries involved in the multilateral negotiations will be able to find sufficient consensus on the issues to strike the bargains necessary for a successful outcome. There is no doubt that it is significantly easier in a bilateral negotiation to establish the interests and the objectives of the parties.

The GATT, of course, has continued to operate while the multilateral negotiations are under way. Perhaps the most important change discernable during this period is in the area of dispute settlement. GATT has entered an era of greater legalism. The contracting parties are increasingly concerned with the interpretation of their rights and obligations in dispute resolution proceedings. This is in marked contrast to the earlier concern of promoting the settlement of disputes in a manner which may not have necessarily been consistent with a strict interpretation of those rights and obligations.[40]

GATT dispute settlement has become surprisingly effective (although there are some problems with compliance). During the period 1985 to 1990, three major Canadian trade policies were examined and found wanting by GATT dispute settlement panels: provincial liquor distribution practices, export restrictions on unprocessed salmon and herring, and restrictions on importation of processed dairy products.[41] Canada was not the only contracting party to suffer defeats in such proceedings. The U.S. lost its share: the *Superfund, s.337 of the Trade Act of 1974,* the *Customs User Fee,* the *Pork from Canada* and *Swedish Anti- dumping* cases all went against it. Japan lost the *Semi-conductor* case. The European Community lost *Oil Seeds,* the *Anti-circumvention measure,* and other cases.[42]

Ironically, perceived problems with GATT dispute settlement had been a major reason for Canada's interest in a bilateral agreement. Canada believed that two countries with strong legal traditions would be better able to make advances in dispute settlement than in the more unwieldy multilateral negotiations.[43] Whether Canada's appraisal of GATT's deficiencies was correct or the GATT has evolved to become more effective in dispute settlement is a matter of debate. I am inclined to think that the answer lies somewhere in between. In my view, the problems of GATT dispute settlement were not as great as some Canadian officials believed. At the same time, it seems that GATT has become much more precise and demanding in its interpretation of contracting parties' obligations.

WHAT HAS BEEN THE EXPERIENCE UNDER THE FTA TO DATE?

The FTA is first and foremost a tariff elimination agreement. Tariff cuts took place with the agreement's entry into force and will take place on each subsequent anniversary until they are all eliminated in 1998. In addition, there have been two rounds of tariff acceleration negotiations.

The two governments have moved cautiously; they will not accelerate the reduction of a tariff from that set out in the schedule to the agreement unless domestic industry supports it.[44]

Work has begun in the working groups established under the FTA. Nine technical standards negotiating groups were established pursuant to Chapter 7 (Agriculture). Their objective is to harmonize standards where possible or, alternatively, to seek functional equivalency. No substantive results have been achieved to date.[45]

Although the two sides appointed negotiators, there have as yet been no real negotiations on subsidies and trade remedies. The two sides are waiting to see the outcome of the MTN negotiations on the revisions to the Subsidies and Anti-dumping Codes. It is unlikely that negotiations will take place until after the two countries have had an opportunity to reflect on the progress achieved in the GATT negotiations and determine whether meaningful progress can be achieved in further bilateral negotiations.

With respect to dispute settlement, two cases have been decided under the Chapter 18 general dispute settlement procedures. Interestingly, both involved not distinctive provisions of the FTA but, rather, three basic provisions of the GATT: national treatment (Article 3), general elimination of quantitative restrictions (Article 11), and the general exceptions article (Article 20).

The first case, *Salmon and Herring*, arguably would not have been decided in the same way by a GATT panel (although the outcome was a sensible one). In my view, the result may have been different because instead of answering the question put to it in a 'yes or no' fashion, the panel held that a Canadian landing requirement which required that 100 per cent of the salmon and herring caught in Canada's Pacific waters be landed in Canada for catch verification, inspection, and sampling was a restriction on the sale of fish for export, contrary to GATT Article 11 and not saved by Article 20. The panel held, however, that the measure could be brought into conformity with Canada's GATT obligations, as incorporated into the FTA, if somewhere in the order of 10 to 20 per cent of the catch was made available for direct export at sea. This attempt to recommend how the non-complying measure could be brought into conformity with the GATT was a departure from GATT dispute settlement practice. The outcome of the second case, *U.S. Size Restrictions on Lobsters*, was generally consistent with GATT jurisprudence and was unremarkable.[46]

The Chapter 19 panel process has operated in a relatively interesting fashion.[47] All the cases to date have consisted of Canadian parties involved in U.S. anti-dumping or countervailing duty cases. Only one American respondent even began to initiate binational panel review, and it eventually withdrew the application. Generally, the panels have acted similarly to courts acting in a judicial review function. They have tended to show appropriate deference to the administering authority.[48]

To date there have been two victories for Canadian exporters. In *Red Raspberries* the U.S. International Trade Administration (ITA) was instructed to revisit its calculation of dumping margins and, in so doing, revised its margin down to zero.[49] Two cases were filed to challenge the ITA's subsidy determination and the International Trade Commission's injury determination in respect to imports of Canadian pork. Recently, the injury panel proceeding rendered a decision which strongly criticized the ITC's injury determination on a number of counts and remanded the determination back to it.[50]

The *Pork* case is noteworthy because at the time the FTA proceedings commenced, Canada launched a GATT challenge of the U.S. law under which its exports were countervailed. Canada argued that a 'deeming provision' whereby a subsidy to the primary producer (of hogs) was deemed to be passed on to the secondary processor (of pork) was contrary to the GATT, which expressly requires that the subsidy be 'determined to have been granted.' The GATT panel agreed with Canada and found that the United States had acted inconsistently with its GATT obligations in applying the deeming provision to Canadian pork exports.[51] The fact that the *Pork* case has been split into different forums illustrates a predictable phenomenon, namely, the possibility of 'forum shopping.' Both parties will consider which forum, the GATT or the FTA, is more likely to advance its interests in a particular case.

One effect of the FTA has been to stimulate a rethinking of the Canadian 'common market' and the barriers to trade created by provincial legislation and regulation. A number of federal-provincial meetings have been held to attempt to come to grips with interprovincial trade barriers. In the aftermath of the Meech Lake crisis, it is not clear what will happen insofar as Quebec's participation in the interprovincial trade discussions is concerned. The interprovincial issue has been highlighted in the Heileman Brewing Company's s.301 complaint recently accepted by the United States trade representative. Heileman has complained that an array of provincial practices which the GATT has already found discriminate against foreign beer have not been eliminated as required by the contracting parties' decision to accept the GATT panel's decision. The complaint underlines the problems that interprovincial barriers have caused for Canadian industry. They have constrained industry's ability to respond to increased international competition because of their balkanizing effect on an already small domestic market. Ultimately, they have made industry more vulnerable to foreign competition and have inhibited its ability to adjust.

CONCLUSION

One important point learned in the negotiations was the converse of the well-accepted 'principle' of bilateral negotiations between a large country and a small one. It has been almost an article of faith in postwar Canadian diplomacy that where unequal bargaining power exists, the smaller country is unlikely to fare as well as the larger country. The free trade negotiations demonstrated that there is a converse to this 'principle.' What was not clear at the outset of the negotiations was that the larger party would also be constrained, not necessarily in the exercise of its power, but in the *desirability* of exercising it.

The point which was not well understood was that the larger party must consider whether it makes sense to engage in wide-ranging negotiations and seek deep concessions from the smaller when it will be obliged to make reciprocal concessions to the smaller country. In my view, the fact that the FTA was essentially a peripheral issue to the United States, one which was not as important as was its relationship with the Community and Japan, led it to be more wary of making concessions to Canada than might have been expected. This was not only due to a relative disinterest in making such concessions because of the smaller 'payoff' but also because of their precedential effect on the claims of other trading partners. This hesitancy often inhibited U.S. negotiating demands.

The second fundamental point to note is that the GATT is deeply embedded in the FTA. The conceptual basis of the GATT formed the basis for the free trade negotiations and the resulting agreement. GATT pervades the FTA; one cannot understand the effect of FTA obligations without referring to the General Agreement. The FTA incorporates the concept of tariff bindings which is found in GATT's Article 2. The FTA directly incorporates the GATT Article 3 national treatment principle. The specialized trade remedy laws, the application of which is disciplined in Chapter 19, are derived from GATT Articles 6 and 16 (and the GATT Anti-dumping and Subsidies Codes). The notion of transparency contained in Chapter 20 of the FTA is drawn from GATT Article 10. Chapter Four on border measures is largely derivative of GATT Article 11 obligations. The Article 20 exceptions to GATT obligations are directly incorporated into the FTA. In addition, the MTN Codes on anti-dumping, subsidies and countervailing measures, government procurement and technical standards are all generally incorporated in the FTA. As noted earlier, the interaction between the bilateral and the multilateral agreement was evident in the first two disputes. Given the pervasive influence of the GATT and the MTN codes, it is perhaps not surprising that the first two panel proceedings involved GATT articles.[5]

The third important point to note was that the free trade negotiations proved that there were limits to bilateralism. The reality of the negotiations was that some issues simply could not be reconciled bilaterally and were shunted over to the Uruguay Round negotiations. For example, irreconcilable differences between Canada and the United States on compulsory licensing meant that there could be no agreement on trade-related intellectual property. (There is a GATT negotiation on that subject.) In addition, while some issues were highly relevant to the bilateral negotiations, it made little sense to proceed with them. The best example is agriculture, where there was little incentive to negotiate a multilateral problem bilaterally.

Finally, there is the precedential effect of the bilateral negotiations. The FTA's proponents believed that in view of the significant overlap of agendas between bilateral and multilateral negotiations, the fact that Canada and the United States would be able to address certain 'new' issues prior to the multilateral negotiations would enable the two countries to establish precedents for those negotiations. It is still too early to determine whether or not there was any merit to that contention, because the Uruguay Round negotiations are still very much in a state of flux. It is certainly true, however, that the work undertaken in preparation for the bilateral negotiations proved to be valuable in refining the thinking of both Canadian and American negotiators in the multilateral negotiations.

CHAPTER THREE

Canada and the Ongoing Impasse over Agricultural Protectionism

Theodore H. Cohn

The drafters of the General Agreement on Tariffs and Trade (GATT) had very little to say specifically about agriculture, and there was little distinction made in theory between trade in agricultural and industrial products. Nevertheless, the drafters were well aware of the major trading countries' commitments to domestic agricultural support programs, and the small number of clauses in the agreement exempting agriculture (and other primary products) have proved to be of major significance.[1] In addition, 'restrictions and distortions in this area of trade have spread far beyond the bounds permitted by the special dispensations from the normal GATT rules.'[2]

While tariffs generally have been decreased through successive rounds of GATT negotiations, there is an incredible array of non-tariff barriers and trade-distorting subsidies in agriculture. Non-tariff barriers are often more restrictive, ill-defined, and inequitable than are tariffs. They are also difficult to reduce through international negotiation because of their close linkages with domestic agricultural programs and because of problems with quantifying and measuring their impact. Canada has been one of the strongest supporters of agricultural trade liberalization throughout the postwar period. However, Canada's position at the Uruguay Round of GATT negotiations is somewhat inconsistent, since it is defending certain agricultural policies that are in fact quite protectionist. Before discussing Canadian views and policies regarding agricultural protectionism, it is first necessary to examine the characteristics of the regime regulating agricultural trade.

THE AGRICULTURAL TRADE REGIME

International regimes may be defined as 'sets of implicit or explicit principles, norms, rules, and decisionmaking procedures around which actors' expectations converge in a given area of international relations.'[3] Regimes can be differentiated 'according to function ranging from specific, single issue to diffuse multi-issue,' and specific regimes are 'nested' within more diffuse regimes.[4] Principles are 'general guidelines that concern how states should behave in international issue areas,' and the principles of specific regimes are derived from the principles of more diffuse regimes. Norms are 'the most general prescriptions and proscriptions' of a specific regime, and rules and decisionmaking procedures 'are designed to reflect or implement the norms.'[5]

In this paper I examine 'agricultural trade' as a specific regime nested within the relatively more diffuse international trade regime.[6] As a result, the principles of the agricultural trade regime are drawn from the more general international trade principles of liberalization, non-discrimination, reciprocity, exemptionalism, special treatment for developing countries, multilateralism, and the role of major interests in negotiations.[7] States differ in their support for various principles, and the *nature* of a regime is determined by the relative importance attached to them. In the agricultural trade regime, there has been persistent tension between the principles of 'liberalization' versus 'exemptionalism.'[8] For many years the main focus of liberalization was on reducing tariffs, but more attention is now given to the intractable problems of subsidies and non-tariff barriers. I define exemptionalism as an agreement to release, on a temporary or more permanent basis, a sector of trade or a state from an obligation required of other sectors or states. Exemptionalism is an essential principle underlying the agricultural trade regime and a major factor in the weakness of the regime.

Although exemptionalism has produced glaring loopholes in countries' GATT obligations, some important contracting parties generally committed to trade liberalization felt that this principle should be recognized. Thus, 'the agricultural exemption was drafted by the American... negotiators, who were keenly aware that no treaty that impinged upon the U.S. farm program could receive the constitutionally-required senatorial approval.'[9] More specifically, some provisions in the General Agreement were designed largely to meet U.S. domestic policy requirements. Although GATT Article 11 calls for the elimination of quantitative restrictions on imports, such restrictions are permitted for agriculture when they are needed to enforce governmental measures that limit the quantities or 'remove a temporary surplus of the like domestic product.' Article 16:4 bans the use of export subsidies for manufactured goods but allows them for agricultural and other primary products. The only limitation on agricultural export subsidies is an ambiguous provision (in Article 16:3) that they should not permit a contracting party to gain 'more than an equitable share of world export trade.'[10] Within a few years, even the GATT exceptions did not satisfy the U.S. Congress, and it amended Section 22 of the Agricultural Adjustment Act to permit the imposition of farm import quotas regardless of any international agreement. The president then imposed some quantitative restrictions on agricultural commodities which violated the GATT requirement that concomitant domestic measures, such as supply management, must be adopted. As a result, in 1955 the United States sought and received an unusually broad waiver (that has no time limit) from its Article 11 obligations.

In addition to the GATT exceptions, some matters relating to agricultural trade were largely excluded from the GATT's determinations. For example, when the United States enacted its Public Law 480 program to dispose of food surpluses through concessional transactions, some contracting parties were concerned that PL 480 would infringe on their commercial exports.[11] Australia proposed that a new article on concessional sales be added to the General Agreement, calling for mandatory prior consultations and compulsory arbitration to protect competing exporters, but the United States was unwilling to accept a major GATT role in this area.

Frustration with the GATT led to the use of additional international forums to deal with agricultural trade issues, including the Food and Agriculture Organization, the Organization for European Economic Cooperation (and later the Organization for Economic Cooperation and Development), and the United Nations Conference on Trade and Development. However, while other international organizations have performed some useful functions in this area, 'negotiations leading to legally binding commitments are the domain of the GATT.'[12] For example, the issues of concessional food exports and surplus disposal were passed on to the much less demanding Food and Agriculture Organization (FAO). In 1954 the major trading nations had adopted the FAO Principles of Surplus Disposal to ensure that programs such as PL 480 did not interfere with normal trading patterns. To assist it in monitoring adherence to the principles, the FAO's Committee on Commodity Problems established the Consultative Subcommittee on Surplus Disposal (CSD). The FAO principles 'represent a commitment by signatory countries,' but they 'are not a binding instrument.'[13] Since the legal status of the principles is unclear, their effectiveness depends on the willingness of members to accept the FAO's suggestions.

GATT's ineffectiveness in agricultural trade also contributed to the development of various bilateral (and plurilateral) arrangements to deal with these issues. For example, the United States and Canada developed a duopolistic arrangement in the 1950s to limit their competition in the wheat trade and to co-operate in expanding markets and managing prices. This duopoly was closely linked with the maintenance of the international wheat agreements. Jon McLin has described the Canadian-American duopoly as a 'surrogate system' of world food security, since it functioned in the absence of an international arrangement with explicit multilateral obligations and administrative responsibilities undertaken by an international secretariat. Although the duopoly had some beneficial effects, the decision to terminate it depended on only two states (and primarily on the U.S.) that became less supportive when co-operation in international wheat trade declined in the mid-1960s. Thus, surrogate international arrangements often lack political, legal, and institutional restraints against unilateral decisionmaking, and they are unreliable substitutes for a regime with formalized principles and regulations.[14]

Since 'exemptionalism' (as well as 'liberalization') has been a basic principle of the agricultural trade regime, the regime has been riddled with protectionist policies. The European Economic Community (EEC) and Japan have also emerged as important actors in the regime, and their agricultural policies generally have been even more protectionist than are those of the United States. Furthermore, a number of new international practices in agriculture violate the spirit and sometimes the letter of the GATT. Prime examples of these practices include variable levies, voluntary export restraints, and some forms of state trading. Thus, Dale Hathaway noted in 1983 that the patterns of trade in agriculture were 'moving even further from the liberal trade concept.'[15]

Most analysts assume that international regimes are more likely to develop and prosper in areas where there is a considerable amount of interdependence. For example, Ernst Haas defines regimes as 'arrangements peculiar to substantive issue areas in international relations that are characterized by the condition of complex interdependence.'[16] Food and agriculture are generally considered to be interdependence issues, and one would therefore expect a resilient regime to develop in this area.[17] One characteristic of interdependence issues is that they are 'intermestic'; that is, they are 'simultaneously, profoundly and inseparably both domestic and international.'[18] Nevertheless, governments have often been unwilling to recognize the intermestic nature of agricultural issues and to expose their domestic policies in this area to strong international influence. This attitude stems from the special characteristics of agriculture, including the unpredictable fluctuations in supply and demand; the chronic problem of food surpluses in relation to effective demand; the threat of serious social problems resulting from structural change in rural areas; the political influence of farmer, agribusiness, and other rural groups; and the importance countries attach to food self-sufficiency.[19] As a result, national governments have never permitted a strong agricultural trade regime to develop.

Since 'the growth of interdependence increases the capacity of all relevant actors to injure each other,' regimes are necessary for managing conflict in highly interdependent areas such as food and agriculture.[20] When states refuse to recognize their interdependence and prevent a strong regime from developing, serious conflicts such as the current agricultural export subsidy 'war' between the u.s. and the European Community become more likely. The lack of an effective regime for limiting injury in agricultural trading relationships has been particularly problematic for smaller country exporters such as Canada.

CANADA'S STAKE IN A MORE EFFECTIVE
AGRICULTURAL TRADE REGIME

Canada has a major stake in agricultural trade liberalization as a result of its long-term tradition of dependence on agricultural exports. The country's agricultural production greatly exceeds domestic requirements, and 30–35 per cent of its agricultural output is exported; this includes about 77 per cent of its wheat, 59 per cent of its canola (rapeseed), and 36 per cent of its barley. Although Canada's trade in farm and food products represents only about 6.5 per cent of its total merchandise trade, the agrifood trade balance is an important positive contributor to the overall merchandise trade balance. In the period from 1957 to 1988, Canada's agricultural balance was *positive* every year except one (1969), and it exceeded $4 billion annually from 1982 to 1984; the non-agricultural balance, by contrast, was *negative* in sixteen of these years.[21]

In terms of commodities, Canada's commitment to agricultural trade liberalization stems largely from the importance of wheat to a major region of the country as well as to the overall economy. Wheat is the only major traded agricultural commodity in which Canada has a large share of world trade, and it clearly dominates the country's crop production. Canada is a significant exporter of barley and canola as well as of wheat, but its share of production and trade in all grains and all fats and oils is relatively small. Thus, a former Saskatchewan Wheat Pool president once stated that 'when Canada talks about grain production and exports we really talk about wheat.'[22]

Unlike the United States in the 1950s to 1960s, Canada could not contemplate adopting costly price support and surplus disposal measures to assist its wheat producers. With a smaller domestic market and economic base, Canada was far more dependent than was the u.s. on exporting wheat at satisfactory prices. It would be incorrect to assume that Canadian agriculture was completely unsupported in this period. Indeed, price support legislation was introduced in 1944 to protect dairy, hog, and egg farmers from postwar price decreases such as those experienced after the First World War. Furthermore, the Agricultural Stabilization Act of 1958 was designed to maintain the prices of nine commodities at 80 per cent of the previous ten-year average market price. Government intervention was, nevertheless, rather limited, and Canadian wheat production in the Prairie provinces did not qualify for price supports. The Canadian Wheat Board is a crown corporation that controls the foreign marketing of wheat and barley grown in Manitoba, Saskatchewan, Alberta, and the Peace River region of British Columbia.[23] Producer returns depend on the wheat board's success in moving wheat at remunerative prices, and Canada clearly has a comparative advantage in the production of wheat. This dependence on wheat exports helps to explain the country's consistent support for an effective agricultural trade regime that promotes a liberal trading environment.

Since the 1960s, the leading markets for Canadian agricultural products have been Britain, the United States, the European Community, Japan, the Soviet Union, and China. Among this group of countries, only the u.s. and the eec have been major competitors for Canadian agricultural markets, and both of these 'trading giants' have amply demonstrated their ability to interfere with Canada's export prospects. Smaller countries, such as Canada, prefer regimes because of 'their potential for exerting indirect control over other countries' actions... [Regimes] serve to control large countries' behaviour toward small countries. We would expect small countries to be the strongest advocates of rule systems as they might prevent the use of overt power.'[24]

Canada's reaction to the agricultural trade policies of the United States and the eec therefore should tell us a great deal about Canadian views of protectionism and about the type of agricultural trade regime it favours. Three areas in particular are examined in the following discussion: GATT exceptions and waivers, export subsidies, and trade relief measures.

GATT *Exceptions and Waivers*

Canada opposed the U.S. waiver of 1955 and the GATT exceptions for agriculture (discussed above), largely because of its dependence on agricultural exports and its inability to match the export subsidies of larger countries. In the 1950s the Canadian delegation to GATT maintained that 'it could not agree to permit the United States to exclude imports to any extent considered necessary to protect any programme of the United States Department of Agriculture.'[25] Canada's criticisms of the U.S. waiver have never ceased, and its October 1987 submission regarding the Uruguay Round agricultural negotiations called for 'the provision of equitable rights and obligations among contracting parties, such that all exceptions and waivers would be phased out.'[26]

Export Subsidies

Despite its early contribution to agricultural protectionism, the United States became increasingly concerned about the growing impact of protectionist policies of others, especially the EEC. As a result, the U.S. and Canada joined in pressuring for agricultural trade liberalization and insisted that agriculture be included in the Kennedy and Tokyo rounds of GATT negotiations. Nevertheless, the European Community maintained that the basic tenets of its Common Agricultural Policy (CAP) were not negotiable, and the results of the Kennedy and Tokyo Rounds in agriculture were disappointing.[27]

Canada had special reasons for its strong opposition to EEC protectionism. Britain had been the largest market for Canadian agricultural exports during the 1940s and 1950s and, in all but two years, in the 1960s. When Britain joined the EEC in 1973, the Community then became Canada's largest agricultural market until the end of the decade. However, the Community has been a market of declining importance, and it was Canada's fourth largest agricultural customer from 1982 to 1986. In 1988, the EEC dropped further to become the fifth largest Canadian agricultural market, after the United States, China, Japan, and the Soviet Union. In the view of Agriculture Canada, 'this decline reflects the continuing trend in the EEC to greater self-sufficiency as a result of the high level of support prices under the Common Agricultural Policy.'[28]

However, EEC competition for third-country markets of interest to Canada eventually became more of a concern than did the declining importance of the Community as an agricultural importer. The CAP established a fully controlled European market with relatively high target prices set for major crops. To insulate the market from world prices, a variable levy system was adopted which ensured that Community products always enjoyed a competitive advantage over imports. To dispose of mounting surpluses, the EEC provided export subsidies (known as 'export restitutions'), which were posing a major threat to North American markets. The U.S. share of global wheat exports declined sharply from 45.0 per cent in crop year 1980-1 to 29.6 per cent in 1985-6, and while a variety of factors accounted for this decline (including the high value of the U.S. dollar), a major issue was the steadily growing market share of the EEC. In May 1985 the United States therefore established an Export Enhancement Program (EEP) to regain what it viewed as its fair market share and to force the European Community to the bargaining table. The EEP authorizes the Commodity Credit Corporation to offer government-owned commodities as bonuses to U.S. exporters to expand sales of agricultural products. The bonuses are a form of export subsidy, since the exporters can sell commodities at prices that are well below domestic levels. The ensuing U.S.-EEC export subsidy contest contributed to lower prices, and smaller exporters, such as Canada, could not even contemplate competing with the subsidy practices of these two agricultural giants.

In contrast to the EEC and the U.S., Canada generally does not provide export subsidies except for a few products such as skim milk powder. Canada therefore joined in a diverse coalition of smaller country exporters to form the Cairns Group of so-called fair traders in August 1986.[29] While the Cairns Group pressured for an end to the U.S.-EEC export subsidy war, Canada was more inclined than some members to view the EEC as the main source of the problem. Prime Minister Mulroney described President Reagan's July 1987 proposal for the elimination of all farm subsidies that distort trade as a 'bold move,' and Canada's agriculture minister stated that 'it is important that we do not undercut the U.S. position... because they are the driving force at the GATT.'[30] Canada's 1987 GATT proposal, which was closely aligned with the American plan, stated that 'a major reduction in all trade-distorting subsidies... should be phased in over, say, five years.'[31] In June 1989, Canada also submitted to GATT a proposal for the 'extension of the existing GATT prohibition on industrial export subsidies [in Article 16] to primary products, notably agriculture.'[32]

Trade Relief Legislation

Although American presidents have been basically supportive of trade liberalization, U.S. deficits since 1971 have contributed to demands from Congress that other states adopt 'fair trading practices.' Agriculture was one of the few areas where the United States continued to maintain a healthy export position, and it aggressively sought to bolster its natural advantages in this area. In the early 1980s, however, the favourable American balance in agriculture was steadily eroded, and protectionist sentiments gained support among farm groups.

The increased U.S. concern with 'fair trade' was evident from the growing support for trade relief actions. In the first three decades after the Second World War, American industries seeking trade relief through countervailing (CVD) and anti-dumping duties usually lost their cases.[33] However, the U.S. Congress responded to pressure from producers by changing the rules and procedures so that industries could obtain relief more easily. There was a markedly increased use of trade relief legislation after the rules were revised in the 1979 Trade Agreements Act, and this had a major effect on Canadian agricultural producers. From 1 January 1980 to 30 June 1986, the U.S. International Trade Commission (ITC) and International Trade Administration (ITA) of the Department of Commerce completed six CVD and six anti-dumping investigations against Canadian agricultural commodities (including fish products). While the American complainants were unsuccessful in several cases, duties were eventually imposed on Canadian sugar, raspberries, dried salted codfish, live swine, and groundfish.[34] More recently, the ITC and ITA reversed an earlier decision and imposed a countervailing duty on Canadian pork exports.

Canada has its own trade relief legislation, and it was in fact the first country to introduce anti-dumping duties in 1904.[35] Until the mid-1980s, Canada relied on anti-dumping rather than on countervail legislation to protect its producers. However, Canada's Special Import Measures Act of 1984 included countervail regulations patterned after those of the U.S., which were 'designed with a distinct procedural bias in favour of domestic complainants.'[36] In 1984, Canada pursued two countervail cases against the EEC, and in 1986 a CVD case against imports of American corn was begun.

Despite Canada's use of trade relief measures, American countervail 'can have a severe impact' on Canada while Canadian countervail is likely to be 'little more than another irritant to the United States.'[37] Thus, 'rewriting and strengthening the GATT subsidies and anti-dumping codes probably has a higher priority in Canada than in any other country because of the continuing harassment of ... [its] agricultural exports by the United States.'[38] The different perceptions in the two countries are even evident from the terminology that is used. In the United States, countervail and anti-dumping laws are normally referred to as 'trade remedy' legislation, a term that clearly has positive connotations.[39] Some Canadian analysts, by contrast, describe the U.S. laws in more negative terms as 'contingent'/'contingency protection' measures. Since trade relief legislation can provide both a remedy for unfair trading practices *and* an excuse for protectionism, I follow the practice of those authors who use more neutral terms such as 'import relief' or 'trade relief' laws.[40] Canada's main motivation in seeking the bilateral free trade agreement was to gain more assured access to the American market, and a major concern in this regard was U.S. trade relief law. Furthermore, in its 1987 submission concerning the Uruguay Round, Canada proposed that there should be 'agreement to enshrine in the GATT, rules which would clarify what...counteraction practices would be allowed.'[41] In June 1989 Canada also tabled the first comprehensive proposal to clearly identify the criteria for legitimate countervail measures, so that the growing trend towards disruptive trade actions could be controlled.[42]

In summary, Canada has a major stake in agricultural trade liberalization, and its position has been shaped partly in reaction to the policies of central actors such as the United States and the EEC. A growing sense of crisis in the agricultural trade regime deepened the feeling that there was an urgent need for reform. The Canadian government, therefore, took the lead in having agriculture placed on the agenda of the 1986 Tokyo Economic Summit, played a major role in the formation of the Cairns group, and ensured that the priority to agricultural reform was reaffirmed in the GATT, the OECD, the Economic Summits, the Quadrilateral Group, and other international forums. In explaining Canada's objectives, the international trade minister stated that 'as a middle power with a small domestic market, it is absolutely critical that we support the goal of an open world economy, based on respect for the rule of law in multilateral trade.'[43]

AGRICULTURAL PROTECTIONISM IN CANADA

The Punta del Este delaration opening the GATT Uruguay Round states that

> negotiations shall aim to achieve greater liberalization of trade in agriculture and bring all measures affecting import access and export competition under strengthened and more operationally effective GATT rules and disciplines...by:
> (i) ...the reduction of import barriers;
> (ii)... increasing discipline on the use of all direct and indirect subsidies.[44]

Although Canada has a major stake in the success of these negotiations, the government has nevertheless defended some highly protectionist agricultural programs. This apparent contradiction stems from the wide diversity of interests in Canadian agriculture. While some sectors (grains, oilseeds, and live animals and red meats) are export-oriented, others (dairy and poultry products, and fruits and vegetables) depend on the domestic market to absorb most of their production. The diversity of interests is also regionally based, with the regional interests reflecting the types and nature of commodity production in each province. For example, the protectionist dairy and poultry industries are concentrated in central Canada (Quebec and Ontario), where 78 per cent of industrial milk, 64 per cent of fluid milk, 64 per cent of poultry, and 55 per cent of eggs are produced.[45] It is not surprising that the general farm organizations in Quebec and Ontario (the Union des Producteurs Agricoles and the Ontario Federation of Agriculture) were strongly opposed to the Canada-U.S. Free Trade Agreement. Western Canadian farmers, by contrast, are heavily involved in grains, oilseeds, and beef production for export and are therefore more inclined to favour trade liberalization. One should nevertheless be careful not to over-generalize about the different Canadian regions. For example, Ontario's protection levels in the livestock and red meat sector are low, and its rates of protection in the grains and oilseeds sector are less than those in western Canada.[46]

The changing nature of GATT negotiations could force the Canadian government to confront these contradictions in its policies. Prior to the Tokyo Round, negotiations focused primarily on 'border measures' that directly affected trade flows, such as tariffs, import quotas, foreign exchange restrictions, and export subsidies. However, the Tokyo Round negotiators began to place more emphasis on the 'trade effect' of national policies; that is, 'if a policy has an "important" impact on trade flows, it would be classified as an international policy regardless of the particular instrument used.'[47] Three policy areas that were previously considered to be mainly domestic were therefore included in the Tokyo Round: government procurement, subsidies, and standards. The Uruguay Round continued this approach and extended it more explicitly to agricultural goods. Thus, the Punta del Este declaration calls for negotiations on 'all direct and indirect subsidies, and other measures affecting directly or indirectly agricultural trade.'

Since domestic policies are now more subject to negotiation, a number of Canadian agricultural programs could be affected by the Uruguay Round, including stabilization and other safety net programs, transportation subsidies, provincial government subsidies, some technical regulations, and supply management. The Canadian government has already moved towards reassessing and/or reforming some of its policies in areas such as transportation subsidies and safety net programs. However, this chapter focuses on one area where inconsistencies with trade liberalization objectives are especially evident: Canadian supply management policies for dairy and poultry products. Indeed, a 1987 OECD study of Canadian agriculture concludes that 'a significant level of import protection exists, which is not entirely consistent with the [country's trade liberalization] policy objectives ... this is particularly the case for dairy products, poultrymeat and eggs.'[48] In view of limitations on the length of this article, I draw most of my examples from the dairy sector, which the OECD describes as receiving 'relatively higher protection' than do other sectors.[49]

Canada's import quotas on poultry, eggs, and dairy products are closely linked with supply management plans. National and provincial boards administer marketing schemes for these products that include production/marketing quotas, formula pricing which guarantees production costs, and government subsidies for the dairy sector. The marketing boards are designed to provide adequate and stable incomes for producers, partly by imposing limitations on the entry of lower-priced imports.

Federal-provincial co-operation is essential to the effectiveness of these supply management programs, because the Canadian constitution gives the two levels of government concurrent jurisdiction over agriculture. In addition, jurisdiction over the marketing of commodities is divided as a result of judicial review. Provincial involvement with agricultural policy has increased in recent years, and this change could adversely affect the federal government's ability to meet its obligations resulting from international agreements. This problem could be especially serious in negotiating agreements for dairy products. Dairy policy in Canada is divided into industrial (or manufacturing) and fluid milk categories, the former including skim milk powder, butter, cheese, ice cream, and yoghurt. Industrial milk policies, which involve movement of goods among provinces and outside the country, are mainly established at the federal level and administered by the Canadian Dairy Commission and the provinces. However, fluid milk production and pricing is almost completely under provincial jurisdiction.[50]

Supply management supporters in Canada maintain that such programs provide a number of advantages domestically. They strengthen the bargaining power of producers and reduce their risk, provide market security, and increase stability. Although consumers (and taxpayers) pay costs for supply management, they may also receive some benefits through more stable prices. Furthermore, there is evidence that egg and chicken marketing agencies have helped to limit vertical and horizontal integration, leaving farmers to control egg and broiler production. Nevertheless, 'the list of negative results of the ways in which supply management systems have been operated is long too and provides reason enough for contemplating reform.'[51]

In international terms, it is evident that supply management programs can have a number of trade-distorting effects. For example, the Canadian Dairy Commission Act permits the federal government to control imports that would interfere with actions taken to support the price of any dairy product. Cheese imports are governed by quota, a small amount of buttermilk is imported under licence, and imports of most other dairy products are generally prohibited. These controls on dairy product imports are justified under the GATT Article 11 provisions relating to supply management. Furthermore, the federal government has a policy of balancing supply and demand for milk on a butterfat basis. Manufactured milk contains a fixed per cent of butterfat and of skim milk solids, and the definition of self sufficiency in terms of butter generates chronic surpluses of skim milk powder.[52]

Canada's supply management policies have sometimes evoked a strong negative reaction from the United States. In 1975, for example, the U.S. government sought a GATT ruling regarding the legality of Canadian import quotas designed to facilitate the establishment of a national egg marketing board. The Canadian producers in question feel that supply management protects them from American competitors who have a number of production and marketing advantages. In the case of the poultry industry, the U.S. benefits from cheaper wages, economies of scale, and a more favourable climate. It is not surprising that American exports of poultry meat to Canada were valued at U.S. $31.5 million in fiscal year 1986, while Canadian exports to the U.S. amounted to only $3.7 million.[53]

Under the Canada-U.S. Free Trade Agreement (FTA), tariffs will be eliminated over a ten year period on a number of processed poultry and dairy products such as chicken dinners and frozen pizza.[54] Article 706 of the FTA also calls for a small increase in Canadian global import quotas for chickens, turkeys, and eggs to reflect recent increases in imports from the U.S. (i.e., when demand for these products in Canada exceeded domestic supply). Despite the increased quotas, Canada's agriculture minister noted that in the FTA negotiations 'we pressed for, and won, specific reference to Article 11 under the ... GATT – that is, reference to the right of countries to impose import controls in order to protect the integrity of their supply management systems.'[55] Thus, Article 710 of the FTA states that 'the Parties retain their rights and obligations with respect to agricultural ... goods under ... GATT Article 11.' The United States and Canada both follow protectionist policies in the dairy sector, and dairy products are not specifically covered in the Free Trade Agreement. In its synopsis of the FTA, the Canadian government provided specific assurances that 'dairy farmers will continue to benefit from supply management programs since these are not affected by the agreement and are consistent with Canada's GATT obligations.'[56]

Many Canadian farmers are not convinced, however, that marketing boards involved with supply management will remain intact after the free trade agreement is fully implemented. Their suspicions are understandable in view of the considerable opposition to these boards in both the United States and Canada. Indeed, the U.S. trade representative indicated that 'in the course of the FTA negotiations we sought to have Canada's supply management scheme for poultry and eggs eliminated, but the Canadians were unwilling to go beyond a quota increase.'[57] Canadian consumer groups also feel that the FTA should have dealt with the problems of marketing boards since consumers are paying a cost for them through higher prices. These higher prices are in effect a tax on consumers, which is sometimes described as a negative 'consumer subsidy equivalent' (CSE). The OECD has estimated that the highest levels of consumer transfer (or the most negative CSE's) are found in the Canadian dairy and chickenmeat sectors.[58]

Canadian food processors are also dissatisfied with the exclusion of supply management schemes from the FTA, since they must use higher-priced Canadian commodities as raw materials. It is difficult to ignore this issue, since food processing is Canada's second most important manufacturing industry. Canadian exports of processed foods increased by 300 per cent in just over a decade to $2.8 billion in 1987. Nevertheless, in a November 1989 report Agriculture Canada indicated that 'there appears to be substantial potential for further diversification when we recognize that only 2 per cent of our total agri-food exports consist of highly processed products.'[59] During House of Commons hearings on the FTA, food processors repeatedly warned that they would not be able to compete with their U.S. counterparts. For example, the president of the Grocery Products Manufacturers of Canada stated that:

> Our greatest concern centres on the availability of input commodities such as poultry, eggs, milk, wheat and fruits and vegetables to Canadian food processors at prices no higher than those paid by our competitors in the United States, if there is to be a free trade agreement between our two countries...Under the proposed free trade agreement, packaged processed food products will flow freely between Canada and the U.S. within 10 years, but non-tariff barriers will be retained, presumably to protect higher-priced regulated agricultural commodities in Canada.[60]

The processing issue is particularly sensitive in the case of dairy products. Dairy farmers had been concerned that the removal of tariffs on processed goods under the free trade agreement would put pressure on Canadian dairy boards to sell their raw product to processors at lower prices. After the FTA was concluded, the Canadian government, therefore, added processed dairy products (i.e., ice cream and yoghurt) to the Import Control List. This decision was taken to assure dairy producers that supply management would not be affected and also to deal with the concerns of Canadian food processors. The move was politically astute; the Conservatives subsequently won the November 1988 election with a sweep of Quebec rural seats.[61] However, when Ottawa turned down the Pillsbury Company's application to export Haagen-Dazs ice cream from the United States, the U.S. requested (in December 1988) that a dispute settlement panel be formed to determine whether the quotas were inconsistent with the GATT. American officials argued that ice cream is not covered by GATT Article 11, since it is a processed food rather than a raw dairy product.

In September 1989, the panel determined that Canadian import restrictions on ice cream and yoghurt did not conform with GATT obligations, and in early December the GATT council formally adopted the panel's report. Canada could have vetoed the decision, but such action would have undermined its position as a supporter of strengthened trade rules and would have caused strained relations with the United States. Instead, Canada accepted the decision but deferred action, maintaining that 'it would be premature to act on the Panel recommendations before the conclusion of these [Uruguay Round] negotiations.'[62] There was a precedent for this action; the U.S. had used similar delaying tactics when it failed to implement an earlier decision of the GATT Council.

While accepting the panel decision, Canada criticized it on a number of grounds. The agriculture minister argued that the decision was unfair in view of the waiver, which has given the United States 'an exemption from the GATT for its import quotas since 1955.'[63] Canada also viewed the panel decision as an indication of the need to revise GATT Article 11 so that processed as well as raw agricultural products could be protected. Agriculture Canada did offer some proposals for reforming the supply management system in a November 1989 document initiating a review of the country's agri-food policies. For example, the document stated that the system should become 'more market responsive' and meet 'the changing needs of consumers.' Furthermore, the department acknowledged that the prices of supply-managed commodities 'have been higher than many international prices,' and that this 'is of particular concern to further the processing industry in Canada.' Nevertheless, the government remained firmly committed to 'retaining border protection necessary to ensure that our supply management programs can function.'[64] On 14 March 1990 Canada tabled a proposal in Geneva for strengthening and clarifying GATT Article 11. The proposal states that import restrictions should be permitted for 'those processed products which are made "wholly or mainly" from the fresh product under domestic supply control.'[65]

Domestically, both the supply-managed and exporting farm sectors are concerned that the federal government is engaging in a 'balancing act' between them, and that their interests might be traded off in the Uruguay Round.[66] Internationally, the government's expressed commitment to strengthening Article 11 has created a rift with its traditional free trade allies. A particular problem for Canada has been the (November 1988) U.S. proposal for a process of 'tariffication'; that is, that non-tariff barriers be converted to bound tariffs, which would gradually be reduced. Tariffication would eliminate the need for treating agriculture as an exception under Article 11, since quantitative restrictions would be phased out. At a Cairns group meeting in November 1989, a tariffication proposal was accepted by all fourteen members; but Canada's trade minister added that the rule must not apply to import restrictions maintained in conformity with Article 11.[67] The rift with other Cairns group members widened when Canada refused to initial the October 1990 Cairns group Proposal for a Multilateral Reform Program for Agriculture. In this proposal the Cairns group called for converting all non-tariff import measures to tariff equivalents. Canada issued its own proposal in October 1990, indicating that quantitative import restrictions should continue to be permitted under GATT Article 11.

Canada sought support for its Article 11 position from some unlikely allies, including Western Europe, Japan, and the Nordic countries. The EEC registered the view that it might be necessary to retain the Article 11 exceptions in some form to accommodate countries with internal supply control programs. This view was also shared by the Nordic countries, Japan, Austria, Switzerland, Israel, and South Korea. However, even the EEC and the Nordic countries have expressed willingness to consider partial tariffication under specified conditions.[68]

In December 1990 the Uruguay Round negotiations were suspended because of seemingly irreconcilable differences between the U.S. and the EEC over the issue of agricultural subsidies. As a result, pressures on Canada to adopt a less protectionist position regarding GATT Article 11 were temporarily alleviated. The renewal of GATT discussions in early 1991 raised hopes that a Uruguay Round agreement on agriculture might eventually be concluded. If the major agricultural traders do arrive at a consensus, attention might again focus on Canada's supply management related import barriers.

It should be mentioned that most trade arrangements accompanying Canada's commodity policies conform with GATT regulations, and that supply management is no exception. One would expect this of a middle-sized trader 'for such countries must look to the rule of law in international commerce since they will surely lose in a world characterized by the rule of power.'[69] Thus, a former agriculture minister has stated that 'Canada supports GATT. And Article 11 is a distinct provision in GATT. The U.S. waiver is not. The European Community's variable levies are not. Trade-distorting subsidies are not. Phony sanitary and phytosanitary non-tariff barriers are not.'[70] However, William Miner and Dale Hathaway have pointed out that Canada has 'maintained or increased restrictions on imports of various agricultural products by measures that are more or less consistent with the letter, if not the spirit, of the GATT rules.'[71]

FUTURE OPTIONS FOR CANADA

As a smaller country which is extremely dependent on exports, Canada has an overriding objective to promote agricultural trade liberalization. Nevertheless, the discussion of supply management in this chapter indicates that Canada is also maintaining and defending some highly protectionist policies. There is a variety of strategies that the country can employ to achieve these (somewhat inconsistent) agricultural trade objectives, which may be generally categorized as unilateral, bilateral, plurilateral, and multilateral. Since the results of the GATT Uruguay Round are still uncertain, the following discussion examines Canada's future options in the event of both a successful and unsuccessful outcome. A 'successful' agreement would result in a substantial amount of trade liberalization in agriculture and in a stronger and more effective agricultural trade regime.

Unilateral Strategies

Canadian policies obviously have far less impact on global trade issues than do the policies of the 'Big Three' in the GATT: the United States, the European Community, and Japan. Canada may choose to employ some unilateral strategies, but (unlike the Big Three) the influence it can exert individually on the outcome of the Uruguay Round is minimal.

Since the other Cairns group members and the U.S. strongly oppose Canada's efforts to include processed agricultural products in the GATT Article 11 exceptions, there is little chance that this proposal will be approved. If the multilateral negotiations result in an agreement, it is in fact possible that the exceptions for agriculture will either be abolished or be subject to greater restrictions. The EEC and Japan both have been supportive of some Article 11 exceptions, and Canada's supply management system might, therefore, be accepted by others in modified form. Producers of supply-managed commodities might be pressured to reduce domestic output and to accept a larger market share for imports. Furthermore, raw farm products might have to be sold to food processors at lower prices so that they can survive in a more competitive global environment.[72] If the EEC agrees to (partial or complete) tariffication, the major trading nations might decide to dispense with the agricultural exceptions under Article 11. Canada would then have to decide whether to implement the GATT ruling against it on processed dairy products or to ignore it and risk U.S. retaliation. The question arises whether it is a viable option for Canada to unilaterally maintain its supply management-related import barriers in such circumstances.

Because of its smaller economic size and capacities, Canada could not consider emulating many of the unilateral strategies adopted by the United States and the EEC. In a recently completed study, I found that Canada normally has resorted to bilateral, plurilateral, and multilateral (rather than unilateral) strategies to achieve its agricultural trade objectives. Examples of this preference include Canada's opposition to most GATT waivers and exceptions, its support for a duopolistic arrangement with the U.S. (and later for a plurilateral arrangement) to stabilize wheat prices, its consistently strong support for the GATT and the FAO's Consultative Subcommittee on Surplus Disposal, its membership in the Cairns group, and its endorsement of the bilateral free trade agreement.

Canada has not been averse to unilateralism in certain areas. For example, it has adopted some innovative practices in providing agricultural export credits and credit guarantees, and it has sometimes acted unilaterally (as have other countries) in limiting agricultural imports.[73] Nevertheless, even in these cases Canada has been careful to abide by GATT regulations. As discussed, Canada has repeatedly indicated that its supply management system meets the legal requirements of Article 11. Canada's support for the GATT, despite its own array of protectionist policies, results in no small degree from its relatively limited power resources. Since Canada often 'cannot directly influence the imposition of national controls by other countries,' it frequently is willing 'to tie its own hands – as long as it is able to tie the hands of others as well.'[74]

Given its traditional preference for group strategies, Canada would feel strong pressures to abide by a multilateral agreement to dispense with the agricultural exceptions in Article 11. It is understandable that there is skepticism regarding the federal government's long-term commitment to supply management. Thus, Barry Wilson has stated that Canada 'first will have to be seen fighting the good fight to defend supply management in Geneva before conceding defeat in the face of overwhelming odds.'[75] Nevertheless, the political problems confronting the Canadian government if it makes major concessions on the supply management issue should not be underestimated. The Union des Producteurs Agricoles (UPA) is a powerful farm interest group to which all Quebec farmers with sales over a minimal amount must pay dues, and it is fully committed to the maintenance of supply management related import barriers. The UPA is also highly nationalistic, and the Mulroney government must pay particular attention to its concerns in view of the failure to ratify the Meech Lake accord. Farmers supportive of supply management have considerable influence on the Ontario as well as on the Quebec government. Thus, the Ontario minister of agriculture and food has stated that 'it is imperative for Canada to state its demand that Article 11 of the General Agreement be strengthened and clarified,' and that Canadian producers must be 'assured of the Federal Government's commitment to supply management.'[76]

Countries may adopt unilateral strategies for trade liberalization as well as for protectionist purposes. Since Canada's most basic commitment is to freer trade, the question arises as to whether it might unilaterally reduce trade barriers even if the GATT talks are a failure. As Robert Paarlberg notes, too little attention has been given to unilateral liberal policy reform because of the predispositions of most international relations scholars:

> Among liberal internationalists...'unilateralism' has a bad name. The opposite approach – 'co-operation' – is taken as something close to a supreme value. There is some historical basis for this association between *unilateralism* and *illiberal* policy (in the 1930s), and then in the post-war period between *multilateralism* and *trade liberalization* (at least in areas other than agriculture). But unilateral policies do not have to be illiberal, as the repeal of the Corn Laws by itself would seem to indicate. Nor do 'cooperative' multilateral policies always reduce barriers to trade – witness the multifiber arrangement.[77]

There are strong domestic pressures for agricultural trade reform, and Canada seems prepared to take some steps towards liberalization even without a GATT agreement. Domestic reasons for discontent with the status quo include 'the huge expense, the many failures, the unwanted perversities, and the regional inequities in what we are doing now for farmers.'[78] The Mulroney government's ideological preference for deregulation and greater market orientation is an additional factor pointing towards decreased government intervention in agriculture. However, agricultural reform in Canada would have definite limits in the absence of a multilateral agreement. When larger states undertake unilateral policy reforms, others might be inclined to follow their example, but Canada probably has insufficient influence to be the trend-setter in this area. Canada would therefore be running the risk of simply losing its competitive advantages because of its unilateral concessions. While Canadian consumers, taxpayers, and food processors would benefit from agricultural reform, the opposition to change among a number of farm groups would be great. It is therefore unlikely that the government would take major initiatives to liberalize agricultural trade if the GATT talks end in failure.

Bilateral Strategies

There is a long history of Canadian-American co-operation in the agricultural trade area, and bilateral consultations on grain issues have been almost continuous since the Depression of the 1930s.[79] A bilateral approach to agricultural trade issues 'offends multilateral purists, but recent experience shows that in several respects it has been more likely to produce trade-liberalizing results.'[80] A prime example of trade bilateralism, which is relevant to a discussion of Canada's future options, is the Canada-U.S. Free Trade Agreement. To assess the importance of the agreement, it is first necessary to provide some background on bilateral trading relations.

The significance of Canadian-American agricultural trade is often underestimated because of the types of commodities exchanged. For example, in 1988 over 40 per cent of Canada's agricultural exports to the U.S. (by value) were live animals and red meats, while 42 per cent of Canada's agricultural imports from the U.S. were fruits and vegetables. Commodities of this nature have a lower profile than do grains and oilseeds, which account for about 75 per cent of Canadian and 65 per cent of U.S. farm exports. Nevertheless, Canadian-American interdependence is evident when trade in *all* agricultural commodities is considered. The United States has been the largest single country market for Canadian agricultural exports in a number of years, including 1950-2, 1968-73, and 1983-8. In 1988, the U.S. accounted for 28.4 per cent of Canada's agricultural exports, followed by China (16.2 per cent), Japan (14.1 per cent), the Soviet Union (9.5 per cent), and the EEC (8.9 per cent). In addition, the United States has been the largest supplier of Canadian farm imports every year in the postwar period (supplying 56.7 per cent in 1988). Since Canada and the United States export some agricultural products almost exclusively to each other, this trade also helps to maintain the vitality of particular geographic regions and farm commodity groups.

The Free Trade Agreement therefore could help to further some of Canada's trade liberalization objectives. Although agricultural provisions in the FTA are limited, they call for the elimination over ten years of bilateral tariffs on agricultural goods; the conditional opening of bilateral trade in wheat, oats, and barley; the exemption of the two countries from each other's meat import laws; an agreement not to use export subsidies in bilateral trade; the elimination of rail subsidies on Canadian agricultural goods moved to the U.S. through west coast ports; and an agreement to decrease technical barriers to trade.[81] In addition, Chapter 19 of the FTA deals with binational dispute settlement, which is relevant to agriculture because of the large number of trade relief cases involving agricultural products. Canada viewed dispute settlement as the single most important negotiating issue, since it wanted more assured access to the U.S. market. While Canada wanted a binding arbitration panel to resolve all trade complaints, it did not achieve this objective. Instead, trade complaints are to proceed through normal domestic channels in each country, with access to a binational dispute panel only after the domestic process has been completed. The panel decisions will be limited mainly to determining whether or not the country in question has made a countervail or antidumping decision in accordance with its own laws. This panel system will exist for five to seven years, during which time the United States and Canada will try to develop a new set of joint rules for the use of trade relief legislation.

It should be noted that bilateralism can sometimes detract from a country's ability to pursue multilateral trade options. Thus, some analysts feel that the Canada-U.S. Free Trade Agreement marks a reversion from the GATT system to a system of regional trading blocs. The planned consolidation of the EEC in 1992 could be viewed as yet another step in the regionalization process. The U.S. tendency to deal with some major trade disputes on a bilateral basis can also interfere with Canada's (and other countries') multilateral options. Under Section 301 of the 1988 U.S. Trade Act, the United States names countries for particular attention which (allegedly) create barriers to its exports. Other GATT members have been concerned about the time and effort the United States has devoted to such bilateral matters. Despite the potential pitfalls of bilateralism, the agricultural trade provisions were in fact included in the FTA largely in the hope that they would provide a stimulus to multilateral reform. Thus, a U.S. department of agriculture official has stated that 'if our two nations - both of which have highly developed systems, and both of which have a big stake in freer and fairer agricultural trade - cannot resolve the issues that trouble our trade, what chance for success will there be for the Uruguay Round?'[82]

If the Uruguay Round has a successful conclusion, discussions as a follow-up to the FTA should complement and facilitate discussions in the GATT because the bilateral and multilateral negotiations have dealt with many similar issues. These include efforts to stem the increase of agricultural trade barriers and to phase out the barriers that now exist; to clarify what subsidies are trade-distorting and therefore countervailable; to develop a consensus on measuring and comparing subsidy practices in different countries; to freeze trade-distorting agricultural subsidies at their present levels and then decrease them over time; to harmonize the differences in technical regulations, standards, and certification procedures regarding health and product safety that hinder trade; and to improve dispute-settlement processes.[83]

If the Uruguay Round does not result in a successful agreement, it is likely that Canada will rely more on resolving certain agricultural trade issues bilaterally with the United States. Indeed, Canada has displayed a distinct tendency historically to adopt bilateral strategies in this area when the multilateral option was closed off.[84] Some major agricultural trade problems for Canada, such as those relating to U.S. countervailing duties, might eventually be resolved in a bilateral setting. Furthermore, bilateral problem solving could be effective for commodities that Canada and the United States export almost exclusively to each other.

Nevertheless, the most important agricultural commodities that the U.S. and Canada export – grains and oilseeds – are sent primarily to third countries. Some fundamental agricultural trade disputes would therefore be difficult to resolve in the absence of a multilateral agreement. For example, in Article 701 of the FTA the U.S. and Canada agree to take account of each other's interests when using export subsidies in sales to third countries. Critics in Canada maintain that the United States is not taking this provision seriously since it is continuing to subsidize grain exports to Canadian markets. However, the United States is simply unwilling to scale down its export subsidies without similar concessions from the European Community. The U.S. and Canada have also been reluctant to make substantial concessions to each other on non-tariff barriers to imports before third countries have also offered concessions. In summary, Canada has some bilateral trade options in lieu of a multilateral agreement, but they have definite limitations.

Plurilateral Strategies

A plurilateral approach involves more countries than a bilateral approach but fewer countries than a multilateral approach. States pursue a multilateral strategy by acting through international organizations which do not limit their membership according to geographical areas, cultural groups, or economic/political criteria. Plurilateral groupings are more limited in membership and include such bodies as the Cairns group, the OECD, and the Group of Seven.

In view of its predilection for group strategies, Canada has at various times been attracted by plurilateralism. For example, in earlier research this author found that Canada was far more favourable than was the United States to an exporters' pricing agreement if efforts to negotiate an effective International Wheat Agreement (involving importers as well as exporters) in the late 1970s failed. Indeed, after the IWA negotiations were suspended in February 1979, the Canadian Wheat Board minister invited the other major wheat exporters (the U.S., Australia, and Argentina) to a ministerial meeting in Saskatchewan to discuss the possibility of concluding an exporters' agreement. However, for a variety of reasons the United States was opposed to an arrangement limited to exporters, and the Canadian efforts were unsuccessful. Even if the U.S. had felt otherwise, an exporters' pricing agreement bypassing consumer states would be extremely risky, since the market power that foodgrain exporters can exert is limited.[85]

Plurilateral groupings, such as the OECD, have often complemented (rather than competed with) the GATT in dealing with agricultural trade problems. For example, OECD discussions have sometimes led to binding agreements in subsequent GATT negotiations. While preparations were underway for the Uruguay Round, two OECD committees were conducting a Ministerial Trade Mandate (MTM) study which helped to set the agenda for the multilateral negotiations. When the preliminary report of the MTM work was released in May 1987, the OECD Council of Ministers issued a communique 'committing' its members to reforming their domestic agricultural policies and to confronting agricultural trade problems in the GATT. The Cairns group is another plurilateral grouping that is closely linked with the GATT negotiations. This group has permitted its members to wield more influence at the Uruguay Round than any of them could exert individually.

On various occasions, Canada has used its membership in plurilateral groupings, such as the Group of Seven, the Quadrilateral Group of Trade Ministers, the OECD, and the Cairns group, to push for a common approach on agricultural trade in the GATT. For example, in 1987 Prime Minister Mulroney raised the issue of agricultural subsidies at the Venice Economic Summit, and the minister for international trade persuaded the other members of the Quadrilateral group to give priority to agriculture on the world trade agenda.[86]

It is nevertheless unlikely that plurilateral groups can 'substitute' for the GATT in any sense if the Uruguay Round is a failure. First, these groups do not have the legal authority that rests with the GATT. Second, plurilateral groups, such as the Group of Seven, the Quadrilateral group, and the OECD, all have as members the main industrial state protagonists on current agricultural trade issues in the GATT: the U.S., the EEC, and Japan. The Cairns group is an exceedingly diverse body composed of Western industrial states, less-developed countries, and one East European state. Canada's attempt to protect its supply management system has done much recently to expose the major differences among Cairns group members. As a result, it has been easier for these groupings to issue declarations in support of agricultural trade reform than to ensure that such reform will in fact occur.

There are, of course, plurilateral options for Canada that may present themselves in the future. Foremost among them is the possibility of a Canada-U.S.-Mexico free trade agreement. Canada's exports to Mexico are largely composed of agricultural products and transportation machinery. However, Mexico is Canada's fifteenth largest export market for agri-food products, accounting for only about one per cent of such exports. While Canada has important interests to safeguard in the case of a trilateral free trade agreement, the opportunities such an accord present for an expansion of Canadian agricultural exports should not be overestimated. In conclusion, plurilateralism can complement but not substitute for the multilateral option through the GATT.

Multilateral Strategies

There is a widespread feeling that the agricultural trade regime is in a state of crisis, and Canada is certainly feeling the effects.[87] Indications of the crisis include the buildup of surpluses and deterioration of prices for major agricultural commodities, the increased levels of protection and subsidy in most industrial states, the serious economic problems confronting farmers, the persistence of hunger and malnutrition in important regions of the Third World, and the heightened levels of conflict as revealed in countervailing duty cases, the U.S.-EEC export subsidy war, and other disputes.

The crisis situation has demonstrated that there is an urgent need for more effective regime principles, rules, and decisionmaking procedures to resolve disputes and dismantle protectionist barriers. As a result, the major trading nations have acknowledged more directly than ever before that 'national policies, which are geared to achieve what are seen as essentially domestic objectives ... have an important impact on international trade.'[88] It is recognized that domestic policies must be altered if there is to be some resolution of the impasse in agriculture. Instituting domestic reforms in the context of multilateral negotiations has some important advantages, including the following:

> There are opportunities for eliminating those interventions which were introduced to counter the subsidies, distortions and instabilities attributable to other countries' policies; concerted policy-disarmament by all countries reduces the size of the adjustments required of each; reform is more politically acceptable if the economic costs of adjustment are seen to be widely and equitably shared; and externally-specified obligations can provide the political 'cover' needed to effect changes that are desired but which are too politically sensitive to be tackled solely in a national context.[89]

A major task of the Uruguay Round negotiations is to produce an agreement that promotes agricultural trade liberalization and desubsidization. To further the process of desubsidization, GATT members must agree 'on the types of policy instruments that are least trade-distorting and begin to reshape farm programs accordingly.'[90] To achieve this objective, many liberal or free trade economists feel that farm programs must be 'decoupled.' These economists maintain that decoupled programs would provide support to farmers without distorting production, consumption, and trade. If programs were decoupled, they argue, domestic agricultural policies would have only minimal trade-distorting effects on foreign countries. Some critics of this approach, on the other hand, express doubts that agricultural programs could be genuinely decoupled and still provide adequate support to farmers over the long term.

In accordance with its support for trade liberalization, Canada has endorsed the decoupling concept and has expressed its willingness to decouple its own farm programs if other GATT members take similar actions. To some extent the effects of decreased support for farmers would be offset by increases in effective demand and trade. Nevertheless, the effects of decoupling on Canadian farmers would vary widely according to the commodities produced. Livestock producers, for example, have received relatively little government support, and they would actually benefit in a decoupled age. However, the negative effects of decoupling on some other producers could be substantial. Grain producers might benefit from an increase in export prices, but this would not compensate for the loss in payments if the transport subsidy, the Special Canadian Grains Program, and the Western Grains Stabilization Program were removed. There would also be a definite decline in prices and the number of producers in supply-managed sectors.[91] While some Canadian producers would suffer losses as a result of trade liberalization and the termination of government programs, Canadian consumers and taxpayers would benefit from lower prices and reduced government expenditures.

Depending on the negotiations, agreement might be reached to engage in partial decoupling or in phased decoupling. If Canada decoupled in phases, transition payments could be provided to farmers to ease their adjustment to the changes. There is also a variety of policies the Canadian government could adopt to provide income security to producers in decoupled forms. These include 'direct government transfer payments unrelated to current production, land-use conversion programs to encourage conservation, recreation and wildlife use, early retirement programs in exchange for rights to future farm program benefits, and individual and community adjustment programs to encourage the development of alternative employment for rural people.'[92] It is likely, however, that a considerable number of farmers would view some of these measures as a disguised form of welfare.

As discussed, Canada's credibility in pushing for agricultural trade liberalization and desubsidization has been undermined recently by its support for supply-management related import barriers. The Canadian government must realize that it may not be possible to restrict U.S. and EEC export subsidies (under GATT Article 16) without also extending Article 11's limitations on quantitative restrictions to agriculture. If export subsidies were constrained, the EEC would have to absorb more of its agricultural surpluses in the home market and there would be pressures to decrease imports. Since EEC variable import levies are not covered by current GATT rules, it would therefore be necessary to alter Article 11 to ensure that the use of variable levies did not increase. In such circumstances, it is inconceivable that GATT members would support Canada's proposal to broaden Article 11 coverage for agriculture.[93]

Canada has proposed that GATT adopt a 'comprehensive approach' to the removal of import barriers, in which 'all exceptions and waivers would be phased out, access under each tariff line would be bound, and variable import levies, minimum import price systems and all other measures affecting access to markets would be brought under the purview of effective and enforceable GATT disciplines.'[94] If other GATT members decide to adopt this 'comprehensive approach,' it is highly doubtful that they would permit Canada to maintain the status quo with regard to its supply management system. Whether Canada's trading partners would accept Agriculture Canada's proposal to retain import barriers as part of a supply management system that was more 'market responsive' remains to be seen.[95]

Canada is certainly not alone in following contradictory policies, and all major trading nations share the dilemma of balancing domestic against global political realities. For example, even though the u.s. administration has pushed aggressively for tariffication, C. Ford Runge notes that 'the idea of tariffication has not gone down well in Congress.'[96] All major GATT members must face the reality that domestic and international agricultural reforms are closely linked, and that one is not likely to occur without the other. Farm support will continue to be necessary and desirable, but it will need to be decoupled as much as possible from production, consumption, and trade.

The fact remains that the GATT has an extremely poor record in dealing with agriculture, and the Uruguay Round agricultural trade negotiations might ultimately fail. Canada is already embarked on a major review of its agricultural policies and is beginning to scale down its farm support programs, actions which are premised on the assumption that the GATT talks will succeed. Even if the negotiations fail, there will be domestic pressure for major reform, because 'Canadian society will surely question whether there is any sense in participating indefinitely in the costly subsidization of the incomes of people and the value of assets engaged in the production of agricultural products in chronic excess supply.'[97] As discussed, Canada could pursue certain unilateral, bilateral, and plurilateral strategies if the Uruguay Round ends in failure.

In the absence of GATT reform, however, a major dismantling of Canada's support programs could have serious economic consequences for many farmers and serious political consequences for the government in power. It would seem, therefore, that Canada's best option is to do its utmost to ensure that the GATT talks succeed. The discussion in this chapter demonstrates that unilateral, bilateral, and plurilateral strategies to promote trade liberalization are often complementary with the multilateral route, and that Canada would be best advised to pursue a variety of these 'options' simultaneously. As a smaller state that has a comparative advantage in the production of some major agricultural commodities, Canada (and large segments of its farm community) is in dire need of a stronger agricultural trade regime.

CHAPTER FOUR

Canada and the Private International Trade Law Regime

A. Claire Cutler

As a trading nation, Canada has traditionally been committed to the principles underlying the multilateral, rule-based trading regime and actively involved in efforts to regulate international trade practices. The belief that participation in multilateral forums such as the General Agreement on Tariffs and Trade (GATT) strengthens Canadian leverage in negotiating trade issues and promotes an open trading environment that enhances Canadian trade opportunities are identified as among the benefits flowing from Canadian participation.[1] It is indeed curious that in spite of Canadian interest in the evolving framework for the regulation of international trade, until quite recently there has been very little interest or involvement in the regime governing private international trade relations. The law of private international trade is concerned with the international sale, transportation, financing and insurance of goods, as well as dispute resolution. These transactions are designated as 'private' because 'the relations with which we are here concerned are primarily between individual traders themselves, involving the state or the international community only as regulator.'[2]

Today, Canada is an active participant in the unification of private international trade law. The unification of trade law may be defined as 'the process by which conflicting rules of two or more systems of national laws applicable to the same international legal transaction is replaced by a single rule.'[3] The unification movement began in Europe in the second-half of the nineteenth century and involves the creation of uniform or model laws, the adoption of international conventions, and the unification of trade customs and practices governing international transactions and dispute resolution. While Canada is now active in this movement, such participation is recent. It is only in the last twenty years or so that Canada has shown an interest in the private international trade regime and really only since the beginning of the past decade that Canada has actively participated in the process of rule creation. As recently as 1980, a noted Canadian trade law authority commented on the passive role played by Canada in the United Nations Commission on International Trade Law (UNCITRAL), the main contemporary inter-governmental agency for the formulation of private international trade law. He observed that 'as one of the world's leading trading nations it is distinctly anomalous that we have not so far sought full membership in the organization. Smaller states with far less at stake are members.'[4]

This chapter will review Canadian attitudes and policies regarding the regulation of private international trade and explore the reasons for earlier disinterest in the regime. In reviewing Canadian policies it will be necessary to examine the main characteristics of the regime. In doing so we shall see that in some areas Canada has been particularly active, while in others there has been minimal interest and little in the way of articulated policy. Various explanations of Canadian policies will be considered, as will future policy options. It will be argued that a significant impediment to Canada's implementation of new conventions and model laws lies in the constitutional division of legislative powers. The fact that many private trade law issues involve matters that fall within provincial legislative competence limits the federal government's capacity to unilaterally enter into binding international agreements and conventions. However, the constitutional problem is not insurmountable, as evidenced by federal-provincial co-operation in the unification of the law governing international arbitration. Further obstacles were derived in the past from the unity provided by Anglo-American legal traditions and the policies and attitudes towards the unification movement held by Canada's major trading partners. In transactions with British and American traders there was little perceived need for greater uniformity. Moreover, the United States, Canada's major trading partner, was also rather late in joining the unification movement. Recognition in Canada of the benefits generated by uniform laws really only began to occur when it became clear that whether Canadians liked it or not, their trade relations would be drawn into the international regulatory framework by virtue of Canada's trade relations with the United States and the latter's participation in the regime. In addition, the changing composition of Canada's trading partners and the proclivity of many new partners, particularly Pacific Rim countries, to submit their trade transactions to international regulation suggests that there will be an even greater need for Canadians to familiarize themselves with the regime in the future.

OVERVIEW OF THE PRIVATE INTERNATIONAL TRADE LAW REGIME

International regimes may be defined as 'sets of implicit or explicit principles, norms, rules, and decisionmaking procedures around which actors' expectations converge in a given area of international relations.'[5] Functional theories of international regimes posit that such arrangements reduce information and transaction costs among participants.[6] The private international trade regime functions to facilitate international trade through the unification of diverse national rules of law and practices. The unification movement presumes that uniformity and transparency in the laws regulating commercial transactions produce gains for all participants by reducing uncertainty as to the applicable system of law and by reducing the costs of doing business.

> The impetus for the unification of law of international trade stems from the difficulties typically faced by those who engage in international commercial transactions as a result of the multiplicity of, and divergencies in national laws. A single transaction involving multiple legal relationships (for example, a contract of sale, payment provisions, insurance, transportation, etc.) may be subject to divergent rules of different national laws, seldom known in all their particulars to all the parties directly involved. On questions of performance, interpretation and applications, the parties require adequate knowledge of the legal conditions governing the performance of the general obligations.[7]

By providing for uniform performance and enforcement standards, model laws, and standardized contracts and contract practices, the private international trade regime helps to reduce legal uncertainty and the costs of transacting.[8] Indeed, the values embodied in regime principles, norms, rules, and decisionmaking procedures emphasize the priority given to maximum transparency and predictability, while at the same time retaining the flexibility and informality required for the expeditious conduct of commercial relations.[9] While a full discussion of the normative basis of the regime is beyond the scope of this chapter, it will be useful to identify the main principles that provide the foundation for the regime and review the key formulating agencies that constitute the decisionmaking framework.

Regime Principles and Formulating Agencies

Four principles provide the foundation for the regime: the autonomy principle, the sanctity principle, the informality principle, and the arbitration principle. The principle of the autonomy of the parties' will, or freedom of contract, provides that 'the parties are free, subject to limitations imposed by national laws, to contract on whatever terms they are able to agree.'[10] The sanctity principle provides that 'once the parties have entered into a contract, that contract must be faithfully fulfilled (*pacta sunt servanda*) and only in very exceptional circumstances does the law excuse a party from performing his obligations.'[11] The informality principle requires that international transactions be regulated and enforced with minimal formal and procedural requirements.[12] The arbitration principle provides 'that arbitration is widely used in international trade for the settlement of disputes and the awards of arbitration tribunals command far-reaching international recognition and are often capable of enforcement abroad.'[13] These principles reflect the emphasis placed upon the creation of a voluntary, suppletive framework for the regulation of private international trade relations. While some of the regime rules are of a mandatory and prohibitory nature, the majority are optional and empower or permit the parties to transact or settle their disputes according to prescribed terms. It would thus be inaccurate to characterize the regime in terms of injunctions and prohibitions, for the model laws, codes, and contracts operate at the option of the parties, and the parties are free in many instances to contract out of the application of international conventions.[14] In addition to reflecting the value of providing the parties with maximum scope to define the terms of their agreements (limited, of course, by national public policy constraints), the regime principles reflect a disdain for formalities and a suspicion of the insularity and potential partiality of national courts and national legal systems. The preference for arbitration as the principal mechanism for dispute resolution and the avoidance of formal procedures in the conduct of arbitrations attests to the regime emphasis on the informal, impartial, and expeditious settlement of disputes.[15]

Canadian attitudes and policies regarding the regulation of private international trade exhibit a commitment to these regime principles, though as mentioned earlier, Canada was rather late in joining the unification movement. The federal Department of Justice has primary responsibility for the unification of private international law. However, the department consults widely with other federal government departments, the Uniform Law Commission, the Advisory Group on International Law, provincial and territorial governments, and Canadian business groups.

Efforts to unify private international trade law began in the second half of the nineteenth century in the work of private organizations such as the Hamburg Bourse for Corn Traders (1868), the Bremen Cotton Bourse (1872), the Silk Association of America (1873), and the London Corn Trade Association (1877). In the twentieth century, a number of international inter-governmental and non-governmental organizations became involved in the unification movement. The activities of the following, most significant agencies, will here be considered: the Hague Conference on Private International Law, the International Institute for the Unification of Private Law (UNIDROIT), the United Nations Commission on International Trade Law (UNCITRAL), and the International Chamber of Commerce (ICC).[16]

The Hague Conference on Private International Law

The first inter-governmental body to undertake the unification of commercial law was the Hague Conference on Private International Law, which was established in 1893 but only attained the status of an international organization in 1955.[17] The Hague Conference works towards the progressive unification of the conflicts of law rules relating to a number of private law areas. With regard to international trade law, its main unification efforts concern the enforcement of foreign judgments, the international sale of goods, and procedural matters.[18] However, as one author has noted, acceptance of the Hague Conventions by member states has been 'slow.'[19] This is attributed to a lack of public interest in the subject matter and the fact that the delegations are rarely constituted by individuals able to exercise influence in their national political systems. In addition, the essentially European and civil law orientation of the Hague's earlier unification efforts no doubt contributed to the disinterest of common law countries. Canada only became a member of the Hague Conference in 1968, and, to the author's knowledge, there was no official Canadian policy regarding the work of this organization prior to that time.[20] The United States, though invited to attend Hague Conferences held in the latter part of the nineteenth century and after the First World War, did not attend.[21] American participation in Hague Conferences only began in 1964, following congressional approval of membership.[22]

Today, Canada participates actively in the Hague Conference. While the unification of trade law has largely been taken over by UNCITRAL, the Hague Conference has adopted conventions on civil procedure that have a bearing on trade relations. Canada is party to the Convention on the Service Abroad of Judicial and Extrajudicial Documents in Civil or Commercial Matters (1965).[23] This convention facilitates the service of documents by contracting states by providing rules for service of documents abroad and by establishing a system of central authorities to receive service in each jurisdiction. While the federal government decided to become party to the convention in the early 1970s, it did not come into force in Canada until 1 May 1989. The delay was due to the fact that the convention deals with matters that fall within provincial jurisdiction and, thus, requires implementation in the provinces and territories. The absence of a federal-state clause enabling application of the convention to only those jurisdictions that have enacted implementing legislation dictated waiting upon commitments from the provinces and territories.

The Department of Justice is presently consulting with the provinces on the implementation of two other Hague conventions of relevance here: the Convention on the Taking of Evidence Abroad in Civil and Commercial Matters (1970),[24] which facilitates the transmission and enforcement of rogatory commissions, and the Convention on Abolishing the Requirement of Legalisation of Foreign Public Documents (1961), which simplifies and accelerates the process of authenticating public documents.[25]

These three conventions establish a procedural framework for international commercial transactions that embodies the regime principle of informality and emphasizes the expeditious conduct of commercial transactions. By standardizing and streamlining procedures they contribute to greater certainty, lower costs, and less delay.

UNIDROIT

Further efforts to unify private international trade law have been undertaken by the International Institute for the Unification of Private Law (UNIDROIT), an inter-governmental organization established in 1926 within the framework of the League of Nations. UNIDROIT engages in the harmonization and unification of private law and the preparation of uniform rules. UNIDROIT has worked on a variety of trade subjects including, for example, the preparatory work for a conference held at The Hague in 1964, which produced two conventions on the international sale of goods: the Convention Relating to a Uniform Law on the Formation of Contracts for the International Sale of Goods (ULF) and the Convention Relating to a Uniform Law on the International Sale of Goods (ULIS), both known as the Hague Sales Conventions.[26] The Hague Sales Conventions have not received broad support. Most of the countries who participated in drafting the conventions were European, and of the twenty-seven states who signed the Final Act of the Hague Conference twenty-two were European.[27] Canada did not attend the Hague Conference and did not participate in the drafting of the conventions. Though, today, Canada participates fully in UNIDROIT and has a representative on the governing council, Canada only became a member in 1969. Nor did the United States participate significantly in the drafting of the 1964 Hague Sales Conventions. Congressional approval of u.s. membership in UNIDROIT came at the same time as did approval of membership in the Hague Conference, at which point the drafting process was more or less finished.[28]

UNIDROIT's unification efforts have extended to a number of other areas of commercial law.[29] Its efforts to unify the laws governing agency in the international sale of goods resulted in the adoption of the Convention on Agency in the International Sale of Goods in Vienna in 1983, which is not yet in force.[30] The Department of Justice has deferred consideration of this convention, pending its consideration of the Vienna Convention on Contracts for the International Sale of Goods, to be discussed shortly.

In 1988, Canada hosted a diplomatic conference for the adoption of the final texts of draft conventions on international leasing and international factoring, prepared under the auspices of UNIDROIT with Canadian participation. The conventions were designed to fill a gap in the law governing those methods of financing that have developed in 'financial circles to meet newly-perceived market needs characteristic of the move towards a credit economy' and which are 'largely untrammeled by legal regulation.'[31] The Convention on International Financial Leasing is intended to harmonize existing domestic laws governing such transactions as well as to serve as a model for domestic law in jurisdictions where such activity is new and unregulated.[32] The Convention on International Factoring is intended to provide uniformity among states with respect to their domestic laws governing international factoring.[33] Both conventions embody the autonomy principle in that they provide a permissive legal framework within which the transacting parties are left considerable freedom of contract to add to or modify the rules, or to opt out of the application of the conventions if desired. The conventions are not yet in force; eight states have signed but not ratified them.[34] The Department of Justice intends to review the merits of becoming a party to the conventions and will consult with the provinces, territories, and relevant business groups. The Uniform Law Conference of Canada has been asked to draft uniform law that will serve as a model for implementation.

UNIDROIT is presently working on the law on franchising. After consultations with provincial governments and business groups, Canada recommended that work proceed towards preparing a legal guide on the franchising contract, expressing doubt as to the value of attempting to develop an international convention unifying the law in this area.

Other areas of UNIDROIT activity of interest to Canada include assessing the feasibility and desirability of unifying the law governing security interests in mobile equipment, proposed by Canada in 1988,[35] and the drafting of non-binding rules and principles governing international commercial contracts.

The real impetus to the unification of trade law came with the establishment of the United Nations Commission on International Trade Law (UNCITRAL).[36] UNCITRAL was established by the United Nations General Assembly in 1966 and given a mandate to 'further the progressive harmonization and unification of the law of international trade.'[37] This mandate includes, among other undertakings, the preparation or promotion of international conventions, model laws and uniform laws, and the promotion of codification and wider acceptance of international trade terms, customs, and practices.[38] UNCITRAL was created in response to observations made by Professor Clive Schmitthoff, who is regarded as the 'conceptual father' of UNCITRAL,[39] as consultant to the United Nations Secretariat in the preparation of its report cited earlier on the progressive development of the law of international trade. Schmitthoff observed a lack of co-ordination among organizations involved in the unification of trade law. He further observed that unification efforts failed to achieve universal application due to the lack of participation of developing countries and the European, civil law basis of earlier unification efforts.[40] UNCITRAL was thus created with a view to representing 'the principal economic and legal systems of the world, and of the developed and developing countries.'[41] Membership in the organization is designed to represent all major legal systems in the world and states of various levels of development, including both planned and market economies. Membership is determined on the basis of regional representation,[42] and, pursuant to the rules of procedure adopted by UNCITRAL, decisionmaking proceeds by way of two-thirds majority vote. However, according to Canadian representatives at UNCITRAL, no decision has yet been put to a vote. The commission has always reached decisions by consensus.[43]

Work proceeds in working groups, which are assigned specific areas of the law for unification. In the earlier years, the working groups were composed of only a portion of UNCITRAL members. The remaining members and international organizations were able to participate as observers. However, in later years all UNCITRAL members came to be represented in the working groups, and observer status was extended to include non-members as well. As a result, a review of the working methods of UNCITRAL conducted by the United Nations Secretariat concluded that 'since all States are invited to attend either as member or as observer, the principal of regional representation may have less practical significance than it did in earlier days.'[44] Given the broad interpretation[45] of the role of observers and the norm of reaching decisions by consensus, these observations may indeed be accurate.

However, Canada, participating only as an observer in the 1970s and 1980s, did seek full membership, replacing Australia in 1989, reflecting the belief that full membership enhances visibility and influence in the commission.[46]

UNCITRAL has created five working groups, of which two are no longer active. The Working Group on Time-Limits and Limitations (Prescriptions), created in 1969, went out of existence after the preparation of the Convention on the Limitation Period in the International Sale of Goods (New York 1974).[47] The convention came into force in 1988, among ten contracting states, and has been referred to as UNCITRAL's 'first born.'[48] It provides uniform limitation or prescription periods within which parties to an international sales contract may exercise claims arising out of the transaction, unifying an area of law known for the disparate approaches adopted by common and civil law jurisdictions.[49] 'Domestic limitation periods range from 6 months to 30 years, and conflicts rules in this area are unusually diverse and unclear, with obvious opportunities for forum shopping. To meet this problem, UNCITRAL and a Diplomatic Conference of 66 States unanimously agreed on a limitation period of 4 years.'[50] The unification of limitation periods reflects the regime values of promoting certainty in and transparency or visibility of the parties' obligations in an international contract for the sale of goods. By establishing a uniform time period within which claims must be exercised, the convention creates a certain and visible time limitation on the parties' obligations. Canada has not acceded to the convention and accession remains unlikely until the federal government moves to accede to the companion Convention on Contracts for the International Sale of Goods. As of July 1989, the United States had not adopted the convention, although the American Bar Association has been soliciting opinions from the business law community regarding the need for uniform rules in the area.[51]

The Working Group on International Shipping Legislation, also created in 1969, was similarly phased out after preparation and adoption of the United Nations Convention on the Carriage of Goods by Sea (1978), the 'Hamburg Rules.'[52] The working group undertook this project, at the request of the United Nations Conference on Trade and Development (UNCTAD), where preparatory work for a convention was already underway. The Hamburg Rules create a mandatory legal regime regulating the liability of ocean carriers for damage, loss, and delay in the delivery of goods and modernizing the rules governing bills of lading. The mandatory nature of the Hamburg Rules constitutes a departure from the autonomy principle in that signatories cannot contract out of their application. They are intended to replace the Hague-Visby Rules (International Convention for the Unification of

Certain Rules relating to Bills of Lading, Brussels 1924 and Visby Protocol 1968) and seek to establish a more equitable allocation of risks between cargo owners and carriers.[53] The Hague Rules were regarded by many as favouring the interests of carriers at the expense of cargo owners. The Hamburg Rules raise the limits of liability and increase the responsibility of carriers by providing that the carrier is to be responsible for damage or loss unless it can prove that it was not negligent. Although Transport Canada has in the past recommended Canadian accession to the Hamburg Rules, considerable opposition from Canadian industry has frustrated accession.[54] By January 1989, only fourteen of the twenty ratifications or accessions required to bring the Hamburg Rules into effect were in place. As of that date, the United States had signed but not ratified the convention.[55]

The Working Group on the International Sale of Goods was created in 1969 and renamed the Working Group on International Contract Practices in 1979, after completing work on the unification of sales law. The Working Group on International Contract Practices is involved in a number of unification projects. It has prepared uniform rules on liquidated damages and penalty clauses, an undertaking in which Canada has not taken much interest.[56] The working group has also drafted a Convention on the Liability of Operators of Transport Terminals in International Trade, which will go to a diplomatic conference for review in 1991.[57] This convention harmonizes the laws governing the liability of transport terminal operators and is intended to fill a lacuna in the liability regimes established by other international transport conventions. These conventions govern the liability limitations of carriers but not that of non-carriage intermediaries, such as warehousemen or stevedores, whose liability would be governed by national law. It is believed that harmonization of limitations will make insurance needs more predictable and will facilitate recourse actions by carriers' multimodal transport operators, and freight forwarders against non-carriage intermediaries. Canada actively participated as an observer in this project and is presently consulting with industry and the provinces on the merits of adhesion to the convention. A diplomatic conference will be held in Vienna in April 1991 for the finalization, adoption, and opening for signature of the convention.

The working group's preparations of uniform law on independent guarantees and standby letters of credit proceeds with active Canadian participation. Of particular concern is a resolution of the differences in national laws governing fraud as a grounds for non-payment.[58]

By far, however, UNCITRAL's most successful unification efforts to date include the unification of sales law and arbitration law undertaken by the Working Group on International Contract Practices. Indeed, success in these areas can be explained by the fidelity of the Convention on Contracts for the International Sale of Goods (Vienna Sales Convention) and the UNCITRAL Model Law on Arbitration to the autonomy, sanctity, and informality principles.

The 1980 Vienna Sales Convention[59] concluded lengthy unification efforts that began many years ago and led to the 1964 Hague Sales Conventions mentioned earlier.[60] As stated by a member of the UNCITRAL Secretariat, the Vienna Sales Convention 'is the result of a truly global effort, with balanced representation of all the regions and economic and legal systems of the world.'[61] The Vienna Sales Convention entered into force on 1 January 1988 among signatory states[62] and governs the formation of the contract of sale and the rights, obligations, and remedies of parties to international sales contracts.[63] The automatic application of the convention to transactions that come within its sphere of application may suggest a departure from the autonomy principle.[64] However, the autonomy principle is upheld for 'freedom of contract ... is a fundamental principle of the convention and it provides expressly that parties to international sales contracts may opt out of the convention or vary the effect of any of its provisions.'[65] In addition, the informality principle is embodied in the absence of a writing requirement for the formation and variation of contracts.[66] The sanctity principle is reflected throughout the convention in the various provisions governing the performance obligations of the parties.

Canada has not acceded to the Vienna Sales Convention, though accession is definitely on the agenda. This suggests that there has been a shift in attitude towards the convention, for there was little initial support for accession. Federal legislation was introduced in the House of Commons on 26 September 1990, implementing the convention for certain federal entities.[67] Eight provinces and one territory have thus far enacted legislation implementing the convention.[68]

While it appears that Canada had a 'principal role' in drafting the federal-state clause, which allows a country with a federal system of government to exclude the application of the convention for some of the territorial units,[69] Canada did not participate actively in the drafting of the balance of the convention. Much of the work was finished before Canada began participating earnestly in UNCITRAL proceedings and certainly before Canada became a member. Furthermore, Canadian attitudes towards the convention at the time of its adoption in Vienna were lukewarm. Professors Jacob Ziegel and Claude Samson, two of the Canadian delegates at the Vienna Conference, in a Report to the Uniform Law Conference of Canada, questioned whether the convention would serve the needs of the Canadian business community.[70] On the basis of responses to a questionnaire seeking reactions to the convention, the paucity of litigation in Canada involving international sales agreements and the fact that about two-thirds of Canadian trade is with the United States, they concluded that 'it is difficult to see how this trade would be assisted by an international sales convention.'[71] Further reservations were expressed concerning the automatic application of the convention to contracting states and to those who have not signed the convention but come under its scope by virtue of transacting with a contracting state. It was felt that a regime requiring parties to expressly opt out of the application of the convention would draw in small importers and exporters. Rather than reducing transaction and information costs, the report suggests that the opting out requirement would add to the costs of doing business.

> As a loyal supporter of the UN and as a major trading nation, Canada has strong reasons to support UNCITRAL's goals and the concept of a uniform law of international sales. But sympathy should be combined with realism and practicality, and support should not be based on a misplaced form of idealism. The question that needs to be asked is whether the gains to Canada and the Provinces, both short term and long term but particularly long term, will exceed the costs of adopting a convention that contains some unfavourable features. Particularly worrisome from Canada's point of view is the need for contracting parties to opt out of the convention if they do not wish to be bound by its provisions. We have suggested that this requirement would particularly affect small exporters and importers (or those only incidentally involved in the importing and exporting of goods) who are least likely to know of the convention and who could normally be expected to prefer to be governed by a law more familiar to them.[72]

The report recommended a 'wait and see' approach and consultation with Canada's major trading partners and Canadian export and import interests before acceding to the convention. It concluded that 'Canada was seriously handicapped in making significant input into the UN Convention because Canada was not a member of UNCITRAL and has not sought to play an active role as an observer at the organization's meetings.'[73]

In contrast to Canada's limited participation in the preparation of the Vienna Sales Convention, the United States played a leading role. The experience as 'Johnnies-come-lately' at the 1964 Hague Sales Conference and the resulting inability to significantly adapt the civilian-based regime to the needs of common law sales prompted greater American activity in the unification movement.[74] In fact, John Honnold, one of the U.S. representatives to the 1980 Vienna Sales Conference, was head of the UNCITRAL Secretariat during the drafting of the convention, while Allan Farnsworth served as a U.S. representative to the conference and to UNCITRAL and served on the working group.[75] The extent of American influence led Honnold to conclude that 'the 1980 Sales Convention bears a much closer resemblance to the UCC [U.S. Uniform Commercial Code] than to any other legal system.'[76]

The Working Group on International Contract Practices began work on the unification of international arbitration law in 1981, leading to the adoption in 1985 of the UNCITRAL Model Law on International Commercial Arbitration.[77] The model law 'is intended to serve as a model of domestic arbitration legislation, harmonizing and making more uniform the practice and procedure of international commercial arbitration while freeing international arbitration from the parochial law of any given adopting state.'[78] The model law embodies the autonomy principle in the freedom it accords parties 'to tailor the "rules of the game" to their specific needs.'[79] For example, the parties are free to specify arbitrable subject matter and to choose institutionalized arbitration and rules,[80] the procedures governing the conduct of arbitrations, and the applicable law.[81] Party autonomy is also reflected in the strict limits placed on judicial intervention into arbitration proceedings. The 'approach of the model law, which allows limited prompt recourse to court during arbitral proceedings, but simultaneously permits the arbitration to go forward, represents a balance between the potential for delay through dilatory tactics of a recalcitrant party, and the futility and high cost of arbitral proceedings in which the award is ultimately set aside by the court.'[82] The informality principle is reflected in the wide powers over procedural matters given the arbitral tribunal. In tandem with the New York Convention on the Recognition and Enforcement of Foreign Arbitral Awards (New York Convention 1958),[83] the model law provides a comprehensive and voluntary regime for informal, expeditious, and impartial dispute resolution and enforcement.

Canada acceded to the New York Convention in 1986. The New York Convention permits the enforcement in Canada of awards made outside Canada in states that are parties to the convention and the enforcement of Canadian awards made abroad.[84] The enforcement of awards has been described as 'the cornerstone of the legal regime governing international commercial arbitration since the claimant is not resorting to arbitration as an academic exercise.'[85] There is little incentive to rely on arbitration in dispute settlement if the parties are unable to satisfy the award through enforcement proceedings. Indeed, enforcement is an integral component of the arbitration principle. It has been noted that, prior to accession to the New York Convention,

Canadian business persons were at a disadvantage in negotiating arbitration clauses in their contracts. This difficulty arose from the fact that Canadian business persons were unable to guarantee the rapid recognition and enforcement of foreign arbitral awards in Canada. This may have hindered the ability of Canadian business persons to compete on an equal footing with foreign competitors as foreign parties preferred to deal with business partners in countries where they could be guaranteed that there would be no problem with enforcement of their contracts (ie. those who are party to the New York Convention).[86]

The fact that all jurisdictions within the country have now enacted arbitration award enforcement legislation attests to the priority attached to the principle. However, Canada was the last of the major industrialized countries to accede to the New York Convention. The United States ratified the convention in 1970, Japan in 1961, Great Britain in 1975, the Soviet Union in 1960, and West Germany in 1967. While Canada was one of the 'last holdouts' among the major industrialized countries to accede to the New York Convention, we were the first to enact the model law.[87] Legislation has been enacted at the federal level, in all the provinces, in the Yukon and the Northwest Territories, incorporating the model law or variations of it into local law.[88] It has been noted that until these recent amendments, the common law provinces followed English law on arbitration, which allowed considerable scope for judicial intervention. The reform thus constitutes a 'U-turn' in policy regarding arbitration, for it significantly curtails judicial review of arbitral awards and, at the federal level, for the first time allows the Crown and its agencies to agree to arbitration.[89]

The Canadian response to the activities of the remaining UNCITRAL Working Groups has not been nearly as dramatic, with the exception of the work on international payments. The Working Group on International Payments (formerly the Working Group on International Negotiable Instruments) undertook the work leading to the adoption in 1988 of the United Nations Convention on International Bills of Exchange and International Promissory Notes.[90] Canada was the first state to sign this convention, and, as of October 1990, the only other signatory was the United States. The convention requires ten ratifications or accessions to come into force, and federal implementing legislation will be necessary. The Canadian delegation was particularly active in this unification effort, reflecting the concern expressed in the Canadian banking community regarding the need to unify the common and civil law approaches to international payments.[91] The leadership exhibited as first signatory to this convention stands in marked contrast to the delay in acceding to the New York Convention.

The Working Group on International Payments is also attempting to develop a model law on international credit transfers, reflecting the perceived need to regulate the electronic transfer of funds. The draft under negotiation at present has generated much opposition, largely from the United States, which would prefer a regime closer to that of the U.S. Uniform Commercial Code. There does not appear to be an articulated Canadian position at the moment.[92]

The Working Group on the New International Economic Order has produced a Legal Guide on Drawing Up International Contracts for the Construction of Industrial Works.[93] The guide is intended to assist the less developed countries in the negotiation and drafting of construction contracts. Canada participated actively in the preparation of the guide, which took several years, and is also participating in the current work on a Model Law on International Procurement, which seeks to render procurement practices more uniform, visible, and equitable.[94] Government procurement policies 'have become increasingly important non-tariff barriers to trade' and are of concern to Canadian exporters seeking access to foreign markets.[95] The Department of Justice is consulting with federal and provincial government departments regarding the interests at stake. It appears that Canadian priorities in the negotiations include ensuring the consistency of the model law with the GATT Procurement Code and the Canada-U.S. Free Trade Agreement and recognition of the right to employ socioeconomic factors in procurement practices.[96]

UNCITRAL is also currently working on a Legal Guide on Countertrade, though this project has not as yet been assigned to any particular working group.[97] This is an area of particular interest to Canada, for 'Canadian resource exporters are facing more and more demands for countertrade.'[98]

Before moving on to consider Canadian policy in greater detail, it should be noted that unification efforts are also being undertaken by other organizations. At a regional, inter-governmental level, Canada, now a member of the Organization of American States (OAS), is reviewing the work of the Inter-American Specialized Conferences on Private International Law with a view to the possibility of acceding to conventions governing commercial arbitration and civil procedures. Two European conventions adopted by the Council of Europe on service of documents and obtaining evidence abroad in administrative matters have been submitted to the provinces for review. Canada is also considering acceding to the convention between the European Economic Community and the European Free Trade Association on the jurisdiction and enforcement of judgments, which permits the accession of non-European states.[99]

In addition, the International Chamber of Commerce (ICC), a private, non-governmental organization, has developed standardized rules and procedures governing documentary credits, terms of trade, contract guarantees, arbitration, and conciliation.[100] These guidelines are of voluntary application, reflecting the operation of the autonomy principle which underscores the emphasis placed by the regime on self-regulation by the international business community. The ICC Uniform Customs and Practice for Documentary Credits and Uniform Rules for Collections are widely used by Canadian banks in their international transactions.[101] In addition, Canadian traders regularly adopt the ICC Incoterms that regulate and standardize the terms of trade governing the transfer of risk, carriage, insurance, and the like in international contracts of sale.[102]

EXPLAINING CANADIAN POLICY

The discussion has thus far shown that it is only in recent years that Canada has been active in the unification movement. Today, Canada participates actively in all UNCITRAL working groups, though some unification efforts have attracted more interest in Canada than have others. Canadian interest is most evident in the areas of international sales, payments, and arbitration. Canada was the first to sign the Convention on International Bills of Exchange and International Promissory Notes but was among the last to accede to the New York Convention and has not yet acceded to the Vienna Sales Convention. How might this be explained?

The explanation commonly offered to account for Canadian policy is that constitutional limitations on the federal treatymaking power are posed by the division of legislative powers between the federal and provincial governments. The well-known Labour Conventions case[103] established that the federal government cannot implement international conventions in areas falling under provincial jurisdiction under section 92 of the BNA Act.[104] Indeed, the speed with which the federal government was able to act with regard to the Convention on International Bills of Exchange and International Promissory Notes may well be accounted for by the fact that bills of exchange, promissory notes, and banking fall within federal legislative competence under the Constitution Act (ss. 91 [15], [18]) and thus do not require provincial co-operation. In contrast, the sale of goods and arbitration are regarded as matters of a private nature and are governed by provincial property and civil rights (ss. 92 [13], [16]). This explanation has been offered in the past: 'The federal government has taken the position from the beginning that domestic implementation of the Sales Convention is a provincial responsibility and that the federal government cannot accede to the Convention without provincial concurrence.'[105] So, too, with regard to the New York Convention, the federal Department of Justice in 1982 cited the need for provincial co-operation before accession was possible:

> While I am not aware that this Department has ever taken a formal position, we have been concerned that the subject matter of the Convention may be primarily one falling within provincial jurisdiction. In that case in order for this Convention to be implemented effectively in Canada, without restricting its application to matters within the legislative jurisdiction of Parliament it would be necessary not only to have federal legislation, but also to have all the provinces and the territories adopt uniform implementing legislation and rules of practice and procedure. I am not aware that any provincial government has ever urged accession by Canada into the New York Convention or evidenced any interest in the Convention.[106]

Indeed, the breakthrough on the New York Convention occurred when British Columbia took the lead in pushing for speedy accession and in being the first to enact provincial legislation implementing the New York Convention and the UNCITRAL Model Law.[107] It has been noted that: '[I]n the face of compelling arguments by the Attorney General of British Columbia, then Attorney General of Canada, John Crosbie, QC, took the unprecedented action of acceding to the UN Convention before all the provinces had the necessary implementing legislation in place.'[108]

One might question why similar federal action did not occur sooner with regard to the Vienna Sales Convention. As mentioned earlier, eight provinces and one territory have already enacted implementing legislation. Furthermore, as Professor Ziegel notes, the federal-state clause in the convention that enables accession on behalf of only the jurisdictions that have enacted such legislation 'does not specify a minimum number of component units to which the convention must apply upon accession beyond the threshold figure of one.' He notes further that the federal government does not appear to have adopted a firm policy regarding the acceptable minimum number of concurring provinces.[109] There is no reason why federal-provincial co-operation in the unification of the law governing international commercial arbitration cannot be duplicated in the international sale of goods and other areas involving provincial jurisdiction.

In addition to constitutional reasons for earlier disinterest in the unification movement, the insularity and self-sufficiency of the Canadian legal system have been cited as posing obstacles to Canadian participation in the movement. The feeling that the existing legal framework could adequately meet the country's needs frustrated participation in the unification of commercial arbitration law and sales law: 'Over the years Canada's international economic relations have been largely with the United States and most of the disputes arising out of this relationship have been settled by conventional modes, that is through settlements or litigation. The substantial similarity of the Canadian and United States economies had created a relatively insulated trading environment in which few perceived the need for change.'[110] It is possible to detect a shift in perceptions regarding the commercial need for unification in response to changing American attitudes towards unification and the diversification of Canada's trading partners. In fact, it was precisely these realities that prompted Professor Ziegel to reverse his position on accession to the Vienna Sales Convention:

> I think the provinces were right to bide their hands until it was clear which way the United States would jump. Now that we know the answer, there are strong reasons, in my view, why we should follow the u.s. lead. One pragmatic reason is that Canadian sellers and buyers will be drawn into the Sales Convention even without Canada's accession. This is because the convention applies to contracts of sale where either the contracting parties have their places of business in different contracting states of the Convention, or, if only one of the states is a contracting state, where the rules of private international law applied by a court in that state lead to the law of a contracting state.[111]

Thus, a contract of sale between a merchant in a foreign state which is party to the Sales Convention and a merchant in Canada could be brought under the scope of the convention, even though Canada had not acceded, if the foreign court found its law to be the proper law of the contract under the conflicts of law. The possibility that Canada's international sales transactions will be submitted to international regulation whether we like it or not simply by virtue of contracting with someone in a state which is party to the convention, should force Canadians to reassess the adequacy of existing laws and grapple with the uniform laws.

The change in attitude towards unification is bound to be intensified as Canadians explore commercial opportunities in other countries: 'The significance of arbitration and other non-judicial means of dispute resolution has increased as the focus of Canadian trade and investment has turned away from western Europe and the United States and towards Asia and the Pacific. In the case of many Asian countries, trade often follows long-term contractual arrangements... where litigation as a means of settling differences may be inappropriate and unappealing to both sides.'[112] China and Japan, for example, share an aversion to the adversarial system, preferring non-confrontational methods of dispute resolution such as arbitration and conciliation.[113] Canadian jurisdictions adopted unified arbitration laws in order to make Canada a more hospitable venue for international commercial arbitration. Once a 'no man's land'[114] for international arbitration, Canada is now equipped with the legal and institutional framework to meet the dispute resolution needs of the international business community. Recent developments in the adoption of unified international sales law suggest that this will be the next major unification achievement. While Canadian recognition of the benefits afforded by the adoption of unified private international trade law has been late in coming, it has finally arrived.

FUTURE POLICY OPTIONS

Constitutional limitations on the federal treatymaking power have inhibited the ability of the federal government to exercise leadership in the unification of private international trade law. The division of legislative competencies between federal and provincial governments in many areas of international trade dictates a co-operative approach to the formulation and enforcement of regime norms, principles, and rules. Domestic constitutional restraints on Canada's ability to participate in the regime governing private international trade have broad implications for Canadian participation in international economic regimes in general. Many areas of international economic exchange involve both federal and provincial jurisdictional competencies and thus raise the constitutional issue. However, federal-provincial co-operation has made the adoption of unified international commercial arbitration law possible, and similar co-operation in the area of the international sale of goods will likely produce a similar result. There is no reason why similar co-operation cannot occur in other areas in the future. The use of a federal-state clause is of some assistance in facilitating Canadian participation in regimes governing matters where provincial implementation is required but is not forthcoming or where only some of the provinces or territories enact implementing legislation. However, objections to the use of such clauses have been raised on the grounds that they function to create even further disunity in Canadian laws. It has been noted that 'the federal-state clause is not an entirely satisfactory approach to the problem as it is still possible to have territorial units within a State which do not implement the Convention and therefore uniformity across the country as a whole cannot be achieved. In addition, even if all units do implement the Convention, there may be some differences from unit to unit in the implementing legislation.'[115] The same author makes the case for a broad interpretation of federal treatymaking power, which includes implementation, arguing that: '[N]owhere is this need for a broad treaty implementation power more evident than in the area of those international agreements which can affect Canada's economic well-being and commercial livelihood.'[116] Another alternative has been suggested in greater recourse by the federal government to the trade and commerce power provided for in the Constitution Act, 1867 (s. 91[2]), though this may be a rather heavy-handed approach and may pose some constitutional difficulties.[117] Unilateral federal action could frustrate unification efforts by generating animosities and conflicts and could create the risk of further disunity in Canadian law by creating dual systems of law for many areas.[118] This could ultimately undermine the achievement of uniform results, thereby weakening the regime. The preferred approach to achieving uniformity in the laws regulating international trade is through federal-provincial co-operation and negotiation. While this is a more cumbersome process, it is the most likely means of enabling Canada to participate more actively in the development and formulation of regime principles, norms, and rules.

Domestic constitutional problems will not be the only factors determining future Canadian unification efforts and participation in the creation and enforcement of regime standards. Future initiatives are likely to be influenced significantly by the moves of Canada's major trading partners, in particular those of the United States. The adoption of regime principles, norms, and rules by Canada's trading partners will have the effect of imposing regime discipline on many more bilateral commercial transactions. Canadian commercial actors will be drawn into the international regulatory regime simply by transacting with parties subject to regime discipline. This has particular significance for bilateral trade relations with the United States. There is growing support in the United States for the creation of a strong regime governing international commercial transactions. Whereas prior to the Second World War the United States regarded the unification movement with 'benign aloofness,' the success of U.S. postwar domestic commercial unification efforts produced greater awareness of the benefits generated by uniformity in commercial law and practice. 'The last hundred years have seen a dramatic shift in American attitudes from isolationist disinterest to active participation in the process.'[119] Today, the United States participates fully and exercises leadership in the development of the regime. While it is beyond the scope of this discussion to consider the broader issue of the impact of u.s. leadership on the creation of international regimes in general, the participation of the United States in the creation of the regime governing private international commercial transactions has been instrumental in strengthening the regime by universalizing the unification movement beyond its essentially European origins.[120] American policies and attitudes concerning the regime are likely to be of further relevance to Canada in light of the commercial, legal, and institutional integration that is occurring under the Canada-u.s. Free Trade Agreement.

Finally, it should be noted that Canada's capacity to influence the direction or substantive content of the unification movement is probably consistent with our status as a 'small state' with 'little capacity to affect the international economic system as a whole or the international economic regimes that provide rules that regulate the imposition of national controls on international transactions.'[121] However, Canada can contribute to the strength of the regime by developing domestic decisionmaking mechanisms that encourage federal-provincial co-operation, thereby facilitating accession to and uniform implementation of regime conventions, model laws, and the like. Furthermore, the regulation of a number of issues that are now on the agenda for unification are of substantial consequence to Canada. The regulation of government procurement policies and countertrade are two such issues. It might just be that Canada's recently acquired status as a full member of UNCITRAL, in combination with the organization's practice of consensus based decisionmaking, will provide Canada with greater opportunities to influence outcomes and will enhance Canada's participation in the unification movement.

PART TWO

Regulation of International Financial Transactions

CHAPTER FIVE

Canadian Foreign Investment Policy: Issues and Prospects

James A. Brander

INTRODUCTION AND BACKGROUND

From the time European settlers first came to what is now Canada, inflows of foreign investment have played an important part in Canada's development. The role of foreign investment has been a topic· of significant public policy concern, particularly in the past twenty-five years,[1] and has featured prominently in several recent election campaigns. During the 1970s and 1980s both the New Democratic Party and, to a lesser extent, the Liberal party have incorporated anti-foreign investment (or, more accurately, anti-U.S. investment) themes in several election campaigns, while, conversely, the Conservative party has incorporated a clear pro-foreign investment stance in its campaigns of the 1980s.

Actual policy towards foreign investment has been relatively non-interventionist over most of Canada's history.[2] Foreign investment has been restricted in some particular industries, notably banking, but in general Canada has always been one of the world's most open countries with respect to investment flows. The principal departure from this general policy openness occurred under the Liberal governments of the 1974-84 period, particularly as manifested in the formation of the Foreign Investment Review Agency (FIRA) in 1974.

This chapter will review some of the salient features of foreign investment in Canada and offer a summary of the concerns that have been raised about foreign investment, with the focus on 'domestic' as opposed to 'international' aspects of policy. It will be argued that there are legitimate concerns about foreign investment that should be raised and addressed by policy. It will also be argued, however, that the interventionist argument of the 1970s was largely misguided, and that the political debate over investment has therefore failed to bring out the important issues.

DEFINING AND MEASURING FOREIGN INVESTMENT

Foreign investment flows are generally divided into several categories, the most important of which are direct investment and portfolio investment. Conceptually, foreign direct investment (FDI) is investment that confers control over how real assets are used. Foreign portfolio investment (FPI) is investment that does not confer control over real assets but simply establishes a claim to (private sector) financial returns. In practice, this means that most direct investment is in the form of equity (stock), while most portfolio investment is in the form of debt (corporate debentures, bonds, loans, etc.). An American takeover of a Canadian firm would be direct investment, whereas an American purchase of a long-term corporate bond issued by an 'arm's length' Canadian firm would be portfolio investment.

The equity versus debt distinction is not, however, a perfect guide to distinguishing between direct and portfolio investment. Canadian authorities define equity holdings of less than 10 per cent as portfolio investment, and they define long-term debt as a direct investment if the creditor owns more than 10 per cent of the stock of the debtor firm.

In addition to direct and portfolio investment, there are other investment flows as well, mostly government flows. For example, if foreign residents buy Canadian government savings bonds, that is a foreign investment in Canada. Similarly, changes in holdings of foreign exchange by Canadian governments, corporations, or individuals, and changes in the holdings of Canadian dollars by foreign governments, corporations, or individuals are also investment flows (i.e., when a foreign government holds Canadian dollars it is 'investing' in Canada in that it is holding a claim [dollar bills or bank accounts] over Canadian resources). I will refer to the sum of all investment flows other than direct investment as 'indirect' investment.

Most of the political concern over investment arises over direct investment. The Foreign Investment Review Agency, for example, dealt strictly with direct investment. Figure 1 is a bar graph showing the recent evolution of foreign direct investment in Canada (1950-88). The taller set of bars represents the stock of gross foreign direct investment in Canada as a percentage of Gross Domestic Product (GDP). The smaller set of bars shows the stock of net foreign direct investment: direct investment by foreigners in Canada minus direct investment by Canadians abroad.

Figure 1 shows that foreign direct investment is important in Canada, equalling close to 20 per cent of GDP in 1988. (This compared with about 9 per cent for the U.S.)[3] However, while the relative importance of (gross) foreign direct investment rose rapidly in the 1950s, it has fallen substantially since then. Gross direct foreign investment in Canada has, of course, been growing, but it has been growing less rapidly than has gross income.

The difference between the two sets of bars shows the amount of direct investment undertaken by Canadians in foreign countries. This relative importance of Canadian direct investment abroad has grown, with the result that net FDI in Canada has fallen more rapidly than has gross FDI and, by 1988, was down to about 9 per cent of GDP – only about one-third its 1960 level.

It would not be reasonable to argue that the decline in the relative importance of foreign direct investment is necessarily either good or bad. If, however, the level of FDI is viewed as a problem in itself, then it was much less a problem in 1988 than it was in 1960.

Figure 1 might come as a surprise to some, as it is conventional wisdom that the world in general and Canada in particular are becom-

FIGURE 1
Foreign direct investment to GDP

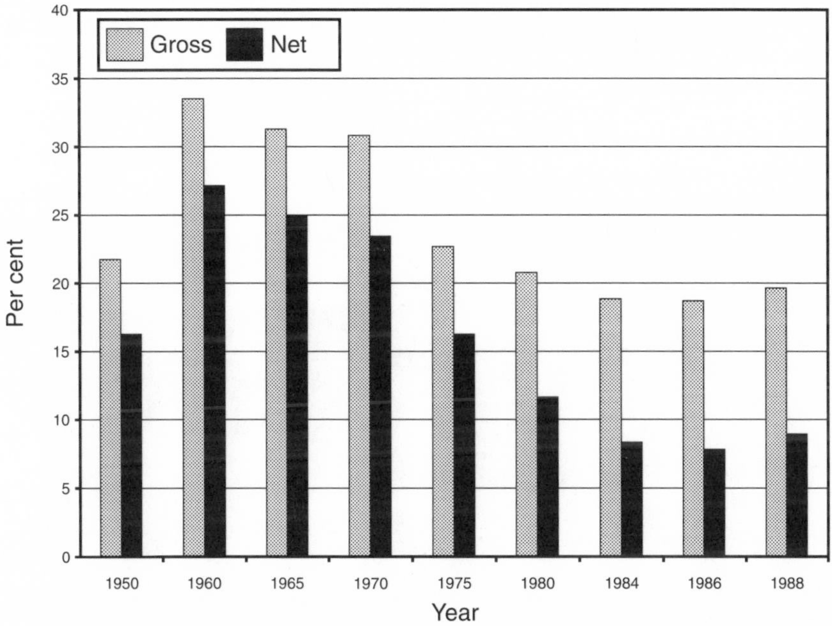

SOURCES: Statistics Canada publications 67-001 and 67-202

ing more internationally integrated, not less. How can this be true at the same time that direct investment has fallen in importance? The answer is that while foreign direct investment has been falling in relative importance, increases in indirect investment have more than fully compensated for this fall. Figure 2 shows gross foreign investments in Canada and net foreign investments (i.e., gross investments in Canada minus Canadian investments abroad).

Figure 2 indicates that the relative importance of international investment has grown in Canada over the past forty years. All of this growth has occurred in the area of indirect investment. Part of the growth of indirect investment is due to the great expansion of pension funds and other institutional investors (in Canada, the U.S., and elsewhere), whose investments are of the portfolio type. In addition, the increasing growth of Canadian government indebtedness (federal and provincial) has contributed to the growth of indirect foreign investment in Canada.

One important inference to be drawn from Figure 2 is that net foreign investment in Canada has grown since 1950 and, after a long decline, has been growing since 1975. This means that Canada's net foreign liabilities have been growing in proportion to total income.

FIGURE 2

Foreign investment to GDP

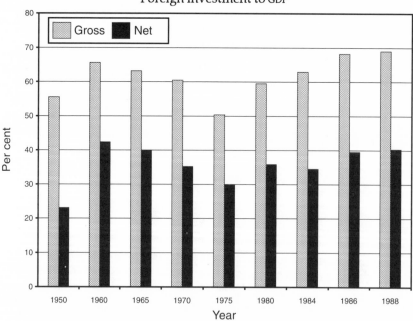

SOURCES: Statistics Canada publications 67-001 and 67-202

FOREIGN DIRECT INVESTMENT: CONCERNS AND RESPONSE

As mentioned above, most of the concern over foreign investment has focused on direct investment. The nature of this concern arises from several sources: (1) possible loss of 'economic welfare,' (2) loss of economic sovereignty, (3) loss of political sovereignty, and (4) compromise of Canadian social and cultural objectives

In order to understand the first concern it is important to have a clear definition of 'economic welfare.' In this context economic welfare is usually defined as real income (or, equivalently, real purchasing power). Economic welfare in this sense simply measures the amount of goods and services that a typical Canadian is able to buy. This is not the same thing as what economists refer to as 'utility,' although economists normally assume that higher purchasing power implies higher utility, other things being equal. In addition, many observers might argue that the economist's notion of utility is much narrower than is that in which we are really interested, which might be some conception of 'happiness,' and which might incorporate other considerations as well.

The concern is simply that Canadians might have lower real incomes as a result of foreign direct investment than they would otherwise have. This might come about if foreigners were exploiting us in some way; if they were extracting wealth from Canada that would be better kept at home. This claim seemed particularly relevant in the aftermath of the 1973-4 OPEC-inspired rise in oil prices, which allowed foreign (and domestic) owners of Canadian oil reserves to earn substantial windfall profits.

The argument that foreign investment is a tool of international exploitation was popular among Marxist and other leftist intellectuals during the 1960s and early 1970s but never had much credibility among Canadian policymakers, even among those who favoured foreign investment controls. In fact, of the four concerns listed above, the economic loss argument is regarded as the least credible by opponents and proponents of foreign direct investment alike. For example, the Gray Report[4] (1972), which was the precursor to the establishment of FIRA, made the following observation: 'It [foreign investment] has contributed in an important way to the growth of production, employment, incomes, and government revenues in Canada.' My reading of the international evidence since the early 1970s is that it provides about as strong a rejection of the 'investment as exploitation' argument as one encounters in the social sciences.

Mainstream economic reasoning concerning the role of foreign investment runs as follows. Allowing liberalized foreign investment results in more real investment in Canada than would otherwise take place. More investment leads to more real capital per worker and to technological improvement (particularly through technology transfer). This acts to raise labour productivity and real wages (or, equivalently, to increase the availability of 'high wage' jobs) and to improve the quality of consumer goods. Therefore, Canadians are economically better off as a result of foreign direct investment.

This is not the only mechanism through which foreign investment might affect economic welfare, and, although some mechanisms may have negative effects, most economists would focus on the 'capital-deepening' and 'technological progress' aspects of foreign investment as being, empirically, the most significant. The fact that some foreign firms make large profits is not inconsistent with this. Some firms do well, some do poorly. On balance, there is no evidence that foreign firms earn an abnormally high return from operating in Canada. They seem to earn 'normal' returns on average. Furthermore, even if firms did make 'above-normal' returns, it is possible that Canadians would still benefit. After all, if investments create net value we expect all parties to the investment, including the foreign investor, to be made better off.

The second concern, loss of economic sovereignty, refers to the idea that Canadians are somehow worse off if 'foreigners' are making major economic decisions in Canada. Sometimes this idea is expressed by claiming that Canadian industry is excessively 'dependent' on foreign influences. I have never been able to identify a reasonable economic foundation for this argument. The main economic point is simply that business firms are in business to make profit. By and large they seek profit-maximizing strategies. Whether the individuals making decisions are Canadian or American will not significantly affect which decisions are profit-increasing and which are not. For example, if the profit-maximizing price of some product is $10 per unit, then we should expect the firm producing it to charge $10 – irrespective of where its head office happens to be located.

It is conceivable that foreign firms might act systematically differently from domestically owned firms, and it is often alleged that foreign firms engage in less domestic R&D than do domestic firms, or that foreign firms provide fewer 'good jobs' than do domestic firms. I think that this claim shows a confusion between cause and effect. Foreign firms who are successful in R&D will reap the benefits of that R&D by using it in investments in Canada and elsewhere, just as successful innovative Canadian firms will incorporate their R&D in investments in other countries. We expect to observe that foreign firms operating in Canada will use a lot of the technology they have developed elsewhere. This is a very important agent of economic growth in Canada and should be regarded as a benefit of foreign investment, not a cost. If we insisted that all technology used in Canada be developed in Canada, we would be much poorer – closer to the Albanian solution than anything else.

Very often, especially in less developed countries, reducing 'foreign dependence' really amounts to a substitution of domestic government control over economic decisions for foreign private sector control. The motive is often more socialist or populist (or merely expedient for political élites wishing to increase their personal wealth) than national-ist. Once a domestic government has operational control over produc-tive assets it might well behave differently than would a private sector firm (domestic or foreign) and might, for example, get involved in elaborate subsidization or employment schemes. One important ad-vantage of foreign investments is that they normally increase the level of competition in the domestic economy.

These two concerns get a relatively unfavourable treatment from economists. The main concerns about foreign direct investment might therefore arise from sources other than economic mechanisms.

The third concern is loss of political sovereignty. Foreign investment can undermine the political authority of a domestic government in several ways. One way domestic government authority is undermined is through 'extraterritoriality,' which arises when one government imposes rules on the operations of firms based in that country on its operations in other countries. Probably the most extensive use of extraterritoriality has been the imposition of rules on the operations of North American firms investing or operating in South Africa. The importance of extraterritoriality operating in Canada is very much open to question. During the 1970s much effort went into trying to find examples of u.s. extraterritoriality operating in Canada. For example, a few u.s. firms operating in Canada obeyed the 1960s u.s. embargo on trade with Cuba, even though Canada did not join this embargo. On balance, however, there are very few such examples, particularly in recent years. Canada has, in any case, adopted legislation making the extraterritorial policy of other governments invalid in Canada (al-though Canada does continue to apply its own extraterritorial require-ments).

The second way in which foreign investment may undermine do-mestic authority is that the foreign firms doing the investing may be large and influential and may be in a position to directly influence the conduct of domestic government policy so that it acts in their interests rather than in the interests of domestic general welfare. This is an important concern, but whether this is more of a concern with foreign rather than with domestic corporations is an open question. Certainly some of the greatest abuses of the lobbying process in Canada have involved domestic rather than foreign corporations.

A third source of loss of domestic sovereignty arises from the government-to-government level negotiations that are the byproduct of international investment flows. More precisely, foreign investment flows bring the taxation, regulatory, competition policy, and trade policy regulations of different countries into contact with each other. It is necessary to formulate tax treaties, trade treaties, some harmonization of regulation, and so on, if the legal systems of two countries are to dovetail smoothly in the handling of international investment flows. Such agreements, as with all international agreements, place constraints on the behaviour of any one national government. It is far from clear that this is a bad thing. Technological progress continues to make the world a smaller and smaller place – a place in which getting along with other countries becomes increasingly important. Agreements between countries, by their nature, limit the scope for any one country to take unilateral action; that is, they limit its sovereignty. That is what they are supposed to do, and we are generally better off as a result.

It does seem to be true that foreign investment compromises political sovereignty to some extent. However, it is worth emphasizing what is not compromised. Foreign ownership of an asset in Canada does not, of course, provide exemption from Canadian law. A foreign-owned operation in Canada is subject to Canadian environmental legislation, to Canadian labour law, to Canadian taxation, and so on. Furthermore, these laws can be changed at any time, and foreign and domestic firms alike will have to follow them. A foreign-owned domestic asset is subject to exactly the same political control, through the legal system, as is a domestically owned asset.

The fourth concern, compromise of social and cultural objectives, is more amorphous than are the others, and is something of a catch-all for other concerns. Reducing the level of foreign ownership sometimes seems to be regarded as a good thing in itself, quite apart from its economic or political effects. Much of the anti-foreign investment literature emphasizes ownership statistics (such as: 'more than half the oil industry is foreign owned' or 'nearly half of the manufacturing sector is foreign owned') as though these facts in themselves, quite apart from any economic consequences they might have, are supposed to make us feel worse off.

Carrying this point slightly further, if the Seagram family were to change its nationality from Canadian to American, this should make us feel worse off because 'Canadians' would then own fewer real assets. Thus, promoting domestic ownership becomes a social objective in itself. There may be something in this argument at a psychological level, but it is hard to pin down any economic consequences. Whether the Seagram family is American or Canadian, the (profit-maximizing) behaviour of the Seagram corporate empire is unlikely to change, and any assets or individuals that reside in Canada must pay Canadian taxes and obey Canadian laws.

As for culture, it can be argued that foreign (especially American) investment in Canada has shifted business culture and popular culture in an American direction. Put slightly differently, foreign direct investment is part of a general process of internationalization which serves to reduce the cultural distinctiveness of individual countries, especially relatively small countries such as Canada. While this effect undoubtedly does exist, it is far from clear that the cultural evolution induced by foreign investment is necessarily bad. Furthermore, its significance for the process of cultural change in Canada seems slight compared to other forces, particularly direct communication through cultural media (especially television) and immigration.

As might be inferred from the above discussion, my view of the traditional concerns raised about foreign direct investment is that they are either misleading (alleged economic damage) or very small and perhaps ambiguous in effect (political and cultural sovereignty). Canada has followed an open investment policy for most of its history, and my view is that this has played no small part in Canada's economic success as a nation. It is perhaps worth remembering that Canada has arguably the highest standard of living of any country in the world[5] and a very low level of violent social and cultural conflict by international standards.

A BRIEF HISTORY OF CANADIAN POLICY TOWARDS FOREIGN INVESTMENT[6]

Prior to the 1950s, there was relatively little policy controversy over foreign investment. Indeed, the high tariff barriers that had been in place in Canada since the formation of the 'National Policy' in the late nineteenth century had acted to encourage foreign investment in manufacturing. High tariffs on manufactured goods induced U.S. firms, who would otherwise have exported to Canada, to 'jump' the tariff walls and produce in Canada instead, even though such production facilities might be unable to realize economies of scale. Thus the Canadian manufacturing sector was characterized by high U.S. investment levels of the 'branch plant' or 'miniature replica' type. While most economists would argue that the national policy of high tariffs was damaging to Canadian economic development, they would also argue that it would have been a lot more damaging if it had been coupled with restrictions on investment flows.

In 1957 the Gordon Royal Commission on the state of the Canadian economy[7] recommended legislatively mandated increases in Canadian participation in foreign-owned subsidiaries operating in Canada. The Gordon Commission reflected a growing but still relatively weak sense of economic nationalism in Canada, and it did not have broad support. In 1965 the government published the Watkins Report,[8] the first major study of foreign investment per se. The report focused on the application of U.S. extraterritoriality through U.S. subsidiaries operating in Canada and recommended that extraterritoriality be explicitly forbidden in Canada and that the future conduct of foreign-owned firms in Canada go through some sort of formal review process.

A further report, the 1970 Wahn Report, reflecting the increased emphasis on economic nationalism (and a general anti-U.S. sentiment), advocated more extreme measures, including a legislatively mandated repatriation process. Finally, the Gray Report of 1972 provided the blueprint for a general reformulation of policy towards investment, leading to the passage of the Foreign Investment Review Act of 1974.

The political background to this legislation is fairly interesting. The Liberal party under Pierre Trudeau formed the government from 1968 to 1979, then again from 1980 to 1984. At times the Liberal party led a minority government supported by the New Democratic party, and at times it held a majority. Within the Liberal party itself, Trudeau was associated more closely with the interventionist and anti-American left of the party than had been the previous prime minister and party leader, Lester Pearson.

The NDP in general favoured a more interventionist and more anti-American approach to investment than did even the interventionist wing of the Liberal party. Thus, much of the policy debate actually consisted of the centre-right of the Liberal party resisting the strong interventionist position taken by the Liberal left and the NDP, as the Liberals required the tacit support of the NDP to stay in power during much of the period.

The increase in concern over direct investment that occurred in the late 1960s and early 1970s is understandable, at the political and psychological level, as a response to the anti-American and anti-business sentiment that peaked in this period. The unpopularity of the Vietnam War was an important contributing factor, as was the popularization of environmental concerns and the general fashionability of socialism. In most of the developing world there was a reaction against foreign investment. The World Bank estimates that over 1,200 firms lost investments in expropriations between 1960 and 1980.

In the case of Canada, however, this rise in concern over foreign direct investment contained a certain irony, because, as indicated by Figure 1, foreign direct investment was declining in relative importance during this period. In the 1950s and 1960s, Canadian trade barriers had fallen substantially (and continued to fall throughout the 1970s) as a result of multilateral trade agreements negotiated and implemented under the General Agreement on Tariffs and Trade (GATT). As a result, the 'tariff-jumping' rationale for direct investment was weakening significantly, and the 'branch plant' or 'miniature replica' type of investment in manufacturing was disappearing.[9]

The Foreign Investment Review Act came into force in 1974, creating the Foreign Investment Review Agency (FIRA). The act created a requirement that all direct foreign investments above a certain threshold level[10] must be approved by the federal Cabinet. The mandate of FIRA was to gather information about foreign direct investment in Canada, to counsel foreign firms making applications, to review the applications, and to make recommendations to Cabinet concerning the applications. The basic criterion for approving an application to make a foreign investment in Canada was that the proposed investment be 'of significant benefit to Canada.' The applicant had the obligation to demonstrate 'significant benefit,' but the act did not specify how this was to be done, although it did provide a list of activities that would be looked upon favourably, including undertaking to purchase domestically produced inputs in preference to imports. The U.S. appealed various aspects of the act to GATT, arguing that FIRA was inconsistent with Canada's pre-existing international agreements. GATT did find that FIRA contravened GATT agreements in certain respects, including mandated preference for domestic over imported inputs, but did not rule against the basic principles incorporated in FIRA, reflecting the lack of general principles concerning investment in GATT.

FIRA had four basic effects. First, it simply turned down (i.e., it recommended to Cabinet against) quite a few investment proposals. Second, it modified the structure of many investment proposals which were accepted. Third, it increased the time and expense associated with making an investment in Canada, and, finally, the existence of FIRA discouraged a large number of investment projects in that the foreign firms decided not to bother making an application. In its first full year of operation (1975) FIRA turned down 67 per cent of resolved cases but by the early 1980s was approving about 90 per cent of resolved cases.[11] This increase in the approval rate was due, in part, to the fact that applicants were able to learn from observation what kinds of proposals were likely to be accepted, then either tailor their proposals appropriately or not bother applying. In part, however, it seems that FIRA itself became less strict in the face of strong criticism from the business community and other sources. During the election campaign of 1979, the Conservative party took a negative view of FIRA, and, when it was elected to a near majority, it seemed likely that FIRA would be watered down or dismantled. The Conservative government did not, however, last long enough to implement much policy of any sort, and the Liberals were elected in 1980, after including in their campaign a pledge to strengthen FIRA. (In neither 1979 nor 1980, however, was FIRA a major election issue.) In 1981, the Liberal government reversed its campaign position on FIRA and promised to ease FIRA's review process and to introduce no new legislation to expand or strengthen FIRA's mandate.

In 1984, the Conservative party ran against FIRA as a major campaign position. Shortly after being elected, the Conservative government abolished FIRA and replaced it, under the 1985 Canada Investment Act, with a new agency (Investment Canada), whose principle aim is to encourage investment, although it does retain a review function. Its approval rate is very close to 100 per cent. The act itself makes the following statement of purpose: 'Recognizing that increased capital and technology would benefit Canada, the purpose of this Act is to encourage investment in Canada by Canadians and non-Canadians.'

In 1988 Canada and the U.S. concluded negotiations over the Canada-U.S. Free Trade Agreement (FTA), which established further principles of investment freedom concerning flows between the two countries. A general election was fought in 1988 largely over ratification of the agreement. Once again the Liberals and NDP took a strong anti-free investment position in the campaign. When the Conservatives were returned to office, the FTA was ratified and went into effect on 1 January 1989. The FTA establishes the principle of 'national treatment,' meaning that investors from either country must be treated the same by the domestic government. Thus, Canada may have different investment laws than the U.S., but the same laws must apply to U.S. and Canadian firms operating in Canada, with some exceptions. One exception is that Canada reserves the right to review and, if necessary, reject large takeovers.

INVESTMENT AND INTERNATIONAL COMPARATIVE GROWTH

Across the world as a whole, a wide variety of approaches to foreign investment have been tried. It is difficult, however, to draw inferences from the comparative economic growth experience because so many other factors also vary across countries. I do think, however, that it is useful to at least consider the broad empirical evidence concerning economic growth. Figure 3 shows percentage increase in per capita real income over the 1960-85 period for a selected group of countries.

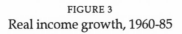

FIGURE 3
Real income growth, 1960-85

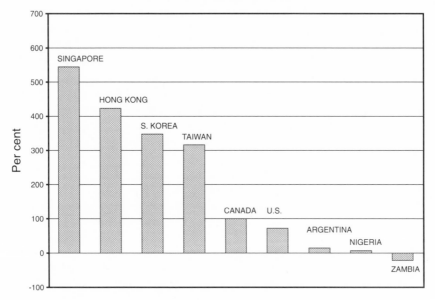

source: Robert Summers and Alan Heston, 'A New Set of Comparisons of Real Product and Price Levels: Estimates for 130 Countries, 1950–1985,' *Review of Income and Wealth* 34(1988):1-25

The world's fastest growing country, Singapore, had a 1985 per capita real income over six times its 1960 level. Even allowing for measurement problems, it is clear to anyone who is familiar with Singapore that the standard of living has been completely transformed in twenty-five years. It achieved in this twenty-five years about the same real income improvement experienced in Canada in the period from Confederation to about 1975. Singapore is not alone: Taiwan, Hong Kong, South Korea, Thailand, and, more recently, Malaysia, have, along with Japan, experienced a similar transformation. In all of these cases technology transfer seems to have been a very important contributing factor to economic growth, and foreign direct investment seems to have been an important vehicle of technology transfer for most these countries.

Conversely, a large number of countries, particularly in Africa and Latin America, but also in Asia, have actually had stationary or even declining real incomes over the 1960-85 period. Many of the countries with the worst performance have been countries with high levels of government control of investment. The contrast in Asia between the open market oriented economies and the socialist closed economies of North Korea, Vietnam, and Cambodia is particularly striking. Perhaps the most interesting case is China itself. From the period of the 'Great Leap Forward' to the end of the Cultural Revolution (1959-75) China had very poor economic performance. In 1976 a dramatic reversal began, referred to as the 'Open Door Policy.' This policy re-established markets and private ownership in the agricultural sector, allowed the formation of private enterprise in selected geographic areas and economic sectors, and encouraged foreign investment. Between 1976 and 1985 China experienced the most rapid per capita income growth of any country in the world, approximately doubling per capita real income in a mere ten years.

I would not suggest that policy towards investment is the major factor in explaining this differential performance, but it does seem that, generally, both socialist and populist policies of government intervention have had a poor record of economic performance over the past thirty years. The success stories, on the other hand, are associated with pro-investment, market-oriented policies. The relationship between total investment (domestic and foreign) and economic growth is fairly strong.[12]

Another group of countries did, however, have pro-investment policies and still had serious problems. These are the so-called 'debt crisis' countries of Latin America, Africa, and elsewhere. These countries received large (mostly portfolio) investments during the 1970s. When an international capital shortage began in the early 1980s, exacerbated by increasing government budget deficits in many countries, real interest rates rose sharply. Most of the heavily indebted countries were unable to repay their debts and, even after interest rates fell, could still not repay them. As a result, these countries have been unable to take advantage of international capital markets in the 1980s and have poorly functioning (or non-functioning) domestic capital markets. Their economic performance has been very poor, as they have paid the price for the profligacy of the 1970s.

The problem experienced by these countries was that they took in large capital inflows but did not use the inflows to finance sound investment projects. In many countries, inflows were used to finance food subsidies, high wages, and other 'populist' initiatives that raised current consumption at the cost of high future liabilities. In some countries incoming capital was invested, but instead of being invested where it would bring the highest return it was invested in politically inspired projects of questionable economic value. In addition, of course, large amounts of the investment inflow was, in many countries, skimmed off by private individuals, particularly political leaders.

FOREIGN INVESTMENT AND CANADA'S POSSIBLE DEBT CRISIS

Canada is still a long way from the experience of the 'debt crisis' countries, but their example is instructive. Just as a household or a business will get into trouble if it continually borrows to finance current consumption, the same is true of a nation. The natural counter-argument is that efficient private portfolio decisions may lead to high net foreign investment levels. If, for example, large capital inflows are being used to finance real assets that will earn income in the future, then there is no reason to be concerned. Debt will be rising but so is the ability to pay that debt. If the investments are good ones, the latter will be rising by more than the former.

In Canada, most of the inflow has been invested in economically sound projects, but a large portion has gone into financing current consumption, particularly government consumption. It is an accounting identity that the government budget deficit plus the difference between investment in Canada and Canadian savings must equal the net capital inflow. Thus, high levels of government borrowing and/or low domestic savings tend to induce a capital inflow. While the government budget deficit as a share of GDP has been reduced from its alarmingly high level of 1984, it remains very high and is still at an unsustainable level. The Conservative government inherited a major financial imbalance from the Liberals: entrenched expenditure commitments greatly exceeded entrenched revenue sources, and they have not done enough to improve the problem. The tax system continues to be biased against saving, because the inflationary part of interest income is fully taxable (although the generous tax treatment of registered retirement savings offsets this to some extent). The goods and services tax (GST) would bring improvement on both counts. Thus, there is some hope that the Canadian fiscal and savings position will be put on a firmer foundation. If so, then the growing level of net overall investment in Canada (i.e., of net liabilities) will decline.

A CASE FOR A TAX ON FOREIGN INVESTMENT IN FIXED ASSETS

So far I have argued that a relatively open approach towards investment, as Canada has followed throughout most of its history, is appropriate. However, different categories of investment do perhaps call for different policies. Rather obviously a country may want to discourage environmentally damaging investments, for example.

A more subtle argument is that it may be in the interests of one country, like Canada, to use its market power to extract a higher return from foreign investments than would be the case under pure non-intervention. Specifically, in investments that amount to foreign purchases of fixed real assets, such as natural resources and real estate, domestic economic returns can be obtained by placing a special tax on such investments. As long as the demand for such investments is downward sloping (i.e., as long as the tax does not eliminate all foreign demand), then the domestic economy can benefit. This is analogous to the ability of OPEC to extract higher returns from oil sales by using its market power in the oil market.

The case for a tax on foreign investment in fixed assets is relatively straightforward. It is less obvious that we would want a comparable tax on investment in 'augmentable' assets, such as factories. The difference is as follows. If a foreign resident buys a given piece of land, that land will be available for use in Canada. There is no use value lost if the land is not sold to foreigners. Thus, there is no reason not to charge foreigners the full monopoly price for the land. It is impossible for a single seller to do this because of general competition in the market. The government, however, could do it by using a general tax on foreign land purchases. (This would, incidentally, lower the price for domestic purchasers.) Such a policy might not be desirable in the case of investment in a factory, because any investments that are discouraged will result in Canada having fewer productive assets than it otherwise would.

If two similar countries with a lot of two-way investment use this policy, then both may be worse off. Thus it might make sense for two countries, like Canada and the U.S., to agree not to use monopoly taxes of this type. If, however, the investment flow is largely one-way, as is true of the East Asian real estate purchases in North America, both Canada and the U.S. could be better off by taxing such investment inflows. Investors in the source countries would be worse off. Basically, Canadians would simply be extracting a higher net return for their land.

CONCLUDING REMARKS

We are living in a smaller and more interdependent world than we once did. It is no longer unambiguous what we mean by 'foreign' as opposed to 'domestic' investment. A new investment by Alcan is regarded as a

Canadian investment because Alcan is a 'Canadian' company. However, more than half of Alcan's shares are owned by non-residents of Canada and more than 80 per cent of its revenues come from foreign sources. Alcan operates in over 100 countries, is the world's largest producer of aluminum products, and has only a small fraction of its labour force in Canada. Alcan has its head office in Canada but is increasingly an 'international' corporate citizen.

Correspondingly, it is hard to identify Shell as a Dutch company, Honda as a Japanese company, or General Motors as a u.s. company. All these firms are international firms whose ownership is widely dispersed, whose shares can be purchased by citizens of almost any country (including Canada), who pay taxes and employ workers in many countries, and whose ownership might easily change hands in tomorrow's corporate merger. All of them are broad organizational networks spanning many countries. Trying to distinguish some small subset as 'Canadian' and others as 'foreign' based on the location of the 'head office' might be to miss the essence of today's international corporate world.

Canada is part of an integrated international investment community. Private sector financial integration has moved ahead of government level co-ordination of international regulation. The need at this stage is not for unilateral investment restrictions but for a broadly based international framework for investment regulation so as to prevent tax avoidance and to keep different political jurisdictions from competing away the benefits of investment in tax and subsidy concessions. In addition, a secure regulatory environment that protects the economic rights of investors is important. Canada is a party to a variety of agreements through GATT, the UN, the International Monetary Fund (IMF), the Organization for Economic Cooperation and Development (OECD), and the Canada-u.s. FTA. However, the current round of GATT negotiations has made disappointingly little progress on a general investment agreement to mirror the agreements on trade.

Canada's biggest domestic concern is not that 'foreign investors' will somehow abuse their host, but that the aggregate level of savings (private and government) is not high enough to sustain high investment levels without incurring large net debts.

Canada and International Legal Regimes for Foreign Investment and Trade in Services

Robert K. Paterson

INTRODUCTION

Despite a well-publicized era of foreign investment controls during the 1970s, Canada, throughout its history, has remained relatively open to foreign investment and trade in services. In international forums Canada has also, often passively, supported initiatives to remove restrictions on such economic activity. This posture is best evidenced by comparing the high levels of foreign investment that have existed in Canada for decades with the restrictive laws and policies existing in many other countries.

With the imminent conclusion of the Uruguay Round, where, for the first time, trade in services (though not investment) is squarely on the GATT agenda, it is appropriate not only to consider what form new accords might and should take, but also what has been and should be Canada's role respecting such initiatives.

Unlike those of many other countries, Canada's restrictions on foreign investment and trade in services are usually transparent, taking the form of accessible legislation, regulations, and published policies. Furthermore, such rules normally affect areas of the economy that are restricted from foreign access in most countries – such as banking, broadcasting, insurance, and transportation. Most Canadian restrictions are of long standing. The most significant restrictions in recent times arose as a result of the Foreign Investment Review Act and the National Energy Policy of the 1970s and have now been virtually disbanded. The Canada-United States Free Trade Agreement of 1988 (FTA) has led to further liberalization of Canadian laws as far as American investors and service traders are concerned. Despite this relative openness, Canadian investment policy still contains two major planks which support the retention of controls. First, there is a continuing commitment to restrict foreign investment in areas of the economy which are seen as having strategic significance. This concern was well illustrated, during the debate surrounding the conclusion of the FTA, by heated discussion about whether the agreement obligated Canada to engage in sales of water to the United States. Strategic concerns are clearly evidenced by the provisions of Chapter Nine of the agreement – dealing with trade in energy. Second, there has been a long-standing debate in Canada about foreign investment and the protection of cultural industries such as television and book publishing. Again, this concern is intensified by the physical proximity of the United States and popular perceptions about the dangers of cultural asphyxiation.

The specific risks posed by foreign investment and open trade in services have been the subject of extensive debate in Canada for several decades. They have been well articulated in several published government reports and have been translated into federal legislation and policy. Much of this debate has been driven by long-standing Canadian concerns about our cultural and economic relationship with the United States. The current liberalism towards foreign investment controls represents the position of the Conservative party government. Of the three federal political parties, the Conservatives are least concerned with investment controls based on economic theory. The present government does, however, show some readiness to protect cultural industries, and, thus, the FTA contains an explicit exemption for cultural industries from all provisions of the agreement, allowing Canadian laws that restrict American investment and services trade affecting such industries. This development is less the result of an attempt to develop new multilaterally-agreed upon standards than it is a product of domestic political pressures inside Canada to place limits on American investors in light of what are seen as specific threats posed by such investors. The current Conservative party government appears less concerned about such threats from American investors than do the parties in opposition.

What is striking about these specific Canadian investment concerns is that they do not appear to have been advanced by Canada with the same degree of concern at the multilateral level. This is probably in large measure due to a lack of major international initiatives affecting services and investment – until the current GATT round. However, it also reflects a structural separation of national foreign investment policy and the formulation of Canada's international position on investment issues. The latter appears to consist of passive support for continuing liberalization of existing restrictive measures as well as restrictions on the introduction of new measures. Canada's special concerns about the

United States as a source country would explain this dichotomy but other reasons probably include the small scale of Canadian private investment in developing countries (which often have the most restrictive regimes) and the large scale of Canadian investment in the United States and Western Europe (where investment restrictions are relatively modest or, at least, visible). This passive stance may be about to change as a result of the conclusion of the Uruguay Round and other developments (such as the recent execution of investment promotion agreements). If Canada remains passive in multilateral debate, however, it risks having the international legitimacy of its well-articulated investment restrictions (in federal and provincial law) undermined by changing multinational norms.

Another risk of Canadian passivity in the international arena concerning trade in services and foreign investment is that it could eliminate this country's credibility in what is shaping up as a heated debate between developed and developing countries over these issues. Canada may find itself permanently aligned with the developed countries (particularly the United States) in a confrontation with the developing states. Furthermore, concessions extracted by the latter countries in multilateral accords may not be made available to Canada in a politicized solution. The long-standing strategic and cultural concerns advanced to justify domestic restrictions in Canada may be undermined by multilateral agreements on other norms.

This chapter will start by examining the international accords currently applicable to controls affecting foreign investment and trade in services and will then gauge what Canadian policy has been towards the major issues involved. The problems of competing expectations and interests of host states and source investors in formulating new agreements will be discussed. Finally, changing Canadian policy on investment issues will then be discussed and suggestions will be made about the development of that policy.

PROBLEMS OF DEFINITION

We are now at a point where both international and domestic legal regimes concerning international trade in goods have reached a relatively settled and mature stage. Considerably less certainty surrounds the regimes affecting overall international economic relations. In the case of foreign investment, at least in its present form, this uncertainty may arise because such investment is largely a post-colonial phenomenon. The identity of colonial governments and their European masters eliminated political risk in earlier times. Also, the absence of modern forms of transport and communications meant that managing an integrated overseas business was considerably less feasible than it is now. The main reason foreign investment controls have been the longest awaiting rule-making consensus is almost certainly political. Trade in goods, and, to a less degree, services, seems to many to involve less risk of compromising national identity and dictating certain immigration policies. We are now, therefore, at a stage when the economic pressures for a more open global investment environment have never been stronger, but there is almost a complete absence of a liberal framework to support the dismantling of existing national investment controls.

Two practical terms have emerged to describe the new forms of international economic activity – 'foreign direct investment' and 'trade in services,' The former is usually defined as a transfer of business assets from a source country enterprise to a host country enterprise, with the former retaining control over these assets.[1] Such investments are usually effected through a subsidiary corporation (or its equivalent) that is incorporated under the laws of a host country but is owned and managed by a source country enterprise.

Now that restrictions on 'trade in services' have been placed on the Uruguay Round agenda, the need for a broadly based definition of that phrase has arisen.[2] One overriding consideration must be that only services that can be materially restricted in some manner need to be within the scope of a definition – services whose provision is virtually undetectable cannot be meaningfully regulated. The main problem of defining services, however, arises from their intangibility. Many restrictions on foreign direct investment will operate as restrictions on trade in services, since some form of establishment is needed to provide many services. At the other extreme will be services that are encapsulated in tangible goods (such as computer discs), which may be subject to restrictions on trade in goods. In between are services traded through the temporary presence of individuals in the importing country. This middle category will constitute the services trade requiring separate regulation.

International agreement on both trade in services and foreign direct investment will require conceptually based definitions of both terms. This means that trade in services will be best defined negatively as any activity that falls short of an agreed definition of foreign direct investment. In most instances, trade in services will involve some temporary movement of capital or labour not amounting to the implementation of a permanent form of establishment. Even services as intangible as telecommunications will probably demand some level of personal residency in most instances.

The rapid progress in international rule-making, extending to impediments to trade in services, has necessitated some level of consensus about how trade in services should be defined. At the same time, tentative steps are being taken to introduce the reduction of barriers to foreign direct investment onto the international agenda. This phenomenon has revealed the essential artificiality of any definitional exercise and has produced a realization that, with the prospect of extending GATT rules to these two forms of economic activity, virtually no impediments to international business relations necessarily lie outside multilateral regimes. While for business and economic objectives the continued separation of trade in services and foreign direct investment may be debatable, these categories remain useful for legal and institutional purposes, though it is impossible to consider progress in one to the exclusion of the other. In liberal economic terms, protectionist measures affecting investment may be as abhorrent as are those concerning trade in goods, but non-economic factors concerning cultural, political, and strategic concerns will need to be addressed before a new legal regime emerges.

INTERNATIONAL ACCORDS AFFECTING RESTRICTIONS ON FOREIGN DIRECT INVESTMENT AND TRADE IN SERVICES

Customary Public International Law

Customary international law does not limit a state's ability to restrict the entry of foreign investment.[3] This is often described as the absence of a 'right of establishment.' It not only allows states to prohibit the entry of foreign investment but also to regulate and restrict such investment as is allowed entry. This appurtenance of sovereignty needs to be balanced against the law of state responsibility for injuries to aliens and alien property. The doctrine of state responsibility requires that host states observe international minimum standards in the treatment of aliens and alien property and has been extended to cover foreign corporations and businesses.[4] Insofar as this has led to requirements respecting the expropriation of foreign property and the prescription of nondiscriminatory treatment of aliens and alien property, it has been rejected by Latin American officials and jurists, by the socialist states of Eastern Europe, and by many developing states in Asia and Africa. Their main concern, however, is whether they may not only treat aliens less favourably than nationals but whether there is an international minimum standard below which such treatment must not fall. Such arguments have surrounded the search for a new international economic order and the concept of permanent sovereignty of states over natural resources.[5] Whichever view one takes of the current state of customary international law, one cannot ignore extensive state practice, including that of Canada, instituting significant restrictions on foreign investments and service providers. Traditional international legal theories of state responsibility, however, would seem to require the equal treatment of aliens and nationals under international law – in effect, a national treatment standard. Short of this, however, states (under customary international law) are free to restrict, or indeed prohibit, the entry of foreign investment according to their own national policies.

The Havana Charter and the GATT

The provisions of the GATT do not deal comprehensively with restrictions on foreign investment or trade in services, though several of them have some impact on these forms of economic activity.

The charter of the proposed International Trade Organization (ITO), considered at the Havana Conference of 1947-8, recognized the right of states to determine whether foreign investment should be permitted and, if so, on what terms.[6] The charter, of course, was never operative, but under Article 29 of the GATT, the right of establishment contained in the ITO Charter is to be recognised by GATT contracting parties 'to the full extent of their executive authority.'

Article 29 was considered by a GATT panel in a case involving allegations by the United States that undertakings obtained by Canada from American investors, concerning the purchase of goods in Canada and the maintenance of certain export levels, violated several provisions of the GATT.[7] The panel concluded that undertakings to purchase goods of Canadian origin treated imported goods less favourably than domestic products and were inconsistent with Article 3:4 (the national treatment obligation). The panel noted that the provisions of the ITO Charter had never entered into force but thought that the ITO Charter provisions, taken together with Article 29, were consistent with increased international co-operation to reduce barriers to foreign direct investment. While the views of the GATT panel are consistent with the conclusion that there is no recognized right of establishment under international law, they are also a rejection of the Canadian argument that Article 29 can be used to diminish any obligations otherwise arising under the GATT.

The GATT panel's findings in relation to certain aspects of Canada's former foreign investment screening mechanism (the Foreign Investment Review Act) clearly show that no provisions of the General Agreement restrict the ability of a contracting party to control the entry of foreign direct investment, either in general or in specific sectors of a host economy. The panel's findings were limited to certain purchasing requirements established by administrative means. Attempts to invoke other GATT provisions (Articles 11 and 17) failed. These purchasing requirements were modified following the GATT panel findings, but their existence suggests Canadian unreadiness to adhere to a national treatment standard for foreign investment. Typically, Canada has maintained and introduced discriminatory measures against foreign investors while supporting the prohibition of such measures under international law.[8] This somewhat schizophrenic position means that Canada remains continually at risk of international legal challenges like that in the GATT FIRA panel decision. While the dismantling of the restrictive Canadian investment controls of the 1970s has increased American investor confidence in particular, there remains the possibility that changes of government in Canada could see new restrictive regimes once again affecting foreign investors. Americans are only free of this risk to the extent that they have guaranteed rights under the Free Trade Agreement.

The GATT has somewhat more relevance in relation to barriers to trade in services than to foreign investment controls; motion pictures are exempted from Article 3 insofar as domestic quotas are concerned, and Article 5 deals with non-discrimination in regard to goods in transit. Trade in services is further affected by several of the accords negotiated during the Tokyo Round. This arose because these accords go beyond tariff reductions and deal with a variety of non-tariff barriers in greater detail than they did previously. For example, the Government Procurement Agreement includes certain services whose provision is 'incidental' to the supply of goods.[9] Canada has signed the agreement and implemented its provisions at the federal level through revised administrative procedures. Similarly, the 1979 GATT Subsidies Code allows for the imposition of countervailing duties on imported goods that have benefited from subsidized services.[10] Canadian accession to these accords suggests greater flexibility on the removal of barriers to services trade than reduction of barriers to foreign investment.

The Organization for Economic Co-operation and Development

Canada has participated in various OECD initiatives to develop standards regarding certain aspects of foreign investment and trade in services. These developments have acquired more significance than might otherwise have been expected given the relative inactivity of the

GATT in these fields, but they still lack force of law and emanate from an organization with only specialized developed country membership.

The Declaration on International Investment and Multinational Enterprises[11]

This 1976 declaration attempts to establish minimum voluntary standards for the treatment of foreign investors by providing that, so far as is compatible with essential security interests, members should accord foreign-controlled enterprises operating in their territories treatment that is no less favourable than that accorded in like situations to domestic enterprises (national treatment). Canada, in adhering to the declaration, reserved the right to take action respecting foreign investment, and specific mention was made of the now repealed Foreign Investment Review Act and other laws. Under the declaration, Canada may also continue to provide preferential assistance or special incentives to domestic firms in keeping with its modern practice. The declaration contains a set of guidelines for multinational enterprises, which are intended to promote minimum standards of corporate behaviour regarding such issues as disclosure of corporate information, labour relations, transfer pricing, and restrictive trade practices. Countries which have signed the OECD declaration have established systems of 'contact points' (in Canada this is the Department of External Affairs) to which nationals can refer concerns about the activities of source country enterprises in light of the declaration. There are no reported instances of any utilization of this system in Canada, though labour union references to the State Department of the United States have led to representations being made to the governments of Sweden and Japan. The declaration represents a series of separate unilateral commitments by OECD members, but the Decision on National Treatment accompanying the declaration is an OECD council resolution and may, therefore, not only carry more weight than does the non-enforceable declaration but may, arguably, also be evidence of a national treatment obligation at the level of international law. Under the OECD Decision on National Treatment, the Committee on International Investment and Multinational Enterprises (CIME) is to act as a forum for consultations between members over exceptions to the national treatment obligation.

Work is presently continuing on a new OECD National Treatment obligation respecting investment, which will carry more legal weight than do the above instruments. Canada apparently supports this initiative, subject to its special concerns about cultural industries and federal states.

At the time of its adoption of the declaration in 1976 – and again on its reaffirmation in 1979 – Canada made statements to the effect that it retained the right to take measures it considers appropriate concerning foreign investment. These statements have been interpreted as suggesting that Canada did not favour international progress on the reduction of barriers to direct investment, but such statements hardly seem to accurately reflect Canada's present position in light of its accession to the OECD Capital Movements Code and provisions in the Canada-U.S. Free Trade Agreement.[12] A better assessment of Canada's present position is that it still regards the OECD codes as non-binding but now favours international negotiation of a binding investment regime. Unfortunately, this conclusion must be inferred in the absence of any expressed articulation of Canadian policy towards restrictions on foreign investment.

Trade in Services and the OECD

Three specialized OECD codes relate to trade in services and are part of the resolve of the organization to reduce or eliminate barriers to trade in services, current payments, and capital movements. Obstacles to trade in services are the special subject of the committee on Capital Movements and Invisible Transactions (CMIT). The committee, assisted by CIME, has an ongoing role in examining code reservations and derogations, with the object of having members withdraw them.

The Invisibles Code. The 1961 Code of Liberalization of Current Invisibles Operations provides that members must eliminate restrictions among themselves on 'current invisibles transactions and transfers' subject to various reservations and derogations made according to the agreement.[13] The word 'transactions' describes contractual obligations and the word 'transfers' refers to their discharge by transfers of funds. Thus, rather than specifically relating to trade in services, the Invisibles Code relates to invisibles transactions in the balance of payments. Annex A to the code enumerates the transactions to which it applies. These include such services as films, insurance, transportation, and tourism but exclude banking, education, health, and computer services. Members are permitted to make reservations to the code (as Canada did on adhering to the code in 1961) when its obligations conflict with domestic legislation or the protection of a particular industry. Derogations are permitted if justified on economic or financial grounds. The code is also unconditional to the extent that members are required to apply liberalization measures to all IMF members as well as to all OECD members.

The Capital Movements Code.[14] On 18 July 1985, Canada became the last OECD country to become party to the December 1961 OECD Code of Liberalization of Capital Movements. This OECD code seeks to liberalize restrictions on foreign direct investment through eliminating restrictions on medium and long-term financial movements. If Canada had been party to the original promulgation of the code, it is difficult to see how, consistent with such participation, it could have introduced the Foreign Investment Review Act. As well as requiring the liberalization of restrictions on the entry of direct investment, the code contains a principle of non-discrimination that obliges signatories to treat all non-resident owned assets equally (though not necessarily the same as domestic ones). The breadth of these obligations is reduced by the fact that all party states have lodged reservations concerning inward direct investment and establishment. In March 1991, Canada replaced its full reservation on foreign investment under the code with a more specific reservation addressing the Investment Canada Act and specific sectors of the economy, such as financial services, energy, telecommunications, and marine transportation.

The Declaration on Transborder Data Flows. This OECD declaration was adopted in 1985 and seeks promotion of access to data and information services and the avoidance of domestic barriers to their international movement. The detailed provisions on this topic contained in the services chapter of the Canada-U.S. Free Trade Agreement represent the manifestation of this commitment on the part of Canada. The declaration is now being reconsidered by the OECD in the light of European concerns about lower legal standards respecting privacy in Canada and elsewhere.

Investment Promotion and Protection Treaties and the World Bank Centre for the Settlement of Investment Disputes

While expropriation has never been a recurrent issue in Canadian investment law, it is of long-standing concern internationally, where there have been several attempts to resolve the complex legal questions surrounding this topic. In recent years many bilateral investment treaties have been signed between capital-exporting and capital-importing countries. These treaties are designed to afford some level of legal guarantee about levels of investor protection. Until very recently, Canada has shown no interest in entering into such accords, but this seems to be changing with the signing in 1989 of an investment promotion and protection treaty between Canada and the Soviet Union and with the signing of a similar agreement in 1990 with Poland.[15]

Bilateral Investment Promotion and Protection Treaties (BIT's)

The Bilateral Investment Promotion and Protection Treaty (or BIT) seeks to achieve comprehensive protection for foreign direct investment by means of specific undertakings granted on a reciprocal basis. The BIT constitutes a more sophisticated arrangement than do the old paternalistic treaties of Friendship, Commerce, and Navigation (FCN) and other rather amorphous commercial accords signed by Canada.[16]

The American model BIT and the Canada-USSR accord on investment both define 'investment' in a broad sense that may include certain categories of trade in services.[17] Under Article 1(b) of the Canada-USSR BIT, the term investment includes a broad range of contractual rights, such as those which arise through licensing agreements and intellectual and industrial property agreements.

BIT's usually provide for protection against expropriation and for compensation for loss due to war, revolution, state emergencies, and restrictions on the transfer of capital and profits. BIT's do not confine themselves to outright expropriatory actions but seek to provide protection against any measures that significantly impair investment rights – such as creeping expropriation. In the Canada-USSR BIT, for example, expropriation must be 'for a public purpose, under due process of law, in a nondiscriminatory manner and ... accompanied by compensation ... based on the real value of the investment at the time of the expropriation.'

Most BIT's do not go as far as to extend a right of establishment but do provide for the free transfer of capital and profits and for national treatment by the host state of investment activities by nationals and corporations of the source country. The Canada-USSR BIT extends national treatment to contractual performance and enforcement, copyrights and patents, and personal property rights.[18]

Dispute Settlement and the World Bank Centre

Provision for dispute resolution is typical of most BIT's. In many instances, where a dispute is between an investor and a host government, reference is made to submission to the International Centre for the Settlement of Investment Disputes Between States and Nationals of other States (ICSID).[19] ICSID was set up in 1966 as part of the interest of the World Bank in encouraging the flow of capital to developing countries. Canada has not yet ratified the ICSID Convention. ICSID is not itself an arbitral institution, but it facilitates the establishment of arbitral tribunals to resolve investment disputes between contracting states and nationals of other contracting states. ICSID constitutes a novel form of dispute settlement in addition to adjudication, private arbitration, and diplomatic protection.

ICSID arbitral tribunals decide investment disputes according to the rules of law agreed on by the parties or, in the absence of agreement, the law of the state party and applicable rules of international law.[20] Once a dispute is submitted to ICSID, the source country is precluded from pressing its investor's claim through diplomatic channels. American BIT's require compulsory arbitration of disputes between investors and host governments, under ICSID auspices, and ICSID awards must be recognized as binding and enforceable by all contracting states.[21] This framework is clearly designed with the political dynamics of a host state/private investor dispute in mind. In contrast, the Canada-USSR BIT, in Article 9, provides for arbitration under the 1976 United Nations Commission on International Trade Law (UNCITRAL) Arbitration Rules. Since the UNCITRAL rules were primarily designed for private arbitrations, they would seem much less suitable than would ICSID procedures to resolve investment disputes where one side is a sovereign state.

It is remarkable that, apart from the provisions of the FTA, the most significant development in Canada relating to dispute resolution in international business arose from a provincial initiative. During 1986, as part of its attempt to enhance the credibility of Vancouver as a financial and business centre in the North Pacific, the government of British Columbia repealed its outmoded arbitration legislation and enacted a statute based on the 1985 UNCITRAL Model Law on International Commercial Arbitration. The legislation, since adopted by parliament and all the other provinces, applies to the arbitration in British Columbia of international commercial disputes and, in a series of detailed substantive and procedural provisions, places considerable limits on the scope for local judicial intervention in the conduct of such private arbitrations.[22] This should enhance Canada as a suitable venue in a dispute involving a Canadian investor and a host country or its citizens.

The provincial initiative just described also led the federal government to expedite Canada's accession to the 1958 United Nations Convention On The Recognition and Enforcement of Foreign Arbitral Awards (the 'New York Convention'). Such accession means that awards brought down in Canada must be enforced under the convention in the territory of countries party to it. Again, this development should enhance the willingness of foreign parties to arbitrate investment and other international commercial disputes on Canadian soil. Accession to the New York Convention significantly undermines the federal government's long-standing explanation for Canada's non-accession to ICSID on the basis that it relates to a matter within provincial legislature competence.

While most OECD countries have entered into BIT's, Canada has in the past been reluctant to do so. There has never been a well-articulated policy explanation for Canadian inactivity, though several reasons suggest themselves. First, the level of private Canadian investment in countries with a history of expropriatory measures has been low. Second, some of the security afforded by such agreements has been provided through foreign investment insurance against political risks offered by the Export Development Corporation (a federal Crown corporation). Finally, and perhaps most convincingly, Canadian non-participation reflects our schizophrenia concerning foreign investment controls. While Canada has a long history of host-country status – a character that is likely to continue as long as budget deficits mandate capital importation – it is also increasingly seen as a source country. The liberalization of Canadian investment laws, following the passage of the Investment Canada Act and the coming into force of the FTA, suggests that Canada now increasingly favours limits on the restrictions states may impose on foreign investors. It was in the context of this more liberal investment policy era that Canada signed its recent investment accords with the Soviet Union, Poland, and others.

The Canada-U.S. Free Trade Agreement

A major manifestation of Canadian policy towards foreign direct investment and trade in services is the 1988 Free Trade Agreement between this country and the United States. The FTA, unlike the GATT, contains extensive provisions on such matters as energy, trade in services, investment, and financial services. The FTA does not, of course, replace the GATT as the legal foundation of the Canada-U.S. trading relationship, but some regard it as a prototype for future multilateral economic accords to be developed under GATT auspices. Whatever Canadian policy might be extracted from its activity inside the OECD and its inactivity regarding investment dispute settlement procedures, the FTA signals at least a qualified commitment on Canada's part to the multilateral reduction of barriers to investment and trade in services.

Trade in Services (Chapters 14 and 17)

Chapter 14 merely represents a standstill in barriers to bilateral trade in services between the two countries – existing barriers to services trade remain in place. Thus, a general national treatment obligation is put in place – each country must treat residents of the other no less favourably than it treats its own residents respecting covered measures – but this obligation does not apply to existing measures.[23] Discriminatory treatment of service providers is permitted if necessary for prudential, fiduciary, health and safety, and consumer protection reasons.[24] The FTA does not, therefore, establish a right of establishment for service providers but merely guarantees national treatment and non-discrimination in future.

While the FTA provisions on trade in services may, at first, appear to represent a radical shift in Canadian trade policy, closer examination shows that they only amount to a limited application of two basic GATT principles (national treatment and non-discrimination) to services trade between the two countries. The provisions of the FTA are less extensive than are those of the Protocol on Trade in Services to the Australia New Zealand Closer Economic Relations Trade Agreement of 18 August 1988. That protocol extends to all but expressly excluded services (the FTA only extends to 'covered services') and builds on a higher level of present access for service providers than exists between Canada and the United States. The FTA nevertheless represents significant progress both in terms of the bilateral relationship and an apparent Canadian commitment to freer trade in services in the context of the Uruguay Round.[25]

Foreign Direct Investment (Chapter 16)

While the substantive content of the services accord may seem modest in scope, this deficiency is ameliorated by the existence of a separate agreement on investment. This accord may well be regarded as the first Canadian BIT – though it probably owes its existence more to the complex bargaining that was part of the FTA and less to independent Canadian resolve to enter into an investment agreement with its largest foreign investor. The United States has argued longest and loudest for the easing of Canadian investment controls. While legal restrictions on foreign investment in the United States related to sectors of special concern (such as transportation and banking), Canada still maintains a generic review system (the Investment Canada Act).

The FTA effects immediate amendments to the Investment Canada Act, giving preferential levels of review for American investors in Canada. The agreement also effects a standstill concerning any future restrictions on United States investment and expands concepts developed in relation to trade in goods and services to cover American direct investment. In this respect, the FTA exceeds the agreement also reached, and currently the subject of GATT negotiations, about trade related investment measures (TRIM's). Like Chapter 14, however, Chapter 16 does not apply to existing non-conforming measures. As with restrictions on trade in services, both countries may amend existing non-conforming measures short of decreasing their level of conformity.

The scope of Chapter 16 is largely determined by the definition of the term 'business enterprise,' which requires a place of business, a work force, and assets used in carrying on a business. The establishment or acquisition of a business enterprise constitutes an investment under the agreement. This means that 'investment' has a narrower meaning in the agreement than it does in most BIT's, where it includes intangible property rights arising out of contractual agreements.

The FTA comes nowhere close to granting reciprocal bilateral rights of establishment in respect of foreign direct investment. Nor does it do much to dismantle existing controls, though it does effect significant reductions in thresholds for American investors. The essential element of the agreement that is concerned with investment is that no more restrictive Canadian regime than that imposed on Americans by the Investment Canada Act can be reimposed.

Finally, reference should also be made to Chapter 15 of the agreement, which complements the above provisions by liberalizing physical access for business travellers of either country. Simplified procedures are established for temporary entry by professional and business persons but not for other providers of labour services.[26] The principle of Chapter 15 is stated in Article 1,501 as being 'the desirability of facilitating temporary entry on a reciprocal basis and of establishing transparent criteria and procedures for temporary entry, and the need to ensure border security and protect indigenous labor and permanent employment.' While Chapter 15 introduces procedural and administrative changes, the substantive immigration laws of both countries remain unchanged. In essence, labour certification and equivalent procedures which presently apply to business visitors will no longer apply. The ambiguity of much of Chapter 15, however, makes uncertain just how significant its effects will be on trans-border movement of business persons. It is not clear, for instance, how long temporary entry status can be maintained or whether a person can qualify simultaneously under more than one category of temporary visitor.

The investment and services provisions of the FTA would suggest that Canada is squarely in favour of the liberalization of restrictive measures affecting these areas of international economic activity. However, when one considers the already close economic relationship between Canada and the United States, the level of agreement reached in the FTA seems relatively modest. Most existing investment and services trade restrictions remain in place; many of the treaty provis-

ions have not been implemented and may become casualties of constitutional arguments over the scope of federal legislative power in Canada. Furthermore, the provisions of the FTA (such as those dealing with
financial services) often reflect unique aspects of the Canadian-American regulatory relationship and may not be transferable to an agreement of general application. This harks back to a concern mentioned
earlier, that Canada's foreign investment policies have often been
reactive to popular political concerns with the level of American investment in this country rather than with a concerted response to the
problem of foreign investment in a multilateral context. Pressures from
host countries to protect restrictions on foreign investment and trade in
services may force Canada into a stance favouring the elimination of
such restrictions. Other OECD countries have already started to press
Canada to extend to them the benefits conferred upon the United States
under the FTA regarding investment and services. Once such a process
gets underway, it will be insulated from the ambiguities of Canada's
relationship with the United States and resistant to changes affecting
that relationship.

THE URUGUAY ROUND AND TRADE IN SERVICES

Even though foreign direct investment is not a subject for negotiation,
the consideration of a regime for trade in services will involve the GATT
in issues affecting the right of establishment. Whatever system of rules
does emerge will significantly pre-empt the codes and accords discussed earlier insofar as they overlap with any GATT agreement.

The present round of GATT multinational trade negotiations is the
first to specifically include trade in services on its agenda. In the
ministerial declaration initiating the Uruguay Round it is stated that:

> Negotiations in this area shall aim to establish a multilateral framework
> of principles and rules for trade in services, including elaboration of
> possible disciplines for individual sectors, with a view to expansion of
> such trade under conditions of transparency and progressible liberaliza-
> tion and as a means of promoting economic growth of all trading partners
> and the development of developing countries. Such framework shall
> respect the policy objectives of national laws and regulations applying to
> services and shall take into account the work of relevant international
> organizations.[27]

The ministerial declaration thus suggests three central elements for
a framework agreement; a general framework agreement of principles

and rules, separate codes for certain services sectors, and a process of progressive liberalization.

It should be parenthetically noted that the Declaration on Trade in Services itself is a decision of ministers representing individual governments, unlike the accompanying declaration on Trade in Goods which is a decision of the contracting parties. This procedure reflects the intent of some developing countries to separate the two sets of negotiations so that benefits achieved on goods trade could not be used to bargain for concessions in trade in services. While the Group on Negotiations on Trade in Services reports to the Trade Negotiations Committee, it is otherwise autonomous.

Prior to the Uruguay Round, little preparatory work had been done inside the GATT on the topic of trade in services because of uncertainty about whether the subject would be on the MTN agenda. Nevertheless, it is clear that the GATT, with its large membership and proven authority to enforce agreements entered into by its members, is probably best suited to regulate international trade in services. Other factors which support a GATT role in the area of services include the organization's record in trade obligations, its relative freedom from ideological controversy, and the value of existing GATT principles and procedures as a basis for a new framework of international legal obligations respecting trade in services.

While the outcome of the Uruguay Round negotiations on trade in services remains uncertain, it became clear by the mid-term review at Montreal in December 1988 that three concepts were highly likely to form part of a framework agreement: national treatment, non-discrimination, and transparency.

National treatment, as set out in Article 3 of the GATT, is premised on the fact that goods are normally subject to tariffs as they cross national frontiers. Accordingly, this level of measurable protection should not be eroded by internal discriminatory measures. The principle of national treatment has, however, increasingly become an independent principle of non-discrimination against foreign suppliers into markets, and, in this sense, it is argued that it prohibits all internal measures, such as taxes and regulations, that operate as protectionist measures against foreign suppliers of goods and services. Once certain minimum quality standards (premised on such permissible objectives as preservation of competition, consumer protection, or social welfare) are satisfied, then it becomes difficult to justify any further differential treatment of foreign suppliers into a domestic market.[28] The Montreal Interim Ministerial Decision on Services of December 1988 defines national treatment as 'the services exports and/or exporters of any signatory are accorded in the market of the other signatory, in respect of all laws, regulations and administrative practices, treatment "no less favourable" than that accorded domestic services providers in the same market.'

The GATT principle of non-discrimination, as incorporated in the most-favoured-nation clause, ensures the openness of the world's trading system. The main issue regarding its application to trade in services is whether it should be made unconditional (meaning concessions should be extended to all members of a services agreement irrespective of reciprocity) or conditional (meaning concessions should extend only on the basis of reciprocity). Unconditional most-favoured-nation treatment could either be in the form of equal rights of access to all or a limited right of access without discrimination on the basis of national origin. These alternatives could provide a basis for the reconciliation of the position of certain developed and developing countries, in that market access could be granted regardless of reciprocity, with certain restrictions on the degree of access allowed but without discrimination on grounds of national origin. For instance, Canada would be obliged to allow entry of foreign financial services without discrimination on the basis of national origin but with restrictions on the degree of access to the domestic industry permitted foreign suppliers overall.

A concern with liberalization on this basis is that foreign-supplied services may not meet the quality standards expected of domestic services providers.[29] It has been suggested that governments will be under pressure to relax their regulatory stringency in order to increase their international competitiveness. The answer should lie in the corrective effect of market forces, but, if these are thought to be ineffectual, the permissible minimum quality standards referred to above should be sufficient without the need to withhold unconditional most-favoured-nation treatment.

The United States has taken the position that liberalization affecting services (and perhaps also investment) will expand business opportunities and world trade in general, leading to improved overall economic development. This conclusion is partly based on the perception of the United States and some other developed economies that their comparative advantage is moving from industrial production towards the production of services. The United States is concerned that there exists a growing area of world trade and investment that is not subject to an established body of rules (GATT) with effective remedies and procedures for dispute resolution.

Developing countries fear that the benefits of this ongoing change in the world economy may not be captured by them, at least in the short term.[30] Having relatively recently asserted their political and economic independence, the developing states fear that if they give in to American pressures they may lose their new found freedom. Canada has similar concerns, but they have greater significance for less developed countries, where government control of certain sectors of the economy may be part of a deliberate strategy to achieve economic as well as cultural independence.

The developing countries have suggested that, precisely because of their lack of economic development, they will not receive, at least in the short term, the same levels of benefit from economic liberalization that should accrue to the developed states. Many developing countries fear the influence of transnational corporations over both their economic and cultural identities. Specifically, there is concern about the need to provide protection and incentives for fledgling local industries, which might fail if exposed to international competition. Brazil and others are pessimistic that technical developments in the communication of information will lead to increased centralization and deprive them of the expected benefits of an expanded service sector. On the other hand, they argue, factors such as labour resources, in which they may enjoy comparative advantage, may not be made the subject of liberalization.

Many of these types of concerns are long-standing, while others are a product of the negotiations leading up to an agreement on trade in services in the Uruguay Round. That process has already revealed a certain level of flexibility on both sides. While the issues are profound and deeply felt, there are indications that the sorts of compromises reached between Canada and the United States in the context of the FTA might also be possible in respect of the developed and developing nations in a multilateral context.[31]

It is clear at this stage of the negotiations that whatever concerns Canada might have had about the risks of foreign investment in the 1970s have now receded – Canada has joined the United States in broadly supporting liberalization measures. This would seem to mean that Canada is no longer viewed as sharing some of the concerns of developing countries set out above.

CHANGING CANADIAN POLICY ON FOREIGN DIRECT INVESTMENT

Since the 1970s there has been a perceptible shift in Canadian attitudes to restrictions on foreign investment. The Trudeau governments of the seventies saw the growth of economic nationalism in Canada. Many Canadians questioned whether economic benefits were being secured to Canada by transnational corporate investment. Examples were cited which indicated that American companies chose not to locate their research and development departments here but in the United States, and that such firms tended to source their inputs from American manufacturers rather than from Canadian suppliers. Other specific arguments included the drain on the balance of payments through dividends and royalties, the export of unprocessed primary products, and the extraterritorial application of United States laws through the activities of American corporations in Canada. These arguments closely resembled those advanced by developing host countries about foreign investors. In the case of Canada, however, they were reinforced by arguments based on cultural and social values.

In direct response to these concerns were Canadian laws and policies of the period: the Foreign Investment Review Act, the National Energy Policy, and provincial and federal legislation dealing with the extraterritorial application of American antitrust laws and corporate management directives. Internationally, Canada's investment perspective was reflected in its lack of participation in many arrangements designed to facilitate investment dispute resolution. Canada did not enter into any BIT accords and has still not become party to the ICSID Convention. Even while adopting the 1976 OECD Investment Declaration, Canada expressed its firm intent to retain the right to impose further restrictions on the entry of foreign investment.

By the mid-1980s, however, there had apparently been a distinct change in Canadian foreign investment policy. This change was symbolized for many by the prime minister's sentiment that Canada was now 'open for business.' The Foreign Investment Review Act was repealed and replaced by the Investment Canada Act in 1985, thus limiting the categories of reviewable investments. Along with a new foreign investment screening agency, Investment Canada, amendments were also made to the Bank Act, expanding the scope for foreign banking operations in Canada. Canada's international positions regarding investment also reflected this change in policy. In 1985, as we have seen, Canada became part of the OECD Code on Capital Movements. The Uruguay Round, commencing in 1986, also saw Canada more or less allied with the United States in supporting liberalized trade in services and related GATT initiatives. In 1988, the FTA sent another signal of Canada's willingness to agree to freer rights of establishment – at least as far as the United States was concerned. The decade closed with Canada's first bilateral investment treaty (BIT) being signed with the Soviet Union.

Why did Canadian investment policy undergo the major shift just described? At least three factors suggest themselves. First, American investment in Canada had largely stabilized by 1980, and investment from other countries – especially Asia-Pacific – was increasing at a faster rate. Also, Canada itself was becoming a more significant investor abroad, especially in the United States. Second, there was a greater realization in Canada by the early 1980s that its continued economic growth was dependent on international competitiveness. The Canadian government increasingly saw this growth as better secured by Canada participating in effective international agreements than by reacting to isolated domestic concerns. Finally, deregulation of the Canadian economy in the 1980s increased the likelihood that Canada would enter into international accords to reduce barriers to economic transactions.

CONCLUSION

Canadian foreign investment policy has apparently entered a period of ongoing support for the liberalization of restrictive measures – both in Canada and elsewhere. While this policy – which evolved during the 1980s – has not been the subject of as detailed an articulation as was the restrictive policy of the 1970s, it is evidenced by the ongoing removal of restrictions.

As the conclusion of the Uruguay Round approaches, bringing with it the likelihood of an accord on trade in services, the question arises as to what sort of accord Canada should support and how Canada's approach will differ from that of the United States. Finally, how will such an accord likely influence Canada's position on future investment liberalization measures?

Even the United States, which has spearheaded the removal of investment restrictions, has not unequivocally asserted that a right of establishment should exist under international law.[32] Canada's own treaty practice and its repeated reservations to OECD instruments suggest that Canada is not likely to support a general right of establishment. If multilateral agreements are proposed for isolated economic sectors, however, Canadian practice suggests that it might support a right of permanent entry in specific areas – such as banking, where Canada presently allows such access on the basis of reciprocity.[33]

The provisions of Chapter 14 of the FTA (Trade in Services) and Canada's joinder in OECD instruments suggest that Canada would favour a services accord which requires that foreign service providers be accorded the same treatment as local service providers (national treatment). The FTA shows that Canada is willing to extend national treatment to foreign direct investment. There is no apparent reason why this principle should not extend to foreign direct investment, notwithstanding that no right of establishment is extended. This was the approach adopted in the FTA.[34]

Canadian investment policy appears to differ markedly from that of the United States on the issue of cultural industries. While the FTA marks a significant reassessment by Canada of its attitude to foreign investment, it can hardly be said that this includes the so-called cultural sector.[35] The amendments to the Investment Canada Act designed to liberalize access for American investors do not apply to the acquisition of 'cultural businesses,' which include the publishing, film, video, music, and radio and television industries.[36]

While Canadian domestic law protects the cultural sector against foreign control, the Canadian government has not made clear how it supports such protection in the international context. This reticence is part of the perception, mentioned earlier, of the lack of a well-articulated Canadian position on investment controls.

Many governments promote various cultural policies some regard as adversely affecting trade in services and foreign investment. With a move by the United States to include cultural industries among those whose services should be freely traded, the opportunity arises for Canada to use its domestic experience for the benefit of the international community.[37] With the extension of the GATT agenda to trade in services and perhaps investment, restrictions based on cultural sovereignty must be directly addressed in the GATT context. This will afford the opportunity to increase the international legitimacy of such concerns, which heretofore have primarily been addressed in more politicized forums, such as the United Nations and its agencies. Canada should have the opportunity to explain some of its long-standing domestic practices and reinforce its support for similar concerns on the part of many other countries.

While there have recently been major international undertakings on Canada's part concerning foreign direct investment (the FTA, the OECD codes, and BIT's with the Soviet Union and others), these developments have not taken place in the context of a clearly articulated Canadian policy on the subject. Canada is at risk of being perceived as having an investment policy no different from that of the United States, unless it explains its position on the changes that have occurred and the basis of future international activity on Canada's part to reduce restrictions on foreign direct investment. In the absence of such an express statement of policy, observers may be excused for thinking that nothing about Canadian investment policy has changed since the 1970s, except in relation to the privileges granted American investors under the FTA. It may be that pressures from third countries for the same advantages as American investors have been granted will eventually precipitate a clear expression of Canada's position regarding foreign direct investment – both here and abroad. While no such expression has occurred,

Canada has entered into several new international legal regimes that are liberal in character. These agreements represent structural changes that will make it difficult for Canada to reverse its position and take a protectionist stance on foreign investment – whatever political changes might occur within the country.

CHAPTER SEVEN

Canada and the International Monetary Regime

Michael C. Webb

This chapter provides a description and assessment of Canadian policy towards the international monetary regime over the period since 1945. According to the consensual definition, an international regime is a set of 'principles, norms, rules, and decisionmaking procedures around which actor expectations converge'[1] in a particular issue area. The international monetary regime is the set of principles, norms, rules, and decisionmaking procedures relevant to the issue of how governments reconcile national macroeconomic objectives with international constraints.

The need to reconcile national objectives with international constraints arises because the ability of any country to achieve its macroeconomic objectives depends on the policies pursued by its international economic partners and the nature of market linkages between the country and the international economy. National monetary and fiscal policies that diverge from those of the country's main trading partners generate adverse international market flows that may prevent the country in question from achieving its domestic economic objectives. Expansionary policies generate trade deficits and capital outflows, and the resulting payments imbalance puts downward pressure on the exchange rate; restrictive policies generate trade surpluses and capital inflows, leading to pressure for exchange rate appreciation.[2]

At the same time, policies that states could use to insulate their policies from adverse international market pressures can impose burdens of adjustment on foreign countries and undermine international economic stability. For example, countries experiencing external deficits caused by expansionary policies could impose trade restrictions or devalue their currencies, thereby 'exporting' the costs of their macroeconomic policies to foreign countries.

This danger has been the stimulus for international efforts to create and sustain an international monetary regime. The basic purpose of this regime throughout the period since 1945 has been to reconcile the pursuit of national macroeconomic objectives with international trade liberalization and international economic stability.

The international monetary regime is of considerable importance to Canada because of the openness of the Canadian economy. Openness is apparent in the relatively high level of exports and imports relative to gross domestic product in Canada and the integration of Canadian capital markets with American capital markets. This openness means that Canadian macroeconomic policymaking must be highly sensitive to conditions in the international economy and to foreign government policies. Canadian policies that do not take the international context into account are likely to generate adverse trade and capital flows and will not be sustainable.

This chapter examines Canadian efforts to shape the international regime and the consistency of Canada's own international monetary policies with the prescriptions and proscriptions of the regime. Because the scope of the international regime is so broad, the relevant Canadian 'policy' is also wide-ranging. It includes the government's stated policy towards specific international institutions and norms as well as concrete Canadian actions in all of the policy areas described below as relevant to the international monetary regime.

This examination of the record of Canadian policy will serve as a basis for evaluation. Policy in the areas covered in this chapter ought to promote Canada's collective national interest in long-run economic stability and prosperity. Has this been the case? This assessment will of necessity be highly subjective. I will suggest that Canadian policymaking in recent years has focused too much on domestic considerations, with too little attention paid to the opportunities and constraints arising out of the international monetary regime.

Canadian policy can also be evaluated in light of arguments that have been made about Canada's general interests in international economic co-operation. The dominant tradition in the study of Canadian foreign policy depicts Canada as a strong and active supporter of multilateral institutions.[3] Multilateral institutions are supposed to benefit middle-sized powers like Canada by providing opportunities to band together with like-minded states to pursue interests that diverge from those of dominant countries, especially the United States. Furthermore, the rules incorporated in international regimes (see below) are thought to benefit smaller countries by making it harder for larger countries to pursue unilaterally determined policies intended to export burdens of international monetary adjustment to foreign countries.

In contrast to this view, I will argue that Canada has been no more supportive of the international monetary regime than have other countries. Canada has frequently violated regime norms and rules when these norms and rules were inconsistent with policies the government of the day thought were necessary to achieve its domestic objectives.

On a related point, the record of Canadian policy also reveals a preference for bilateral deals with the United States over multilateral co-operation when vital Canadian interests are at stake. Canadian leaders have found that multilateral institutions are not very responsive to specifically Canadian concerns. This means that, in practice, there are few opportunities for Canada to use multilateral forums to build coalitions in support of international policies favourable to Canada. In contrast, the United States has often been willing to negotiate arrangements that satisfy both Canadian and American objectives.

The record of Canadian participation in the international monetary regime also provides a basis for evaluating arguments about Canada's status in the international economic system. Some analysts have argued that Canada has recently achieved 'principal power' status in the international system, playing a key role shaping international order.[4] But, I will argue, Canada has never had a substantial influence on the character of the international monetary regime, despite its participation in important forums like the Group of Ten (G10) and the Group of Seven (G7).

Before turning to Canadian policy, a few words about the scope and nature of the international monetary regime are in order. As already stated, the international monetary regime consists of the principles, norms, rules, and decisionmaking procedures relevant to how governments reconcile national macroeconomic objectives with international constraints. A number of different types of policies could be used to achieve this reconciliation. These can be described in three categories; external, symptom management, and internal.[5]

External Policies. Governments could seek to eliminate payments imbalances by manipulating trade and capital controls. Deficit countries might restrict imports and capital outflows; surplus countries might encourage imports and restrict capital inflows. Alternatively, governments could adjust exchange rates; deficit countries might devalue, while surplus countries might revalue.

Symptom Management Policies. Governments might try to manage payments imbalances by financing them (using national reserves, international borrowing, or both) and by intervening in foreign exchange markets to manage the international market flows that are symptomatic of different macroeconomic policies in different countries.

Internal Policies. Governments could adjust monetary and fiscal policies to eliminate imbalances between savings, investment, and consumption that generate trade imbalances and to eliminate cross-national interest rate differentials that generate speculative international capital flows.

As is apparent from this list, the international monetary regime deals with economic policies that have enormous domestic political ramifications – especially monetary and fiscal policies.[6] Consequently, the regime has always been rather loosely defined, as few governments have been willing to accept formal international constraints on their freedom to select policies that serve their domestic political interests. The regime has also changed substantially over the course of the postwar period. There has been continuity only at the level of basic principles. These principles have been aptly summarized as 'embedded liberalism.'[7] The basic purpose of the international monetary regime has been to reconcile the pursuit of domestic macroeconomic stabilization with international trade liberalization. Changes in the regime can be largely explained as adaptations designed to permit this reconciliation as international capital markets have become increasingly integrated.[8] Changes have been considerable at the levels of norms, rules, and decisionmaking procedures.[9] These characteristics of the regime have frequently been weak, in the sense of not providing clear, agreed prescriptions and proscriptions that actually influence national behaviour. Furthermore, actor expectations frequently converge around patterns of behaviour that reflect the preferences only of the most powerful countries – and especially of the United States. To call this a regime, therefore, implies nothing about whether it is desirable according to some normative criteria.

The international monetary regime could influence the manner in which domestic macroeconomic stabilization is reconciled with international liberalization by setting rules or guidelines for government policy and by promoting information-sharing and consultations. We can identify changes in the importance of both categories of influence over the postwar period. Formal rules were important in the 1950s and the 1960s, particularly with respect to exchange rates, but these rules did not seriously constrain national macroeconomic policymaking. Information-sharing and consultations were limited compared to the 1970s and 1980s, as most governments felt that detailed discussions of monetary and fiscal policies infringed on national sovereignty. By the late 1970s and the 1980s, formal rules existed only within the European

Monetary System, although interest in the use of internationally agreed indicators and targets for national policies revived in the mid-1980s. At the same time, information-sharing and consultations have become more important, and certain norms about how macroeconomic policies ought to be conducted have developed. Leading governments often have not followed these norms in national policy, but there has been significant co-ordination of policies on an ad hoc basis.

The empirical section of this chapter is divided into four periods, in each of which the international monetary regime took distinct forms. In each period, the norms of the regime and the behaviour of leading states will be discussed briefly, as background for describing Canadian policy. A concluding section evaluates Canadian policy according to the criteria outlined above.

1944-58: THE POSTWAR RECOVERY PERIOD

The international monetary regime designed by the United States and Britain in the 1940s was intended to overcome the perceived defects of the interwar system. Countries were expected to fix exchange rates at internationally agreed levels and to liberalize trade controls, exchanging them for current account purposes (while controlling so-called 'speculative' capital flows) after a brief postwar transition period. Temporary international credits would be provided through the International Monetary Fund (IMF) to give deficit countries time to restore their respective payments balances gradually, without resort to drastic trade controls, currency depreciation, or domestic deflation – all of which had been common and devastating in the 1930s.

None of the norms or rules of the Bretton Woods regime were widely respected before the late 1950s. Most countries outside North America relied on the transitional provisions of the IMF agreement to impose comprehensive, discriminatory trade and exchange controls in order to insulate ambitious national reconstruction programs and full employment policies from international market pressures. Exchange rates were chosen and adjusted unilaterally. Enormous European, Japanese, and Canadian trade deficits with the United States were managed on a bilateral basis. Foreign aid financed American and Canadian exports to Europe and Japan and encouraged a slow acceptance of trade liberalization norms outside North America.

Thus, international practice in the postwar recovery period diverged sharply from international norms embodied in the IMF and the General Agreement on Tariffs and Trade (GATT). Canada's record in this area was also mixed. Canada strongly supported the establishment of an international regime, and Canadian diplomats worked hard to achieve a compromise between British and American positions in the Bretton Woods negotiations. Canada had an enormous stake in the creation of a liberal, multilateral economic system as a way to restore prewar trading patterns (when Canada's trade surplus with Europe had financed its trade deficit with the United States) and to discourage the United States from returning to isolationist foreign policies.[10]

Canada provided generous financial aid to Britain and other European countries in the immediate postwar period, both to finance Canadian exports and to encourage those countries to move towards currency convertibility. By 1951 Canada had eliminated its own comprehensive exchange controls, thereby becoming one of the first countries to establish currency convertibility and to accept the full obligations of IMF membership.

These actions all demonstrated strong support for the norms of the regime designed at Bretton Woods. But when Canada faced severe external payments pressures, it adopted measures that violated the nascent regime's norms, rules, and decisionmaking procedures, just as did overseas countries.

This first became apparent when Canada faced a balance of payments crisis in 1947 caused by a deficit in its trade with the United States at a time when Canada's exports to Britain and continental Europe were not earning hard currency. On 17 November 1947 (the same day that agreement was reached in the Geneva trade talks),[11] Ottawa announced measures to deal with the crisis that violated regime rules and norms. Canada imposed discriminatory restrictions on imports from the United States, despite the recognized danger that overseas countries would view Canada's action as further justification for their own reliance on discriminatory controls that hurt Canada.[12]

Strikingly, Ottawa entirely bypassed multilateral institutions in favour of direct bilateral talks with the United States. Ottawa did not turn to the IMF for a loan, even when American officials suggested that Canada do so.[13] The problem was seen, in Ottawa, as one that could be solved only by the United States.[14] Bilateral negotiations with the United States preceded the introduction of trade restrictions. Canadian officials gained Washington's sympathy and a $300 million loan. Ottawa also relied mainly on bilateral measures to restore external payments balance in the long run, persuading the United States to spend some Marshall Plan dollars in Canada and encouraging inflows of American foreign direct investment.[15]

A more long-lasting Canadian departure from regime norms began in 1950, with the decision to let the dollar float. Speculative capital inflows had made it difficult for the Bank of Canada to maintain Canada's fixed parity of 90.5 cents u.s. without relaxing monetary policy in Canada. The solution most compatible with the norms of the Bretton Woods regime would have been to revalue the exchange rate to some new fixed level, but the government feared that it would not be able to predict what level would dampen speculation.

Consequently, Ottawa decided to let the Canadian dollar float.[16] The Bank of Canada would no longer adhere to the IMF rule that it keep the currency within plus or minus one per cent of a fixed parity. The decision was taken without prior consultation with the IMF. The IMF staff strongly disapproved of Canada's intention to permit the dollar to fluctuate and recommended instead that Canada impose tighter controls on speculative capital flows and conduct open-market operations to prevent increased foreign reserves from inflating the domestic money supply.[17] The Fund feared that the 'use of floating rates by a major developed country could undermine the credibility of the Bretton Woods system and lead to widespread disregard for its rules.'[18]

Nevertheless, the executive board decided to accept the Canadian action and hope that no other countries followed Canada's example. When the executive board discussed the Canadian decision, the representatives from the United States and Britain spoke in support of Canada – indeed, the executive director for the United States would have preferred a stronger board decision, explicitly citing the Canadian action as 'an appropriate step' in the circumstances rather than merely accepting the Canadian action.[19] At this time, the United States and Britain dominated the IMF, holding 30.5 per cent and 14.5 per cent, respectively, of the votes on the executive board.[20]

With these powerful countries on its side (it is most likely that Canada had consulted both before making its decision, although there is no public documentary evidence of prior consultations), Canada was able to evade the central rule of the Bretton Woods regime. International concern about Canada's action was also mitigated by the fact that it was intended to achieve broader objectives shared with the Fund, namely, on non-inflationary macroeconomic policies and currency convertibility – and Canada did make its currency fully convertible in 1951. By the mid-1950s, the Fund had come to accept that the unique features of the Canadian situation – especially the close integration of the Canadian and American economies – meant that a fluctuating exchange rate was appropriate for Canada and that Canada's behaviour did not set a precedent for other countries.[21]

Most other leading countries did not become as open to international capital flows as Canada was in 1950 until the late 1960s. In the early 1970s, other countries made the same decision as Canada had in 1950; they chose to permit their currencies to fluctuate rather than maintain exchange rate stability at the expense of domestic macroeconomic objectives.

Overall, we can see that Canada gave qualified support to the international monetary regime in the period 1944-58 – and that Canada had little impact on the evolution of the regime. The actions of the United States and the European countries were much more important in shaping the norms and rules of the regime and patterns of practice during this period. Canada was able to violate a key international norm – non-discrimination in trade – and one of the central rules of the regime – fixed exchange rates – without its actions setting precedents for other countries. In 1947 and 1950, Ottawa showed that it was willing to violate regime injunctions even though Canada's own export interests would have been severely damaged had Canada's policies encouraged other countries to maintain similar policies. Finally, Ottawa's decision to rely on bilateral measures in 1947 reveals the limits to Canada's commitment to multilateralism. Despite their theoretical attractions, multilateral arrangements appeared unable to meet pressing Canadian needs.

1958-70: THE BRETTON WOODS SYSTEM

The late 1950s and the 1960s were the golden years of the Bretton Woods system. The international monetary regime designed in the mid-1940s came closest to functioning as intended during these years. Fixed exchange rates were maintained by all leading countries until the early 1970s. Trade and exchange controls did become significantly more liberal. International co-ordination of balance of payments lending was extensive, as was co-ordinated intervention to maintain fixed exchange rates.

Other policies of leading countries were not consistent with regime norms. Exchange rates were fixed to the point of rigidity. Macroeconomic policies were made independently, and countries rarely adjusted macroeconomic policies to reduce external imbalances.[22] This pattern is inconsistent with the oft-heard notion that fixed exchange rates forced countries to pursue domestic policies that were consistent with international equilibrium.[23] Multilateral surveillance in the Organization for Economic Co-operation and Development (OECD) was supposed to encourage countries to pursue policies that were consistent with international equilibrium, but it had no impact on monetary and fiscal policies.[24]

The United States experienced a substantial balance of payments deficit for most of this period, a deficit which simultaneously eased immediate political conflicts and undermined the long-run stability of the system. The United States did have a substantial trade surplus until the late 1960s, but this was more than offset by overseas military spending, foreign aid outflows, and capital outflows. The American payments deficit provided liquidity to the system, permitting foreign countries to achieve the balance of payments surpluses that many desired. Confidence in the United States dollar inevitably eroded, however, and as the dollar holdings of foreign central banks kept rising, the drain on American gold reserves became so great that the United States Treasury closed the gold window (informally in 1968 and formally in 1971).

None of the governments concerned were willing to alter macroeconomic policies to correct the situation. The United States rejected foreign demands for deflation, and surplus countries rejected American demands for currency revaluation and domestic reflation (Canada was an exception; see below). Consequently, international monetary negotiations in the 1960s were dominated by efforts to manage the symptoms of fundamentally incompatible national policies. These efforts included foreign lending to the United States, controls on capital movements, and the creation of Special Drawing Rights as an alternative form of international liquidity. These symptom management policies stabilized exchange rates and permitted continuing trade liberalization for most of the 1960s. But by the end of the decade, capital flows through the Euromarkets had become too large to be reconciled with fixed exchange rates and autonomy in macroeconomic policymaking simply by co-ordinating exchange rate and balance of payments policies, and fixed exchange rates were abandoned.

Canada's policies towards the international monetary regime were largely supportive during the late 1950s and the 1960s. Canada participated in the mechanisms of symptom management that were developed to maintain fixed exchange rates in the face of divergent national macroeconomic policies. Canadian dollars were borrowed by deficit countries through the IMF, Canada was a party to the General Arrangements to Borrow (created to help the IMF meet very large requests for drawings), and Canada participated in co-ordinated foreign exchange market intervention.[25] Canada also supported initiatives to expand international liquidity and to reduce the system's reliance on the United States dollar. In all of these areas, Canada was a minor player; the main diplomatic battles were fought among the United States, leading European countries, Japan, and the developing countries.

When Canada experienced international payments problems of its own during this period, its actions were largely consistent with regime norms, although Canada also turned to bilateral arrangements with the United States that went well beyond these norms. In May 1962, Canada restored a fixed parity for the Canadian dollar. The government hoped that this action would reduce speculative attacks by investors who lacked confidence in the Diefenbaker government. Pressure from the IMF, and the IMF's argument that a fixed parity would reduce speculation, probably contributed to the government's decision. The new rate (92.5 cents U.S.) was chosen unilaterally by the Canadian government, which was consistent with international practice – if not with IMF rules and decisionmaking procedures.[26]

Speculative attacks resumed immediately after Diefenbaker was returned with a minority government in the June 1962 election, and Ottawa turned to the IMF and the United States for help, borrowing $300 million (U.S.) from the former and $750 million (U.S.) from the latter.[27] The loan from the IMF was small enough relative to Canada's quota not to require policy conditions, but Canada did simultaneously tighten fiscal and monetary policies – measures that the IMF recommended to countries experiencing deficits. In all of these respects, Canadian policies were consistent with, and probably influenced by, the norms of the IMF-centred regime.[28]

Canada also imposed a temporary tariff surcharge to help manage its trade deficit. This measure violated GATT rules, which permitted quantitative restrictions to deal with balance of payments emergencies but did not contain a comparable exception to the binding of tariffs. But Canada's action was consistent with regime norms, even if not with the letter of the rules; a tariff surcharge distorts international trade less than do quantitative restrictions, and the surcharge was quickly phased out as Canada's payments position improved. Other GATT members criticized the decision to impose a tariff surcharge, but no sanctions were imposed on Canada.[29] As in the earlier Canadian decision to let its currency fluctuate, the regime proved sufficiently flexible to accommodate policies that violated regime rules yet were consistent with broader regime norms.

The single most serious international monetary problem in the 1960s was the American payments deficit. In 1963, the United States introduced the Interest Equalization Tax (IET) to slow capital outflows from the United States by discouraging foreign borrowing on American capital markets. This was one of a number of palliatives introduced by Washington to reduce the American payments deficit without altering domestic macroeconomic policy or overseas military spending. The IET posed a severe threat to the Canadian economy, as Canadian corporations and governments were heavy borrowers on American capital markets. Ottawa immediately sent a team of senior officials to Washington to negotiate a bilateral exemption for Canada. The same pattern was followed when Washington imposed controls on the operations of American transnational banks and corporations in 1965-8.[30]

The Canadian government's instinct in these cases was to seek special treatment for Canada in bilateral talks, not to rely on multilateral institutions or negotiations. This policy made sense because the stakes for Canada were so high, and there was little likelihood of a multilateral solution to a problem that was specific to Canada. Key continental European governments were quite willing to accept controls on capital outflows from the United States, since those controls simultaneously reduced capital inflows that were inflating their payments surpluses. American capital controls therefore reduced pressure on foreign surplus countries to reflate or revalue their currencies. Thus, there would have been little support from key foreign countries for a Canadian initiative to retain open access to American capital markets.[31] Longer-term multilateral reform efforts intended to find alternatives to American payments deficits, as the source of international liquidity did nothing to ease immediate Canadian needs. Thus, it is not surprising that Canadian leaders sought a solution to their problem in bilateral negotiations with the United States. Nevertheless, Ottawa's reliance on bilateral negotiations does counter the traditional view that Canada's interests are best pursued in multilateral forums in which Canada can influence American policies by combining forces with other countries.

The United States did grant Canada an exemption from the IET but, in return, required that Canada take action to strengthen the American balance of payments. Most important, the United States insisted that Canada not permit its reserves to exceed their June 1963 level of $2.7 billion (U.S.). This occasionally meant that when Canada achieved a surplus in its accounts with third countries, the resulting addition to its reserves had to be offset by worsening Canada's payments balance with the United States. When this happened, 'Canada's third country surplus was being contributed to the United States reserves.'[32]

The reserve ceiling was in effect from 1963 to 1968.[33] In combination with the IMF commitment to maintain the Canadian dollar at a level that increasingly appeared undervalued, the ceiling did constrain Canadian monetary policy in the mid-1960s. After 1964, inflationary pressures began to build in Canada, and the Bank of Canada favoured monetary restraint to contain inflation. But on a number of occasions, the bank found that it had to pursue a more relaxed monetary policy in order to prevent either the dollar from appreciating or the reserves from exceeding the ceiling.[34] Thus, Canada's macroeconomic policies in the mid-1960s were constrained by international arrangements – but because of bilateral understandings with the United States not because of the multilateral international monetary regime.

Overall, Canadian policies were consistent with the norms of the international monetary regime in the period 1958-70. Canada participated in international co-operation to stabilize exchange rates and manage international payments imbalances, adopted the kinds of policies the IMF expected when Canada's own payments position went into deficit, and returned to the fixed exchange rate system. At the same time, Canada continued to address its most serious international monetary problems in bilateral negotiations with the United States rather than through multilateral arrangements.

1970-84: FLUCTUATING EXCHANGE RATES AND THE SEARCH FOR DOMESTIC AND INTERNATIONAL STABILITY

The fixed exchange rate system was abandoned by leading countries in the early 1970s. The succeeding decade was characterized by severe domestic and international economic instability as governments cast about for new approaches to international macroeconomic adjustment compatible with increasing international economic interdependence and capital mobility. Leading countries adopted fluctuating exchange rates to maximize their freedom to use monetary and fiscal policies to achieve domestic objectives. Countries also borrowed and lent heavily on private international capital markets to avoid adjusting internal policies to correct external imbalances.

The international monetary regime went through an extended period of turmoil in the 1970s and early 1980s. Regime norms and rules were weak, but none of the leading countries deliberately pursued a policy of competitive depreciation. The widely feared breakdown of the liberal international trading system did not materialize, even during the recession of the early 1980s – the most severe since the 1930s. The principle of 'embedded liberalism' was maintained, but the combination of increasing capital mobility and serious economic problems in all leading countries proved highly destabilizing for the international economy. Domestic macroeconomic stabilization continued to be accorded a high priority, although emphasis shifted away from fiscal demand management to stimulate growth and towards monetary restraint to stabilize prices.

In contrast to the weakness of regime rules, international consultations became more intensive and contributed to a convergence of views about appropriate policies by the late 1970s. But the perverse unilateral policies pursued by the first Reagan administration (1981-4) blocked the emergence of substantive international norms and rules (outside Europe) that constrained national policymaking freedom. This section will briefly describe the evolution of international monetary arrangements in the 1970s and the first half of the 1980s and review developments in Canada in light of international trends.

The move away from fixed exchange rates can be traced back to 1969, when France and Germany unilaterally adjusted their exchange rates after international negotiations to co-ordinate exchange rate adjustments failed. Canada allowed its currency to float in May 1970 (see below), and Germany followed in May 1971. Most significant, the United States announced in August 1971 that it would no longer exchange foreigners' holdings of dollars for treasury gold, imposed a temporary import surcharge, and demanded that surplus states revalue their currencies.

In all of these cases, states were motivated by the desire to avoid the constraint on macroeconomic policy imposed by commitments to fix currency values. Surplus states preferred appreciation to reflation, while deficit states preferred depreciation to deflation. In the early 1970s, it was widely believed that fluctuating exchange rates would smoothly and gradually adjust to accommodate different national rates of inflation caused by different national macroeconomic policy choices. Fluctuating exchange rates therefore appeared to hold the promise of restoring macroeconomic policymaking autonomy. New fixed exchange rate parities were established in the December 1971 Smithsonian Agreement, but by February 1973 all leading countries had abandoned efforts to maintain fixed exchange rates.

Prolonged debates over reforming the international monetary system failed to produce agreement on new international rules to guide national policymaking. The Articles of Agreement of the IMF were amended in 1976 to legalize the shift to fluctuating exchange rates that had already occurred. IMF guidelines for fluctuating exchange rates adopted at this time were weak and unenforceable, and co-ordinated foreign exchange market intervention was rare.

In contrast to the weakness of regime injunctions during these years, international consultations and information-sharing regarding monetary and fiscal policies became more intensive and influential. In 1973, the finance ministers of the Group of Five (G5) countries (the United States, Germany, Japan, Britain, and France) began to meet regularly to discuss monetary policies in the so-called 'Library Group.' In 1975, the first of the annual economic summit meetings was hosted by France. In 1976-8, the United States, Britain, and the OECD Secretariat pressed for the adoption of a co-ordinated, growth-oriented strategy by the largest countries. This was accepted at the 1978 Bonn summit; Germany and Japan agreed to stimulate growth with tax cuts and spending increases, while the United States agreed to foreign demands that it restrain monetary policy and decontrol oil prices. However, after the second oil shock of 1978-9, this attempt to apply a Keynesian approach at the international level was blamed for stimulating inflation and was temporarily discredited.[35]

International consultations after 1979 tended to stress the need for tight monetary policies and fiscal restraint to fight inflation. Rhetorical consensus did not, however, translate into consistent policies or the creation of norms and rules that constrained national autonomy. Most central banks did pursue tight monetary policies in the early 1980s, and international consultations may well have strengthened their determination to do so in the face of a serious recession. But all of the large OECD countries ran huge fiscal deficits in their efforts to pull themselves out of the recession of the early 1980s.

Moves to strengthen the international monetary regime were also blocked by the views of certain political leaders in key countries. By the late 1970s, economic policymakers and economists in many countries recognized that fluctuating exchange rates had not solved the problem of reconciling national macroeconomic objectives with international market pressures. Fluctuating exchange rates did not permit macroeconomic policymaking autonomy and brought serious problems of their own. Exchange rate volatility interfered with international commerce, and inappropriate exchange rates often stimulated protectionist pressures. But the British government under Margaret Thatcher and the American administration of Ronald Reagan (during 1981-4) took the view that the key issue was for countries to get their own houses in order, not to co-ordinate economic policies with other countries. Consequently, both governments pursued restrictive monetary policies aimed at reducing domestic inflation and ignored the external consequences of their policies. American opposition, in particular, blocked all attempts to co-ordinate macroeconomic and exchange rate policies outside the European Monetary System.

Canadian policies during the 1970s and the first half of the 1980s responded primarily to domestic considerations in an ever-changing fashion, as policymakers struggled to deal with the new environment of capital mobilty, international instability, and domestic stagflation. When Canada permitted its dollar to float in May 1970, it became the first G10 country to abandon fixed exchange rates in the interest of macroeconomic policymaking autonomy. In Canada's case, high interest rates had generated large capital inflows, which threatened to fuel domestic inflation if the Bank of Canada intervened to maintain the fixed exchange rate. So Ottawa decided to let the dollar float, and it quickly appreciated from 93 to 98 cents U.S..

Canada also avoided establishing a new fixed exchange rate in the wake of the Nixon shock of August 1971. When President Nixon imposed an import surcharge to put pressure on foreign governments to revalue their currencies, Ottawa sent a team of senior officials to Washington to try to negotiate a bilateral exemption for Canada rather than simply joining with other Group of Ten countries in a concerted effort to force Nixon to alter course. Washington refused to grant an exemption from the tariff surcharge but did agree to exempt Canada from the American demand that Group of Ten countries formally revalue their currencies against the American dollar. Alone among these countries, Canada did not establish a new fixed exchange rate in the December 1971 Smithsonian agreement. Canada won the exemption, apparently by arguing that the Canadian dollar had already appreciated in line with American demands. Ottawa wanted to retain the freedom to adjust monetary and fiscal policies to stimulate the economy or control inflation as it saw fit as well as the freedom to permit the dollar to depreciate to maintain Canada's competitive position in international trade.[36]

During the 1970s and the first half of the 1980s, monetary policy in Canada fluctuated between trying to achieve a particular exchange rate and trying to reduce domestic money supply growth and inflation. In 1972-3 Canadian monetary policy focused on preventing the dollar from appreciating against its American counterpart because Ottawa feared that this would undermine Canada's international competitive position, but, in so doing, Canada imported American inflation.[37] Then, in 1975, with inflation rising, the Bank of Canada shifted to a policy of 'monetary gradualism' to slow the growth of the money supply in Canada. The bank recognized that it could not control both the money supply and the exchange rate, and it chose to try to control the former while permitting the latter to adjust through the market.[38] Consequently, the Canadian dollar fluctuated wildly in 1975-7.

By 1978, the Bank of Canada had become concerned that exchange rate volatility was having an adverse impact on domestic economic conditions, just as had central banks in other countries. The Canadian dollar depreciated rapidly in 1977, and the bank feared that this would stimulate inflation.[39] On the other hand, excessive currency appreciation was undesirable because it eroded the competitive position of Canadian export industries. Thus, from 1978 to 1984, the Bank of Canada focused on stabilizing the dollar. Before 1980, this policy occasionally necessitated low interest rates and rapid money supply growth that stimulated inflation in Canada. The bank also borrowed heavily on international capital markets to support the Canadian dollar in 1978, consistent with the practice of other deficit countries.

In the 1980-4 period, stabilizing Canadian currency against a rising American dollar required very restrictive monetary policy, thereby also serving the objective of fighting inflation in Canada.[40] This was consistent with international norms, which put top priority on bringing inflation under control using tight monetary policy. But the policy hurt Canada's competitive position in overseas trade, since stabilizing the Canadian dollar against its rising American counterpart meant that Canadian currency also rose against overseas currencies.

Canada's fiscal policies paralleled those in other leading countries and, in so doing, violated oft-stated international norms. Ottawa's spending increased sharply in the first half of the 1970s, generating concern that government spending was out of control and was fueling inflation. In October 1975, Finance Minister Donald Macdonald announced that the government had decided to hold future increases in government spending to no more than the rate of growth of Gross Domestic Product (GDP), and Ottawa's spending actually shrunk as a proportion of GDP in the next few years.[41] However, the deficit grew sharply in the late 1970s because of tax cuts introduced by Ottawa to stimulate growth and meet other government objectives.[42] Thus, budget deficits became a perennial feature of economic policy even before the 1981-2 recession, and by 1984 both the annual deficit and the accumulated debt had reached impressive levels.[43]

Despite the priority attached to domestic concerns in macroeconomic policymaking, Canada did continue to support the basic norms of the international monetary regime. Trade policy remained fundamentally liberal. Then minister of finance John Turner served as chairman of the IMF Interim Committee, the central forum for international monetary reform negotiations. Canada focused on trying to find acceptable compromises between the deeply-held views of the main protagonists rather than on advancing particular proposals. Canadian representatives did support giving the IMF more authority to supervise national exchange rate policies (in the context of rules permitting a greater degree of exchange rate flexibility),[44] but this diplomatic position is difficult to reconcile with Ottawa's demonstrated preference for unilateralism in its own policymaking.

A telling aspect of Canadian policy during the mid-1970s was its determined pursuit of a place at the economic summit meetings. The first economic summit had been called in 1975 by French president Giscard d'Estaing, but active Canadian diplomacy had failed to secure an invitation for Prime Minister Trudeau. When President Ford called the second economic summit in June 1976, he used his prerogative as host to invite Trudeau. Ford wanted to counterbalance the large European presence at the meetings. Canada, like Italy, 'ensured that, once invited, [it] could not be left out in future.'[45] The story of Canada's tenuous place in the leading forum for economic policy co-ordination is worth telling if only to counter assertions that Canada's seat at the economic summit table is a concrete symbol of its status as a principal power.[46] The fact that Canadian participation depends on United States support also makes it difficult to view the summits as a multilateral counterweight to the bilateral relationship. In any case, the economic summits have had little relevance for Canada's policies towards the international monetary regime.

The 1978 Bonn summit produced Japanese and West German agreement to stimulate their economies by cutting taxes. Prime Minister Trudeau came home with a different message. Apparently, personal talks between Trudeau and West German chancellor Helmut Schmidt convinced Trudeau that orthodox fiscal policies were appropriate for Canada, and he subsequently introduced a short-lived austerity package. In this case, Trudeau was acting independently; Canada's summit partners had not put diplomatic pressure on him to change course. The international regime did not constrain Canada, yet the exchanges of information at the summit caused the Canadian prime minister to alter his own perceptions of Canada's interests for a brief period, before domestic politics led his government back to tax cuts and spending increases.[47]

Canada did join with other countries in criticizing destabilizing American policies in the early 1980s. For example, Canada supported French president Mitterand's calls for less restrictive monetary policies in 1982-3.[48] These diplomatic efforts had no impact whatsoever, especially since other large countries (Japan, West Germany, and Britain) favoured monetary restraint. Prime Minister Trudeau also joined his summit colleagues in criticizing lax American fiscal policy and tight monetary policy at the 1984 London summit.[49] This position was hardly consistent with Canada's own policy choices, since the Bank of Canada was itself committed to monetary restraint[50] and Canada's budget deficit in 1984 was substantially larger than was the American deficit (relative to GDP). Not for the only time (and not alone among the Group of Seven), Ottawa wanted to persuade a foreign government to accept a discipline that it was unwilling to accept for itself.

In fact, international meetings and institutions stressed the importance of sound fiscal policies throughout the period, and Canada was not alone in ignoring this advice. Canada escaped the severe criticism that fell on others (especially the United States and France) mainly because Canada constituted a small part of the overall problem. International attention naturally focused on those countries whose policies caused the most damage internationally. Not only was Canada a relatively small player in the international economy, but before 1985 its deficits were financed mainly from domestic savings (i.e., from borrowing within Canada) rather than borrowing from abroad.[51]

Canada did not play an influential role in the economic summits of the early 1980s. International surveillance of national policies at the economic summits and in other forums, like the OECD, focused on the policies of the Group of Five countries, paying less attention to the policies of Italy and Canada.[52] Canada, like Italy, was excluded from the Group of Five process of multilateral surveillance established at Versailles in 1982. Canada's stance in international meetings was formulated on an ad hoc basis; in 1984, one observer noted that 'there is ... no Canadian policy to speak of regarding macroeconomic co-ordination.'[53] Canada was severely buffeted by the international economy in the period 1978-84, and policymaking was dominated by ad hoc efforts to manage successive crises. Nascent international norms did not constrain Canadian macroeconomic policy. The Trudeau government was not even able to use international pronouncements to justify domestic policies, because the market-oriented rhetoric of international meetings conflicted with the more interventionist tone of Canadian government policies in the early 1980s.

1985-91: TENTATIVE STEPS TOWARDS MACROECONOMIC CO-ORDINATION

Macroeconomic policies have been a central focus of economic diplomacy among the advanced capitalist countries since the mid-1980s. Most governments recognize the desirability of international co-ordination to avoid international economic instability, although co-ordination in practice has been difficult to achieve. Non-co-ordinated monetary and fiscal policies have not achieved their objectives without exacting high costs, including international economic instability, protectionist pressures, and growing government debts to domestic and foreign investors.

The international monetary regime has been strengthened since 1985. Procedures for consultations and information-sharing have become more important, clear norms for national policies have been identified (though often not followed), and certain weak rules have been generated, although their impact has generally been short-lived. The key turning point was a change in the attitude of the Reagan administration in 1985. Administration officials recognized that unilateralist policies were not sustainable and had generated powerful protectionist pressure within the United States that threatened the liberal international trading system. Washington looked to international co-operation to reduce the overvaluation of the dollar and the American trade deficit, thereby defusing Congressional protectionism. Most foreign governments welcomed the Reagan administration's change of heart on exchange rates but were wary of Washington's demand that they reduce their trade surpluses by stimulating domestic demand.

Procedures for multilateral surveillance of national policies intensified in response to decisions taken at economic summit meetings in 1982 at Williamsburg and in 1986 at Tokyo. By 1987-8, meetings of G5 and G7 finance ministers, deputy finance ministers, and central bank governors were held on a regular basis. These meetings reviewed trends in economic conditions and national policies, and the discussions were reportedly frank and valuable.[54] The frequency of these meetings and the fact that they were attended by ministers and officials actually responsible for national monetary and fiscal policies both made it more likely that multilateral surveillance could have some impact on national policies.[55] G7 discussions and communiqués have stressed the need to adjust domestic policies, especially fiscal policies, to eliminate external payments imbalances. Countries with current account deficits are urged to deflate, while surplus countries are urged to reflate. Clear international norms have emerged regarding the conduct of fiscal policy, even though they are often not obeyed.

Macroeconomic policies in leading countries were occasionally co-ordinated, as a consequence of these discussions, on an ad hoc basis. In 1987-9, surplus countries – Japan and West Germany – relaxed monetary policies and pursued more stimulative fiscal policies in response to American demands that they do more to eliminate their surpluses and the American trade deficit. The United States Federal Reserve has occasionally co-ordinated monetary policy with foreign central banks. American leaders committed themselves to reducing the American fiscal deficit, but these diplomatic understandings have had little impact on American budgets. In fact, the monetary and fiscal policy adjustments made by overseas governments in response to American pressure have had the perverse effect of permitting the United States to maintain profligate fiscal policies without experiencing the capital flight and currency collapse that would have accompanied similar policies in any other country.[56] Some observers have credited international consultations and information-sharing with strengthening the determination of all central banks to resist inflationary pressures; for example, in 1988 central banks in many OECD countries tightened monetary policy in reaction to the shared perception that easy money after the October 1987 stock market crash and the resulting rapid growth were threatening to bring renewed inflation.[57]

International consultations regarding exchange rates have also been extensive since 1985. Co-ordinated intervention in foreign exchange markets by G5, G7, and other OECD countries has been fairly regular since early 1985 (see below), although this action has frequently failed to have the desired impact in the face of strong contrary market sentiments. The G5 and G7 governments have been able to agree on exchange rate co-ordination even in the face of deep disagreements about monetary and fiscal policy.

Attempts were made to move beyond international consultations and ad hoc co-ordination towards the creation of regime guidelines for the conduct of monetary, fiscal, and exchange rate policies. These nascent guidelines took the form of the establishment of a set of economic indicators to be reviewed in meetings of finance ministers and their deputies from the Group of Five and Group of Seven countries and of target ranges for key exchange rates. The United States wanted to use the review of indicators to signal when policy adjustments were needed in specific countries, hoping that such a system could be used to put pressure on foreign surplus countries (notably Japan and Germany) to ease monetary policy, stimulate domestic demand, and reduce export surpluses. Japan and Germany, recalling that the Carter administration had used similar tactics to pressure them to reflate in 1977-8, resisted the idea. They especially rejected any notion that changes in the indicators, or divergence between objectives and actual conditions, should trigger automatic policy changes. The notion of automaticity was dropped, and the 1986 Tokyo summit directed the finance ministers to review a number of indicators of economic policies and conditions in their regular meetings. Most important, the summit communiqué

> invite[d] the Finance Ministers and Central Bankers in conducting multilateral surveillance to make their best efforts to reach an understanding on appropriate remedial measures whenever there are significant deviations from an intended course; and recommend that remedial efforts focus first and foremost on underlying policy fundamentals.[58]

The system of surveillance based on these indicators has been in place since 1988. The use of indicators has contributed to the consultative and information sharing components of the international monetary regime, but the system is not one of rules that constrain national policymaking autonomy. Representatives of different governments undoubtedly use statistical indicators to back up their demands for changes in foreign government policies, but any co-ordinated policy adjustments that may occur are still on an ad hoc basis.

Target ranges for G7 currencies were established in the February 1987 Louvre accord, supplemented by guidelines for co-ordinated intervention in foreign exchange markets. However, over the next two years the reference ranges were broadened and adjusted in response to market pressures and disputes among governments.[59] Consultations are continuous and there has been frequent co-ordinated market intervention on an ad hoc basis when governments feel that market movements are inappropriate, but no international rules have been established.

Canada has given strong diplomatic support to the international monetary regime that has emerged since 1985, but concrete Canadian policies have often been inconsistent with the norms of the regime. Furthermore, some episodes in Canadian macroeconomic adjustment policy in recent years raise doubts about whether Ottawa is actually reaping the benefits that are supposed to flow from participation in the Group of Seven process of multilateral surveillance.

The Conservative government of Brian Mulroney has been enthusiastic about proposals for multilateral surveillance of national policies to encourage countries to adopt policies that are consistent with international stability. Ottawa welcomed the proposal for a strengthened process of multilateral surveillance advanced by United States secretary of the treasury James Baker at the 1986 Tokyo summit.[60] Officials in the Department of Finance and the Bank of Canada prepared a joint paper setting out a conceptual framework for surveillance of economic indicators and circulated it to other finance ministries in a contribution to the work then underway to design and implement such a system.[61] A former official characterized Canada's general approach to international co-ordination as one which, in favouring changes in fiscal policies and exchange rates to eliminate international imbalances, was consistent with the approach of Japan, Germany, and Britain. In contrast, France and Italy favoured fixed exchange rates backed by extensive co-ordinated intervention in foreign exchange markets; adjustment, in this model, would happen as governments unilaterally altered their macroeconomic policies to achieve external balance.[62] However, the Canadian government's support for such a process for co-ordinating fiscal and monetary policies is difficult to reconcile with its own fiscal policies. As we shall see below, domestic political considerations have led Ottawa to pursue policies that violate the international norms apparent in G7 discussions and that are not responsive to international criticism.

Prime Minister Mulroney also made a determined effort to secure Canadian admission to the then-G5 process of multilateral surveillance,[63] and the G5 countries did agree at the 1986 Tokyo Summit to admit Canada (and Italy) to some, but not all, finance ministers' meetings. As with the economic summit meetings in the mid-1970s, United States support was critical to the success of Canada's efforts to gain admission to the multilateral surveillance process. The United States Treasury favoured Canadian and Italian membership, in part, because both countries supported the American proposal to create an indicator system backed by a stronger political mechanism for co-ordinating policies.[64] Ottawa still has to be vigilant to keep its seat; representatives of the larger countries (especially France) repeatedly suggest that Canada and Italy should be excluded.[65]

The Mulroney government is enthusiastic about multilateral surveillance and the related work of the economic summits, in part, because the ideological tenor of these meetings is so close to the Canadian Conservative government's own ideological beliefs. Summit communiqués and Group of Seven finance ministers' meetings consistently emphasize market-oriented policies, the dangers of inflation, and restraint in government spending. In contrast to the previous Liberal government, the current Conservative government has drawn on these norms of the international monetary regime to defend its own policies in domestic political debates.

Canada's role in the international monetary regime since the mid-1980s has been relatively minor. The G7 has superceded the G5 as the most important forum, although Canada and Italy are still excluded from some G5 discussions of foreign exchange market issues. G7 discussions are dominated by the United States, Japan, and Germany.[66] Even France and Britain are not central to most debates.[67] Important issues are typically discussed over the telephone by American, Japanese, and German officials prior to actual G7 meetings, though Canada is kept informed of such discussions by the United States (as Germany keeps the other European G7 countries informed).[68] The dominance of the three largest countries is also apparent in IMF practices. IMF advice to Canada (and to Britain, France, Italy, and all smaller member countries) is couched solely in terms of what is best for the country itself. In contrast, IMF advice to the United States, Japan, and West Germany also deals with the impact that their policies have on the international economy.[69] Despite its minor role, participation in the G7 process of multilateral surveillance does give Canadian officials privileged access to information and debates about economic trends and policies in the key countries in the global economy. Whether Canadian policy benefits from this access is discussed below.

While Canada has given strong diplomatic support to the G7-centred international monetary regime, actual Canadian policies since the mid-1980s have frequently diverged from the norms of the regime, perhaps to a greater extent than in most other countries. On a number of key issues, Ottawa has been unwilling or unable to act in accordance with regime norms. This is most dramatic in the area of fiscal policy. Canadian leaders have supported international declarations in favour of fiscal restraint and have joined other Group of Seven countries in urging the United States to get its budget deficit under control.[70] Yet Ottawa failed to bring its own deficit under control even when economic growth was strong. By the late 1980s, Ottawa's annual deficit had stabilized around $30 billion – larger as a proportion of gross national product than American budget deficits.

G7 finance ministers' meetings have repeatedly urged Canada to reduce its budget deficit as part of co-ordinated efforts to attack the basic roots of international imbalances. Former finance minister Michael Wilson acknowledged that Canadian fiscal policy had come under criticism in international meetings, but he claimed that Canada's partners were sympathetic to Ottawa's problems in this area because they had confidence in the general thrust of Canadian economic policy.[71] G7 communiqués often include specific policy commitments by each of the seven governments – commitments that are intended to demonstrate how the governments are co-operating to manage international economic problems. Canada's representatives have repeatedly committed the government to reducing the fiscal deficit, but no specific targets have been publicly stated.[72] According to a former Canadian representative to the G7 deputies' meetings, Canadian officials have been 'careful to limit their deficit reduction commitments to what they felt was politically feasible at home.'[73]

Criticism of Canada's budget deficits has also come from the OECD and the IMF in their annual reviews of member states' economic policies.[74] When the IMF suggested in a February 1989 report that the deficit be cut by $9 billion in the next budget, Prime Minister Mulroney and Finance Minister Wilson welcomed the suggestion because it helped them sell the message of austerity.[75] But when the budget came down in April 1989, the projected deficit actually increased from $29 billion to $30.5 billion! The IMF has also criticized Canada's fiscal-monetary policy mix. For example, in its 1990 annual report, the IMF called on the government to make a greater effort to reduce the fiscal deficit, in part to reduce the need to use very restrictive monetary policy to slow inflation: 'Heavy reliance on high interest rates could have adverse consequences for the exchange rate and international competitiveness, as well as for domestic investment.'[76] This, of course, is an argument also made by many domestic critics of Canadian monetary and fiscal policies.[77]

Judging from the record of federal budgets in the 1980s, international criticisms have had little impact. The annual deficit remains at approximately $30 billion (public accounts basis) even after a number of years of strong economic growth in the late 1980s.

Even if Ottawa is unwilling or unable to directly co-ordinate fiscal policy in the G7, participation in the multilateral surveillance process should improve Canadian policymakers' knowledge about developments in the international economy, thereby helping them select appropriate policies. However, it appears that fiscal policy does not take international developments into account in any serious fashion. A critical failure of Canadian fiscal policy in recent years entailed missing an opportunity to reduce the budget deficit while the economy was prosperous and international conditions were favourable. American fiscal policy was highly expansionary in the 1980s, and Japanese fiscal policy became quite expansive after 1986. Expansion abroad tends to stimulate exports from Canada, thereby stimulating the Canadian economy as a whole – especially since exports account for a high proportion of Canadian gross national product.

If fiscal policy had taken this international context into account – and Canadian policymakers would have known about the expansive nature of American and Japanese policies from Group of Seven meetings if not from reading the newspapers – it could have focused on drastic deficit reduction in the years 1987-9. The political costs of deficit reduction are much higher now than they would have been in those years because the accumulated debt is larger and the economy is in recession.

The costs of missing this opportunity were substantial. The absence of fiscal restraint meant that the entire burden of containing inflation was left to monetary policy, leading to very high interest rates. High interest rates added to the annual debt service burden and the budget deficit. High interest rates and the high dollar (viewed by the bank as a necessary part of its anti-inflation strategy) also had a severe impact on Canada's export and import-competing sectors, making it difficult for them to reap the purported benefits of the Canada-United States Free Trade Agreement. Long-term planning in the mid-1980s, taking into account what could be learned about foreign government policies from Group of Seven meetings, could have mitigated all of these problems.

Recent budget documents indicate that Ottawa continues to neglect the international context in which fiscal policy operates. For example, the 1990 budget document stated that Canadian growth was expected to be export-led in 1990 as domestic growth would slow. But the discussion of the external economic environment predicted that the American trade deficit would shrink substantially, and that American growth would slow as the United States reduced its fiscal deficit.[78] These projections are internally inconsistent. The projections about the United States economy implied that Canada's exports to its largest market would decline, not increase. Thus, Canadian growth would also decline unless it was offset by demand growth in Canada or very strong export growth overseas. Perhaps this inconsistency (and the general lack of attention in the budget papers to international developments) simply reflects the fact that budget documents are intended mainly to sell the government's policy to an uninformed public. But it also seems to indicate that international developments are not an important consideration in the budgetary process.

The limited influence of the G7 on Canadian fiscal policy can be attributed to international and domestic factors. Internationally, Canada has not come under intense pressure to reduce its deficits, simply because Canada is too small for its policies to have much impact on foreign countries. American budget deficits that are smaller as a proportion of GDP than are Canadian deficits[79] have attracted severe international criticism because American deficits threaten to destabilize the international economy in ways that Canadian policies could not; Congressional protectionism and the volatility of the United States dollar posed direct and immediate threats to the prosperity of foreign countries. In contrast, imprudent policies in Ottawa hurt mainly Canada. In this case, not being large was a virtue for the Canadian government (if not for Canadians) because it meant that Ottawa could escape criticism that would have befallen a larger country pursuing similar policies.

Domestically, the limited influence of international monetary regime norms can be attributed to the political paralysis of budget policy and institutional decisionmaking structures that are oriented primarily to domestic considerations. The fiscal policymaking process does have room for consideration of the international implications of the budget and is, in theory, open to input from the G7 process. The Department of Finance is responsible for the preparation of a fiscal plan which is supposed to set the basic framework for revenue and spending. In preparing and revising this plan, finance officials review conditions in the domestic and international economies, project future trends based on different fiscal measures, and prepare macroeconomic policy recommendations. These are incorporated in the minister of finance's fiscal plan after consultations in the Cabinet.[80] Both the minister of finance and the associate deputy minister of finance, who attends G7 deputies' meetings, are involved in the preparation of the fiscal plan and, therefore, provide a direct link between the multilateral surveillance process and domestic policymaking.

However, macroeconomic considerations, domestic and international, play little role in determining actual revenues, spending, and budget balances. Recent Canadian governments have been incapable of using fiscal policy as macro-policy because of pressures imposed by the deficit and demands for spending. Political considerations, rather than macroeconomic policy concerns, determine the balance between revenues and spending. The macroeconomic impact that budgets have is now merely the unintended consequence of a long-standing political inability to make difficult decisions to cut spending and raise taxes, even in prosperous times. As one finance department official expressed it, 'at times one wonders how we manage to get the purpose of our fiscal policy backwards. The deficit and politics now determine how much the government will spend. Very little else seems to matter.'[81] Thus, the lack of Canadian compliance with international regime norms in the area of fiscal policy is caused, in part, by the domestic political paralysis of fiscal policymaking – a paralysis that is undisturbed by other G7 countries, which have little interest in Canadian policies.

The traditional secrecy of central bankers makes it difficult to assess what impact, if any, the international monetary regime has had on Canadian monetary policy. Since early 1984, Canadian monetary policy has been geared primarily to achieving domestic objectives, in contrast to the focus on exchange rate stability that predominated in the 1978-84 period.[82] Interest rates were eased in the years 1984-7 to facilitate economic recovery. Since 1988, monetary policy has focused increasingly on containing inflation. This is consistent with international trends; beginning in 1988, discussions among central banks stressed the need to tighten monetary policy to prevent a resurgence of inflation.[83] Very restrictive monetary policies have generated intense criticism in Canada, and the government has tried to draw on the anti-inflation rhetoric of the IMF and the G7 summits to justify its policies at home.

Canada, like most countries, has been reluctant to co-ordinate monetary policies explicitly with other countries, even when there are good domestic and international reasons for doing so. This was apparent in the spring of 1990. During the first four months of 1990, the Japanese yen fell sharply because of concern about rising inflation and the falling stock market. Canada did join in co-ordinated foreign exchange market intervention to shore up the Japanese currency.[84] But when Japan's finance minister asked for a co-ordinated reduction of international interest rates to help support the yen at an April 1990 G7 meeting, Canada joined the other countries in rejecting the request. After the meeting, Finance Minister Michael Wilson explained the reason for Canada's stance: 'In the end, everything really starts with our domestic policy ... We can't change our policy as a base for doing something for another country.'[85]

This dismissal of international monetary co-ordination may have missed the point.[86] Interest rates were high in Canada in April 1990 not just for domestic reasons but because high international interest rates had led the Bank of Canada to push Canadian interest rates even higher to prevent the dollar from falling. Avoiding dollar depreciation was an essential part of the Bank of Canada's anti-inflation strategy, since a high dollar put severe pressure on Canadian tradeable goods industries not to raise wages or prices.[87] Wilson and Bank of Canada governor Crow had both admitted that Canadian interest rates were high, in part, because of high interest rates in other countries.[88] Consequently, a co-ordinated reduction of international interest rates could have improved the circumstances of all countries, including Canada – and, in fact, Canadian interest rates were gradually reduced after April 1990. It is also hard to argue that a decline in the value of the yen would be good for Canada, since this would only make Japanese manufactured goods more competitive in international trade and would reduce the amount of money that Japanese investors have to buy Canadian treasury bills.

For all of these reasons, Canadian assent to Japan's request might have served Canadian domestic interests better than did independent policymaking. The failure to recognize the international context, in which seemingly domestic policy choices are made, caused Canadian officials to miss an opportunity to co-ordinate policies in a way that would have helped both countries.

Canada's exchange rate policies have demonstrated a mixed pattern of consistency and inconsistency with international regime norms. Internationally, there has been extensive co-ordinated intervention in foreign exchange markets to stabilize exchange rates since 1985. There has also been a trend towards emphasizing exchange rates as a target for monetary policy.[89] Canada does participate in co-ordinated foreign exchange market operations. The Bank of Canada joins other central banks in concerted operations to stabilize the exchange rate for the United States dollar against the deutschmark and the Japanese yen. Interestingly, the Bank of Canada conducts most of this intervention in those three currencies, not in Canadian dollars. The overall level of Canadian reserves is not affected, and domestic monetary policy is also not affected.[90] This sort of exchange rate policy co-ordination is therefore consistent with continued independence in Canadian monetary policymaking.

Target ranges for the Canadian dollar against the American dollar have been assigned in Group of Seven meetings since the Louvre accord in February 1987. These ranges, and the target ranges for the British, French, and Italian currencies, are of secondary importance to relationships among the three key currencies – the United States dollar, the Japanese yen, and the deutschmark.[91] The target range for the Canadian dollar was probably determined only by Canada and the United States, with American leaders arguing in 1987 that the Canadian dollar should appreciate to reduce the 'unfair' competitive advantage a low dollar gave to Canadian exporters. Critics of the Free Trade Agreement have argued that Ottawa agreed to revalue the Canadian dollar in response to American demands in the trade negotiations.[92] There is no public evidence to suggest that Ottawa made an explicit trade-off involving the exchange rate, although it is likely that the United States would not have accepted the Free Trade Agreement had the dollar remained as low (around 70 cents U.S.) as it was in 1986-7. American trade negotiators and members of Congress had publicly identified the low Canadian dollar as an unfair trading practice, and larger countries like Japan and Germany were having to revalue their currencies in response to American pressure.[93] Canadian officials have argued, in response to their critics, that the exchange rate could not have been part of the Free Trade Agreement because exchange rate discussions are held in the multilateral G7 context, not in bilateral relations.[94] This argument is somewhat disingenuous, since the United States is the only G7 country that had any interest in the exchange rate for the Canadian dollar. Nevertheless, American pressure probably was not the key factor causing the appreciation of the Canadian dollar after 1986. The Bank of Canada's anti-inflationary high interest rate policy drove the dollar up from a level that Ottawa itself felt was too low.

Multilateral surveillance and G7 policy co-ordination since 1985 have encouraged central banks in most of the large countries to use the exchange rate as a target for monetary policy; a declining currency is thought to signal future inflation and the need to tighten monetary policy, while an appreciating currency is thought to signal policy that is too restrictive.[95] In contrast with this view, the Bank of Canada has explicitly stated that it does not target the exchange rate in setting monetary policy. High interest rates have driven the Canadian dollar up since 1987. The Bank of Canada intervened heavily to slow the rise but did not peg the dollar.[96] Bank of Canada governor John Crow argued that using monetary policy to keep the dollar from rising at a time of strong demand and rising real incomes in Canada 'would have had frighteningly severe inflationary consequences.'[97]

In practice, however, the Bank of Canada does target the exchange rate. In mid-January 1990, the Bank of Canada eased monetary policy in response to its assessment that inflationary pressures were easing,[98] causing the bank rate to fall from 12.41 per cent to 12.14 per cent. This triggered a sharp decline in the Canadian dollar, from 86.5 to under 83 cents U.S.. The bank subsequently pushed the bank rate up to well above its level of early January in order to stabilize the dollar at 85-86 cents U.S..

There are a number of lessons to be learned from this episode. First, it demonstrates that the Bank of Canada does target the exchange rate, in the belief that a high dollar helps to dampen inflation in Canada. As governor Crow explained,

> currency depreciation had two main kinds of economic effects, both of which were an offset to domestic monetary restraint through interest rates. It raised returns from exports and was therefore expansionary for the Canadian economy. In that way it was an easing force in overall monetary conditions. Also, it had a direct effect on prices paid by Canadians that was in addition to the inflation pressure already coming from domestic forces.[99]

The cautious lowering of interest rates since late spring 1990 also demonstrates the importance the bank attaches to stabilizing the dollar in the mid-80 cent U.S. range; cuts in the bank rate have tracked cuts in American interest rates, and, when the dollar came under selling pressure in October 1990, the bank actually increased interest rates slightly.[100]

Second, the fact that the decline in the dollar was met with a policy change in Canada rather than co-ordinated intervention in foreign exchange markets by the G7 countries reveals Canada's standing in the international monetary regime. Volatility of the Canadian dollar is a Canadian problem, whereas volatility of the American, Japanese, and German currencies is an international problem.

Third, the episode raises doubts about whether Ottawa is taking advantage of participation in multilateral surveillance and meetings of central bankers in the Bank for International Settlements (BIS) to improve their knowlege about developments in the international economy and in foreign government policies. The Bank of Canada does pay close attention to developments in the United States,[101] and declining interest rates in the United States in late 1989 and early 1990 encouraged the January 1990 cut in the Bank of Canada rate. However, had the bank looked abroad more widely, it could have seen that interest rates were moving up in Japan and Germany, and that the United States Federal Reserve was under pressure to raise interest rates to prevent the American dollar from collapsing. This context makes the January 1990 action especially puzzling. One reason markets reacted so sharply to the interest rate cut was that it was inconsistent with trends in international interest rates.[102] The Bank of Canada ought to have known about the trend in international interest rates, since credit conditions are surely one of the main topics for discussion at BIS and G7 meetings.

Overall, Canadian policy towards the international monetary regime since 1985 has been marked by inconsistency. Ottawa has given strong diplomatic support to a strengthened G7 process of multilateral surveillance and has petitioned successfully for participation in what had been a G5-only process. However, Ottawa's own fiscal and monetary policies have frequently violated the norms that have emerged from the G7 process and have been largely immune to explicit international criticism. The government has also failed to take advantage of opportunities to adjust Canadian policies, either unilaterally or in co-ordination with other governments, in response to opportunities and information generated from participation in the G7 process.

CONCLUSIONS: EVALUATING CANADIAN INTERNATIONAL MONETARY POLICY

Canada has consistently supported the evolving norms of the international monetary regime, but it has also consistently avoided conforming with those regime injunctions that interfere with its domestic macroeconomic objectives. The ideal regime, from the Canadian perspective, would be one that constrains other countries while leaving Canada free to choose its own policies independently. This attitude, of course, is no different from that of other leading countries.

Has this policy served Canada's national interests? The pursuit of autonomy was beneficial through the early 1960s, as floating exchange rates gave Canada greater freedom to reconcile its macroeconomic objectives with pressures imposed by close economic integration with the United States. Ottawa was able to use monetary policy to maintain domestic price stability without generating unmanageable speculative inflows. In the mid-1960s, Canada did lose some monetary policy autonomy as a consequence of bilateral agreements to exempt Canadian borrowers from United States capital controls. But this was a choice made by Ottawa apart from international regime commitments, and it was made because Ottawa valued Canadian access to American capital markets more highly than it valued strict price stability.

Canada's efforts to evade regime norms and rules in the 1940s, 1950s, and 1960s could have hurt Canada had they weakened the international monetary regime, since the regime was so important for Canadian prosperity. But Canadian action had no such effect; for example, no country followed Canada's lead in 1950 and abandoned fixed exchange rates. Similarly, Canada's willingness to accede to American demands in bilateral negotiations in the 1960s did not help the United States to persuade other foreign countries to adjust their monetary policies to support the American balance of payments. Canada's behaviour did not undermine the international regime when Canada evaded regime norms and rules, nor did Canada's behaviour strengthen the regime when Canada agreed to innovative measures of co-ordination. Canada was too small and too peripheral to central debates about the international monetary system for others to see Canadian policy as a precedent.

During the Trudeau years, from the late 1960s through the early 1980s, few international norms existed to constrain Canadian policy. Canada could not have done more to create a new regime because divisions among the larger countries were so deep. This was also a period of turmoil in the international economy, when there was no consensus inside Canada or abroad about what policies were appropriate. In these circumstances, Canadian policymaking was dominated by ad hoc efforts to manage successive crises, some of them self-inflicted.

Since 1985, Canada would have been much better off if Ottawa's policies had conformed more closely to the norms of the international regime. This is because Ottawa's policies have been so damaging to the country itself, not because these policies weakened the international regime. The Canadian government has correctly given strong support to the creation of a rigorous system of multilateral surveillance but has erred in not adjusting Canadian policy to conform with the remedial measures proposed for Canada. Persistent budget deficits, and erratic monetary policy that pays attention to both domestic conditions and the exchange rate in an ad hoc and unpredictable manner, have not served Canada's collective national interest. Tailoring national policies to fit the international environment is critically important to the success of monetary and fiscal policies in a country like Canada (that has little influence over international economic conditions), but all the evidence suggests that macroeconomic policymaking in Ottawa is dominated by parochial domestic considerations.

Canada's international monetary policies should also be examined to see what they reveal about Canada's approach to international economic co-operation. Some specific questions drawn from the literature on Canadian foreign policy were identified in the introduction. First, has Canada's vulnerability to international economic shocks and foreign government policies led it to be a dedicated and effective supporter of multilateral co-operation? Here the conclusion is quite clear: Canada has not been an unusually dedicated supporter of the international monetary regime, not even during the so-called 'golden years' of Canadian diplomacy in the late 1940s and the 1950s when the rhetoric of Canadian diplomacy was dominated by liberal internationalism. Canada has pursued a fundamentally liberal international economic strategy and has been more open to trade and capital flows than have many countries during most of the postwar period. But Canada has also been willing to violate regime rules and norms throughout the postwar period when this was necessary to achieve key Canadian domestic objectives (e.g., the floating exchange rate of 1950-62 and the unwillingness to follow international advice on fiscal policy in the 1980s). Canada gives strong rhetorical support to the norms of the international regime but is no different from other countries in preferring a regime that constrains foreign countries rather than itself.

Furthermore, Canada has not consistently supported multilateralism in the international monetary regime. Paradoxically, this tendency was manifest most clearly in the 1940s and the 1960s, years in which Canada is commonly thought to have been especially committed to multilateralism. This is the opposite pattern to that suggested by advocates of the view of Canada as a 'principal power,' who argue that Canada became more willing to seek bilateral deals after the 1960s. Canada turned to bilateral deals with the United States in the late 1940s and sought bilateral exemptions from American policies in the 1960s and early 1970s. Multilateralism has been advocated as a way for Canada to avoid domination by the United States, but in the case of international monetary policies Canada has often relied on bilateral negotiations with the United States to achieve its most important objectives. In the 1970s and 1980s, Canada relied on the support of the United States to gain admission to the G7 economic summits and the G7 finance ministers' meetings over the opposition of other G5 countries. American leaders perceived, usually correctly, that Canada shared many interests with the United States and would therefore be a source of support for the United States in multilateral diplomacy. This makes it difficult to see the G7 as a forum in which Canada can join with other countries to resist American pressures regardless of other advantages of G7 membership.

A number of reasons can be identified for Ottawa's interest in bilateral arrangements. Most important, multilateral institutions are not responsive to Canadian concerns, dominated as they are by the United States, the large European countries, and Japan. Consequently, when Canada faces serious international problems, Canadian political leaders turn for help where it is most likely to be quickly forthcoming – the United States. This is so even though Canadian diplomats and officials (who can afford to be less preoccupied by pressing political problems) pay a great deal of attention to the evolution of the multilateral regime. Reinforcing the bilateral tendency is the fact that most of the international economic problems faced by Canada are essentially problems in its relations with the United States – the dollar shortage in

1947, speculative inflows from the United States undermining the fixed parity in 1950, the desire for access to the American capital market in the 1960s, the Canada-u.s. exchange rate in the 1980s, and so on.

Finally, the historical record raises serious doubts about the proposition that Canada is a 'principal power.' Canada has had very little influence over the evolution of the international monetary regime – indeed, we would be hard-pressed to find any evidence of Canadian influence beyond its attendance at international meetings. Canada's weakness has enabled it to evade regime norms without facing severe international diplomatic repercussions and without undermining the strength of the norms themselves. Canadian membership in regime institutions may be important for Canada (although Ottawa does not take full advantage of its membership, as suggested by the continuing neglect of the international context in fiscal and monetary policymaking). But Canadian membership is less important for other countries, some of which are constantly trying to exclude Canada. Despite its membership in the Group of Seven, Canada is not one of the key countries shaping the international monetary order.

PART THREE

Regulation of International Service Industries

CHAPTER EIGHT

Canada and the Changing Regime in International Air Transport

Martin E. Dresner and Michael W. Tretheway

INTRODUCTION

From the end of the Second World War until the late 1960s, international air transport was governed by a stable regime. That regime was based on bilaterally negotiated aviation treaties and a cartel-like operation by the air carriers' International Air Transport Association (IATA). The regime fixed routes which could be flown, prices which could be charged, and (usually) capacities which could be offered.

In the 1970s, the regime was undermined, and a new regime came into existence. The growth of competing air services from charter and non-IATA carriers, coupled with a pro-competitive U.S. aviation policy, brought down the old regime. In its place a new regime emerged – a regime which is fluid and not as precisely defined. Many markets behave more competitively than before, with pricing and capacity levels more freely determined, if not completely unconstrained. Elsewhere, the price fixing abilities of IATA have been severely eroded. Where pricing has not been freed, regional groups of carriers may establish prices within their territory.

As the industry evolves in the 1990s, it may be on the verge of yet another regime change. In many senses, the 1980s regime was bound to be unstable. Markets to/from/within North America were increasingly competitive, while those in Europe and elsewhere were protected. In protected areas, cracks began to appear in the form of competitive freedom: between the UK and the Netherlands in Europe, markets to Chile in South America, and markets from anywhere to Singapore in Asia. There were an increasing number of state owned carriers which were privatized. Airline consolidation forces began to cross borders, the result being the gradual globalization of the airline industry. While it may be too soon to know how the air transport regime will evolve in the 1990s, some clues are evident. The European Economic Community (EEC) is scheduled to deregulate at the end of 1992. In addition, evolving negotiating strategy in the EEC could lead to the reactionary formation of trading blocs in other parts of the world. These trading blocs could turn protectionist in their external negotiations.

The 1980s also brought about major changes to Canadian domestic air transport. Following on the heels of U.S. domestic deregulation, the Canadian domestic air transportation industry was largely deregulated.[1] Canadian international air policy, on the other hand, remained largely unchanged. Unlike the U.S., Canada did not liberalize its international air transport policies and remained one of the few major markets with which the U.S. could not negotiate a liberal bilateral agreement.

This chapter discusses the changed and changing regime in international air transport and focuses on the opportunities and challenges it presents for Canada. The infrastructure of Canadian international air transport policy is still largely tuned to the old postwar regime. A new look and new policies are required.

The next section briefly outlines the institutions and vocabulary of international air transport. The sections that follow discuss the regime which took shape in the late 1970s and the 1980s, further regime changes which could occur in the 1990s, and, to put this into a perspective for Canada, Canadian international aviation policy. The concluding section then proposes opportunities and challenges for Canada.

INTERNATIONAL AIR TRANSPORT REGULATORY INSTITUTIONS

Bilateral Agreements. The international regulation of air transport is largely conducted through bilateral air transport service agreements between pairs of countries. These 'bilaterals' define the terms and conditions under which commercial air transportation may take place between the two countries.[2] The terms and conditions include: the specification of allowable routes for the airlines of each country; the method for determining capacity levels on each route; and the method for determining the tariffs to be charged on each route.

It has been widely considered that the general framework of postwar bilateral agreements was established with the 1946 U.S.-UK 'Bermuda' agreement. This agreement established that (a) traffic rights were to be for 'named' routes[3] rather than for general authority to serve any pair of points in the two countries, (b) pricing by carriers would require approval of both countries, and that this would generally mean adoption of prices set by IATA; (c) fifth freedom rights would be severely limited;[4] and (d) carriers would generally be free to offer as much capacity as they wanted on third and fourth freedom routes,[5] subject to an ex post review by governments and possible orders to reduce capacity. In fact, the Bermuda type agreement generally applied only to routes to/from the U.S. Elsewhere, a major deviation from Bermuda was mandatory ex ante government approval of capacity, with an obligation to roughly split traffic between the carriers of the two countries. Often this would go a step further with approval of (or requirement of) revenue pooling agreements between carriers. These agreements resulted in carriers splitting the market exactly fifty-fifty, each operating an equal number of flights in similar aircraft, with all revenues shared – regardless of whether or not one carrier received more traffic.

International Air Transport Association. In the past, bilaterals often delegated the determination of air tariffs to an international body of air carriers: the International Air Transport Association (IATA). IATA, the 'trade association' of the international scheduled airlines, acted as a rate-maker on international scheduled air routes.[6] Both of Canada's large international air carriers, Air Canada and Canadian Airlines International (CAI), are members of IATA and remain active participants in IATA's ratemaking activities.

International Civil Aviation Organization. The International Civil Aviation Organization (ICAO) is an intergovernmental body, affiliated with the United Nations, and based in Montreal. ICAO, historically, has been actively involved in the establishment of technical standards and procedures.[7] It has been particularly important in such areas as security, airports, and air navigation. More recently it has had a limited involvement in the economic aspects of international air transport. Three air transport conferences, held in 1977, 1980, and 1985, resulted in recommendations advocating co-operative, rather than competitive, approaches to international air transport.

THE CHANGED REGIME IN INTERNATIONAL AIR TRANSPORT

The postwar regime in international air transport existed in a relatively stable form from the end of the Second World War to the late 1960s. It had emerged as a result of a compromise between the major air powers, the United States and the United Kingdom, at Bermuda in 1946 and was accepted by the majority of countries in the world with the capacity-setting modifications discussed above. As noted, the regime was built around the functioning of the three major institutions of international air transport; ICAO, IATA, and the system of bilateral air agreements. In the late 1960s and 1970s, however, the tariff-setting role played by IATA weakened, signalling the first major crack in the regime.

The Decline of IATA's Fare-Setting Role

The weakening of IATA's economic regulatory role was due both to deliberate actions by the United States to undermine the fare-setting ability of the association and to structural changes in the industry and the environment.[8] Competition from new entrants into the industry, including charter carriers from developed countries and non-IATA carriers from developing countries, contributed to 'illegal' discounting of IATA fares by the association's own members.[9]

IATA's price-setting role was further threatened when, in the late 1960s and early 1970s, U.S. economists produced studies questioning the need for the economic regulation of air transport.[10] The economists concluded that the U.S. air industry was not efficient and that its inefficiencies were due to economic regulation. Deregulating the system, the economists predicted, would result in more efficient carriers and in lower prices to consumers. The findings of the economists coincided with a more general movement in the United States towards less government intervention in the economy. President Carter campaigned on a platform of 'less government' in the 1976 election. Once elected, he chose the airline industry as a vehicle for carrying out his policy.[11] Carter promoted legislation to deregulate the U.S. domestic system and, concurrently, presided over policies to liberalize U.S. international air transport.[12] As a result, in 1978, the United States launched a pro-competitive policy which further undermined IATA's tariff-setting role by promoting price competition in the marketplace.

The launching of this pro-competitive U.S. international policy was the final blow to IATA's ability to co-ordinate fares on major routes such as the North Atlantic and North Pacific.[13] The result was a transformed regime in certain parts of the world. Competitive forces replaced IATA tariff co-ordination as the primary means of setting prices.

The Advent of the Liberal Bilateral

As outlined above, the international air industry is largely regulated by bilateral agreements, which establish the conditions of air transport between two countries. The bilateral pattern established by the Bermuda I agreement was fairly restrictive: only 'named' routes could be flown, both countries had to approve fares, carrier capacity levels could be limited, and usually only one carrier of each country would be authorized to fly a route. As part of its pro-competitive policy, the U.S. signed a series of 'liberal' bilateral agreements, starting with the Netherlands agreement in 1978. A liberal bilateral typically allowed the airlines to freely determine capacities without governmental interference and restricted governmental disapproval authority over fare levels. In some of the liberal bilaterals, both governments had to reject fare levels before they were disapproved. In other liberal bilaterals, only the country in which a flight originated could reject a fare. Other features which were often incorporated in liberal bilaterals included:[14] (1) The multiple designation of airlines. This allowed each country to designate a number of carriers to serve routes between the two states; (2) a reduction in route restrictions. More routes between more cities in the two countries were generally allowed. As well, restrictions were eased on incorporating third countries into the routes between or beyond the signatories to the liberal bilateral (fifth freedom rights); (3) the inclusion of charter flights. The traditional bilaterals governed only scheduled services. The liberal bilaterals usually contained a section regulating charter flights. The clause stated that charters were allowed as long as they conformed with the laws of the country in which the flights originated; and, (4) a fair and competitive practices clause. This stated that each designated airline must be allowed a fair and equal opportunity to compete on air routes governed by the bilateral.

The decision by the United States to adopt a liberal, deregulatory approach to international air transport can be viewed as a two-step process. First, the United States made the decision to deregulate its domestic industry. Second, the United States extended the domestic policy to the international sphere, even over opposition from U.S. air carriers and foreign governments. In order to obtain the signature of other countries on bilateral agreements, the United States used a 'carrot and stick' approach to negotiations.

A number of authors have discussed how one state can use its monopoly supply over a good to obtain economic leverage over another state.[15] This was the carrot. The monopoly good possessed by the United States in international air transport was access to U.S. markets. As Hight (1981:21-2)[16] outlined, the United States received practically all the route rights that its airlines needed in bilateral negotiations with various countries following the Second World War. However, other countries only received permission for their airlines to land in U.S. coastal cities, leaving U.S. airlines with monopoly rights to U.S. inland cities. The United States was therefore able to offer other countries the right to designate airlines on routes to U.S. inland cities, in exchange for those countries consenting to liberal bilateral agreements.

As a stick, the United States was able to coerce countries into signing liberal bilateral agreements through the use of economic power. For example, the United States used its economic power to persuade the United Kingdom to liberalize their bilateral agreement. The United States did this by signing liberal bilaterals with Britain's small neighbouring countries, the Netherlands and Belgium. Under the threat of the loss of U.S. traffic to the Netherlands and Belgian gateways, the UK was forced to liberalize.

The United States used its carrot and stick approach to sign twenty-three liberal or quasi-liberal agreements between 1978 and 1982.[17] The United States was, however, unsuccessful in signing liberal agreements with a number of major aviation countries, such as France, Italy, Japan, and Canada.

TABLE 1

Growth of three Asian airlines 1979–88

(passengers in millions, PKP in billions)

	1979	1988
Cathay Pacific		
Passengers	2.5	6.0
Passenger kilometres performed	5.2	19.7
Singapore Air Lines		
Passengers	3.4	6.0
Passengers kilometres performed	12.0	28.1
Thai International		
Passengers	1.5	5.7
Passenger kilometres performed	4.4	16.4

SOURCE: ICAO, *Civil Aviation Statistics of the World*, 1980, 1988

The Growth of Non-IATA Airlines

Table 1 shows the rapid growth of three Asian airlines: Singapore, Thai International, and Cathay Pacific. These carriers operated outside the IATA cartel until 1990. Through their aggressive pricing and capacity policies their traffic soared, forcing 'cartel' carriers to respond with non-IATA-sanctioned fares. The result has been a set of Pacific Rim markets which are competitive in many ways. The impact has been dramatic. In 1982, CP Air, the predecessor of Canadian Airlines International, operated two nonstop flights per week from Canada to Hong Kong. Within a few years, in response to entry by Cathay Pacific, CP operated ten flights per week in this market during the peak season, and Cathay did the same.

Summary

A new regime developed in international air transport in the 1970s and 1980s. That regime can be characterized as follows:

- competitive pricing on routes to/from/within North America, on some Asian routes, and in a few European markets (e.g., UK-Netherlands),
- capacity setting freedom for carriers on the same set of routes,
- continued cartel pricing elsewhere, either through IATA or regional airline associations,
- growth of charter services (e.g., within Europe) and non-IATA carriers where scheduled markets continue to be protected.

FUTURE CHANGES IN THE INTERNATIONAL REGIME

A new regime emerged in air transport during the past twenty years, but that regime is currently unstable, and further change is inevitable. The European situation cannot persist for long with some routes competitive (e.g., UK-Netherlands) and others protected. Similar problems exist in Asia and South America. Eventually, market forces will precipitate further regime changes.

Future role of IATA

It seems evident from many developments of the 1970s and 1980s that it would be difficult for IATA to resume the pre-eminent role it played prior to this period in the co-ordination of international air tariffs. Developments which weakened IATA's control over tariff co-ordination included (a) the growth in the number of airlines operating international air services, many of which do not adhere to IATA pricing; (b) the increasing diversification of product offerings by carriers,[18] which makes price co-ordination more difficult to achieve; (c) the maturity of the airline industry, which contributed to lower growth rates in the demand for air services, thereby exacerbating problems of overcapacity which, in turn, has led to problems concerning the illegal discounting of IATA fares; (d) the continued opportunities for secret price-cutting through the offering of rebates to travel agencies; and (e) the advent of the liberal bilateral, which substantially lowered the barriers to entry on many important international routes, resulting in competitive, rather than co-ordinated, price setting. Given these developments, it is unlikely that IATA will resume its formerly pre-eminent role as price-setter on most major international air routes.

Alternative Pricing Schemes

In recent years, IATA has had to contend not only with economic developments which have weakened its fare setting ability but also with three alternative methods of establishing tariffs. The first method, a pro-competitive or market-based approach, was initiated by the U.S. in 1978. Adherents to this pricing method assume that individual airlines competing in the 'free market' should determine tariffs. Liberal bilaterals make this approach possible.

A second alternative is the determination of tariffs through a process of government negotiation. A 1982 agreement between the United States and twelve European countries provided for pricing zones on North Atlantic air routes to be established by an intergovernmental working group.[19] Within these zones, airlines have complete freedom to set fares. Outside the zones, fares are approved subject to the terms of the bilateral between the United States and each European state. It is evident that this agreement represents a compromise between the U.S. competitive or 'free-market' position and the more restrictive pricing philosophy shared by many European states.

The third alternative is price-setting by regional associations of air carriers, used mainly in the developing world.[20] This activity has been attributed to the dissatisfaction of some developing countries with IATA.[21] IATA has attempted to accommodate regional interests by changing the rules governing traffic conferences. Traditionally, unanimous agreement on fares was required among airlines in IATA to change prices. The rules were changed in 1978 to permit 'limited agreements' and 'sub-area agreements.' However, given the size and complexity of the international airline industry in the 1990s, it is doubtful that a single organization, such as IATA, can satisfy all concerned interests.

European Deregulation in 1993

Most of the political debate over the merit of international air regulation has occurred in the developed world. Europe is currently the major battleground over international deregulation. Consumer groups, on one hand, view enviously the relatively low u.s. air fares and promote European deregulation as the vehicle for bringing lower fares to Europe. IATA and the airlines, on the other hand, have claimed that u.s.-style deregulation cannot be exported wholesale to the multi-country European market, and that, when cost differences are taken into account, European fares are comparable to u.s. fares.[22]

Two intergovernmental bodies, the European Civil Aviation Conference (ECAC) and the European Community (EC), have been deeply involved in the debate over the regulation of air transport for many years.[23] The two bodies have advocated replacing the current pricing system, in which IATA establishes minimum fares for different classes of air travel in Europe with a zonal system. Reference fare levels would be established, subject to government approval, and 'zones of freedom' around these reference levels would then be set. In 1987, a zonal system was approved by both the ECAC and the EC Council of Ministers.[24] The agreements covered discount and deep-discount fares but not regular economy fares. In addition to these efforts, there have been bilateral governmental initiatives. Most significant were the liberal bilaterals signed by the United Kingdom with Luxembourg, the Netherlands, West Germany, and Ireland. The agreement with Luxembourg, for example, provided that a joint decision of the United Kingdom and Luxembourg was necessary to veto fares. The traditional system requiring the approval of fares by both governments was abandoned.

Most recently, within the EC, agreement was reached by the twelve countries' transport ministers to eliminate constraints on third, fourth, and sixth freedom flights. The elimination of the constraints on sixth freedom traffic would allow Air France, for example, to enplane traffic in London and carry it to Rome via France.[25] As well, the eventual removal of all restrictions on capacity is part of the new agreement. Pricing within increasingly broader zones has been established. The effect of these changes could be dramatic for the carriers of the twelve EC countries. Routings may change for many passengers and the availability of significant numbers of discounted tickets could tap a new market segment for Europe, just as deregulation did in the u.s. If these reforms are successful, the EC will become an airline growth market in the mid 1990s.

The Emergence of Trading Blocks in Air Transport

Ever since the failure of the 1944 Chicago Conference to reach an agreement on the economic multilateral regulation of international air transport, the primary form of regulation has been bilateral air transport agreements. The proposed 1992 single European market offers the prospect of replacing bilateralism with regionalism, if not multilateralism. At present, each European Community member negotiates its own air transport agreements. As the barriers to free trade in European air services are removed, the EC may move one step further and begin to negotiate agreements with other countries on a regional or bloc basis. Such negotiations have already been authorized and conducted with Norway and Sweden.[26]

What are the implications of European (or other) bloc negotiations? First, non-European carriers that currently fly between European Community countries on a fifth freedom basis may find that these flights will not be permitted under bloc negotiations. An integrated European Community may preserve all intra-community routes strictly for community carriers. (An exception may occur if equivalent rights are granted to European carriers, such as cabotage rights in the U.S.)[27] Second, the weaker European carriers, such as Sabena of Belgium and Luxair of Luxembourg, may only be able to survive if they join forces with larger carriers (e.g., British Airways, Air France, Lufthansa) and play a subsidiary or feeder role within a carrier group. Finally, the European bloc may provide the incentives for other countries to enter into regional blocs to protect their intra-regional routes from outside competition.

Globalization

In the mid-1980s, a wave of mergers swept the U.S. airline industry, resulting in the formation of eight 'mega' carriers.[28] Shortly thereafter, consolidation came to Canada, resulting in a duopoly consisting of Air Canada and Canadian Airlines International. Some consolidation is also taking place in Europe, with the takeover of British Caledonian by British Airways and the acquisition of Air Inter and UTA by Air France. BA and Air France have joined what had been an exclusively American $7 billion club. The question now is whether this consolidation movement will cross international borders. Will truly global carrier systems emerge? If globalization does come, what form will it take? Will there be outright mergers, or will the consolidation take the form of strong or weak carrier alliances? Tretheway[29] addressed these issues and identified three forms which a global carrier could take.

Corporate Merger

The most obvious way to build a global network is to buy airlines in various countries and merge them into a single corporate entity. Some precedent exists for such multinational airlines. SAS is owned by government and private interests in Denmark, Norway, and Sweden.[30] Air Afrique services twelve countries in western Africa. While a few other examples can be found, all involve pooling the traffic-generating ability of small countries within a close geographic region. Some attempts have been made by airlines to purchase airlines of other countries. SAS, for example, bid for British Caledonian as well as Aerolineas Argentinas but was unsuccessful in both attempts.

From an operational point of view, outright merger is the most desirable form of consolidation. It allows full advantage to be taken of fleet and crew utilization possibilities, amasses purchasing and borrowing power, and allows the adoption of a single consumer identity. International mergers, however, meet with many political obstacles. For example, Canada and the United States have laws restricting foreign control of their respective carriers. For many countries, national identity is tied to the existence of a 'flag' carrier. Many highly skilled managerial and technical jobs are linked to the city with the corporate headquarters of the flag carrier. For these reasons, it is hard to envision many outright mergers taking place, at least at present. Would the French government allow Air France to disappear by being swallowed up by American Airlines, Lufthansa, or Japan Air Lines? While global merger may be attractive from the airline managers' point of view, it seems to be an idea whose time has not yet come.

Simple Carrier Alliances

Simple carrier alliances involve 'marketing agreements' between carriers of different countries for preferential exchange of traffic. Air Canada, for example, may sign an agreement with Cathay Pacific whereby it books Canadian travellers going to various Asia Pacific destinations on Cathay. Similarly, Cathay books passengers going to destinations east of Vancouver on Air Canada flights. Both carriers may gain traffic which would have gone to rival Canadian Airlines International, which serves both domestic Canada and the Asia-Pacific region, or to U.S. carriers serving both Asia and Canada.

Marketing agreements may go further than this, specifying frequent flyer participation or code sharing. A travel agent in Seattle, for example, may see a British Airways flight to London listed on the Computer Reservation System (CRS). In fact, it could consist of a United Airlines flight from Seattle to Chicago (using BA's CRS code) connecting to a BA flight to London. (Until recently, United had no Chicago-London rights and BA did not fly to Seattle on a daily basis.) By being listed via code sharing as a single airline service, the flight will appear in the CRS display with a high priority. In addition, a United Airlines' patron may prefer this 'BA' flight if it earns United frequent flyer award credits for the entire journey.

While carrier agreements undoubtedly are effective marketing tools, they are limited, since they may easily be cancelled. BA could switch to another carrier to provide feed to its Chicago-London flight. United could win or purchase rights (and, recently, has done so) to fly the route as well. A parallel for this volatility existed with the U.S. feeder carriers in the immediate post-deregulation years. Some trunk carriers enlisted feeder service at various hubs, only to see the feeder switch its allegiance to a different trunk. The trunk carriers needed to stabilize their feeder arrangements and did so by taking equity positions in the smaller carriers.

Strong Airline Alliances Involving Equity Swaps

This strategy might be referred to as the 'strong alliance' option. Carriers of different countries maintain their own corporate identity but are affiliated in order to provide a global service network. In order to take advantage of the potential of the global network, the component carriers need to engage in much co-ordination of their marketing efforts. This includes routing decisions, schedule timing, the establishment of joint fares, code sharing in CRS data bases, common frequent flyer programs (where allowed), and some co-ordination of dynamic seat management decisions.[31] There could also be co-ordination on the cost side, with joint purchasing of fuel, catering services, and, possibly, aircraft. In order to take advantage of these benefits, the carriers need to make substantial investments or to relinquish some previous functions (or routes) to the other carriers. Such undertakings are not easily made and can only be justified when a strong commitment is made by all parties.

A logical form for this commitment involves the purchase of an equity stake in one carrier by another or, possibly, mutual equity stakes. Examples that have taken place include the Dutch carrier KLM's investment in the U.S. carrier Northwest and cross investments between Swissair and the U.S. carrier Delta. The intent of these equity positions is not so much for one airline to control another (which may not be permitted by one or both countries) but rather to solidify an operating relationship.

It should be pointed out that many of the benefits to be gained from building a global network depend on shared information systems. The core of airline information technologies is increasingly becoming the computer reservation system. This suggests that affiliated carriers need to share the same CRS system. When this argument is carried to its most extreme, it suggests that global carrier networks will be built around the existing CRS systems.[32]

Summary

It is likely that the international air transport regime will continue to evolve over the next ten years. Several forces are at work which are undermining the status quo. IATA is unlikely to regain its pricing powers. Regional groups, especially in the developing countries, may replace IATA's price setting duties. Europe is rapidly moving towards deregulation and could start to bargain as a bloc, changing the bilateral foundation of the air transport regime. Finally, a number of carriers themselves have started to globalize by building alliances with other carriers.

CANADIAN INTERNATIONAL AVIATION POLICY

The Canadian air transport market is less than one-tenth the size of the U.S. market. The two largest Canadian carriers combined are smaller than is the seventh largest U.S. carrier, Pan American, in terms of passenger-kilometres performed.[33] Canada is neither a major destination for world travellers nor a major generator of traffic on the world scale. In summary, Canada and its carriers are relatively small participants in world air transport, especially when compared to the United States.

Unlike the United States, Canada has not played a leadership role in shaping the international air transport regime. Canadian negotiators do not have the bargaining power necessary to force regime changes to Canada's benefit. Canadian policy has emphasized market sharing arrangements between Canadian and foreign carriers. For example, in many of Canada's bilateral agreements, each country is authorized to designate only one carrier to fly on routes covered by the agreements. The markets are then shared relatively evenly between the two carriers.[34]

Two important aspects of Canada's international air policy are discussed below. These are: the 'spheres of influence' policy for designating which carrier will fly where and the nature of existing Canadian bilateral air service agreements. Due to its importance, the U.S. bilateral is given special attention.

Spheres of Influence

Much like the Pope divided the world between the Spanish and Portuguese centuries ago, the Canadian government divided the world between Air Canada and Canadian Pacific Air Lines [now Canadian Airlines International].[35] Each carrier was designated areas of the world, or 'spheres of influence,' in which it could operate. The precise manner in which the world was divided between the two airlines was outlined in a ministerial statement issued in 1973.[36] Routes over the Pacific Ocean, for example, were assigned to Canadian Pacific Air Lines, while most of northern Europe was assigned to Air Canada. In the late 1980s, this policy was slightly modified. For example, Air Canada was assigned Korea in the Pacific, and Wardair (now part of Canadian Airlines International) was designated as the second carrier to London. The basics of the policy, however, continue to exist.[37]

Bilateral Agreements

Canada signed thirteen new bilateral air agreements between 1 January 1978 and 30 April 1986.[38] A listing of these agreements, along with the specification of some of their features, is shown in Table 2. Eight of the thirteen agreements allow each country to designate only one air carrier to operate services on a given air route. The other five agreements allow each country to designate more than one carrier per route. Single designation limits competition to a maximum of two carriers per route; multiple designation allows more carriers to compete on a given route.

In contrast to the United States' pro-competitive policy, which challenged the ratemaking authority of IATA, ten of thirteen Canadian bilateral agreements specify IATA as the preferred means for establishing tariffs. The other three agreements state that the designated airlines should jointly establish tariffs. In all thirteen cases, competitive pricing was discouraged in favour of a system of co-operative pricing.

Seven of the thirteen Canadian bilaterals specify that there must be interairline or intergovernmental agreement on capacity levels prior to the operation of air services.[39] This precludes airlines from unilaterally establishing capacity levels in response to market forces. In addition, three agreements (Greece, Israel, and Yugoslavia) make provisions for revenue sharing between the designated airlines of the two countries. These agreements allow the designated airline of one country to obtain a share of revenues accruing from an international route even if the airline does not operate on that route.[40] These agreements effectively reward airlines for *not* operating services.

TABLE 2

New Canadian bilateral air agreements: January 1978–April 1986

Date in force	Country	Designation per route	Preferable means of fare setting	Required agreement on capacities
12 Oct 1978	Haiti	Single	IATA	Yes
8 May 1979	Argentina	Single	IATA	Yes
31 Aug 1982	India	Single	IATA	Yes
6 Jan 1984	St. Lucia	Multiple	'Airline Agreement'	No
12 Jun 1984	Singapore	Single	IATA	Yes
20 Aug 1984	Greece	Single	IATA	Yes
9 Nov 1984	Rumania	Single	IATA	Yes
16 Nov 1984	Yugoslavia	Multiple	IATA	Yes
4 Sep 1985	New Zealand	Multiple	IATA	No
18 Oct 1985	Barbados	Single	'Airline Agreement'	No
18 Oct 1985	Jamaica	Multiple	IATA	No
18 Oct 1985	St. Christopher & Nevis	Multiple	'Airline Agreement'	No
13 Apr 1986	Israel	Single	IATA	No

SOURCE: Bilateral air agreements

U.S. Bilateral Position

An especially important bilateral for Canada is the agreement with the U.S. Not only is the U.S. Canada's largest international air market, but there is a threat of Canadian overseas traffic travelling via U.S. gateways and a corresponding opportunity for Canadian carriers to divert U.S. traffic.

Current Status

Although it has been amended on a number of occasions, the primary agreement regulating transborder scheduled air services remains the air services bilateral signed by Canada and the U.S. in 1966. This agreement established the primary rules for the regulation of scheduled air routes, capacity levels, and prices – rules which have largely remained in effect.

Air Routes. The Canada-U.S. air agreement followed the practice of the Bermuda agreement signed between the U.S. and the UK in 1946 and established specific routes which could be flown by Canadian and u.s. carriers. u.s. carriers were allowed to operate on sixteen route groups, while Canadian carriers could be designated to operate on twelve. Each country could designate only one carrier to operate on most routes unless permission to designate extra carriers was afforded by the other country.

It should be noted that the route schedules in the 1966 agreement were more restrictive than were the schedules in many other Canadian bilateral air agreements in that service was confined to specified route pairs. A more common specification of allowable routes would have been points in Canada to specific u.s. destinations for services by Canadian carriers and points in the u.s. to specific Canadian destinations, for services by u.s. carriers.

The 1966 agreement has been revised on a number of occasions, allowing services to be operated between additional route pairs, but the border has not been opened to services that could be operated at the discretion of carriers. Except under specific circumstances, such as routes of a regional or local nature, all transborder routes must still be specifically vetoed by both governments.

Capacity Levels. The Canada-u.s. air agreement has an unrestrictive capacity clause. Section 12 of the agreement states that neither government can unilaterally impose restrictions on the carriers of the other country with respect to capacities, frequencies, or type of aircraft employed. Airlines, therefore, have the leeway to set capacities and frequency levels as they see fit, without input from the other government.

Pricing. As opposed to the capacity clause, the pricing provisions are restrictive. All fares must be submitted by airlines operating transborder routes for approval by the governments of both countries. This approval process allows either government to reject a fare submitted by an airline for approval.

Charter Air Transport. Charter, or non-scheduled air transport, is regulated under a separate Canada-u.s. bilateral air transport agreement, signed in 1974. Non-scheduled air transport was defined, for the purpose of the agreement, as 'commercial air transportation of traffic on time, mileage or trip basis by a carrier or carriers, where the entire planeload capacity of one or more aircraft has been engaged.' The pricing and capacity clauses contained in the agreement were reasonably liberal. Airlines were permitted to establish 'reasonable rates' without prior approval from the foreign government. If one government was dissatisfied with the rates, it could enter negotiations with the other government to find satisfactory solutions. Governments could not impose restrictions on flights, frequencies, capacities, or the type of aircraft used by airlines of the other country, although it was stated that non-scheduled services should not substantially impair the operations of the other country's carriers, whether scheduled or non-scheduled. A further clause stated that the volume of non-scheduled traffic originating from one of the countries should be reasonably related to the volume of traffic carried by its own non-scheduled carriers. Since the vast majority of non-scheduled traffic was Canadian-originating, this would imply that the vast majority of traffic should be carried by Canadian non-scheduled airlines. This Canadian advantage was mitigated by a contradictory requirement that u.s. carriers achieve between 25 and 40 per cent of the market share of non-scheduled carriers to sun destinations by 1978.[41]

Local Services Agreement. On 21 August 1984, the Canadian and u.s. governments signed an agreement on regional commuter air services. Its objective was 'to introduce greater predictability and automaticity in the approval of applications,' and 'to facilitate and encourage the provision of additional transborder services of a regional, local and commuter nature.' Previously, new services had to be approved by the aeronautical authorities of both countries. This agreement, in contrast, implemented an automatic approval system wherein a route application to one country would receive an automatic approval from the other if five criteria were satisfied.

First, the aircraft capacity was no more than sixty passengers and the payload capacity no more than 18,000 pounds. Second, the city-pair was not among those named in the 1966 Agreement. Third, at least one city had a metropolitan population of less than 500,000 in Canada or 1,000,000 in the u.s. Fourth, the stage length of the proposed route did not exceed 400 statute miles to and from points in central Canada and 600 statute miles to and from all other points in Canada. Fifth, the proposed service was not already authorized to an airline of the same country. It should be noted that the aeronautical authorities could approve a route application even if the above criteria were not met, but this would require approval of both countries.

Experimental Transborder Air Transport Program. On 21 August 1984, the Canadian and u.s. governments established an experimental transborder program in order 'to foster new transborder air services,' and 'to gain experience with innovative pricing and service mechanisms.' Under this programme, designated carriers were given unrestricted automatic access to Mirabel Airport from any point or points in the u.s. other than seven international gateways (Boston – Logan; Chicago – O'Hare; Los Angeles; New York – JFK; San Francisco; and Seattle). All flights had to originate or terminate at Mirabel, and points in third countries could not be served on single-plane services.

Unlike the Air Transport Agreement of 1966, this agreement contained liberal pricing provisions. Fares would only be disallowed if they were rejected by the aeronautical authorities of both countries. This marked a change from the previous situation, where fares had to be filed for approval by both governments' authorizing bodies. It was further agreed that the u.s. government would propose a u.s. airport which would have the same transborder privileges as did Mirabel, and the airport at San Jose, California, was subsequently chosen.

The Canadian and u.s. Position Papers

On 18 December 1984, Canadian and u.s. aviation officials agreed to exchange concept papers in preparation for future negotiations. Matters to be addressed included the expansion of the allowable number of routes between the two countries and the amalgamation of the scheduled and non-scheduled air agreements. The concept papers which were exchanged on 13 June 1985 envisaged the creation of an open transborder system governed by market forces. However, different approaches were proposed.

The u.s. government proposed that a free trade market be established, in which carriers would be permitted to operate services between any point in Canada and any point in the u.s. This approach would eliminate such questions as whether all or specific routes should be single-tracked (designated to only a u.s. or a Canadian carrier but not to both) or double-tracked (designated to carriers of both countries), which cities could serve as intermediate points on routes, and to what extent Canadian airlines should be able to penetrate u.s. markets. To offset the structural advantage to its national airlines, the u.s. government would consider certain enhancements for Canadian carriers, which could include full stopover rights and change of gauge operations in the u.s. Change of gauge rights would allow an airline to use an aircraft on one section of the route which was different in capacity from that used on another section of the route. The aircraft could be leased or operated under a contractual relationship with one or more u.s. airlines.

Pricing procedures and non-scheduled services were also addressed. Under the existing double approval pricing regime, scheduled airlines were unable to change fares or respond to competitors' changes freely and quickly. As a result, the u.s. noted that it would be interested in a double disapproval pricing regime, where prices are approved unless rejected by both governments. In addition, scheduled airlines should be allowed to match charter fares and vice versa.

With respect to non-scheduled services, the u.s. government stated that the present arrangement should be updated so that it provided a more open operating environment for existing and potential services, including split passenger-cargo charters and air freight forwarder charters. In addition, charter services, which operated in a regular pattern, should be converted to scheduled authority.

The Canadian concept paper differed from the u.s. paper in that it envisaged the creation of one common market or, as referred to in the concept paper, a fully integrated North American civil aviation system. This proposal not only allowed carriers to operate services between any point in Canada and the u.s., but it also allowed the free movement of factors of production. In other words, Canadian carriers could serve intra-American traffic and vice-versa (i.e., cabotage rights would be permitted).

According to the Canadian government, a common market would minimize or eliminate the structural advantage of u.s. airlines and, thus, provide an equal opportunity for airlines of both countries to participate in a pro-competitive environment. As stated in the concept paper, the structural advantage of u.s. airlines stemmed from their ability 'to accumulate and aggregate traffic originating from or destined to points behind u.s. gateways at airline hubs in the u.s. and then connect these hubs to the principal population centres in Canada.' In addition, the pre-clearance program at Canadian airports (where u.s.-bound passengers pre-clear u.s. customs in Canada) further enhanced the attractiveness of u.s. airlines in the transborder marketplace, particularly for through-plane services.

The Canadian concept paper stated, as well, that an agreement on routes should be the 'centrepiece' of any new Canada-u.s. air agreement. Hence, 'subsidiary' issues, like non-scheduled services, pricing, and all-cargo services would be considered at a later time.

Recent Developments

The two governments were unable to reach a compromise on a comprehensive liberal air transport agreement. Neither concept paper was acceptable to either party, nor could any compromise agreement be reached. Transborder air traffic remains regulated by the 1966 bilateral, the separate charter agreement, and the two limited agreements reached in 1984. Canada was unwilling to accept the u.s. proposal for the free determination of transborder routes because of perceived advantages this would afford to u.s. carriers. The u.s. was unwilling to accept the Canadian cabotage proposal because u.s. carriers were concerned, at least in part, that it would be a precedent-setting move which could result in the u.s. market being opened to cabotage by carriers of other countries, resulting in a loss of business for u.s. carriers. It was likely that this disagreement also contributed to air transport being left out of the Canada-U.S. free trade agreement.[42]

The most recent negotiations between Canada and the United States over a new air transport agreement are taking place at the time this paper is being written (May 1991). Both the U.S. transportation secretary and the Canadian minister of transportation announced the 'open skies' talks which, again, could include the discussion of cabotage arrangements. The major Canadian aim in the discussion appears to be to increase the access Canadian carriers have to U.S. markets.[43] A major U.S. goal is to increase the routes available to U.S. carriers so as to allow them to better connect Canadian cities into their hub-and-spoke networks. An important impetus for negotiations from the U.S. side is the desire of a group of U.S. airports to increase the number of international markets served from their cities.[44] Those opposing a major revision to the bilateral agreement, especially a cabotage arrangement, include Canadian Airlines International, the U.S. and Canadian pilots' unions, and the Canadian charter tour operators.[45] It remains to be seen what results will arise from these talks, but they will likely last several months, if not years.

Summary of Canadian International Air Policy

As a general rule, the major aim of Canadian international air policy has been to negotiate the best deal possible for Canadian carriers. The Canadian government has attempted to meet this goal by restricting competition on Canadian international routes, thereby guaranteeing Canadian carriers a 'fair share' of available revenue. The restrictions have kept Canadian carriers from competing between themselves (through the spheres of influence policy) and from competing too vigorously with foreign carriers (through restrictive bilateral agreements and a permissive attitude towards Canadian carriers engaging in revenue pooling). The bilateral agreement with the U.S., with its pricing restrictions and limited number of designated routes, is a good example of Canada's restrictive approach.

OPPORTUNITIES AND CHALLENGES FOR CANADA

As was discussed above, Canadian international air transport policy has remained relatively unchanged over the last several decades. While other countries have adopted a free-market approach to air transport, Canadian policy has been conservative; the government has been content to divide international routes between Canada's largest two carriers and, within markets, between a Canadian and a foreign carrier. In this section, three alternative approaches to viewing Canadian air transport policy are examined. In each case, there are opportunities for Canadians (either carriers or passengers or both) to gain, given the changing air transport environment.

Consideration of Consumer as well as Carrier Interests

An opportunity exists for Canada to develop a new air transport policy based not only on the interests of airlines but on the interests of air travellers. Canada could begin this approach by reaching a liberal air transport agreement with the u.s. A comprehensive liberal agreement between Canada and the u.s. will likely not be reached as long as airline interests are placed above consumer interests in the negotiating process and as long as Canadian carriers are unwilling or unable to better adapt to the changing air transport regime. It would seem evident that transborder air travellers would benefit from a free transborder market, either with or without cabotage, through lower prices, greater frequencies, and improved routings. Canadian airlines, on the other hand, would likely lose a share of the transborder market to their u.s. competitors. In our opinion, the u.s. market has been well developed by the u.s. carriers, and their positions would be easily defended against cabotage incursions by foreign airlines, whether Canadian or others. To date, authorities on both sides of the border have chosen to attempt to negotiate an agreement favoured by their carriers and, therefore, have neglected the interests of air travellers. Is this likely to change in the future?

The answer seems to be maybe. Canadian bilateral negotiations have traditionally been airline-driven. The carriers accompany the official government of Canada negotiating team. Consumer representatives have not. New bilateral agreements are signed when Canadian carriers wish to establish new routes. Consumer interests have traditionally played a secondary role, if any, in Canadian bilateral negotiations. However, in the current Canada-u.s. negotiations, for the first time, labour and community representatives have been asked to participate in the negotiations. Prior to the negotiations, public hearings were held by Parliament to assist in the development of the negotiating mandate. This suggests that the Canadian government may be willing to take a new direction in international airline policy.

Viewing Air Transport as a Logistical System

Air transport routings may be thought of in terms of global networks or 'logistics systems,' not just as country-to-country origin-destination pairs. Canadian domestic and international traffic can be routed through the U.S. Similarly, Canada's airlines can carry increasing amounts of non-Canadian global traffic flows by restructuring their route networks. Better network connections for Canada could result in lower costs for moving goods and people into and out of Canada.

While logistics is normally thought of as a discipline for optimizing the movement of freight, it is also relevant to passenger traffic. Business passengers are mainly concerned with getting from origin to destination on a timely basis. Before deregulation, much of the U.S. was served by nonstop, but often infrequent, air service. Since deregulation, airlines are providing more frequent one-stop routing through major hubs. Many travellers feel that the 'cost' of increased time spent in flight is more than offset by the 'benefit' of more frequent service. The traveller has thus made a choice between competing logistical systems. Tourists can also be thought of as purchasing complete logistical packages. For example, tourists from Japan may wish to see the Rockies and spend some time shopping in a large city. They may be indifferent to the choice between a package which routes them through Vancouver and one that routes them through Seattle.

An airport, as part of a logistical system, facilitates the flow of goods and people into and out of a region. It can also act as a transfer node (or an in-transit node) between two very distant regions. An airport is an intermodal facility, transferring passengers or freight from one mode of transport, air, to another, usually motor transport. An airport, as part of a logistical system, competes with other logistical systems. Air freight can be flown to Seattle and then be trucked to a firm in Vancouver as an alternative to being flown directly into Vancouver.

To illustrate how one country's air transport system fits into a broader logistical system, consider the traffic routing in Figure 1A. A traveller from an 'off-line' (i.e., non-hub) point, such as Taipei in Asia, wishes to travel to an off-line point in South America, such as Quito. The historical routing pattern using Vancouver requires no fewer than five stops, a minimum of three airlines, and, depending on the day of the week, two to four days travel. It is now technically possible to fly directly from Tokyo to Toronto (see Figure 1B). This flight pattern eliminates one stop and hours of flying and in-transit time. Alternative methods of improving the routing through Canada exist. Off-line points in Asia can be connected to Vancouver (Figure 1C), and Vancouver can be directly connected to hubs with access to off-line South American points (Figure 1D) or directly to South America (Figure 1E). Any of these alternatives will likely be preferred by the consumer.

How can Canada benefit from viewing international air transport as a logistics system? Canada and the U.S. are currently negotiating a new

FIGURE 1

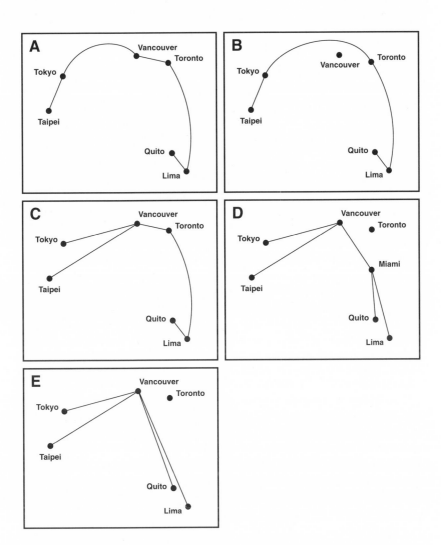

(A) Historical routing: off-line Asia to off-line South America; (B) potential routing bypassing Vancouver; (C) potential routing using Vancouver to off-line Asia; (D) potential routing using Vancouver to off-line Asia via hub to South America; (E) potential routing using Vancouver to off-line Asia direct to South America bilateral air transport agreement which, if concluded, will provide Canadian carriers with better access to U.S. markets. Canadian carriers can attempt to use this access in order to route passengers between the U.S. and Europe and the U.S. and Asia. Canadian airports are ideally located to serve as hubs for both North Atlantic and North Pacific traffic flows.

Foreign Ownership Policy and the Implications for Canadian Participation in Globalization

The National Transportation Act stipulates that non-Canadians may not exercise controlling interest over Canadian domiciled carriers.[46] In a series of decisions in 1988 and 1989, the National Transportation Agency has strictly enforced this limitation. Similar foreign ownership limitations appear throughout the world. The U.S., for example, has almost identical requirements. Almost all bilaterals stipulate that any carrier designated by a country to fly a route must be controlled or owned by nationals of that country. This is to prevent Greece, for example, from designating British Airways to fly Athens-New York.

It is too early to determine the effects of globalization on the air transport industry. However, the early 1990s are likely to be dynamic, and Canada should stand ready to adjust its ownership policy to promote the interests of Canadians (consumers and carriers). Rather than simply reacting to whatever the U.S. decides, Canada may be better served by taking a proactive role. If evidence appears that globalization will increase (e.g., if frequent flyer programs spread to other continents), then a pre-emptive move vis-à-vis the U.S. could give Canada an edge in the market. Canadian carriers will be more attractive partners to European or Asian carriers if they are the first carriers available for acquisition or merger in North America. Once U.S. carriers become available, the value added of a Canadian carrier to the global network will fall. A change in Canadian laws, therefore, that would allow greater equity participation by foreign carriers in Canadian carriers could help to better position Canada in a global system. As an example, Canadian cities could be established as North American hubs in a globally based hub-and-spoke system if Canadian carriers become part of a global airline.

SUMMARY AND CONCLUSIONS

This chapter has observed that the international air transport industry underwent a dramatic transition in the 1970s and 1980s in the way decisions are made about markets to serve, prices to charge, and capacities to offer. The regime, meaning the set of institutions and rules governing the market, changed. In many of the most important international markets, cartel price-setting by IATA has been replaced by competitive forces. Bilateral air treaties have also become more liberal in the specification of routes which can be flown and the method of determining capacities.

We present evidence that further regime changes are likely. These changes will tend, on balance, to be pro-competitive. Some of the changes which could occur include free markets in air transport within trading blocs such as Europe or North America; negotiation of rights and conditions of service between trading blocs rather than on a country by country basis; complete breakdown of mechanisms to control prices and capacity levels by other than market forces; and consolidation pressures which cross borders, resulting in a globalization of the industry.

Canada has had an international aviation policy which was consistent with the 1945-70 regime. During the 1980s, only minor changes to Canadian international air policy took place. As the regime continues to evolve, it is doubtful whether Canada's reactive policy evolution will serve either its consumers or its carriers well.

While the exact nature of the new regime is not currently known, some broad trends are discernable. First, competitive forces will play a large role, especially in any market to/from/within North America and within Europe. Second, higher traffic growth rates will likely be experienced outside rather than within North America due to the liberalization of air services in these parts of the world. The U.S., and to a lesser extent Canada, have had over a decade of experience with deregulation. Low-fare customer markets have already been tapped in North America. In contrast, Europe has yet to tap this market segment (with the exception of sunspot charters). Third, as the world's carriers are given greater freedom, they will evolve new logistical patterns for routing passengers and freight. The days of each viable origin-destination combination being linked by nonstop flights may be over. Global traffic flows may be routed through global hubs. For example, Canada-Switzerland traffic could easily be routed via Paris, London, New York, Brussels, Frankfurt, or Amsterdam rather than via direct flights. Fourth, the coming changes create opportunities for consumers, carriers, and economic development. A global hub could be developed just as easily in Toronto as in Chicago, provided Toronto has adequate access to U.S., South American, and Asian points. A global airline hub will be a powerful economic generator. It can offer local consumers a larger variety of direct destinations and fares. Because of this, and similar implications in cargo transport, global hubs will be an attractive place to do business. Carriers domiciled in the country of the global hub will have great opportunities for growth. Fifth, there will be pressures on airlines to consolidate. During the 1990s, these pressures will cross national frontiers, and some degree of globalization will take place.

The forces of change are already at work in international air transport. The task for Canada is to develop a policy which maximizes national benefits to consumers and carriers. In order to maximize total benefits, the policy may be based on competition and global network building in contrast to the current policy based largely on carrier protection and point-to-point networks. There are three main themes which may be pursued.

First, the policy can strive to increase access from Canada to non-North American markets. Being part of a global logistical network requires, absolutely, access to a large number of global points. Existing policy has been reactive: bilaterals are negotiated when point-to-point traffic flows have been built to a point where a Canadian carrier asks for the bilateral. Since bilaterals can sometimes take long periods to negotiate, a more proactive policy may be needed.

Second, the policy can rely to a large extent on competition to determine service levels and prices. When CP Air felt protected on its route to Hong Kong, it did little to develop the market. When faced with significant competition from Cathay Pacific, CP Air quickly responded with much expanded service, benefitting the carrier, the consumer, and the Canadian economy. Competition will induce our carriers to develop markets rapidly and, thus, build a role for Canada in the global network.

Third, the policy can strive for improved access to the U.S. market. This is vital if Canada is to have a role in the global air network. It is beyond the scope of this paper to comment on what form that access should take, for example, transborder-only free trade, versus cabotage, versus an expanded list of named routes. Nevertheless, improved access is required. It seems strange that Canadian carriers and consumers can fly nonstop jets Toronto-Lima or Toronto-Tokyo but not Toronto-Washington, DC, or Ottawa-Washington, DC.

In addition to these three broad tenets, there are a number of secondary issues. Canada's policy should facilitate global carrier alliances, although the extent and nature of these alliances need careful consideration. Related to the globalization issue, some reconsideration of foreign ownership restrictions may be needed.

The international air transport industry has undergone fundamental changes in the past decade and will continue to evolve in the 1990s. Canada needs to have a clear vision as to future policy directions.

CHAPTER NINE

Canada and the Evolving System of International Shipping Conferences

Trevor D. Heaver

INTRODUCTION

Shipping conferences are voluntary associations (cartels) of liner firms engaged in the international movement of trade. They are designed to constrain competition among the member lines and to reduce the effects of competition from 'outsiders.' They usually function in one direction on a trade route, for example, from Australia/New Zealand to North America. Many conferences exist; in 1989, there were thirty conferences in trades through Canadian ports.[1]

Conferences evolved in British trades during the 1870s, but they soon dominated liner trades around the world. The constraints that they place on competition were controversial and have remained so. Consequently, conferences have been subject to many national investigations, including those in Canada. The investigations have consistently concluded that conferences should be allowed, subject to certain limitations, because of their effects in stabilizing rates and services – attributes desired by shipping lines and by most shippers. However, the positions of interested parties have been constrained by the international regime of the shipping services and by the differences in perspective among countries.

Differences among the policies of countries have become more important in the last twenty years. Some governments are protectionist of their shipping interests, while others adopt more liberal, market competitive policies. Governments differ in their views on the best ways to control conference practices. In particular, developing countries have pushed a multinational regime opposed by most developed countries.

The purposes of this chapter are to identify issues in the Canadian policy on liner conferences and to outline the intergovernmental relations affecting the development and implementation of the policy. The development and practices of conferences are described in the next section. Four policy approaches of other governments, which are important in the international environment to which Canadian policies must relate, are then reviewed. This is followed by Canadian policy up to the Shipping Conference Exemption Act of 1987. The experience with that legislation and the current issues are considered in the last two sections of the paper.

THE DEVELOPMENT, STRUCTURE, AND PRACTICES
OF LINER CONFERENCES

The development, structure, and practices of cartels in liner shipping have been greatly influenced by the technology and economics of liner shipping. Therefore, the characteristics of liner shipping are described before the features of conferences are outlined.

The Characteristics of Liner Shipping

Liner shipping provides scheduled services by vessels operating regularly between prescribed ports. The services are designed to serve shippers with a few tons to a few hundred tons of freight per shipment. Prior to 1960, liner services were provided by geared multi-deck vessels for which the loading and unloading of cargoes was a lengthy and costly process. Ship schedules were uncertain. The introduction of containerization led to a revolution in technology during the 1960s and 1970s. Today, liner shipping is dominated by gearless container ships with cellular structures for fast loading and unloading. Ship turnaround time has been greatly reduced and sailing schedules made more reliable. Shippers now expect to integrate liner services more precisely into their logistics systems.

Liner shipping markets are defined by the geography of services. They are not global – like the services for bulk ships that trade in any part of the world on short notice. Competition in liner markets is dominantly among the liner companies on a route. The number of companies may be one or two on a low volume route; it may be twenty or more on a major route.[2] Competition may come, also, from bulk ships when they have surplus capacity and attempt to 'trade up' to larger volume liner shipments with low service requirements. Competition may also come from air freight for high value commodities. Finally, competitive constraints may exist on one route from freight movements on other routes.

When liner shipping was provided by break-bulk ships, liner companies were concerned with moving cargoes from one port to another. Shippers, freight forwarders, or domestic carriers assumed responsibility for the freight to and from the ports. The introduction of container services brought about an important change for two reasons. First, the firms that were leaders in containerization were customer focused and believed in door-to-door service. Malcolm MacLean of Sea-Land brought a trucker's approach to shipping. In Canada, Frank Narby of Cast was successful in penetrating the u.s. Midwest market through Canada by providing door-to-door service. Second, the container facilitated the fast, low-cost handling of traffic so that high volume and reliable movement of traffic could be scheduled and integrated with domestic movements.

These developments brought about radical change in the shipping business. Containerization provided the technology for shipping to provide intermodal service. Traditional service patterns of separate hinterlands served through port gateways gave way to continent-wide competition among transportation systems through widely separated ports.[3] The changes gave rise to new market conditions and the need for a review of the regulation of conferences. The u.s. Shipping Act of 1984 facilitated changes in liner shipping – it did not cause them.

Liner Conferences

Liner shipping routes have been dominated by conferences since the latter part of the nineteenth century.[4] In 1875, liner companies operating from the uk to Calcutta formed the Calcutta Conference, which successfully used deferred rebates to get shippers to remain loyal to conference carriers. Conferences quickly formed on other routes with sufficient traffic to support regular liner services and have retained a dominant position in the provision of liner services since that time.

Conferences covered ranges of ports typical in vessel voyage patterns. In the Pacific, different conferences existed from various trans-Pacific origins and to the east and the west coast of North America. As competitive conditions have changed, conferences have amalgamated to cover wider ranges of ports. This has contributed to the reduction in the number of conferences serving Canada from forty-eight to thirty between 1983 and 1989.[5]

The explicit purpose of conferences is to constrain competition among member lines and to reduce the effects of competition from 'outsiders' – both non-conference lines and bulk ships. The rationale for the anti-competitive measures is to enhance the stability of rate and service levels in the interest of facilitating trade.

Conferences have adopted many different structures and practices.[6] Many conferences are 'closed'; new lines can only gain admission at the discretion of existing members. New members may have limited sailing rights and limited voting power at conference meetings. Some conferences are 'open'; since 1916, the U.S. has required all conferences in its trades to be open. These conferences admit new members on terms similar to those of existing members.

All conferences engage in rate setting, except for short periods. Closed conferences may engage in traffic allocation or pooling arrangements. Some have capacity and port sailing restrictions. Some have other forms of cargo sharing and even revenue or profit pooling. Traditionally, conference agreements were confidential and practices secret. Even tariffs were treated as confidential documents by many conferences well into the 1960s. Contrary to the general reaction of consumers to cartels, shippers have supported the retention of conferences because of the stability they have provided to services and rates. However, they have sought to have the actions of conferences constrained. The approaches to the regulation of conferences by other countries are an important part of the international environment affecting Canada's policy options.

COMPARISON OF GOVERNMENTAL APPROACHES
TO LINER SHIPPING

National policies on liner conferences reflect many factors. They include a country's interests in shipping and in seaborne trade, the policy on business competition, and its perceptions on the effectiveness of competition in liner markets. For Canada and developing countries previously influenced greatly by European policies, new approaches have developed in the last twenty years.

The classification of approaches which follows is based on a dominant characteristic in a country's policy. Four approaches are described. They are: laissez-faire, government-supported countervailing power, regulatory, and multilateral code.

Laissez-faire Policies (Example, United Kingdom)

The first full investigation of conferences was by the Royal Commission on Shipping Rings, which reported in 1909.[7] From that time, government intervention has been spurned in favour of negotiations by shippers' associations with conferences.

Early attempts to establish associations of exporters found conferences reluctant to deal with shippers as a group. It was not until 1955 that the British Shippers' Councils (BSC) was formed to deal with governmental and commercial interests affecting shipping and air services. The BSC encouraged the formation of shippers' councils in other European countries, leading to the formation of the European Shippers' Council (ESC). In 1963, the ESC reached a 'Note of Understanding' with European shipowners for regular consultations and the use of an independent panel to help resolve disputes. However, these developments did not prevent the conduct and effects of conferences from remaining contentious.

The next major UK investigation into liner conferences was the Committee of Inquiry into Shipping, which reported in 1970 (the Rochdale Inquiry).[8] The inquiry arose from general concern about the status of British shipping and not specifically because of issues with conferences. The committee found criticisms of conferences were almost entirely related to the details of their operations and not to the principles of their existence, and that operation 'within a "closed" conference, is desirable for most deep sea routes.'[9] Further, it was the committee's 'strongly held view that both shippers and liner operators should develop their means of consultation and cooperation, so that mutual problems can be solved amicably and the most efficient arrangements made for continuing development for liner services.'[10] For the regime to work effectively, a strong shippers' council and a code of conduct adopted by conferences were considered necessary. The latter was seen as avoiding problems of jurisdiction arising from government imposed codes. Legislation was not passed in the United Kingdom until the British Merchant Shipping (Liner Conferences) Act, 1982. The principal function of the act was to allow the secretary of state for trade to make regulations in response to the multinational Code of Conduct for Liner Conferences, which is discussed later.

The recommendations of the Rochdale Inquiry were in keeping with the policy developments in Europe.[11] For a number of years, encouragement had been given to the resolution of shipper/conference issues through discussions between a shippers' council and conferences. However, significant European Community (EC) policy initiatives were not taken until the mid-1970s. This timing reflected resolution of legal uncertainty about the status of international shipping under the Treaty of Rome, growing concern about international flag discrimination, and the development of the Code of Conduct for Liner Conferences at the United Nations Conference on Trade Development (UNCTAD), hereafter referred to as the UNCTAD Code. The growing need for collective action is evident in various events about this time. In 1973, shipowners' associations from EC member countries formed the Comité des Associations d'Armateurs des Communautés Européennes (CAACE). In 1977, the European Council drew up a proposal so that a member state might accede to the UNCTAD Code as 'it was time to enforce international agreement governing liner conferences and that the existing Code should be taken as the starting point.' Also, it was felt that 'a common Community approach to the UN Liner Code could provide a foundation for a common position vis-à-vis the United States…on the special problem faced by liner shipping on the North Atlantic routes.'[12] This proposal was adopted as the so-called Brussels Package in 1979. The EC support of liner conferences through the UNCTAD Code was seen as a method of achieving 'a worldwide self-policing system based on agreements between the shipowners and the consignors.'[13]

The EC policy to support liner conferences was contrary to the general articles in the Treaty of Rome, which bar cartels. The support was founded on the belief that the economic stability provided by conferences aids trade and on the presupposition that conferences operate in trades which are open to new entrants. The EC was concerned that flag discrimination, including that proposed in the UNCTAD Code, would reduce the competitiveness of liner shipping as well as adversely affect their liner companies.[14] ('Flag discrimination' refers to the reservation of some share of a country's trade to national lines of the country.)

Since 1982, the Consultative Shipping Group (CSG)[15] and the U.S. have been involved in discussions to ensure access for the ships of participating countries to trade between them and to facilitate access to other trades.[16] In 1986, the U.S. and CSG issued a joint statement to resist protectionist activities which impair competitive access to their trades. In February 1987, the council of the OECD approved the Recommendation on Common Principles on Shipping Policy for Member Countries. This policy document, which is non-binding, directs member countries to safeguard and promote open trade in various ways.[17]

In 1986, the EC adopted regulations setting out co-ordinated principles of the policy on liner shipping. They are, first, adherence to competitive access of shipping to international trade; second, allowance of conferences with a minimum of government regulation; and third, the use of bilateral or multilateral mechanisms for the resolution of disputes over approaches to efficient shipping services. These principles are of importance to Canadian policy options.

Government-Supported Countervailing Power (Example, Australia)

Shipping services have always been of special importance to Australia because of the country's distance from markets and dependence on ocean transport to reach them.[18] However, it was not until 1929 that the concern of shippers led to actions independent of the British laissez-faire approach. Following a government-sponsored Overseas Shipping Conference, a shippers' group was organized to negotiate with ship-owners so that tonnage could be rationalized and the rates of closed conferences approved. Subsequently, various initiatives have been pursued to make primary reliance on the countervailing negotiating power of shippers successful.

Part 10 of the Trade Practices Act was amended in 1966 to extend exemption from the competition provision of the act to all outbound conferences, providing that they fulfil certain 'undertakings.' Central to these were meeting with a shipper body and the provision of information reasonably necessary for the purpose of negotiation. The shipper body is similarly obliged. A government official was to be allowed to be present at meetings. In the event of failure of a conference to provide efficient, economic, and adequate services, or if it hindered an Australian flag operator engaging efficiently in overseas trade, the conduct of a conference could be referred to the Trade Practices Tribunal for study. On the recommendation of the tribunal, the government could withdraw the exemption of the conference from the Trade Practices Act.

In 1972, the Australian Shippers' Council (ASC) was formed to strengthen the position of shippers and was named as the representative shipper body with which conferences were required to negotiate. However, in spite of the expertise available to a special shipper association, negotiating strength, in the end, depends on competitive conditions in individual commodity markets and on the logistical alternatives available to shippers. Thus, in the Australian trade, the main negotiating clout is in the hands of the major exporters, such as the Wool Corporation and the Meat Board. The result is both complementary and potentially conflicting interests among commodity groups.

In 1989, the ASC collapsed and the Trade Practices (International Liner Cargo Shipping) Amendment Act modified the regime. Limitations on exemptions from the Trade Practices Act and other changes were introduced to encourage more competition in liner shipping. Reliance on commercial processes continues by recognition of a designated peak shipper body to negotiate broad matters and designated secondary shipper bodies to negotiate for shipper groups. To avoid international conflicts, limited regulation applies to inbound conferences.

Regulatory Policy (Example, the United States)

The U.S. has adopted quite different policies from other developed countries; it has regulated conferences actively. The development of shipping conferences raised the dilemma of reconciling the pro-competitive (anti-trust) principles of the Sherman Act of 1890 with the co-operative (cartel) practices of conference members. The Alexander Report of 1914 resulted in the Shipping Act of 1916, which struck a balance by exempting conferences from the Sherman Act as long as they conformed to certain practices. The legislation followed the pattern of the Act to Regulate Commerce of 1887, which led to the Interstate Commerce Commission (ICC). (Indeed, the Alexander Report recommended that lines be brought under the supervision of the ICC.)

The restrictions in the 1916 act were designed to limit the potential for monopolistic abuse by conferences. All conferences were required to be open; all were precluded from paying deferred rebates and from using fighting ships (ships deliberately operated at a loss by conference members to prevent the entry of non-conference services); and the U.S. Shipping Board (a predecessor of the Federal Maritime Commission) was authorized to disapprove rates that were 'so unreasonably high or low as to be detrimental to the commerce of the U.S.'[19] Conference agreements could be disapproved if they were found to be unjustly discriminatory or unfair between carriers and shippers or to operate to the detriment of U.S. commerce. The act, while allowing conferences to exist, resulted in the extraterritorial application of the law to agreements made in foreign sovereign states and by foreign carriers when those carriers operated services to or from U.S. ports.

Application of the act gave rise to various issues, including the legality of the dual rate system used by conferences to ensure shipper loyalty. In 1958, the U.S. Supreme Court decision in the Isbrandtsen case found a specific application of the dual-rate system illegal. This and other issues led to the Bonner and the Celler reports. The reports concluded that revised methods for effectively controlling the operation of conferences were necessary if the system was to do more good than harm. The Celler Report feared the elimination of the conference system would impose 'severe hardship upon our U.S. merchant marine and [create] substantial rate instability presently undesired by American shippers.'[20] Resulting amendments to the Shipping Act required that the conference agreements had to be in the 'public interest,' and that conference tariffs should be on file with the FMC and available for public inspection. Various restrictions were imposed on procedures for rate changes, and the differential between loyalty contract and non-contract rates (dual rates) was limited to 15 per cent. In 1964, in response to various requests of the FMC for data from British and other foreign shipping companies, the UK passed legislation enabling it to forbid UK companies from meeting certain demands of the commission.

The substantial changes in liner shipping associated with containerization during the 1960s and 1970s led to increasing pressure for change in the U.S. legislation. The general policy thrust to deregulate industry also led to new questions about the appropriateness of the Shipping Act. Reviews of the industry resulted in continued allowance of shipping conferences under new regulated conditions. The greatest change introduced by the Shipping Act of 1984 'involves the clear substitute of regulation by government with a more effective and appropriate regulation by the marketplace.'[21] However, the amount of regulation still exceeds that in other developed countries.

The act has introduced three broad types of change. First, it has introduced measures which reduce burdens on carriers. Conference agreements no longer require FMC approval; they go into effect within forty-five days of filing unless the FMC can obtain a court injunction. The burden of proof is on the FMC to show that the agreement does not meet the 'standard' required for exemption from anti-trust laws. This standard is less demanding than that which existed previously. Immunity is provided, also, for action outside an agreement in effect. This has provided a mechanism for agreements to be entered into between conference and non-conference lines. Finally, the act allows conference intermodal rates, as required for effective conduct of the container business.

Second, the act introduces measures to make conferences more responsive to shippers' needs. Conferences are required to provide carriers with the right of independent action on rates. The authority of shipping lines and conferences to enter into services contracts is made explicit by the act. This authority is not extended to third parties selling shipping space; these are generally known as Non-Vessel Operating Common Carriers (NVOCC). Both independent action and service contracts have become important but sometimes controversial aspects of liner shipping practice since 1984.

Third, the Shipping Act has extended the range of prohibited acts. Many of the prohibitions were intended to ensure that only the rates on file with the FMC would be charged. An important prohibition in the 1984 act is the use of a loyalty contract 'except in conformity with the anti-trust laws.'[22] This has resulted in the end of the dual rate system in U.S. trades.

The effect of the legislation on shipping services is a matter of current debate in the U.S. Some information about detailed commercial matters will be used later in this chapter. However, two policy issues need to be highlighted here. They make clear that liner shipping issues are involved in much wider policy matters, and that they are relevant to a multinational framework.

The first issue is the potentially conflicting response of governments to the evolution of 'superconferences' in the Atlantic and Pacific trades. As argued earlier, competition through various ports, and over various routes, has become continental in scale. This has encouraged the consolidation of conferences. The relaxation of the conditions required of conference agreements in the Shipping Act has made superconferences more likely. Agreements between conference and non-conference lines have also been made legal in the U.S. In both the Atlantic and Pacific trades, this has allowed conference and non-conference carriers to file agreements to discuss various matters, including the reduction of shipping capacity. In the Atlantic, these are in Eurocorde discussion agreements and have led to discussions in the Cross Atlantic Stabilization Agreement.[23] In the Pacific, the Transpacific Stabilization Agreement among thirteen major lines in the eastbound Far East-U.S. line trade has been more successful in achieving a reduction in capacity.[24] Interestingly, these agreements, held legal in the U.S., have been challenged in Canada by the Canadian Shippers' Council as outside the Shipping Conference Exemption Act and in Europe by the European Shippers' Council as falling outside Council Regulation 4056/86. While decisions on these challenges have not been reached, Europe and Canada could adopt more pro-competitive positions than the U.S.

The second issue is the restriction of non-national-flag carriers from trades by government or conference practices. Government practices include: cargo reservation to national-flag carriers; restrictions on the ownership of port or intermodal facilities; discriminatory taxes and port fees; and cargo allocation practices to national-flag lines through government sponsored shippers' associations. Similar effects might be caused by closed conferences precluding entry of a new carrier. Thus, some countries are concerned about the restrictive practices of other governments, for example, the concern of shipping nations with cargo reservation by developing countries, while other countries are concerned about the restrictive practices of conferences, for example, the concern of developing countries about the policies of conferences dominated by lines of developed countries.

The intergovernmental issues raised by differences of policy over liner conferences and over participation of national-flag interests in trades raise broad questions of comity in national shipping policy.

The LDC's and Multilateral Codes

UNCTAD was established to help improve the economic conditions of developing countries. Shipping entered into its deliberations because conference practices might be detrimental to the trade of developing countries and because of the countries' interests in participating in shipping.

UNCTAD's Committee on Shipping produced a report in 1970 which recommended mandatory consultation between conferences and shippers to ensure that shippers' interests are not ignored. A code of conduct for conferences was consistent with the recommendation of the Rochdale Committee, but a number of provisions were opposed widely by developed countries. Most contentious was a cargo reservation proposal.

The development of the UNCTAD Code is significant for three main reasons. First, it was an impetus for a multilateral approach to issues in liner shipping, especially in liner conferences. Second, it helped bring to the fore the role of shippers' associations and councils in user negotiations with conferences.[25] Third, it was an important means by which developing countries could pursue their interest in participating in international shipping activities.

The developments at UNCTAD led the CSG governments to request their shipowners develop details of a code of practice. The consequent Code of Practice for Conferences was supported by the European Shippers' Council and, subsequently, in November 1971, by the CSG governments. Because of the role played by the Committee of European and Japanese National Shipowners' Association (CENSA), the document is usually referred to as the CENSA Code. Consistent with the recommendation of the Rochdale Committee, the CENSA Code set out a framework for voluntary self government by conferences in a regime relying on unregulated negotiations with shippers. The CENSA Code was fated to be received with suspicion by developing countries.[26]

The UNCTAD Code was adopted at UNCTAD in 1974 by the overwhelming support of developing countries. Canada abstained in spite of its consistent 'support of a Code which would be of global scope.'[27] There were two reasons evident in the final statement of the Canadian delegation. First, the code 'is evidently designed to further the development of merchant marines rather than to afford protection to shippers.'[28] Second, 'the legal structure [has] been formulated in considerable haste,'[29] with the consequent uncertainties for its implementation. For the code to come into force required at least twenty-four states to become contracting parties, with at least 25 per cent of the world's general cargo and container fleet. This was achieved after the Brussels Package provided a basis for European Community members to become contracting parties. The code came into force in 1983. However, because of difficulties of interpretation of the code and the change in shipping conditions since the code was drafted, it is not fully implemented anywhere. Nothing has changed since 1985, when Sturmey wrote 'all is in disorder.'[30] One of the difficulties of working with the code is its orientation to liner conferences with no recognition of non-conference carriers. This is in spite of the general reference to liner services in the statement of objectives. Apparently, until near the end of the UNCTAD conference in 1974, there was an 'implied synonymity between conference services and liner services.[31]

Article 52 of the code requires that a review conference be convened five years after the convention comes into force. The Review Conference broke up in 1988 without even reaching agreement on voting rights.[32] This dispute still persists.

The UNCTAD Code has not provided an effective framework for governing the conduct of liner conferences. It has also not been a source of encouragement that a multigovernmental organization can be effective in dealing with shipping issues.

CANADIAN POLICY ON SHIPPING CONFERENCES TO 1987

Canadian policy on shipping conferences has its origins in the investigation by the director of investigation of the Restrictive Trade Practices Commission, as a result of the *Helga Dan* incident in 1959. The *Helga Dan* was an ice-strengthened, non-conference vessel that was able to enter the St. Lawrence during the winter, unlike conference vessels. However, shippers with loyalty contracts with the conference were denied the use of this vessel. The results of the investigation were similar to those of other studies. It was concluded that conferences have positive effects on trade, but their abuse of monopoly powers needs to be constrained. The commission concluded:

> The conferences in the Canada-UK trades have for many years provided reliable regular services for the handling of Canada's manufactures, raw materials, and products of agriculture. Although the member lines lessened competition within the meaning of the Combines Investigation Act, the public interest would not be served by excessive rate competition and instability in the liner trade...the growth of traffic will best be protected if normal commercial practices of shippers and carriers are interfered with as little as possible. Governmental regulation of rates in ocean transport would not be feasible or conducive to the welfare of the Canadian public. The bargaining strength of Canadian shippers and consignees should, however, be further developed, especially in the interests of smaller shippers, and competition should be fostered in the Canada-UK and other trades to the extent consistent with preservation of the advantages of the conference system.[33]

It was not until 1970 that the Shipping Conference Exemption Act (SCEA) was passed; it came into effect in 1971. The act exempted conference agreements from the Trade Practices Act, but it required certain features and precluded others from such agreements. SCEA followed the example of U.S. legislation – for instance, dual rate regulation was similar. However, it provided conferences with greater freedom of action. For example, closed conferences and rebates were legal but, while it required tariffs to be filed, it introduced no specific regulatory measures for them. A sunset clause was included in the act to ensure that the exemption given to conference agreements would be reviewed. However, the three-year time period was inadequate and the act was simply extended for a further five years until 1979.

A 1979 report of the research branch of the Canadian Transport Commission gave a valuable insight into Canadian regulatory policy. Fifty conferences had agreements on file as of December 1977.[34] However, apart from filed information, very little data on the functioning of shipping markets were available. 'In the final analysis, all the documents revealed very little about the general framework or the workings of shipping conferences.'[35] It is evident that the industry had functioned with a filing requirement but with virtually no other government intervention. A study for the Department of Consumer and Corporate Affairs was more critical of conference practices under SCEA.[36] The authors recommended subjecting conferences to more competition but accepted that conferences could not be made subject to the full force of the Combines Investigation Act 'because of the international nature of the industry.'[37] The organization of a powerful shippers' council was suggested 'as a feasible alternative to the dismantling of conferences.'[38]

The Canadian Shippers' Council had been formed in 1966, with the encouragement of the government. However, SCEA did not require consultation of conferences with the shippers. Examination of the Australian experience in dealing with conferences as a potential model for Canada was not undertaken until 1977.[39]

A revision to SCEA in 1979 held that conferences were required to hold meetings, when requested, with a designated shipper group and provide information sufficient for the satisfactory conduct of the meeting. It was hoped that the increased recognition of the CSC would result in the more satisfactory negotiation of issues of general concern to shippers. In particular, bunker and currency adjustment factors had come to the fore as issues since 1973.[40] Unfortunately, they have remained controversial.

The legislation of 1979 contained a five-year period sunset clause. By the time revision to the act was necessary, shippers and government attitudes were undergoing substantial change. SCEA was extended annually from 1984 until 1987.

There were three main influences leading to change. First, there had been a general shift away from government intervention to reliance on market competition. This is reflected in transport in the 1985 policy paper Freedom to Move.[41] Second, deregulation in the u.s. provided an example of change for Canada and also had direct effects because of the integrated nature of shipping services, especially on the North American West Coast, and the competitive relationship of services on the u.s. and Canadian East Coast. Third, the evaluation of liner services was ushering in new competitive alternatives. Freedom to Move states that 'the Government recognizes that it is not feasible to eliminate the conference system. Rather, it is necessary to find the best means of regulating conference operations so as to produce the greatest benefit for shippers...Recent American legislative reform has substantially updated its approach to shipping conferences. The government proposes to establish a more flexible system in Canada.'[42] The primary purpose of new legislation was to ensure that shippers would have 'greater freedom of action with respect to shipping conferences.'[43]

EXPERIENCE WITH THE SHIPPING CONFERENCE
EXEMPTION ACT OF 1987

The revised scea, which came into effect on 17 December 1987, continues to prescribe some conference actions and preclude others. Measures to facilitate the working of competitive forces go beyond those in the u.s. Shipping Act of 1984.

scea addresses a major complaint of shippers. Loyalty contracts continue to be permitted, but they may no longer require a shipper to commit 100 per cent of the traffic. This requirement, and the removal of anti-trust exemption from loyalty contract in the u.s., has resulted in their elimination from North American trades.[44]

Confidential service contracts are allowed but under conditions established by a conference. Only conference contracts are allowed; they may not be established by individual lines. The essential terms of contracts are filed with the nta but remain confidential. In contrast, in the u.s., the essential terms of service contracts are published. Service contracts enable shippers and conferences to negotiate rates and service terms specific to the commodity movement involved and to shippers' and carriers' forecasts of route conditions. The 'service conditions' most frequently included, as revealed by u.s. filings, deal with traffic volumes, not the variety of performance requirements of carriers and shippers found in domestic transport contracts. The contracts should enable more efficient and stable transportation services and rates.

A common feature of u.s. and Canadian law is the requirement that conferences allow their members to take independent actions (IA) on rates after ten days' notice in the u.s. and after fifteen days' notice in Canada. Conferences opposed mandatory IA action, although some conferences had previously introduced it voluntarily. In both countries, IA's are filed with the FMC and NTA, respectively.

In assessing the effects of SCEA, it is useful to compare the Canadian experience with that in the u.s.[45] It is necessary, therefore, to draw attention to further features of SCEA that differ from the regulation in the u.s. First, as in the past, no requirements are imposed on non-conference carriers in Canada; in the u.s., all carriers have had to file their rates since 1961. Canada excludes rate filing by non-conference lines in order to enhance competition; the u.s. requires the filing of rates by all carriers in order to ensure the 'fair treatment' of the shippers and to prevent predatory pricing. Second, SCEA makes rebates illegal on loyalty contracts(which are now unused) but not on tariff rates. Rebating is illegal in the u.s. Allegations of rebating and rates different than filed (less than) have resulted in substantial settlements being paid by shippers and carriers.[46] Third, in Canada, conference agreements and agreements between conferences are exempt from the Competition Act; agreements between conferences and non-conference carriers are not exempt. In the u.s., however, all forms of agreement fall under the Shipping Act and, therefore, may be exempt. Finally, the u.s. attempts to police and enforce its regulations vigorously. Canada does not police the requirements of SCEA; it is presumed that shippers are served and the law upheld as long as no complaints are filed.

These differences are significant and give rise to interesting contrasts between the u.s. and Canadian experience. Service contracts are numerous in the u.s. (459 in 1984, 5,069 in 1988),[47] although their terms and conditions gave rise to commercial and regulatory issues.[48] In Canada, six service contracts were filed during 1988; five were filed in 1989.[49] In comparing these numbers, it is important to note that all carriers' service contracts are filed in the u.s. In Canada, rate agreements between shippers and independent carriers are not filed. In 1984, of 459 filings in the u.s., 93 per cent were filed by independent lines. This changed to 60 per cent in 1987 and 67 per cent in 1988, when the number filed was 5,069.[50]

The number of IA's varies greatly among the trade routes in the u.s. and Canada. Out of a total of 102,363 IA's in the u.s. over the years 1984 to 1988 inclusive, 68 per cent were by members of the Transpacific Westbound Rate Agreement (TWRA) and twenty-eight per cent were by members of the Asia North American Eastbound Rate Agreement (ANERA), which excludes Japan.[51] In Canada, IA was taken by lines in only seven conferences in both 1988 and 1989.[52] Competitive conditions in the Pacific and the effect of U.S. legislation gave rise to 2,258 and 1,064 IA's by members of the TWRA in 1987 and 1988, respectively. Conditions between Japan and Canada led the Japan-West Canada and Japan-East Canada conferences to leave all rates open since mid-1988, although 'minimum revenue requirements' were filed in late 1989.

The actions of conferences have been influenced by the presence of much competition from non-conference liner services. Data on Canadian trade routes with the UK/Continent, Pacific Rim, and Australasia show that although the number of non-conference lines has declined since 1987, their presence is still significant. The number of conference to non-conference lines in the fall of 1989 stood at 23 to 14 on the West Coast and 24 to 29 on the East Coast (including services with Canada through U.S. ports).[53] Conferences carried 62 per cent of the trade with Canadian east coast ports but only 27 per cent of the trade with west coast ports. (These figures do not include Canadian cargoes through U.S. ports).[54] More detailed data are available for the U.S., which reveal that in only three of five trades studied have the number of independents increased between 1984 and 1988. But their share of the traffic was generally significant. For exports, it ranged from only 3 per cent (Brazil) to 44 per cent (Australia); in the North Pacific it was 36 per cent and almost 40 per cent to North Europe.[55] Non-conference carriers have a higher percentage of import traffic, ranging from 7 to 47 per cent on the routes studied. Non-conference competition is least on low-volume routes, which are often with developing countries.

Data for the U.S. reveal that non-conference lines carried lower value commodities than did their conference competitors. Only on the inbound and outbound route with Italy and the inbound route from Australia did the value of commodities carried by non-conference lines exceed that of the value carried by conference carriers. There is no consistent trend for non-conference carriers gaining market share in the higher value commodities.

Conclusions on the effects of the shipping legislation are the same in Canada as in the U.S. The Annual Review, 1989 states that '"Little or no effect" was again the consensus among Canadian shippers, international freight forwarders, and shipping conferences in describing the impact of the Shipping Conference Exemption Act, 1987.'[56] FMC Section 18 Report states:

> There is little evidence to suggest that the 1984 act itself had a significant impact on rate levels. Market supply and demand relationship better explained the movement of rate levels both before and after the enactment of 1984 act. The fluctuation of rate levels in the liner industry were

amplified by the rapidly changing trade flows and exchange rates. Inbound and outbound rate levels moved in opposite directions since 1983, reflecting trade imbalances. The market power of carriers and shippers have shifted back and forth over the years, but the cause of the shifts is to be found in market forces, not in the regulatory changes introduced by the 1984 Act.[57]

Although rate levels may be explained by demand and supply conditions, complaints are likely to be made by shippers when collective decisions are made to increase rates. For example, the contrast in competitive conditions and pricing westbound and eastbound on the Pacific is being linked by shippers to a 'customer-be-damned' attitude on the part of the TWRA.[58] This is in spite of a high frequency of independent action. The Canadian Shippers' Council has also been dissatisfied with the information provided by conferences to justify rate increases.

Formal evidence indicates the importance of competitive conditions in shipping markets. Informal evidence obtained by discussions with a number of carriers and shippers supports the view that SCEA is seen as 'pretty well irrelevant' in day-to-day operations. How much effect the act has on the structure of the liner industry is less clear. Market forces are more effective in Canada because of the lack of rate filing by independents and the lack of policing of rates charged. Consequently, in the trans-Atlantic and trans-Pacific trades shippers are able to get negotiated rate levels and arrangements without resorting to service contracts. Often, various 'off-tariff' arrangements may be made.

Pricing flexibility has been accomplished in various ways. First, some conferences have declared more rates open than was previously the case. The extreme examples are the conferences with Japan, which have declared all rates open. (However, it might be pointed out that the actual level of competition may be lessened by the dominance of Japanese lines in these conferences.) Second, independent actions have been taken aggressively but primarily in Pacific trade. Third, various practices may be used which result in 'off-book, rates' being charged, that is, rates other than those filed in Ottawa: 'commercial/ volume contracts' may be concluded which are not filed as 'service contracts'; subsidiary lines which are non-conference and have a slot charter arrangement may be used to solicit traffic at off-book rates; the payment of freight may be arranged to take place in other countries, with bank clearance possible in yet another country. Fourth, while tariff rates may be charged, services provided may extend beyond those laid down in the tariff. Finally, rebates may be provided which are only illegal under SCEA in loyalty contracts.

However, while there is a substantial amount of actual competition in liner trades, this is not to deny the continuation of frustration by some shippers and the Canadian Shippers' Council with certain conference practices.

ISSUES AND OPTIONS FOR CANADIAN POLICY ON
SHIPPING CONFERENCES

Canadian legislation dealing with liner conferences has been modified over time. In 1970, a limited level of regulation was imposed on a previously laissez-faire regime. In 1979, limited support was provided to facilitate the influence of the Canadian Shippers' Council as a countervailing influence. In 1987, a policy shift to encourage more competitive forces was introduced. In 1992, SCEA will be subject to review. What may be the major issues?

Are Conferences Still Needed?

Conferences have been widely accepted as necessary to provide the rate and service stability needed for trade in general cargo. However, the validity of this argument today is open to new and heightened doubts.

Robust theoretical rationales for conferences are notable by their absence. Various arguments have been used to explain the propensity of the industry to destructive competition. First, the interest of owners to fill ships on berth even at very low rates has been used to explain rate instability. At one time, occasional general cargo ships arriving on berth may have been one reason for such pricing affecting scheduled services. Today, however, the need of shippers for specialized ships and reliable service to meet logistics schedules makes use of occasional vessels much less attractive. Second, it has been argued that the ease of entry into liner markets, subject as they are to growth in trade and to vessel technology offering economies of scale, can produce excessive capacity and waste.[59] Thus, the contestable nature of liner markets could be the source of inefficiency, requiring the intervention provided by conferences.[60] However, this argument, also, seems less tenable today than in the past.

In recent years, the shipping business has become much more like other businesses – it has matured. Ship size has increased to the stage that companies select the ship size which fits a particular service and market strategy. Ships are becoming a part of larger transportation systems in which their costs may be only one quarter of the system costs. These conditions may no longer be consistent with failure in a contestable market. This does not preclude the periodic development of surplus capacity. But it is not clear that the problem is any different in shipping than in the chemical industry, in the pulp and paper industry, or in other industries.

Theory may provide an underpinning for policy, but the actual working of markets and the attitude of participants are important. Changes have taken place recently in the views of shippers. For the first time, a significant number of shippers are opposed to the continuation of conferences. This is true in Canada and the U.S.[61] In Europe, attitudes have also changed. In 1987, the British Shippers' Council indicated, 'it is certainly true to say that the UK shippers' historical acceptance of and support for the conference system is gradually being replaced by a more market-oriented philosophy.'[62] The German Shippers' Council stated: 'In recent years, the shippers' attitude towards conferences has changed. They have taken an increasingly skeptical view of conferences as they have grown accustomed to competition in liner shipping markets.'[63] In the absence of various forms of protection for national-flag lines, even some conference lines might support the demise of the system.[64]

There are many reasons for these changes. First, the improved services of conference and non-conference lines and the working of more competitive practices in many liner trades have raised expectations that competition can work in liner markets as in other previously regulated markets. Second, shippers have become frustrated over the failure of collective processes to resolve to their satisfaction general issues, such as general rate increases, bunker adjustment factors, and currency adjustment factors. Shippers with limited ability to take their business elsewhere do the next best thing – they 'shout!'[65] Third, shippers have become anxious about the development of super-conferences and the agreements of conference and non-conference carriers to reduce capacity.

Measures to eliminate conferences require careful consideration. In a free market environment, it is to be expected that some consolidation of lines would take place. The amount of consolidation has not been studied, but it would not lead to monopolies. The status and effects of slot-charters (pooling by sharing capacity among lines) have not been examined. Rates would no longer be filed and greater reliance would be placed on confidential contracts. Freight forwarders might well play a more prominent role in cargo consolidation to achieve volume rates. However, consideration of the full range of consequences is beyond this chapter. Canadian shippers have not really debated elimination of conferences as a practical possibility, therefore, no definitive answer can be given to the question raised. However, the case for conferences is less robust now than previously. It is the most serious policy question in liner shipping and needs to be addressed.

Section 266 of the National Transportation Act requires that a thorough review of the effects of SCEA be conducted in 1992, including the need to terminate exemption of shipping from the Competition Act. However, some urgency exists for the development of a Canadian position because of the expected review of the UNCTAD Code and the ongoing review of shipping policy in the U.S.

International Comity

International comity has been of considerable importance to Canadian policy on liner conferences. Liner conferences carry our trade to foreign countries, and vessels fly the flags of other countries. Organizations of which Canada is a member, such as UNCTAD and the OECD, are actively involved in discussions about public policy on conferences. Therefore, Canadian action on conferences affects the interests of many countries.

In the past, international support for the conference system has been widespread and has led to the view in Canada that conferences are unavoidable and that Canadian policy should make the most of this system for Canadian trade. Is this position still necessary or appropriate? If Canada were to make shipping subject to the Competition Act, while the policy in other countries remained unchanged, what would be the likely political and commercial consequences?

The political costs of independent action would likely be high, as Canada would be acting against the preference of other countries for a multilateral approach as well as against their policies on conferences. Also, the issues surrounding the elimination of conferences go beyond the efficiency of liner services. For many countries, the regulation of conferences is a mechanism to protect or foster national-flag shipping. Further, some lines receive direct or indirect subsidies, for example, by the carriage of government cargoes, which would distort the results of more competitive markets. The result might be unacceptable in many countries. The elimination of conferences would also threaten the view held in the U.S. that common-carrier attributes of liner services be maintained by regulation. The U.S., which allows confidential contracts in rail service with the associated actual differences in rates, is actively requiring adherence to published ocean rates in the interests of 'fairness.'[66]

The commercial consequences of eliminating conferences would not likely be great for Canada. Particular practices of lines in Canadian trade would change but the structure of services would remain the same. This is because of the minor role of Canadian trade and the current presence of non-conference carriers. On the West Coast, the number of lines and capacity provided is determined by U.S. trade and policies. On the East Coast, the liner services into the St. Lawrence are separate from those with the U.S. East Coast. Nevertheless, the economics of the Canadian services is dependent mainly on the demand and supply of ships in trans-Atlantic trades generally. Also, services on U.S. bills of lading would continue to be governed by U.S. law. It is not likely that shipping lines would withdraw services from Canada. The merit of services depends on the logistics of trade requirements and the consequent commercial viability of services.

A widening of the policy differential between Canada and the U.S. might lead to renewed lobbying by U.S. east coast ports against cargo routed through Canada, especially if, as expected, services would be more, not less, attractive to shippers. The outcome of such lobbying is uncertain, even though the Canadian routing would serve the interests of U.S. shippers.

Change in liner practices in Canadian trades alone are not likely to result in major changes in service levels and rates. On the other hand, international political response would be focused on Canada. Unilateral change in disallowing conferences is possible but its economic effects would be limited and its political costs high.

Strategies for Change

For Canada to pursue the objective of bringing the conference system to an end would be a long process, notwithstanding widespread shifts in policy perspectives. If Canada seeks changes, it should pursue short-term strategies which may bring benefits to Canadian trade, without high costs in international relations. There are two such initiatives.

First, exemption from the Competition Act should not be given to agreements between conference and non-conference lines. The legality of such agreements is being challenged in Canada by the Canadian Shippers' Council and in Europe by the European Shippers' Council.

Second, the policy of requiring conferences to allow independent action on service contracts deserves further consideration. The requirement was dropped from the 1987 SCEA because of international opposition. It provides a mechanism for facilitating the working of competition among shipping lines while maintaining the freedom of lines to meet and discuss service and rate arrangements. The provision could coexist in Canadian trade with different arrangements for service contracts in U.S. trades.

To allow independent action on service contracts does not mean that there would be a rush to service contracts in Canadian trade. But it would allow an extension to liner shipping of the practice common in other modes. Shippers could contract with individual carriers in order to achieve cost and service arrangement fitted to their particular situations. This would be consistent with patterns in logistics management generally, and with the development of reliable and integrated transportation services in seaborne trade.

The strategic implication is for Canada to work now to refine its policies on liner conferences. Liner policy is not a matter to be activated as needed to meet a domestic legislative timetable. Canadian shippers should be proactive in international forums to gain agreements on the conditions needed for the efficient development of liner shipping services. Domestic coalitions of shippers played vital roles in the development of domestic transportation policies in the 1980s. International coalitions of shippers will be necessary if change is to be achieved in pubic policy on conferences during the 1990s.

In the past, Canada has borrowed from the policies of other countries in responding to conditions in liner shipping markets. However, the legislation of 1987 contained some innovative features, such as confidential service contracts for conferences. The opportunity exists for Canada to play a stronger proactive role in the development of the international regime of liner shipping policy. First, a clear policy position must be articulated. Then it can be carried to multilateral bodies such as the OECD Maritime Transport Committee.

Unencumbered by protective shipping policies, Canada can address itself fully to the regime most appropriate to the development of viable and efficient shipping services needed to meet the needs of trade. The growth of world trade in high-valued commodities requires the most efficient and responsive services and provides enhanced opportunities for the development of efficient liner firms.

Canada and the Movement towards Liberalization of the International Telecommunications Regime

Steven Globerman, Hudson N. Janisch, Richard J. Schultz, and W.T. Stanbury

INTRODUCTION

There are two major inter-related imperatives in international telecommunications that are exerting a dominant influence on the policy environment, including the established international telecommunications regime. The first is the growing importance of telecommunications in international business.[1] The second is the emergence and growth of competitive threats to the established regime, which, arguably, are radically changing perceptions about both the utility and feasibility of perpetuating the regime.

The growing importance of telecommunications in international business is a function of several distinct developments:

- An increasing share of international trade is being carried out by multinational companies. The configuration and capabilities of their telecommunications facilities are seen as being important factors influencing their firm-specific competitive advantages.[2]
- With the continued growth of the service sector, and with recent trade liberalization negotiations beginning to encompass service industries,[3] telecommunications is emerging as an increasingly important potential determinant of a country's international competitiveness. This is because service industries are much more intensive users of telecommunications than are primary and secondary industries.[4]
- With increased international competition has come an increased emphasis on decentralization of decisionmaking along with just-in-time production and distribution techniques. These management practices introduce a premium on rapid and accurate information

flows within the multi-branch company and enhance the demand for economical, state-of-the-art telecommunications services.

The increased threats to the established international telecommunications regime come from both outside and inside the established institutions.[5] The established regime can be seen as one which organizes international trade in telecommunications services by regulatory fiat and by cartel-like agreements among national carriers. This regime will later be described in detail. At the other end is a regime organized by the market system in which competitive forces set prices and other conditions of trade in telecommunications services. It will be argued that Canadian policymakers seem to be groping for a position somewhere in between – a position that might be called 'competition without tears.' The Canadian position will be described in detail and the viability of this position will be called into question.

External threats to the established (or traditional posts, telegraph, and telephone (PTT)) regime include the following:

- Technological changes which are reducing costs of competitive entry into the international telecommunications market.
- The growth of telecommunications expertise within large corporations giving them the ability to provision and operate their own private networks.
- The increasingly distance insensitive nature of telecommunications which makes it increasingly economical to locate telecommunications 'production' centres, for example, teleports at greater and greater distances from end users, thus enhancing the potential for direct international competition between telecommunications carriers.
- The development of Common Channel Signalling Systems (CCSS), which make it possible for network operators in one country to control and operate transmission facilities in another country.

Internal threats to the PTT regime relate to actions taken by existing PTT's, as well as other telecommunication carriers, to undercut the 'cartel' prices. Examples include:[6]

- Emergence of private satellite network carriers, for example, PanAm Sat and private cables; these rivals have lower costs and excess capacity.
- Emergence and growth of resellers who can provide small users of services with private line-type services of the global network providers.

- Development of major nodes or hubs on international networks through which international traffic passes. Individual countries, such as Singapore and the UK, by setting up as low cost hubs, threaten to undermine the price setting (and implicit market-sharing) arrangements of the existing regime.
- Policy developments in the United States, and, to a lesser extent, in the United Kingdom and Japan, promoting the adoption of competitive domestic telecommunications regimes.[7] The United States, specifically, is exerting pressure on other countries to implement 'market' regimes.
- More aggressive volume discount pricing by established and major international carriers such as AT&T.

In short, there are grounds for arguing that the potential scope for direct and indirect trade in telecommunications services is expanding, and, indeed, that large business users are increasingly looking for a 'seamless' telecommunications network that is transparent across national boundaries. The existing PTT regime for providing international telecommunications is being threatened by evolutionary technological and economic forces, which favour a market-based regime relying on competition among carriers. Canadian policymakers currently seem unable or unwilling to commit to the new market-based regime. At the same time, they are taking hesitant steps away from the old regime. This chapter discusses the Canadian government's policies to perpetuate the segmentation of Canada's telecommunications industry from international market forces while taking modest steps to allow some degree of competition and suggests the wisdom and inevitability of embracing the new competitive regime.

The structure of this chapter is as follows. First, we briefly describe the companies and institutions which comprise the major players in Canada's international telecommunications regime. We then look at a few of the important changes in technology that are affecting international telecommunications and examine the economics of telecommunications regimes with particular reference to the move towards making telecommunications a part of the international trade in services. Canada's international telecommunications activities are divided into two components. The next section places Canada in the context of international telecommunications regimes. It describes the transborder regime, that is, traffic between Canada and the U.S. and examines the threat of by-pass in international telecommunications. The direct impact on telecommunications of the Canada-U.S. Free Trade Agreement is also discussed. However, the main focus is the traditional international telecommunications regime centred around the International Telecommunications Union. We then focus on the growing importance of telecommunications in terms of trade in services under GATT. Finally, we outline some conclusions and suggestions for Canadian policymakers.

DRAMATIS PERSONAE IN CANADA

By way of background, this section outlines the current telecommunications regime in Canada. At the outset, it should be noted that Canada has a relatively open border for telecommunications services in that international telephone calls can be readily made and received by Canadians through various interconnecting agreements (described below) between Canadian-based carriers and foreign carriers. However, the ability of Canadian subscribers to select how their international telecommunications services will be 'produced,' or, for that matter, how their domestic long distance and local network services will be produced, is severely circumscribed by government and regulatory policies.[8] The forces described in the Introduction, including international bypass and pressure by the U.S. government and U.S. telcos to reduce restrictions on competition in the domestic market are creating pressures to change Canadian policies and regulations governing telecommunications. Nevertheless, the existing policy/regulatory framework constrains the behaviour of participants at the margin.[9] An appreciation of the relevant limitations can be gleaned from a brief overview of Canada's telecommunications industry.

For those unfamiliar with Canada's domestic (and international) telecommunications arrangements – and at the obvious risk of oversimplification – we outline the essential characteristics:

- Each carrier has a monopoly on the supply of local services and public voice long distance service in its territory (usually a single province, but Bell Canada covers most of Ontario and Quebec) and is subject to one regulator.
- Prior to a Supreme Court of Canada decision in August 1989, the geographic scope of federal jurisdiction was limited to telecommunications carriers in BC and most of Ontario and Quebec – notably Bell Canada. These areas accounted for just over 70 per cent of all lines. Now federal jurisdiction applies nationally (to all members of Telecom Canada – see below), although statutory amendments are necessary to eliminate the exemption of two of the three Prairie telcos due to their status as Crown corporations.[10]
- The telcos in Saskatchewan and Manitoba are owned by their respec-

tive provincial governments. Teleglobe Canada, the sole carrier of overseas telecommunications prior to its privatization in 1987, was a federal Crown corporation. The federal government owns 50 per cent of the domestic satellite carrier Telesat Canada, but it announced in February 1990 that its equity will be sold to private sector interests. In September 1990, the province of Alberta sold 56 per cent of the shares of Telus Corp. (for $886 million), which is a new holding company that owns AG Tel.[11] The province has said that the rest of Telus is to be privatized within a few years.

- While the origins of federal regulation of the telecommunications industry can be traced back to 1892, when the Cabinet was given authority to regulate Bell Canada's rates, there was only nominal regulation of telephone rates prior to the 1960s. (Bell was subject to only four rate hearings prior to 1968.)
- Prior to April 1987, Teleglobe Canada's rates were not regulated by the Canadian Radio/Television Commission (CRTC).[12]
- Telecommunications rates are regulated using the rate-base/rate-of-return approach to public utility pricing.
- In general terms, the pricing of telephone services[13] has been based on the following 'principles': flat monthly rates[14] for local services (no local measured services); system-wide average pricing; route-averaged tolls for long distance service; recovery of at least 70 per cent of the fixed common costs of access from large mark ups on monopoly toll services,[15] and interprovincial rates (in relative terms) are strongly influenced by the settlements arrangements[16] established among the members of Telecom Canada (Telecom Canada has never been subject to direct regulation). These arrangements appear to be generous for the telcos across whose territory the calls transit.
- Perhaps the most important objective of federal telecommunications policy is to maintain 'universal access' to the network through 'affordable' local rates.[17] The telephone penetration rate in Canada is one of the highest in the world. (It rose from 50 per cent of households in 1947 to 98.5 per cent in 1987.)
- While competition has been permitted in a number of areas (e.g., private line voice and data transmission – including resale and sharing terminals attached to the network, mobile (cellular) telephones, and the supply of ground equipment for satellite transmission), the members of Telecom Canada have a monopoly on the supply of public voice long distance service (i.e., MTS/WATS).[18]
- The CRTC has engaged in regulatory forbearance in a number of instances since the late 1970s.[19] However, in late 1988, the Federal Court of Appeal put an end to this exercise of discretion by the CRTC.[20]

– The federal Cabinet has authority on its own motion or upon petition to 'vary or rescind any order, decision, rule or regulation' of the CRTC. Resort to this form of 'political appeal' is not uncommon but is only successful in a modest fraction of cases.

Canada has two national telecommunications systems: Telecom Canada and Unitel Communications Inc. (formerly CNCP Telecommunications). Both these systems make use of the overseas network which is operated by Teleglobe Canada Inc.

The Federal-Provincial-Territorial Task Force on Telecommunications Policy estimates that in 1986, of the $5.2 billion in public long-distance revenues for Canadian telcos, 9.7 per cent came from Canada-U.S. traffic while 8.8 per cent came from Canada-Overseas traffic.[21] Given that some 85 per cent of Canada's international traffic is Canada-U.S., it is apparent that the average price of an overseas call is several times that of a transborder call. However, Stern states that as of November 1988 some 200 countries can be dialled directly from Canada.[22] In real terms, the average cost of a one-minute overseas telephone call decreased from $2.15 in 1987, to $1.46 in 1989 – due in part to the fact that Teleglobe came under CRTC regulation in 1987, when it was privatized. Teleglobe's rates were reduced by about 35 per cent in a weighted average basis between 1 January 1988 and 1 January 1990.[23]

Teleglobe Canada

In 1949 the federal government established the Canadian Overseas Telecommunications Corporation, pursuant to its commitments under the 1948 Commonwealth Telegraphs Agreement. The 1945 Commonwealth Telecommunications Conference recommended that there be public ownership of the providers of overseas telecommunications services. COTC took over the operations of Canadian Marconi Company and Cable and Wireless Limited. At that time CN Telegraph, as an agent for Western Union Telegraph, was the third competitor, and it diverted a considerable amount of international telegraph traffic away from Commonwealth to U.S. circuits. COTC was renamed Teleglobe Canada in 1975.

Prior to its privatization in 1987, Teleglobe did not have a legal monopoly[24] (although entrants faced a number of legal constraints) nor was it regulated by the CRTC. Teleglobe is a carrier's carrier with exclusive agreements with Telecom Canada's members, in whose local networks international (overseas) calls originate and terminate. Hence, it would appear to be protected against bypass – particularly when almost 70 per cent of its business comes from residential premises.

It was not until the early 1970s that telephone service accounted for at least one-half of Teleglobe's total revenues.[25] Telephone revenues now account for over 70 per cent of Teleglobe's net revenues. Residential traffic accounts for 75 per cent of the overseas market based on minutes and 59 per cent based on the number of calls in 1989. Between 1980 and 1982 some 19-20 per cent of Teleglobe's outward bound telephone traffic (in minutes) was generated by business. This rose to 25-27 per cent in the period 1988-9. Between 1976 and 1990 Teleglobe's both way traffic grew at an average of 19.5 per cent annually. Over the period 1990 to 1995 it is expected to grow at the compound annual rate of 17.1 per cent.

In 1988 it is estimated that Canada's outgoing international telephone traffic was 358 million minutes while the incoming traffic was 250 million minutes, for a deficit of 108 million minutes. In 1989, about 60 per cent of Teleglobe's business and residential outbound traffic originated in only three cities; about 70 per cent came from seven cities in Canada. One-half of Teleglobe's both way telephone traffic in 1988 was accounted for by six countries. In order of size, they were the UK, West Germany, France, Hong Kong, Italy, and Australia.

Between 1984 and 1987 Teleglobe's average telephone revenue for outward calls was $2.16 per minute. However, it dropped to $1.74 in 1988, $1.54 in 1989, and $1.43 in 1990. The average revenue for inward calls was lower: $0.97 in 1984, rising to $1.17 in 1987, then falling to $0.97 in 1989 and $0.85 in 1990. In December 1991, the CRTC ordered Teleglobe to reduce its rates an average of 6.9 per cent and reduced its allowed rate of return to 13.75 per cent from 14.5 per cent.

Overseas calling rates are grouped into only three very broad categories, are 'postalized,' and are composite (i.e., they do not reflect the relative cost of satellite or cable transmission). Teleglobe makes use of the facilities of two satellite consortia: Intelsat for fixed telecommunications services and Inmarsat (established in 1979) for marine mobile services. Intelsat, created through American initiatives (through the instrument of Comsat), carries two-thirds of the world's overseas telecommunications traffic. Teleglobe has one seat on Intelsat's Board of Governors.

Teleglobe was privatized in March 1987, when Memotec Inc. paid $488 million for all of the shares of the Crown corporation. Two months later BCE Inc., parent of Bell Canada, Canada's largest telco, which operates in Quebec and Ontario, acquired almost one-third of Memotec's shares. It has been argued that BCE has de facto control of Memotec, but BCE denies it, as do DOC officials.[26] When Teleglobe was privatized, it was given a legal monopoly for at least five years, and it was placed under the regulatory aegis of the CRTC.[27]

Teleglobe has a 200-country cable and satellite network that provides data, telephone, telex, and fax services. In October 1989 it joined a 37-member international consortium, laying a $459 million fibre-optic cable linking Canada and the U.S. to Japan (paying $51 million for a 11.7 per cent stake). The 9,800 km cable (TPC-4) will carry 75,000 simultaneous telephone conversations.[28] In 1989 Teleglobe handled almost 400 million minutes of outbound overseas calls and 250 million minutes of inbound calls. The difference represents a deficit of $100-$120 million.[29]

In mid-1989Teleglobe signed a ten-year agreement with three international partners to develop and set up the world's first global aeronautical satellite telecommunications system by 1991.[30]

Telecom Canada

It should be noted that Canada-U.S. calling, which makes up some 85 per cent of all international calls involving Canadian subscribers, is provided by Telecom Canada members. Overseas calls handled by Teleglobe account for only 3 per cent of Telecom Canada members' total revenues.[31] However, they account for about 15 per cent of Bell Canada's originated MTS/WATS revenues, 13 per cent of BC Tel's, and 2.5 per cent to 3.5 per cent of the Atlantic telcos'. Bell Canada claimed, in 1990, that contribution payments accounted for 43 cents of the total 51 cents per minute weighted average settlement rate.[32] Telecom Canada is an association of the largest telephone companies operating in each province,[33] and Telesat Canada[34] is the domestic satellite carrier. It should be noted that while Telecom Canada's member companies are regulated by the CRTC, Telecom Canada is itself unregulated.

> Telecom Canada [is] itself a body of questionable legal pedigree. Telecom Canada has no corporate existence in and of itself and is, essentially, an ongoing agreement to exchange traffic. Unlike AT&T Long Lines in the U.S., which has historically provided interstate long distance service on its own facilities, Telecom Canada has emerged as a unique means of exchanging traffic between separate companies without the existence of a distinct long distance carrier. The Telecom Canada Connecting Agreement provides for terms of interconnection between non-adjacent member companies (leaving arrangements between adjacent companies to be resolved on the basis of bilateral negotiations), a revenue sharing plan, and a commitment to cooperate in the development and implementation of uniform standards and operating procedures, the adoption of new technologies, and in the marketing of new services. It also provides for coordination with U.S. carriers to facilitate the handling of North American traffic and with Teleglobe for the exchange of overseas traffic.
>
> The precise legal status of Telecom Canada is somewhat unclear. This

stems from the fact that Telecom Canada remains an unincorporated enterprise, perhaps best described as a voluntary association of independent telecommunications carriers bound by a common purpose as defined in a set of multilateral agreements. (From an economic perspective, of course, this form of organization exhibits many of the classic traits of a cartel.)

Telecom Canada itself owns neither plant nor equipment, nor does it engage in service provisioning of any kind. Its function is to plan, administer and coordinate, not to operate. Telecom Canada's headquarters are located in Ottawa, with all personnel and premises on loan from member companies. Administrative costs and services are shared among members, as are profits, in accordance with the revenue sharing plan.[35]

The primary service offered by the telecommunications industry is the transmission of voice messages. Voice telephony is provided by public switched telephone services and leased circuits or private lines. The bulk of long-distance voice telephony is provided by the public switched network operated as a monopoly service by Telecom Canada members. Leased circuits and private lines are supplied by both Telecom Canada and Unitel as well as by BC Rail. While data traffic is also carried on the public switched network, the bulk of such telephony is carried on leased circuits and private lines.

For all practical purposes, telecommunications traffic within Canada is carried on facilities owned by either the members of Telecom Canada or Unitel, with over 90 per cent of the traffic being carried on Telecom Canada member facilities. As noted earlier, traffic crossing the Canada-U.S. border is carried to and from the border on the facilities of the two major networks. Overseas calls are carried to or from Teleglobe's facilities at its gateway switches in Vancouver, Toronto, and Montreal. Overseas interconnections involving Teleglobe are governed by other agreements described below.

What is relevant to underscore at this point is that Canadian subscribers using the public network for long distance, including international calling, must use the facilities of Telecom Canada members.[36] Subscribers using leased circuits or private lines have a limited choice among so-called Type I carriers – essentially Telecom Canada and Unitel. Overseas calls must be routed through the gateway facilities of Teleglobe. In essence, facilities-based competition within Canada is restricted to a duopoly in private line services. Moreover, the facilities-based carriers must be at least 80 per cent Canadian-owned,[37] although British Columbia Telephone Company, whose ultimate controlling shareholder is GTE Inc., has a 'grandfather' exemption for its existing facilities.[38]

Issues Awaiting Resolution

In May 1990 Unitel Communications, formerly CNCP Telecommunications, reapplied for permission to provide facilities-based long distance public service.[39] One of its arguments is that the federal regulator, the CRTC, did not reject competition in principle in 1985 but only the particular application before it on the grounds that it had not adequately addressed the issue of support for local service.[40] Indeed, the CRTC itself acknowledged that the following potential benefits could flow from competition in long distance: lower rates, increased productivity, improved customer choice and supplier responsiveness, increased flexibility with respect to pricing and marketing, and better diffusion of new technology.[41]

The established carriers will continue to insist that competition not be allowed in until rates are rebalanced, that is, brought into line with costs. It is argued that without such rebalancing there could only be artificial or contrived competition, and that the regulator would have to allocate market shares by manipulating access costs and levels of contribution. While this argument has much to commend it in principle, it is not at all clear how rate rebalancing can be accomplished in practice. For all intents and purposes, it is impossible for the regulator to increase local rates at a time when telephone companies are obtaining very high earnings without offering the benefits of competitive choice in return. Pressure is rapidly mounting to break this stalemate, in which neither competition nor rate rebalancing can proceed.[42] The CTRC's decision is expected in March 1992.

The larger telephone carriers are acutely aware that as long as there is no rate rebalancing there always will be entrepreneurs who will take advantage of the 'cream' created by long distance rates being so out of line with costs.[43] Their pleas for rate rebalancing demonstrate their lack of confidence in the ability of the regulator to indefinitely hold off cream-skimming new entrants. Only the smaller telephone companies and consumer groups favour the status quo – yet they are the most likely to end up captive of the telcos if the big users are able to leave the public network (engage in bypass).

TECHNOLOGICAL CHANGE IN TELECOMMUNICATIONS

In order to appreciate more fully the discussion of welfare economics, it is useful to highlight the significant technological changes that are affecting the telecommunications industry. As a summary statement, the telecommunications industry over the past decade has been characterized by a relatively rapid rate of technological change, at least in comparison to its earlier history.

While a comprehensive discussion of the relevant changes is beyond the scope of this chapter, several developments need to be highlighted. One is the increasing 'sophistication' of telephone networks associated with the replacement of electro-mechanical network equipment by software-controlled (digital) network equipment. A result is that an increasing variety of services can be offered by suppliers of telecommunications services. Examples include voice mailbox, least cost routing and billing algorithms, message storing and forwarding, data bases, and data networks. Another result is that network capacity can be utilized more intensively by replacing analogue signals with digital signals. The latter take up less 'bandwidth' in transmission facilities and are also capable of being sequenced in 'real time,' that is, multiplexed, so that signals representing different 'conversations' can be processed simultaneously within the same transmission facility. A third is that it is increasingly feasible for networks to be linked and controlled from a centralized location, given commonality of computer standards and protocol. An implication of the latter development is that the 'management' of telephone networks in different countries is increasingly capable of being centralized in a given location.

A second development of note is the emergence of broadband transmission facilities, most notably fibre optic cable, which have the capacity to transmit a much greater 'volume' of information per dollar of investment than does conventional copper wire or coaxial cable.[44] Fibre optics also have other desirable properties, including less signal attenuation and slower rates of physical depreciation. An implication of the implementation of broadband transmission capacity is that an investment of a given dollar amount will contribute to a much greater expansion in potential network capacity than was true with older vintages of technology. Furthermore, services which require large capacity transmission 'pipelines,' for example, videotelephony, are increasingly capable of being economically offered on a widespread basis. One implication of the emergence of fibre optics is that facilities-based entry into the telecommunications industry can take place on a much more significant scale (for a given real expenditure of money) than was true in the past. Another is that competitive entry will be facilitated if entrants can identify and offer broadband services that incumbent carriers are not offering.

A third important development is the emergence and implementation of 'wireless' telecommunications, including miniature aperture satellite, cellular telephony, and personal communications networks. The emergence and development of wireless technology is largely an outgrowth of the conversion of telephone networks from analogue to digital signalling, along with the spectacular growth in the capacity of semiconductor chips, which has allowed both subscriber equipment (e.g., telephone handsets) and network equipment (e.g., satellite earth stations) to grow smaller and more technologically sophisticated as well as cheaper in real, that is, quality adjusted, terms. An important consequence of this development is that an increasing proportion of telecommunications traffic is capable of being carried on alternative (to conventional terrestrial) networks. Indeed, one future vision of the industry sees each individual subscriber having a personal identification number which can be addressed wherever he or she is located. Hence, the subscriber would only need a portable telephone to be reachable on the same telephone number regardless of his or her location. To be sure, limitations on spectrum availability are realistic constraints on how much wireless telecommunications traffic can be carried; however, remarkable improvements have recently occurred in spectrum usage, and further improvements are contemplated.[45]

Several other broad potential implications of the developments cited above might be briefly mentioned, as they are relevant to the economic issues raised in the next section. One is associated with an argument that the changes cited above make it increasingly uneconomical to have multiple suppliers of facilities as opposed to services. Specifically, the technological changes outlined above ostensibly encourage increases in the minimum efficient-sized public telephone network, all other things being constant. A possible inference is that competition in the provision of physical facilities may be increasingly 'wasteful.'

Another implication is that competition in the provision of physical capacity may be increasingly less important than competition in the provision of services, given the growing importance of value added services relative to 'basic' services. An argument might be made that to the extent that network 'intelligence' is embodied in software that is separable from the hardware making up the physical network, relevant competition will increasingly take place among independent suppliers of software to the public network. In this context, it may arguably be sufficient for policymakers simply to guarantee value added suppliers fair and economical access to the physical network in order to ensure workable competition in the telecommunications industry.

The aforementioned implications suggest that preserving the domestic telecommunications network as a Canadian-owned monopoly will have relatively benign consequences for subscribers as long as competition is encouraged in the provision of services carried on the physical network. We will consider this suggestion below in evaluating the economic consequences of segmenting markets for telecommunications services.

ECONOMICS OF TELECOMMUNICATIONS REGIMES

Restrictions on domestic competition have been justified by the need to ensure that suppliers cross-subsidize local exchange service while remaining financial viable.[46] The potential costs of restrictions on domestic competition have been acknowledged by the CRTC. They include reduced rates of technological change in the domestic market. Restrictions on international competition are also motivated by the desire to preserve cross-subsidies; however, an additional concern is national sovereignty in respect to telecommunications systems. Little attention has been paid to identifying the inefficiencies created by restrictions on competition in international telecommunications.

In this section we consider the welfare economics consequences of 'segmented' telecommunications markets. Traditional international trade theory suggests that free trade promotes economic welfare by encouraging a more efficient allocation of resources within the free trading area. Specifically, countries specialize more completely along lines of comparative advantage. Furthermore, to the extent that there are economies of scale in specific activities that are not being fully exploited, free trade can promote the capture of these scale economies by encouraging more complete specialization. Indeed, the additional competition brought about by freer trade should encourage greater efficiencies of all sorts, including greater responsiveness to customer tastes and preferences.[47] These represent potential production efficiency gains from freer trade. More directly, consumers gain from their enhanced access to lower priced foreign goods. Against these gains must be set costs associated with reallocating resources across different sets of activities, for example, retraining workers who are displaced by foreign competition.

Conventional trade theory is applied to trade in goods where production and consumption can be separated in time and space. That is, goods can be produced in one location and consumed in another location with little to no depreciation in the physical attributes of the product. Moreover, consumption does not have to take place identically with production as, say, in the case of attending a live dance performance.

Most service industries, including telecommunications, do not precisely fit the traditional trade-in-goods model.[48] For example, the initiator of a telephone call must obviously initiate the call from where he or she is located in space, and the receiver of the communication is also fixed in a spatial location.[49] In this context, the initiator and receiver of a communication cannot literally choose to initiate or receive the call from any potential supplier located anywhere in the world. However, one should not overstate the extent to which this characteristic constrains the potential for international competition. As noted above, while Canadian-based callers must initiate their communications in Canada, they can have a significant portion of the transmission (and additional processing) of the call done outside Canada. To the extent that telecommunications costs are increasingly insensitive to distance, potential least-cost routing systems will increasingly cut across national boundaries. To this extent, one may not require any major adaptation of traditional trade theory.

Moreover, failure of national governments to make their network architectures compatible with those of other nations/regimes can be likened to the imposition of non-tariff barriers. The issue of technical compatibility will become increasingly important as new technological capabilities emerge, such as ISDN.

Technological change is rendering telecommunications costs increasingly less distance sensitive. Satellite transmission is an obvious case in point. Improvements in the technology have reduced 'echo' effects and other disadvantages of this transmission medium.[50] Fibre optics suffer less attenuation of signal loss than does conventional cable, implying a need for less repeater equipment and other distance-related expenditures. In short, a caller can increasingly justify completing a more distant geographic circuit in order to take advantage of differences in the competitive features of alternative service providers.

For the portion of any communications transmission (terrestrial or satellite) that must be carried over Canadian 'space' before it crosses the Canadian border, potential gains from trade liberalization come from the mobility of factors of production. Specifically, the gains are associated with foreign suppliers establishing in Canada to provide the 'intra-Canada' portion of service at the various nodes in the domestic telecommunications network. The magnitude of the gains in this context are associated with the potential displacement of less efficient domestic suppliers by more efficient foreign suppliers as well as the salutary effects of increased competition on 'x-inefficiency' among domestic suppliers. To this extent, the analysis of the economic impact of unrestricted rights-of-establishment in telecommunications services is analogous to the economic effects of inward foreign direct investment. The evidence here is that foreign direct investment improves economic efficiency in the host country.

In short, trade theory and empirical evidence support the existence of gains to economic integration either directly in the form of trade in goods or indirectly in the form of factor mobility. Telecommunications services are potentially tradeable over a certain spatial dimension of the market. For the 'non-tradeable' dimension, gains ostensibly exist to the extension of unrestricted rights-of-establishment. In principle, gains to closer economic integration of telecommunications regimes will be a function of: differences in factor endowments across regimes; opportunities to exploit economies of scale and scope; and overall size of the relevant market.

Differences in factor endowments should be broadly defined to include differences in technology and other attributes of national carriers in different countries. Telecommunications is a relatively capital and technology-intensive activity.[51] To the extent that prices for these factor inputs differ geographically, telecommunications services could well be cheaper to purchase in one location than another. Equivalently, specific carriers might well enjoy a competitive advantage related to greater technological virtuosity.

It is very difficult to compare costs of service across different national telephone regimes, given the variety of influences on actual costs, including differences in service mix, accounting procedures, and so forth. Even comparisons of rates of new technology adoption and new services introduction are inconclusive, since 'optimal' rates of adoption and introduction may well differ across countries. In any event, there is no persuasive evidence that any specific telecommunications regime enjoys superior technological performance on a consistent basis. Perhaps more to the point, there is no evidence that Canadian carriers are less technologically proficient than are their u.s. counterparts.[52] The evidence is also less than conclusive with respect to total factor productivity differences between Canadian and u.s. carriers. Notwithstanding the limited evidence, one would not want to conclude that all North American carriers are identical with respect to efficiency and other dimensions of performance. Indeed, one might argue that divergences in performance will become increasingly identifiable as the pace of technological change in the industry accelerates and as the market for telecommunications services becomes increasingly specialized on the demand side. In this case, closer economic integration of telecommunications regimes will have greater potential economic welfare gains.

The existence of significant economies of scale and scope suggests the potential for increasing economic efficiency by reducing the number of separately operated telecommunications entities.[53] In this context, one might argue for the organizational integration of American and Canadian telecommunications carriers. Without belabouring the point, the evidence on the magnitude of firm-level economies of scale in the industry is very inconclusive. While the telephone carriers themselves have argued that there are substantial economies associated with planning and provisioning a network,[54] the survival and growth of other common carriers in the United States and Great Britain suggests that economies of scale generally do not exhaust the size of most domestic telecommunications markets, let alone the markets for groups of countries.[55] Nevertheless, one should not conclude that organizational restructuring along north-south lines would not improve economic efficiency. Indeed, one can conjecture that strategic alliances and common ownership arrangements might facilitate the transfer of knowledge and other assets which improve the efficiency and effectiveness with which specific strategies are carried out. For example, private and virtual private networks used by energy companies might be more efficiently provisioned on a worldwide basis by an integrated group of carriers who specialize in such networks.

The more fragmented the demand side of the market for telecommunications services, the less likely it is that telephone carriage can be characterized as a natural monopoly. While there can certainly be argument surrounding the issue, many knowledgeable observers believe that the telecommunications needs of business subscribers are becoming more specialized which, in turn, suggests the potential for greater specialization in the provision of telecommunications services. In this context, small differences in expertise across carriers could be associated with relatively large differences in competitive advantage. In turn, the ability or inability of subscribers to exploit the services of specialized carriers might make a substantial difference to the competitive performances of the subscribers. It is a well known axiom in economics – one that originated with Adam Smith over 200 years ago – that specialization is limited by the size of the market. The more integrated the markets for telecommunications services, the more likely it is that telecommunications firms will find profitable opportunities to offer specialized services.

The larger the overall volume of directly and indirectly traded goods, the larger the potential gains to a liberalized trade regime, all other things constant. Consideration of the potential for international trade in telecommunications is complicated by two factors: first, there is no universally accepted definition of telecommunications trade, and, second, basic data on trade flows for different segments of the communications industry, broadly defined, are lacking. The paucity of data regarding international trade in telecommunications services makes it difficult to evaluate the current status of bilateral trade flows, let alone to assess the potential impact of freer trade on such flows. Statistics Canada data on trade in communications services suffer from two shortcomings. First, the communications data include telephone, telex, telegraph, data transmission, courier, and postal transactions, which is too broad a definition for our purposes. Second, there is no distinction made between basic and enhanced services, which, as discussed above, constitute two different markets, particularly with regard to regulatory conditions.

What can be inferred from the available data is that direct trade in international telecommunications services is (at present) both absolutely and relatively small. Total Canadian exports of communications services, broadly defined as above, equalled $238 million and $304 million, respectively, in 1983 and 1984; total imports were $194 million and $262 million, respectively. The total of exports and imports therefore represent a tiny fraction (less than 1 per cent) of the total revenues of Canada's telecommunications carriers. From these data one is tempted to conclude that an integration of the North American telecommunications regimes is likely to have a small overall effect on economic welfare; however, it should be recognized that the integration of the largely competitive U.S. sector and the largely regulated Canadian sector would likely encourage a major change in Canada's regulatory regime. Specifically, it would encourage deregulation of the Canadian industry. One major consequence would be a convergence of prices and costs. This by itself would have a significant and beneficial effect on allocative efficiency.

As noted in the preceding section, an argument might be made that the integration of international telecommunications markets, or, indeed, even the deregulation of Canada's domestic market, while maintaining existing restrictions on foreign ownership of facilities, will have relatively little impact on the industry's performance given that the physical network is increasingly characterized as natural monopoly.[56] While this argument cannot be exhaustively considered here, several objections might be raised. One is that the responsiveness of facility provisioners might be significantly improved by exposure to competition. It does not seem appropriate to assume that all suppliers of physical capacity will be equally astute in implementing new technology, especially to the extent that different customers have different network needs. Allowing customers to provision their own private networks, while reserving the public network for a single supplier, might be seen as a way of getting 'the best of both worlds.' As a practical matter, it may prove increasingly difficult to prevent private networks from providing telecommunications services to 'outsiders.' Moreover, it is unfair to reserve the benefits of competitive provisioning of facilities to those subscribers who are large enough to afford their own private networks.

Another reservation about the 'benign' monopoly argument is that the division between hardware and software is not precise. Specifically, there is often the potential to build 'intelligence' into either the hardware or the software components of the network. Restrictions on competition in the supply of hardware could unfavourably bias the technological change process in that it would favour diversity in the choice of software associated with providing value added services but would enforce uniformity in the intelligence embedded in the hardware. The concern here is that while it might be more economical in certain circumstances to offer diversity by making adaptations to the relevant hardware components of a telecommunications system, users will be driven by limited competitive alternatives to make the adaptations by utilizing alternative suppliers of software, for example, value added carriers, wherever possible.

Finally, and perhaps of greatest relevance, a monopoly supplier of the physical network would be in a position to extract all of the economic surplus created by advances made by value added carriers unless regulators ensured that a 'fair' price was charged to such carriers. At a minimum, this implies a continuation of the burdensome and potentially inefficient rate-of-return regulation that facility-based competition might obviate. If the physical network is a true natural monopoly, regulation of some sort may be inevitable. However, the potential for entry is ultimately the most robust test of whether output is being supplied at the lowest possible economic cost. The challenge for policymakers would therefore seem to be the implementation of policies that provide maximum potential scope for economical entry into all sectors of the telecommunications industry.

CANADA AND INTERNATIONAL TELECOMMUNICATIONS REGIMES

Canada is a participant in not one but two international telecommunications regimes. One is a multilateral regime created under the auspices of the International Telecommunications Union; the other is the bilateral transborder Canada-U.S. regime. The former is a far more structured, formalized regime than the latter – indeed, it is a legitimate question whether or not the latter is a regime in the conventional meaning of the term.

The purpose of this section is to describe the central components of each regime, the major functions performed by them and the strains they currently confront, and recent initiatives to relieve those strains. While it is the multilateral regime that has been the subject of intense, rather acrimonious, debates and negotiations over the past decade, it is important to note that it is the bilateral (transborder) regime which has greater economic significance for Canada, inasmuch as it governs approximately 80 per cent of Canada's international telecommunications traffic.[57] Our discussion, because of space constraints, will not address the radio spectrum management component of the international regime nor will it deal, except in passing, with issues arising from that part of the regime which governs the operation and provision of international satellite services, particularly those concerned with the International Telecommunications Satellite Organization (Intelsat).[58]

The Bilateral Transborder Regime[59]

The development of the Canada-u.s. telecommunications regime was influenced by a number of factors. Historically, the exchange of telecommunications traffic across the Canada-u.s. border was greatly facilitated by the institutional similarities in the provision of telephone service. While Canada, as noted above, never developed a single separate long distance carrier such as AT&T Long Lines, the existence of provincially-based monopolies made it relatively simple to arrange for the exchange of traffic on a company-to-company basis. Over time, a wide range of agreements was established between Canadian carriers and AT&T which allowed for revenue settlements very similar to those already established domestically. As well, Canada has adopted similar technical standards to those of the u.s., is part of the North American Numbering Plan, and the two countries have fully integrated telecommunications network infrastructures. Indeed, perhaps nowhere in the world are there two more integrated national systems – a fact of fundamental relevance to potential developments in the provisioning of telecommunications services and the consequent policy tensions to be discussed below.

In terms of the nature of the regime, the Canada-u.s. regime has until recently been premised on the same principles as has the multilateral regime discussed below. There have been some striking differences, however. Perhaps the most important is the fact that, unlike the multilateral regime which, given that it is treaty-based, is naturally governmental in nature, the Canada-u.s. regime is non-governmental. Although the Canada-u.s. Free Trade Agreement alters this somewhat, apart from several recent transborder satellite and data agreements, private not public ordering of relationships based on negotiated reciprocal advantages of exchanging traffic has predominated. In many respects, this reflects at the transborder level the role of Telecom Canada on the domestic front. It is worth noting that, since the creation of Telecom Canada, Canadian telephone companies do not have separate agreements with American carriers; agreements are between Telecom Canada and the individual American carriers. Another point of some significance is that Telecom Canada has treated Canada-u.s. revenues as part of its settlement procedures even when only one member is involved, as in a call from Toronto to New York City. This is a further indication of the extent to which the North American transborder arrangements have been treated as, essentially, constituting a domestic, rather than an international, matter.

The second major feature of the transborder regime is the fact that it is deliberately excluded from the larger international regime. In 1988, the United States adopted the following position in the Final Protocol on International Telecommunications Regulations: 'The United States of America formally declares that it does not, by signature of these Telecommunications Regulations, nor by any subsequent approval thereof...accept any obligation in respect of the application of any provision of these Regulations to service within the United States on the one hand, and Canada, Mexico, and Saint-Pierre and Miquelon Islands on the other hand, and to the rates applicable to such services.'

The virtual integration of the two national telecommunications systems is one indication of the highly successful nature of the transborder regime. In the last two decades this highly successful regime has come under growing pressure. This has grown out of the asymmetry between domestic arrangements brought on by the more rapid liberalization of telecommunications in the U.S. The essential issue which is emerging is one of reciprocity.

With the advent of competition in long distance in the U.S., Canadian carriers signed new agreements with MCI and U.S. Sprint to supplement those already entered into with AT&T. However, there have been no new Canadian competitive carriers with which Americans could link up, and this has led to a certain imbalance in cross-border relationships.[60] At the same time, lower long-haul long-distance rates in the U.S. and lower overseas international calling rates have led to entry by entrepreneurs in a manner which has, at least, greatly complicated, if not disrupted, what had been a very straightforward and simple set of transborder arrangements. In the last year the new Canadian entrants have caused concern for both Canadian and American carriers and their respective regulators. The first disruptive threat or opportunity, depending on how one looks at it, is that of transborder bypass of Telecom Canada. This could involve the deployment of computer switches just south of Vancouver and Toronto, giving access to much lower Seattle-Buffalo rates. Given the electronically porous nature of the boundary and the largely uncontrollable nature of modern technology, it would seem that Canadian carriers will find themselves under an increasing threat of bypass. Sharply increased short haul rates to the border (the response adopted so far) will be effective for only so long. We now turn to the threat of bypass in Canada's international telecommunications.

Threat of Bypass in International Telecommunications

Higher telecommunications charges for long distance voice service and broadband data services provide an incentive for intensive long-distance callers to 'substitute' the use of foreign-based facilities carriers for Canadian-based carriage.[61] Three kinds of by-pass involving U.S.-based facilities can be identified: (a) calls from Canada that terminate in the U.S.; (b) calls from Canada that terminate in Canada but pass through the U.S.; and (c) calls from Canada that terminate overseas (e.g., London, Rome, Istanbul) but which pass through the U.S.

Case (a) involves cross-border reselling. This alternative allows Canadian subscribers to access U.S.-based facilities by dialing a number in a nearby U.S. calling zone and then 'patching into' one of the discount U.S. services (e.g., MCI, U.S. Sprint). To date, any such form of resale has been strictly limited to calls terminating in the U.S., since it is illegal for any Canadian carrier to form a Canada-to-Canada circuit through the United States. Nevertheless, it is conceivable that such Canada-to-Canada connections could be made through the use of independent cross-border resellers operating in different regions of Canada. For example, a caller in Vancouver might dial the number of a telephone switch resident in a Washington border town and then dial the number of a switch located in Buffalo, New York, presumably belonging to a second Canadian reseller. Once patched into the Buffalo switch, the caller would dial a number in Toronto to complete a Canada-to-Canada connection. In effect, such combined use of cross-border resellers would be tantamount to the establishment of 'dummy nodes' that large companies might presumably operate for themselves. Obviously, this indirect way of constructing a Canada-to-Canada circuit through the United States involves inconvenience for the caller. Moreover, one would expect Canadian carriers to reconfigure their tariffs to increase short-haul costs to the U.S. border relative to long-haul interprovincial tariffs.[62]

AT&T is trying to halt certain long distance telephone services to the U.S. from Canada, a move that would reduce Unitel's (formerly CNCP's) revenue by 10 per cent.[63] AT&T petitioned the Federal Communications Commission (FCC) to force its competitors to stop selling access to the U.S. network (via MCI or U.S. Sprint) at a discount from government approved rates.[64] AT&T says the deals violate the International Settlements Policy between the U.S. and foreign phone companies. The agreement specifies that Canadians must be charged between U.S. 38 cents to 42 cents a minute for access to the U.S. network. Half of this goes to Telecom Canada. In contrast, the bulk rates AT&T proposed ranged from U.S. 8 cents to 17 cents, none of which is shared with Telecom Canada.

The discount only benefits Canadians calling the U.S. while Canada retains a monopoly at home, so it discriminates against U.S. callers.

In August 1990 AT&T amended its FCC-filed tariffs to permit it to provide its volume-discounted 'Megacom' service to Canadian users.[65] The AT&T tariff provides that Canadian-originated traffic can be carried to destinations in the U.S., back to Canada, or overseas. The other major U.S. carriers (MCI, U.S. Sprint) had provided similar services to Canadian users before AT&T changed its tariff.

AT&T's (1990) recently-lodged complaint with the FCC against Unitel Communications (formerly CNCP) opens up the whole question of the uniqueness of the Canada-U.S. transborder relationship. While it is not a particularly important proceeding in and of itself, its significance lies in that it asks the FCC to treat a Canadian issue as if it were simply part and parcel of U.S. relations with other countries.

At issue is one-way access to the U.S. domestic switched network on a non-reciprocal basis. AT&T alleges that this allows the foreign caller to pay only U.S. domestic rates plus the cost of the international private line, with the foreign carrier avoiding paying the accounting rate for the resulting conversation minutes. It is further alleged that these arrangements provide for non-uniform accounting and settlement rates to the detriment of U.S. carriers and are, therefore, violative of the International Settlements Policy (ISP) and unlawful.

As well, it is claimed that this practice further contributes to a growing imbalance in international settlement payments and allows for 'whipsawing' in that, while U.S. carriers are private and competitive, foreign carriers are generally monopolistic and governmental or quasi-governmental entities, and this gives them an advantageous bargaining position.

Most significantly, AT&T warned that a number of similar proposals to access the U.S. domestic network have been made to foreign carriers in South American, Asia, and Australia, and that, as a result, this 'new concept' in international communications with the U.S. has to be taken seriously.

It is interesting to note that the primary thrust of Unitel's response has been to insist that these concerns for settlement imbalance, undermining of the ISP, and whipsawing, while commonly employed in relation to other countries, are entirely alien to the unique transborder situation. At the same time, it should be noted that Unitel holds out the prospect of greater reciprocity and confidently predicts that its own domestic long distance aspirations will soon be approved. A basic issue in the debate is whether the FCC will maintain the uniqueness of the Canada-U.S. border regime or start down the road of 'internationalizing' the border.

Case (b) involves Canada-to-Canada traffic being carried through the United States. It arises with a network having two nodes in Canada. Double border crossings for telephone calls, that is, calls originating and terminating in Canada, are prohibited by Canadian tariffs and regulatory policies. However, private network arrangements have been designed to circumvent the border-crossing policies established by the major Canadian and u.s. carriers as part of their interconnecting agreements. However, there have been recent reports on 'Canada-Canada bypass,' which uses private lines and switches to route trans-Canada traffic via the u.s. network.[66] People familiar with the technique say a corporate telecommunications manager could rig such a system so it is invisible both to employees and the telephone companies. The practice violates agreements between u.s. telcos and Telecom Canada, but it is not illegal. As much as 20 per cent of the long-distance market is said to be threatened.

The normal arrangement between Canadian and u.s. carriers is that the border crossing, for provisioning purposes, is the one which is nearest the straight line joining the points of origination and termination of the private line. This is significant because, unlike message toll services which are billed on an end-to-end basis, private line services are billed by each carrier, Canadian and u.s., independently, and the distance to the border from the point of origination or termination is the basis for rating. Lower private line rates in the u.s. provide an incentive for users to establish 'dummy nodes' in the u.s. immediately adjacent to the established border crossing point nearest the Canadian origination point of the circuit in order to maximize the use of lower cost u.s. facilities.[67]

To date, there has been relatively little bypass of Canadian-based telecommunications facilities. We believe bypass is likely to increase, given the present regulatory regime. There are at least five forces likely to increase by-pass: recently-introduced international voice services of carriers such as AT&T which offer volume discounts; the growth of resellers which can provide smaller users with private line-type services supplied by global networks; development of major nodes or 'hubs' on international networks through which international traffic can be switched and 'transited'; emergence of private satellite network carriers, for example, Pan Am Sat and private cables, which are undercutting the Intelsat and Immarsat rates; and technological changes that are reducing costs of competitive entry into the provision of international telecommunications services.[68]

In 1988-9 some 25 per cent to 27 per cent of Teleglobe's outward telephone traffic (in minutes) was generated by business. This rather small percentage as to date mitigated the extent of bypass. The growth of international trade and investment relative to domestic business suggests to us that the relative importance of business traffic will increase – and with it the potential for bypass.

Case (c) recently surfaced when Teleglobe Canada applied to the CRTC to put an end to an underground network used by firms to bypass the public long distance network.[69] Teleglobe said several small telecommunications companies (resellers) may be leasing private lines to the U.S. points, from which they route calls to overseas locations, for example, London, Rome, Istanbul. This is the first time Teleglobe has sought to cut off overseas bypass. Teleglobe wants the CRTC to insert a clause in the telco's tariffs prohibiting such bypass. According to the president of Marathon Telecommunications Corp., a reseller, 'there's not a reseller in this room that doesn't do it. By the letter of the law, yes, it is illegal, but it is not being enforced by Bell Canada.' One reseller said that it is large multi-national companies that are the major bypassers. In September 1990 AT&T began offering global electronic message and enhanced facsimile service in Canada.[70] The move angered both the telcos and resellers. March 1991 estimates indicate that bypass via U.S. carriers accounted for about 12 per cent of outward Canada-overseas business telephone traffic in 1990 and would increase even after the introduction of the 'Globedirect' service.[71] In May 1991 Bell Canada applied to the CRTC to introduce a discount calling plan ('Advantage Overseas') for overseas calls similar to its domestic and trans-border long distance plans.[72] The plan would offer a 15 per cent discount to users spending more than $200 per month on overseas calls. A 30 per cent discount would be available to those spending over $10,000 per month on overseas calls. The plan is designed to compete against resellers routing calls through the U.S. Other telcos are expected to follow suit, although opposition to Bell's application is expected. In effect, 'Advantage Overseas' is Bell's response to 'Globedirect,' as Teleglobe and Bell seek to bypass each other.

Both actions draw attention to the relative ease with which Teleglobe can be bypassed and calls into question both the wisdom and practicability of granting a private company a monopoly in the first place. Prior to its privatization in early 1987, Teleglobe's overseas rates were an average of about 25 per cent higher than AT&T's overseas rates. Four years later, the gap was almost closed: on average, AT&T's rates were 2.8 per cent and 5.6 per cent lower for a four-minute and seven-minute call, respectively. Teleglobe's rates for outward calls were about 30 per cent lower than were foreign carriers' inward rates to Canada in early 1991.[73]

Recently, Teleglobe has sought to bypass the domestic telcos. In

November 1989 Teleglobe applied to the CRTC for lower rates based on hooking large corporate customers' networks directly into Teleglobe's facilities.[74] Bell and BC Tel immediately demanded a fee of 43 cents per minute to subsidize local service.

Direct Impact of the Canada-U.S. Free Trade Agreement

The Canada-U.S. Free Trade Agreement (FTA) represents an institutional challenge to Canada's restrictive telecommunications policies. The FTA, which came into effect 1 January 1989, will not, of itself, bring about major changes in the common carrier telecommunications industry. Indeed, it in large measure preserves the status quo. Despite some claims, the agreement does not mandate competition or 'deregulation' along the lines of developments in the United States.[75] Nevertheless, the inclusion of telecommunications as one of only three service areas specifically dealt with in the agreement, and far-reaching tariff reductions with respect to telecommunications equipment, are matters of some considerable importance.[76]

Services

Discussion here will be limited to the treatment of telecommunications services. Attention will be called to what has or has not been included, as exclusion is every bit as important as inclusion in agreements of this kind.[77] The agreement seeks to address, for the first time in any substantial way, bilateral trade in services as distinct from goods, thereby recognizing the enormous growth of the service sector in Canada-U.S. trade in recent years. Although services are not dealt with on a comprehensive basis, this limitation must be viewed in the context of the present total lack of any framework of reference under GATT for the liberalization of trade in services.

The application of the agreement to the service sector is restricted to those services specifically listed.[78] Only three services are the subject of separate Sectoral Annexes to which a more comprehensive set of rules is applied — architecture, tourism, and computer services and telecommunications network based enhanced services.[79]

Two other general provisions governing services should be noted at this point. First, it is stipulated that the agreement is only to have prospective effect (Article 1402:5). This 'grandfathers in' existing statutes, regulations, and administrative practices. Second, there is provision for 'national treatment,' although government procurement and subsidies are excluded from the agreement on services (Article 1402:9).

The agreement is concerned not with telecommunications in general but only with computer services and enhanced services. Why is this so? Briefly stated, it is because of the incompatibility of the respective national approaches adopted towards competition in telecommunications. As already noted, while the u.s. has permitted very extensive competition, Canada has adopted a significantly more cautious approach, especially with regard to competition in public long distance voice. Considerable doubt has been expressed as to whether Canada's relatively modest economy and population base justifies multiple long distance carriers.[80] As well, as we have also seen, Canadian policymakers remain thoroughly alarmed at the prospect of undermining the subsidy believed to flow from long distance to local.[81] Until rates are rebalanced over time and gradually shifted onto a cost justified basis, there will be the greatest reluctance to further facilities-based competition. Indeed, such has been the perception of confusion and disruption in the u.s. with full competition and the divestiture of AT&T, that the Canadian minister of communications was moved to express his condolences to the American people for the pointless destruction of a superb integrated network along with rapid increases in local rates and to promise that Canadians would never suffer a similar fate.[82]

But the incompatibility is not total. Unlike, say, Germany or France, Canada has allowed in competition outside of public long distance voice, at least in the federal sphere.[83] Competition has been allowed in private voice and data services, in resale and sharing, and in terminal attachment as well as enhanced services.[84] It has thus been possible for the negotiators to segment out computer and enhanced services for inclusion in the agreement.

Definitions

Because inclusion is limited, definitions are going to be all-important. Definition-making and construing have been a very difficult process in contemporary telecommunications regulation due to the ever changing nature of technology and the myriad new services it makes possible. One only has to recall the FCC's desperate efforts to distinguish between 'telephones' and 'computers' and, later, 'enhanced' and 'basic' services, or Judge Greene's decisions on the line of business limitations for the Bell Operating Companies, to realize that, whatever definitions are included in the agreement itself, what is going to be crucial is who decides what is, or is not, a 'basic' as opposed to an 'enhanced' service, or what is, or is not, included in 'computer services.'

'Basic' telecommunications is said in the agreement to mean any service, as defined and classified by measures of the regulator having jurisdiction, that is limited to the offering of transmission capacity for the movement of information. 'Enhanced' service is said to mean any service offered over the basic network that is more than a basic telecommunications service as defined and classified by measures of the regulator having jurisdiction (Annex 1404C, Article 7).

An initial reaction might be to believe that basic and enhanced are whatever they are defined to be by the respective national regulators. Does this then mean that a Canadian regulatory agency could define as 'basic' what its U.S. counterpart would undoubtedly consider as 'enhanced,' thereby protecting its monopoly telephone company from competition? It would not appear so. This is because 'basic' is declared in the agreement itself to be limited to the offering of transmission capacity for the movement of information. Should the service, looked at objectively, be more than simple transmission, then the regulator would be without authority to deem it basic. It is instructive to apply this standard to a case dealt with by the federal regulator, the CRTC. Call-Net Telecommunications provides computerized Customer Dialed Account Recording, a type of service held to be 'enhanced' by the FCC, but 'basic' by the CRTC. But Call-Net is not strictly limited to offering long distance transmission capacity for the movement of information. A free trade advocate might say that 'basic' has to be understood exclusively in the context of the agreement; a defensive regulator might say that it is appropriate to give the term a broad meaning in order to block a disguised long distance service, thereby meeting a legitimate Canadian regulatory objective. In the long run, fidelity to the agreement, and not short term national objectives, will have to prevail.

'Computer services' is somewhat more straightforwardly and comprehensively defined as services, whether or not conveyed on the basic telecommunications network, that involve generating, acquiring, storing, transforming, processing, retrieving, utilizing, or making available information in a computerized form, including, but not limited to: computer programming, prepackaged software, computer integrated systems design, computer processing and data preparation, information retrieval services, computer facilities management, computer leasing and rental, computer maintenance and repair, and other computer-related services, including those integral to the provision of other covered services (Annex 1404C, Article 7).

This makes it apparent that the agreement contemplates the direct provision of computer services outside a telecommunications context. With this in mind, it must be read in the wider context of services as a whole, particularly the Sectoral Annex on Temporary Entry for Business Persons, which will greatly ease transborder movement of computer service, sales, management, installation, and maintenance personnel.

Objective

The objective of the Sectoral Annex on Telecommunications-Network-Based Enhanced Services 'is to maintain and support the further development of an open and competitive market for the provision of enhanced services and computer services within or into the territories of the Parties' (Annex 1408 to Chapter 14, Article 1). It is most important to note that the objective is not merely to maintain and support an open and competitive market but to maintain and support the further development of such an open and competitive market.

Monopolies

At the same time as there is this thrust in favour of competition in enhanced and computer services, the sectoral annex responds to Canadian concerns by allowing for monopoly in basic telecommunications (Annex 1408 to Chapter 14, Article 6(1)(b)). In Article 5 these two notions are brought together in the most important provision of the sectoral annex. It provides:

> (1) Where a Party maintains or designates a monopoly to provide basic telecommunications transport facilities or services, and the monopoly, directly or through an affiliate, competes in the provision of enhanced services, the Party shall ensure that the monopoly shall not engage in anti-competitive conduct in the enhanced services market, either directly or through its dealings with its affiliates, that adversely affects a person of the other Party. Such conduct may include cross-subsidization, predatory conduct, and the discriminatory provision of access to basic telecommunications transport facilities or services.
>
> (2) Each Party shall maintain or introduce effective measures to prevent the anti-competitive conduct referred to in paragraph 1. These measures may include accounting requirements, structural separation and disclosure.

From this it may be seen that a positive obligation to prevent anti-competitive conduct is involved; this requires that effective measures be introduced and that these measures include the possibility of structural separation. This last point is worth emphasizing. In Canada, structural solutions have not been favoured apart from cellular radio mobile services, while structural separation would appear to be an idea whose time has come, and gone, in the United States.

Enhanced Services

What, then, is the significance of this concern with competition in enhanced, but not basic, services? Typical enhanced services in Canada include: Datapac Access Arrangements, Radio Paging, Envoy 100, iNet 2000, Telenet, Teltex, Telpost, Store and Forward Telex, and 911 Service.

While only amounting today to a minuscule fraction of telecom revenues, with full penetration of basic service all but achieved, it is probable that future growth will largely be in enhanced and value added services. An analogy may be helpful here. Suppose that Canada and the U.S. had negotiated a broadcasting agreement in 1948, which had excluded radio but had included television. If the future is a world of massaged and manipulated information, does it matter that the basic telecommunications transmission pipes are excluded, provided, as in the case in the Free Trade Agreement, access to basic transmission facilities is assured on a non-discriminatory basis? To analogize to the trucking industry – who cares who owns the roads, provided competing trucking companies have access to them on an equal basis?

Under the FTA, foreign-owned providers of network-based enhanced services enjoy a right-of-establishment. A right-of-establishment includes the establishment of offices, appointment of agents, and the installation of customer premises equipment or terminal equipment for the purpose of distributing, marketing, delivering, or facilitating the provision of an enhanced or computer service within or into the territory of the party. Enhanced services include:

- Access to, and use of, basic telecommunications transport services, including, but not limited to, the lease of local and long distance telephone service, full-period, flat-rate private-line services, dedicated local and inter-city voice channels, public data network services, and dedicated local and intercity digital and analogue data services for the movement of information, including intracorporate communications.
- The sale and shared use of such basic telecommunications transport services.
- The purchase and lease of customer premises equipment or terminal equipment and the attachment of such equipment to basic telecommunications transport networks.
- The movement of information across the borders and access to databases and related information stored, processed, and otherwise held within the territory of the party.

In principle, the right-of-establishment under the FTA should encourage greater indirect international competition in the provision of enhanced services or data services in Canada. Specifically, Canadian subscribers ostensibly have unrestricted access to either domestically-owned or foreign-owned suppliers of such services. In practice, it is still unclear how effectively enhanced service providers can operate if they cannot own and operate at least some of the equipment utilized to create the network.[85] Canadian regulatory policy effectively prohibits the ownership and operation of transmission facilities by non-basic carriers, and this distinction remains under the FTA.[86]

The institutionalization of a right-of-establishment for enhanced service providers in the FTA represents a significant step forward from current treatment under the GATT. Current GATT provisions do not cover trade in service items, such as telecommunications, that are not physically linked to trade in goods (see below). The GATT negotiating program under the Uruguay Round recognized that policy objectives of national laws and regulations applying to services such as telecommunications must be respected. Such objectives include national sovereignty and privacy.[87] Within this context, the scope for the extension of national treatment to any broad class of telecommunications services is questionable.

Grandfathering

As noted earlier, the impact of the Free Trade Agreement will only be prospective. In order to take advantage of this opportunity for grandfathering, the Canadian government announced, in July 1987, a limit of 20 per cent on foreign ownership of Type I carriers (facilities based), with no restrictions on Type II (non-facilities based) carriers.[88] The position on foreign ownership in the U.S. in telecommunications is far more confused, being based on access to the radio spectrum – a matter of ever lessening significance in the brave new world of optical fibre.[89]

The agreement also contains a provision very dear to the hearts of Canadian policymakers who remain concerned that cross-Canada traffic may be carried in large part on American facilities. Nothing in the agreement is to be construed to prevent a party from maintaining or introducing measures requiring basic telecommunications services to be carried on its network within its territory.[90] Canadian authorities have already announced that a statutory obligation will be placed on its carriers to employ Canadian facilities wherever feasible.[91]

Conclusions With Respect to Telecommunications Services

The prevailing conventional wisdom is that the Free Trade Agreement will have little direct impact on telecommunications. It is pointed out that the agreement itself does not require policy changes, that it does not address the crunch issue of competition in public long distance voice, and that it merely confirms existing regulatory policies governing enhanced services. This reflects too narrow a perspective. It underestimates the importance of the inclusion of at least a facet of telecommunications services in a bilateral agreement, and, as we move towards the inclusion, of services in multilateral negotiations, we will have much to learn from this experience.

Five propositions need to be borne in mind. First, the mere inclusion of computer and enhanced services in the agreement is, in itself, an important signal of the centrality of telecommunications services in contemporary international trade. Second, while it is true that the agreement does not change the ground rules governing telecommunications, it does mandate a positive duty to take effective measures to ensure the further development of an open and competitive market in a crucial growth area in telecommunications. Third, Canadian regulators, who might be tempted to play definitional games with respect to 'basic' and 'enhanced,' have had significant constraints placed upon them. Fourth, although not emphasized up to this point, the agreement preserves the status quo of a remarkably open border in telecommunications and will provide barriers against visceral protectionist reflex actions in less prosperous times. For example, the Sectoral Annex applies to the movement of information across borders and access to data bases; this indicates a significant agreement not to impose limits on transborder data flows in the longer run. Fifth, if telecommunications services are to be included in multilateral agreements, there will need to be respect for national concerns to protect basic networks. In this, Canada is really no different from other countries. It will simply not be possible to export the American fully competitive model holus bolus, but it may be possible to adopt the sort of careful delineation and segmentation to be found in the Free Trade Agreement. American-Canadian experience should be of the utmost interest in the on-going GATT negotiations now that trade in services is squarely on the table.

Indirect Impact of the Free Trade Agreement

Thus far we have looked at the direct impact of the FTA on the telecommunications industry. However, it is likely that the indirect impact will be far greater, although it is not yet possible to quantify it with any precision. The most effective arguments for change in the Canadian telecommunications industry have always been those linked to the international competitiveness of Canadian business, especially when compared to its U.S. counterpart. This concern for competitiveness is bound to grow in the years ahead and, with it, the question of whether business is receiving the best possible support from infrastructure industries.

In view of the ever-increasing importance of telecommunications services to business, arguments in favour of choice and the benefits of competition will no doubt receive a more sympathetic hearing than in the past. Canada has to recognize that greater competition has been introduced in the U.S., UK, and Japan without any threat to basic residential services.[92] The 'end of universal service as we know it' Chicken Littles have not prevailed there, and, eventually, will not prevail in Canada.

Although the most recent in a seemingly endless stream of studies glumly concludes along 'competition if necessary but not necessarily competition' lines,[93] the overall post-Free Trade Agreement atmosphere may be fairly said to favour further changes in the provision of telecommunications services in the direction of more competition. It will also create an economic climate which will quicken the pace of change and bring issues to a head more rapidly than might otherwise have been the case.

To conclude this discussion of the Free Trade Agreement as it pertains to the traditional transborder telecommunications regime, a number of observations are pertinent. First, what has hitherto been almost exclusively a non-governmental regime has been supplemented by an explicitly governmental agreement. Moreover, the nature of the principles of that agreement, namely of open domestic markets, albeit qualified, and the right of establishment, the acceptance of the potential for competition between domestic and foreign service providers, and, most importantly, that domestic monopolies must be subject to new forms of discipline to protect foreign competitors are important additions and qualifications to the principles of both the traditional transborder and multilateral regimes. As such, the Free Trade Agreement may be seen as an important potential precedent for transforming the traditional multilateral regime, inasmuch as it treats telecommunications as a service subject to the norms and principles of trade regimes rather than telecommunications regimes. The significance of this can be appreciated when we turn later to a discussion of the GATT round of negotiations and their potential ramifications for the multilateral telecommunications regime.

The Traditional Telecommunications Regime: Weakened or Transformed?

The purpose of this section is to describe in detail the central components of the existing international telecommunications regime and the major functions performed by that regime. We also elaborate upon the strains discussed above that confront existing international telecommunications. We do not address the radio spectrum management component of the regime, nor do we deal, except in passing, with issues arising from that part of the regime which governs the operation and provision of international satellite services, particularly those concerned with the International Telecommunication Satellite Organization (Intelsat).

Although some have claimed that recent international negotiations have radically transformed the traditional regime, we argue that this overstates the extent of the change.[94] The changes that have been made recently to the traditional regime, particularly with respect to the International Telecommunication Union (ITU), although reflecting conflicts over long-standing regime goals and practices, are not so fundamentally inconsistent with historical norms and practices as to constitute in themselves either a transformation or a fundamental weakening of this regime. Further along, however, we discuss the emergence of a potential rival, namely, the imposition of a GATT-type regime on services, particularly on telecommunications services. It could supplant the traditional regime or, more likely, join it in regulating international telecommunications. In either event, if a GATT trade in services regime which covers telecommunications is successfully negotiated, it will result in a profound transformation in the international telecommunications regime. Further, it will have major consequences for Canada. Even if a trade regime covering telecommunications is not successfully negotiated, the basis has been laid for treating telecommunications as a trade issue. Consequently, the traditional regime will face ongoing threats to its dominance.

Here we follow the lead of the major students of international regimes[95] in defining an international regime as a normative-institutional framework around which actor expectations converge in a given area of international relations. In terms of the substantive norms and principles of the traditional regime, three in particular are significant from the perspective of current issues confronting the stability of the regime: the principle of international co-operation; the inviolability of national sovereignty; and the closure of domestic systems to foreign carriers. Although the universe of institutions that play a role in the international telecommunications regulatory regime is rather large,[96] for the purposes of this chapter, we concentrate on the central institution, the International Telecommunication Union (ITU).

Regime Principles

The ITU (originally the International Telegraph Union) dates from 1865, when Napoleon III initiated negotiations to resolve the problems arising from different and conflicting national and regional technical standards, codes, and tariffs for telegraphy.[97] Originally a European-centred organization designed to create an inter-European telegraph network, it now encompasses 166 governments who have contracted to fulfil the necessary treaty obligations.

The ITU as an international regime exemplifies what Young described as a 'negotiated order,' embodying not imposed objectives but what can be described as an international public good: the interconnectivity and interoperability of national telecommunications systems.[98] This good includes the co-ordination of equipment and related technical standards for the transmission and receiving of telecommunications signals, ensuring that users of one system have access to that of other nations, that their calls will be completed as efficiently as possible without causing any technical harm to others, and providing a regulatory framework for allocating the costs of such interconnection and sharing the revenues. All these tasks could, theoretically, be undertaken on a bilateral basis. However, to do so, in the words of one Teleglobe Canada official, would be 'horrendous and tremendously costly.'[99] Moreover, it is conceivable that this understates the problems and overstates the likelihood that the necessary co-ordination, certainly at the worldwide level that is attempted today, would be accomplished. The nature and extent of co-ordination for international telecommunications that has been accomplished under the aegis of the ITU would appear to represent a clear case of the recognition of the validity of Krasner's general comment that 'ad hoc, individualistic calculations of interest could not possibly provide the necessary level of co-ordination.'[100]

Inasmuch as co-ordination of the type required for interconnectivity and interoperability of national telecommunications systems cannot be imposed by any external actor or organization, co-operation among nations has become the central norm of the international telecommunications regulatory regime. The actual development of standards and international agreements has been the product of a consensual process – a process wherein all parties have an equal voice, even if some, particularly for most of the past century, have more influence than others.[101] The point is that, even allowing for an unequal distribution of influence, no single national actor has been able to dominate the process. This is not to suggest that simple-minded, apolitical functionalism alone accounts for the development and longevity of this regime.

Our point is simply that co-operation among nations, the terms and conditions of which are usually the result of difficult and acrimonious negotiations, was the cornerstone upon which the ITU was built and was essential for the degree of international telecommunications co-ordination that has been attained.

Somewhat paradoxically, international telecommunications co-ordination was only accomplished by respecting what would appear to be a diametrically opposite norm: respect for national sovereignty. From the outset it was accepted that the requirements flowing from ITU treaty obligations applied only to the international aspects of a nation's telecommunications system, and that such obligations had no bearing on purely domestic telecommunications. So central was this principle that the preamble to the ITU Convention recognizes 'the sovereign right of each country to regulate its telecommunications.' Membership in the ITU does not derogate from national regulatory control, nor does it confer on any other nation, or the ITU, authority over regulatory or other telecommunications policies of individual members. How an individual nation structures, regulates, costs, or prices the domestic component of its telecommunications system is solely its prerogative. Again it must be admitted that there have been violations of this norm, most notably in the refusal to admit Great Britain into the organization until it had nationalized its telegraph industry in 1875.[102] Furthermore, for many years, United States' preference for private rather than public ownership of its telecommunications companies was a stumbling block to American membership for ITU members. Hence the United States did not decide to join the Union until 1932.

The third principle of the current regime is the closure of domestic telecommunications systems to foreign carriers. The principle of co-operation called for co-ordination of domestic systems. The presumption, valid in almost all cases, was that each nation was served by a single telecommunications carrier. End-to-end international service would not be provided by a single carrier but would be effected through collaborative arrangements between individual national carriers designated by their state as their official international service provider.

Consequently, the objective of the ITU was not the emergence of truly transnational carriers but the interconnection of national systems with one another on the basis of bilateral agreements that respected the terms of the ITU policies. For underseas cables, for example, each national carrier would share joint ownership and be individually responsible for the operation and maintenance of the system from its domestic gateway to the middle point of the cable linking the two countries. In the past two decades, the introduction of satellite systems and, especially, the deployment of high capacity, high cost, fibre optic underseas cable has led to the introduction of multinational consortia, but this has not changed the underlying principle of the international regime.

One of the key intended consequences of the traditional regulatory regime is that customers in one nation are solely customers of their own service providers and not of foreign carriers. The customer has no contact with the foreign collaborator that is used by his/her local or 'national' international carrier to complete a call. Similarly, and most importantly for the traditional regime, 'neither the domestic nor the international carrier has any transnational responsibilities with respect to a customer in a foreign country that originates or receives a call.'[103] One of the central aspects of this structure is that the pricing of international calls is the sole responsibility of national authorities, be they the state-owned firms alone or, as in the case of Canada and the United States, firms and their regulatory agencies. Individual state pricing is influenced by ITU policies governing accounting, collection, and settlement rates, but the ITU has no direct role in telecommunications pricing. The international telecommunications regime, contrary to suggestions from some, is not a price-fixing regime.[104] International rates, particularly the amounts each national carrier must reimburse its foreign counterpart for completion of calls, are set through bilateral negotiations between the two national service providers.

Regime Institutions

For the purposes of this chapter, there are three central institutional components of the existing international telecommunications regulatory regime. The first is the ITU Constitution and Convention, which sets out the composition, structure, and purpose of the union as well as some of the general objectives and conditions governing international telecommunications. Although national concurrence with the constitution and convention is through individual treaties, this part of the regime is not particularly significant from the perspective of the operation of the regime and, especially, the behaviour of the members. The two most behaviourally significant components are the Administrative Regulations and the Recommendations of the International Telegraph and Telephone Consultative Committee (CCITT).

The administrative regulations, which, like the constitution and convention, are treaty-based, set out rules and procedures that have the force of law when incorporated into national legislation. These regulations, for a long period of the ITU's history, were a cause of contention, especially for the United States, which refused to sign the regulations when it joined the ITU in 1932. The U.S. claimed that many of the provisions were in violation of its sovereignty and its right to regulate its domestic, private corporations. The u.s. persisted in its objections until 1973 when, after negotiations, the regulations were drastically reduced in number and confined in content to the stipulation of general behavioural norms. The most contentious rules were transferred to the status of ccitt Recommendations which were non-binding. With these changes, the u.s. signed the international treaty, committing itself to enforce the regulations.

The set of ccitt Recommendations are much more behaviourally significant for the members of the regime. However, their significance is somewhat muted because national compliance with them is voluntary. Members are simply reminded that they 'should comply with the ccitt Recommendations . . . on any matter not covered by the Regulations.'[105] Recommendations are developed by committees of experts composed of representatives, not only of the national carriers but also of equipment manufacturers and users, from all parts of the world. It is through the recommendations that the actual interconnectivity and interoperability of national systems are ensured.

The voluntary nature of the recommendations is also germane to some of the recent conflicts within the regime to be discussed below. Not only do they permit individual national carriers to ignore them, they also allow nations to make special arrangements between them 'on telecommunications matters which do not concern Members [of the itu] in general,' so long as these are not 'in conflict with the terms of the Convention or of the . . . Regulations . . . so far as it concerns the harmful interference with their operation which might likely cause to the radio services of other countries.'[106] The telecommunications provisions of the Canada-u.s. Free Trade Agreement, which were discussed above, constitute an example of such special arrangements.

Note that the central actors in the current regime are states or their designated representatives. Given the treaty-based nature of the regime, this is an obvious point, but there are two aspects of the traditional state representation that need to be underscored. With very few exceptions, telecommunications have been provided within individual countries by monopolies that are publicly owned.[107] In an era of monopoly provision, the identification of the individual carrier and its interests with the individual nation and national interests was not problematical. Indeed, there were no serious problems for the United States with private ownership as long as AT&T, the dominant, if not exclusive, international service provider, was perceived to be a public utility. Ownership patterns may have been different, but there was presumed to be no substantive difference between AT&T and the British, French, or German publicly-owned carriers, for example. Consequently, the domination of telephone or carrier representatives in state delegations for ITU negotiations was not perceived to pose any problems because of the community of interests and objectives that they shared regardless of the state they represented. A related point about the nature of state representation was that technical professionals, particularly engineers, were normally the dominant participants in delegations. This led to a shared language and set of values reinforcing the shared objectives. As we shall see, one of the primary causes of conflict within the present regime has been the move to privatization and its normal concomitant competitive provision of telecommunications. This has led not only to the emergence of new actors within states who want to play an international role but, equally importantly, to a challenge to, and often a displacement of, traditional actors, their common language, and shared objectives.

Recent Strains within the Regime

For more than a century the international telecommunications regime, despite occasional tensions and conflicts, was remarkably stable. Even more significantly, this regime was pre-eminently successful in meeting its objectives. The ITU members met the challenges of expanding from a Europe-centred to a global organization and the even more difficult challenges of confronting several generations of technological change from telegraph to telephone, from copper cable and wireless to microwave, satellite, and fibre optic transmission.

Despite this record of substantial accomplishment, the regime has been riven with considerable tensions and strains within the last decade. In fact, so great were the conflicts that recent renegotiations of the organizational treaties and associated recommendations came close to failure and raised the possibility that the regime would disintegrate.[108] The basic causes of the conflicts will be well known to any observer of domestic telecommunications. Indeed, in most respects they are little more than a transfer to the international arena of domestic battles fought over the past two decades in many industrialized countries. The following constitutes only the most summary list of the causes (with no effort being made to establish any ranking of them): technological changes such as the convergence of communications and computers and the radical changes in transmission and switching capacities; the breakdown of traditional bargains and associated alliances combined with the emergence of new players with telecommunications priorities both within governments and within the private sector; the demand that pricing regimes and market structures be radically transformed; the emergence of new telecommunications services and service providers; and the growing appreciation that telecommunications is central to the competitive advantage of both firms and countries. These and other forces have caused a profound recasting of domestic telecommunications policies and market structures in a number of countries.

As a result of these domestic-based initiatives and the consequent demand that the international regime reflect corresponding changes, the renegotiation of the ITU Convention, Regulations, and CCITT Recommendations initiated at the 1982 ITU Plenipotentiary meeting almost failed. The conflicts centred on the most basic norms and institutions of the traditional regime. Two issues that dominated recent ITU policymaking conferences reflect the challenges facing the traditional regime. The first was drawing the boundary line between regulated and non-regulated telecommunications to determine who and what should be regulated. The second was the issue of permitting special arrangements for private, bilateral telecommunications at the expense of public, multilateral objectives.

Led by the United States, Great Britain, and Japan, and most recently supported by the European Community (if not all its individual members), the last decade has witnessed the emergence of competition between and among international carriers. This competition has been not only between new common carriers, such as that between AT&T and MCI in the U.S. or British Telecom and Mercury in the UK, but between traditionally public common carriers and new private carriers.

One of the major international developments which was seen as a direct threat to the traditional regime was the U.S. decision to license satellite systems outside of, and in competition with, Intelsat. Another major American development, but one endorsed by the UK and Japan, was the licensing of private underseas fibre optic cables that would compete directly with the public systems in a number of areas. The FCC has recently begun to grant applicants greater latitude in determining what facilities to construct and when. What this means is that the FCC is, in effect, deregulating the landing of international cable facilities on U.S. soil. The issues of the number of cables, their destinations, and their capacities are increasingly becoming subject to market forces.[109] This is particularly important in the U.S., where the cable operators have open access to the public switched network. The significance of these developments is a projected large increase in circuit capacity. Table 1 shows that in the lucrative North Atlantic market there will be more than a 600 per cent increase in capacity in the decade 1988-97, and that more than 40 per cent of that increase will come from private circuits which did not exist in 1988.

For many members of the ITU, the actions of the United States, and the few other countries which introduced the competitive provision of

TABLE 1

Transatlantic circuit capacity, 1988-97 (voice circuits, 000)

	1988	1989	1990	1991	1992	1993	1994	1995	1996	1997
Official										
cable links	42.6	42.6	42.6	108.4	107.7	107.7	107.7	107.7	106.1	106.1
INTELSAT	31.2	31.2	69.6	117.6	159.6	159.6	157.6	156.8	156.8	158.0
Total										
traditional	73.8	73.8	112.2	226.0	267.3	267.3	265.3	264.5	262.9	264.1
PanAmSat	—	—	25.0	25.0	25.0	25.0	25.0	25.0	25.0	25.0
Private										
cable links	—	85.0	85.0	85.0	170.0	170.0	170.0	170.0	170.0	170.0
Total private	—	85.0	110.0	110.0	195.0	195.0	195.0	195.0	195.0	195.0
Grand total	73.8	158.8	222.2	336.0	462.3	462.3	460.3	459.5	457.9	459.1

SOURCE: Satellite Systems Engineering, Inc. (SSE Report no. 034), 1988

telecommunications, appeared to be an attempt not only to impose a similar policy at the international level but also to export it to other countries. Recognizing that they could not possibly succeed in forcing a rollback on competition, these countries opted for the alternative, which was to make the new competitors subject to the constraints of the traditional regulatory regime. This option emerged as part of the draft report of the preparatory committee for the ITU negotiations in 1988, which called for the extension of the treaty obligations under ITU to cover 'any entity' providing international telecommunications services.[110] Under the traditional regime, the treaty only applied to government departments or services (administrations) or state-authorized private firms (Recognized Private Operating Agencies or RPOA's). If accepted, this recommendation would have meant that the traditionally-regulated carriers would be joined by private network operators, value added service providers, or any other entity providing an international telecommunications service or facility. The case made for comprehensive inclusion was similar to that made domestically: the principle of having 'a level playing field' in a competitive environment. Of course, the underlying rationale was that international regulation could act as an effective constraint on the development of such competitors and limit their potential harm to traditional service providers.

The U.S. and other pro-competitive countries argued that to extend regulation in this manner was a violation of the respect-for-national-sovereignty principle of the ITU. Their argument was that, inasmuch as these new service providers were not regulated domestically, the ITU could not impose such regulation on the members states. They advocated that the ITU must limit itself to a 'neutral' provision that would permit, but not require, individual countries to decide whether or not to regulate new services and new service providers. The final text was an ambiguous compromise that superficially appears to represent a victory for the pro-regulatory forces but, in fact, concedes the case to the pro-competition countries.

The second contentious issue in the recent negotiations was an American proposal that the ITU permit special arrangements for the establishment, operation and use of special telecommunications networks, systems and services to meet specialized telecommunications needs between providers of such services and facilities in countries which are party to such arrangements. Any 'special arrangements' would be outside the regulatory ambit of the ITU, especially the mandatory regulations. Advocates for this provision defended it on the grounds of 'the greater flexibility and freedom that it allowed private, dynamic, telecommunication business to flourish and to develop new technology.[111] Opponents, not surprisingly, 'were fearful that such arrangements would result in high volume and profitable business traffic bypassing their networks via private, specialized, lower cost networks and that this would lead to an international regime where eventually bilateralism might predominate over multilateralism not only for the value added but eventually also for basic services.'[112] Although a modified version of this provision was accepted, advocates greeted it with enthusiasm because of its intrinsic support for a less restrictive, less regulated international system.

From the perspective of the traditional international regulatory regime, we argue that the changes introduced, or not introduced in the case of the 'any entity' provision, do not constitute a transformation of this regime as others have claimed. The U.S. and its allies were able to block the 'any entity' provision by invoking one of the central normative tenets of the regime – respect for national sovereignty. On the other hand, by seeking to permit and encourage the provision of competitive telecommunications, the norm of international co-operative provision does appear to be threatened. In general, however, advocates of the pro-competition position can argue that competition per se need not undermine international co-operation and, particularly, interconnectivity and interoperability. To support this position they can point to the emergence of international and domestic equipment competition. Previously it had been almost non-existent, and particularly domestic service competition, public and private, in those countries which permit it is evidence that no threat to the fundamental objectives exists.

On the other hand, the extension of the provision for 'special arrangements' does pose a serious challenge to the traditional regime in two respects. First, it places a heightened emphasis on, and legitimacy for bilateral arrangements rather than multilateral agreements. It should be recalled, however, that the new provisions are only an extension of traditional conditions, not a radical departure in themselves and, therefore, are justified by the traditional norms.

Second, the more serious threat posed by the extension of special arrangements is that they permit much more direct penetration of domestic systems by both foreign telecommunications firms and by individual corporations through private systems. Perhaps the most dramatic illustration of the potential in this area is the plan by General Electric, with the assistance of AT&T, to develop a global private network that would link up 1,400 GE facilities in twenty-five countries on six continents. Although no individual nation can be required to permit such private systems, it may be compelled through economic necessity to agree, especially if its corporate users are placed at an economic disadvantage without access to them. An equally important factor that could influence countries to accept such private systems, even over their initial objections, is the potential for their own corporations to use modern technology to 'exit' and 'bypass' domestic constraints that cannot be effectively enforced. The ability of such firms in Canada as Fonorola and Marathon Telecommunications to offer Canadian firms alternative international routes to Teleglobe's statutory exclusive privilege illustrates the limited effectiveness of public controls.

Canada's Role in the International Regime

Thus far we have made no special reference to Canada's role in the operation of the international regime or, particularly, in the recent conflicts. Two points are worth noting in this regard. First, Canada's position on the central issues in the recent negotiations was rather middle-of-the-road, albeit with a slight tilt towards the pro-competitive position.[113] This should not be surprising because Canada's domestic policies and regulatory decisions to date have been to favour competition only in non-public or private services. In 1985, for example, the CRTC rejected an application that would have led to the introduction of public voice competition now allowed in the United States or Great Britain.[114] The federal government's 1987 policy proposals also call for the maintenance of regulation of facilities-based carriers using a 'public convenience and necessity' test.[115] Although Canada rejected the 'any entity' regulatory proposal as extreme, it favoured a regulatory distinction between 'basic' and 'enhanced' services similar to that in the Free

Trade Agreement. Canada also wanted the basic network or means of telecommunications to be subject to the regulations. This was a position which the strongly pro-competitive countries did not support.

The second aspect of Canada's participation in recent conflicts was the composition of the Canadian delegation. This is not insignificant, particularly when compared to the current GATT negotiations. Canada's positions and participation in the recent ITU negotiations were developed primarily by the federal Department of Communications' International Affairs Branch. The primary contributors outside the department came from the telecommunications carriers, particularly Teleglobe, Telecom Canada, and Unitel, the private line competitor to some of the members of Telecom Canada. Their influence, however, was minimal. One of the more interesting developments in the final stages of drafting Canada's position was the demand for membership on the Canadian delegation from a business users' group, the Canadian Business Telecommunications Alliance, which is strongly pro-competitive. The Department of Communications acceded to the request, albeit reluctantly. This user representation, in part, was instrumental in influencing Canada's rejection of the pro-regulatory 'any entity' recommendation. More generally, the decision to include a user representative reflected the presence within Canada of the tensions that are central to current conflicts within the traditional international regime.

GATT: REGIME ADDITIVE OR WRECKER?

In the foregoing section we sought to describe the basic components of the traditional international regime in telecommunications, especially the strains within that regime. Although this oversimplifies the conflicts somewhat, the traditional regime over the past decade has had to cope with strongly divergent, if not incompatible, perspectives. On the one hand, some players have sought to reinforce the normative status quo. Yet they realized that they could only do so by accepting a change in the membership of the regime, that is, subject the new entrants to the embrace of the international regulatory regime. Such an embrace, it was assumed, would diminish any need to change the fundamental principles of the regime. On the other hand, those who sought to change those principles, in a fundamental fashion, realized that there was little prospect of winning the majority over to their point of view. Consequently, they invoked the sovereignty norm to prevent an expansion of the regulatory ambit. As a distinctly second best option, they achieved a moderate extension in flexibility through the expanded 'special arrangements' provision.

Bilateral negotiation to implement 'special arrangements' as an instrument to transform the regime is obviously a cumbersome and costly method and one that offers little hope of success. The modest extent of change agreed to in the Canada-u.s. Free Trade Agreement, whatever the long-term prospects, is a clear example of the limitations of this route. In fact, bilateralism such as this suffers from the same defects as does bilateralism as a means of obtaining widespread inter-national telecommunications co-ordination.

In short, we suggest that, in the ITU negotiations, the United States and its pro-change allies were primarily seeking to defend the gains they had made within the traditional regime in order to pursue, concur-rently, regime change in another arena. That arena was the GATT nego-tiations, particularly in the current Uruguay Round, officially launched in 1986.[116] There bringing trade in services, including and especially telecommunications, within GATT has been made a major priority of the United States.

To understand why the pro-change forces would use the GATT nego-tiations for their challenge to the traditional regime, while adopting what was essentially a defensive posture in the ITU forums, it is import-ant to appreciate one of the most significant developments in the politics of telecommunications that emerged first in the United States and, in recent years, spread to other countries. That development is the emergence of a powerful broad-based telecommunications industry coalition that includes both consumer and producer interests, includ-ing the former monopolies.[117] After considerable domestic success, particularly in the u.s., this coalition is now insisting on commensurate reform not only at the strictly international level but also within other countries. The strength of this new coalition in the United States appears in large part to be a product of the fact that their cause was embraced early on by government officials anxious, for their own reasons, to be 'prominent new supporters of free trade.'[118]

The members of the new coalition and their governmental allies have found that the traditional ITU institutions were antithetical to their interests and the processes heavily weighted against them. Conse-quently, they have sought to transfer debates and decisionmaking to an arena more sympathetic to their cause and, in the process, counterbal-ance traditional actors with new players supportive of their positions. They have, in short, sought to widen the scope of conflict, as is common in domestic interest group politics. The coalition in the United States has clearly had considerable success, for telecommunications was es-tablished as a priority in the 1988 Trade Act. Subsequently, the United States insisted that no new GATT negotiations could begin without placing services, and particularly telecommunications, on the table. It is important to note that the new coalition is no longer a uniquely American phenomenon. Other countries, or at least their trade representatives, including Canada, the United Kingdom, and, most recently, the European Community, have endorsed the basic objectives of the American-based trade in services coalition.

It is important to have a clear understanding of those objectives. The telecommunications services coalition wishes to establish domestically and internationally: the right of private business users (a) to purchase telecommunications equipment from any supplier and to attach such equipment to the public network, (b) to lease private lines, (c) to establish a private network by linking together leased lines, privately owned lines within the premises of the firm, and privately controlled computer switching facilities, and (d) to interconnect private networks with other private networks or public networks.[119]

We argue that the goal is nothing less than to displace the traditional principles of the international telecommunications regime and to replace them with diametrically opposite principles. The objective is an international system premised not on co-operation but on the competitive provision of telecommunications. Domestic systems are no longer to be closed to foreign carriers. They will be penetrated not only by foreign service providers but also by customers who will be able to mix and match public and private systems and services to serve their particular needs. Finally, and most significantly, national sovereignty will have to be drastically diluted to ensure that national service providers are not in a position to exploit any advantage over foreign firms, producers, or consumers. This will require that national policies on industry structuring, standard setting, and service costing and pricing, for example, be subject to some form of international scrutiny and, where necessary, ameliorative mechanisms.

To accomplish these objectives, telecommunications services are, along with other specific services to be negotiated, to be subject to a framework agreement, incorporating the basic principles of the GATT trade regime. These are: transparency of national policies and regulations; no discrimination or the 'most favoured nation' principle; the right of market access to foreign markets; national treatment of foreign-based service providers; and progressive liberalization in order to provide effective market access.[120]

One of the most important developments in the GATT negotiations occurred in March 1990, when the United States tabled a much more detailed and expansive proposal for the telecommunications sector.[121] Prior to this development, negotiations had concentrated on a broad framework which would set out the fundamental principles, such as those just listed, and provide for individual countries to both accept the framework generally and to exempt specific services if they wished. In March, however, the United States put forward a new proposal incorporating both the basic framework and an annex that set out specific principles that signatories would be bound to respect. The overall intent of the annex is to give users and service providers of signatory nations the almost unlimited right of access to, and use of, public telecommunications networks and facilities. Furthermore, any disagreements or complaints about the treatment of non-national users or service-providers would be subject to the GATT dispute settlement process. From Lapointe's perspective, this would result in the signatories 'surrendering, in final instance, regulatory sovereignty over basic domestic, as well as international telecommunications networks and facilities to the multilateral GATT dispute settlement process.'[122] If this happens, he concludes, 'the world will have seen the birth of a new international, legal and institutional framework over the regulation of telecommunications services.'[123]

The possibility of failure in either the general service negotiations or those for telecommunications remains. However, that possibility cannot give much comfort to those who do not wish to see the traditional ITU-based regime displaced, especially by something as different as a GATT trade regime. As Drake and others have noted, 'the impact of the GATT is not entirely dependent on what sort of treaty will emerge.'[124] It seems clear that the mere act of placing telecommunications on the trade table with such force has undoubtedly and permanently altered the international regulatory regime for telecommunications. Henceforth, it cannot be defined as an exclusively domestic issue protected by the umbrella of national sovereignty. It is now irretrievably the subject of trade negotiations. GATT treaty or not, even one less draconian than that currently pushed by the United States 'simply by taking up the matter, the GATT has contributed to liberalization.' Elsewhere, Drake concludes that 'the issue is not that the precise terms of trade have been worked out, but rather that they are now the issue.'[125] It seems inevitable, therefore, that, at a minimum, the traditional international regulatory regime for telecommunications will be supplemented by trade regime principles and processes. In the meantime, pressured by the U.S. and its allies, the ITU acceptance of liberalized 'special arrangements' provides both the legitimacy and the mechanism or 'crowbar' to pursue the benefits of a trade-based regime.

Canada's position on the introduction of a GATT trade-based regime is somewhat surprising, although it should be emphasized that it is difficult to confirm the specifics of Canada's negotiating position. From the outset, Canada was a supporter of the American initiative to put services on the GATT agenda. In 1988, when the initiative seemed to be floundering, the Canadian minister for international trade took a very strong stand at the Montreal ministerial meeting alongside the advocates of a trade in services regime. Beyond this it is not clear what position Canada has taken on either the inclusion of telecommunications in the general framework agreement or, more importantly, on the most recent American proposal. According to confidential sources, Canada favours the general framework agreement which continues to be relatively undefined and, therefore, not inconsistent with Canada's position in the Canada-u.s. negotiations. On the other hand, while some non-Canadian sources have indicated that Canada has unofficially endorsed the recent American proposal, this cannot be confirmed. If Canada did adopt such a position, it would be somewhat surprising – it would indicate a support for far greater competitive provision of telecommunications than has hitherto been the case, certainly in terms of domestic competition, particularly in respect to competition in public voice long distance service.

One of the interesting aspects of the GATT negotiations, and indicative of the pressures facing the traditional ITU-based regime, has been the internal dynamics of Canadian representation for these negotiations. Two aspects in particular stand out. In the ITU negotiations the Department of Communications was not only the lead but also the dominant department in preparing Canada's positions and representing the nation in the negotiations. In contrast, in the GATT round, the Trade Negotiations Office reporting to the minister for international trade (established for the FTA) is the lead department. Although some interdepartmental consultation inevitably must occur, the Department of Communications is only one of several departments consulted, and it is not given any special weight.

The second feature of Canadian representation is the role of private sector participation. It will be recalled that in the final stages of the ITU negotiations a representative of a business user group was reluctantly added to the Canadian delegation. In the GATT negotiations, following the FTA experience where almost twenty sectoral advisory committees were established, similar committees have been formed. Some of these include participants from the FTA negotiations. No advisory committee was set up specifically for telecommunications. Instead, a more inclusive computer and communications (including equipment) committee was formed. This committee includes telecommunications carriers both domestic and overseas, but they are not given any special weight in the process. In fact, there is some concern that the advisory process is somewhat of a charade. The executive vice president of Teleglobe, whose president is on the advisory committee, has recently stated that in order to keep informed of the negotiations he has 'had to establish

[his] own means of accessing working papers, and individuals in-volved in these negotiations, since the consultative process established by the government, until very recently, was apparently conceived to distract those who participate in it.'[126] The sources employed appear to be primarily American, with access to high level u.s. negotiators. Other Canadian participants, in confidential interviews, have also com-plained about limited disclosure of information, inadequate time to prepare, and tight strictures on whom they may consult. All of these problems, they suggest, reduce the opportunity and effectiveness for private sector input in the process. More importantly, the nature of the process would appear to augment the capacity of the trade negotiators to adopt and pursue more independent positions. In the Canadian case, if Canada is supporting the recent u.s. proposal, this would reflect such an outcome because a strong user and/or service coalition has not yet become a presence in the Canadian domestic process.

CONCLUSIONS AND SUGGESTIONS FOR PUBLIC POLICY

In our opinion, as a result of the developments in the ITU and, more importantly, of current trade negotiations, the traditional international telecommunications regulatory regime is about to be transformed. The traditional regime, built on domestically closed and internationally co-ordinated telecommunications systems, will be transformed into one based on domestically fused and integrated systems subject to the forces of competition. The traditional regime, for all the good it has done (and this has been substantial), was premised on the twin princi-ples of co-operation and national sovereignty. The emerging regime will be built on trade principles, competition, and the world as 'the strategic territorial unit for organizing production.'[127]

With reference to overseas (as opposed to transborder) traffic, Mon-itor Company concludes that while Teleglobe has a legislative monop-oly on overseas long-distance service, its 'market power is mitigated for a number of reasons.'[128] First, 'Teleglobe's market is a segment of a larger overseas market that is becoming increasingly, and self-sus-tainingly, competitive.' Second, Teleglobe's market power is reduced by its proximity to the vigorously competitive u.s. long-distance mar-ket, which 'creates rivalry and enhances the bargaining power of business buyers.' Further, Telecom Canada – a major supplier to Teleglobe – has a strong bargaining position. As of the spring of 1991 Monitor Company described Teleglobe's market as 'moderately com-petitive in its business segments and mildly competitive in its residen-tial segments.' However, its underlying structure 'should permit significant competition.' Intven and Salzman note that Teleglobe's market power – which exists only in some segments – 'is largely based on the current DOC and CRTC regulatory conditions.'[129] Because it does not control the feeder/distribution networks at either end of its 'pipe,' the extent of Teleglobe's market power may therefore change rapidly. We note these specific current insights as confirmation of the overall direction of this chapter.

Clearly, there will be some who will maintain that individual nations will be able to insist that national sovereignty must be respected and that regulation be constructed to reflect this. This is not a realistic option. As Eli Noam noted, 'the subject of the regulation – streams of electrons and photons and patterns of signals that constitute information – are so elusive in physical and conceptual terms, and so fast and distance-insensitive, that a regulatory mechanism, to be effective, must be draconian, and for that the traditional system has neither the will nor the political support.'[130] It is reasonable to project that large users will be able to 'escape' from the existing regulatory restrictions sooner and more effectively than other users. The greater opportunities for bypass under the existing regime will leave small users bearing an ever increasing share of the cross-subsidy burden – which, in principle, was intended to benefit them. No country in the world more than Canada must grapple with the fusion of domestic telecommunications systems and the decline in national regulatory control. As we undertake the development of national telecommunications policies, especially those concerning our overseas and satellite carriers, it is imperative that the changing international dynamics be a primary rather than a residual concern.

PART FOUR

International Regulation of Resources and the Environment

Evolution of Canadian Fisheries Management Policy under the New Law of the Sea: International Dimensions

Gordon R. Munro

INTRODUCTION

Of the achievements of the United Nations Third Conference on the Law of the Sea (UNCLOS III), almost certainly the most important are to be found in the area of fisheries. That section of the Law of the Sea Convention, which arose from the conference, pertaining to fisheries – Part 5 the Exclusive Economic Zone – has been universally accepted and is now recognized as customary international law.

As a result of UNCLOS III, large amounts of renewable resource wealth, hitherto international common property, have been transferred to coastal state ownership. The fishery resources within the coastal state 200-mile Exclusive Economic Zones (EEZ's) provide the basis for up to 90 per cent of the world's harvest of fish.

During UNCLOS III, Canada was a strong supporter of Extended Fisheries Jurisdiction (EFJ). While EFJ promised Canada only limited gains off her Pacific coast, the promised gains off her Atlantic coast were very large indeed. Moreover, fisheries were important to the Atlantic Canada economies – economies which historically had suffered from chronic stagnation and unemployment. EFJ thus held out the promise of strong Atlantic coast fishing industries and rejuvenated Atlantic Canada economies.

It is evident, at the time of writing, that the promise has been less than fully realized. There are threats of plant closures in Atlantic Canada due to reduced harvest quotas, which appear, in turn, to be linked with ongoing strife with distant water fishing nations. We shall attempt to assess Canadian fisheries management policy as it has evolved under the post UNCLOS III regime. We shall make the point that, while there have been numerous, well-publicized disappointments,

there have, as well, been successes, which have enjoyed little publicity.

CANADA AND THE UNITED NATIONS THIRD CONFERENCE ON THE
LAW OF THE SEA

Canada implemented its 200-mile Exclusive Economic Zones on 1
January 1977. Prior to that date, Canada's control over fishery resources
was restricted to a zone out to twelve miles from shore, along with
certain additional areas circumscribed by closing lines. All fisheries off
Canada's coasts that were outside these narrow zones constituted
international common property.

Fishery resources have always been notoriously difficult to manage
effectively in economic terms. The difficulty is a consequence of the
common property nature of the resource. While a coastal state may have
property rights to a fishery resource, it is very difficult to assign property
rights to individual fishermen or companies. The consequences of the
common property nature of the resource are that the resource is subject
to overexploitation and/or the fishery sees the emergence of an excessively large fishing fleet and, occasionally, excessively large processing
sectors as well. In either case, severe economic waste is the result.

When fishery resources are international common property, the
common property problem emerges in a particularly virulent form.
One then has not only many fishermen competing for a fishery resource
but many nations as well.

The international common property aspect of fisheries off her coasts
was of moderate concern to Canada in the Pacific. The Pacific salmon,
which she shared with the United States, was subject to possible high
seas fishing. Beyond that, fish tend to concentrate in the waters above
the continental shelf. The continental shelf off British Columbia is
narrow – extending to no more than forty to fifty miles from shore.

Off Canada's Atlantic coast, by way of contrast, the continental shelf
if very broad – extending in some areas, for example, the Grand Banks
of Newfoundland, to well beyond 200 miles. The region has some of the
richest fishery resources in the world – resources which are of fundamental economic importance to the economies of Newfoundland and
Nova Scotia.[1]

The fishery resources consisted primarily of groundfish such as cod,
flounder, and hake. From 1949 until 1977 the fisheries off Atlantic
Canada, beyond Canada's twelve-mile limit, were regulated by the
International Commission for the Northeast Atlantic Fisheries (ICNAF).
Canada and the United States were members of ICNAF, along with

so-called distant water fishing nations such as the Soviet Union, Spain, and Portugal.

Commencing in the late 1950s, there was a massive expansion of distant water fishing nation activity in the ICNAF area off Atlantic Canada. Much of the activity was focused on a cod stock complex extending from southern Labrador to southeast Newfoundland, known popularly as Northern Cod. The complex has been described as constituting the heart of the Newfoundland fishing industry.

The expansion in distant water fishing activity led to a sharp decline in the resource stocks. The decline in the resource stocks had, in turn, a severe impact on Canada's Atlantic coast fishing industry.[2] By 1973-4 the industry was in a deep crisis and required extensive federal government assistance. The experience convinced Canada that international management of fisheries off her Atlantic coast was wholly ineffective. The international common property problem was insurmountable.

By the end of 1973, the formal sessions of the UN Third Conference on the Law of the Sea were commencing. The Atlantic coast experience heightened Canada's interest in the conference and made her a strong supporter of Extended Fisheries Jurisdiction, that is, of increased coastal state control of world fishery resources.

As the Law of the Sea negotiations commenced, there arose two major issues pertaining to Extended Fisheries Jurisdiction. The first was the geographical extent of the coastal state zone. The second was the degree of power which the coastal state would be permitted to exercise within the zone. The initial Canadian position on the extent of the coastal state zone was that it should at least extend to the edge of the continental shelf.[3] If this position were accepted, Canada would be guaranteed full control over Atlantic groundfish resources off her coasts. In the end, Canada was not successful, for numerous political reasons.[4] Rather, the extent of the coastal state zone was set at 200 nautical miles from shore.

The consequence of this outcome was that two segments of the Grand Bank of Newfoundland remained outside the Canadian 200 mile zone. The segments are in the eastern and southern portions of the Bank and are known popularly as the Nose and Tail of the Bank respectively. The presence of these excluded segments caused Canada considerable difficulties.

The second issue was over whether the coastal state was to act simply as custodian for the international community in the zone of extended jurisdiction or whether the coastal state was to be granted full property rights to the fishery resources within this zone. In the end, the proponents of full coastal state property rights prevailed.

The economic significance of this outcome lay in the fact that the economic case for EFJ rested on the severity of the common property problem in international fisheries. EFJ promised to mitigate this problem. The successful approach granted coastal states unambiguous property rights to the resources. The unsuccessful custodial approach did not grant unambiguous property rights to coastal states, and, thus, would not have gone as far in mitigating the common property problem.[5]

As we have noted, the section of the Law of the Sea Convention pertaining to fisheries – Part 5, The Exclusive Economic Zone – has now achieved the status of customary international law. Hence, Part 5 can be viewed as setting forth the accepted international 'rules of the game' for fisheries management in the post-EFJ regime.

The key article in Part 5 of the convention is Article 56, which states that, within the Exclusive Economic Zone (EEZ), the coastal state has sovereign rights for the purpose of exploring and exploiting, conserving and managing the natural resources whether living or non-living.[6] For all intents and purposes, therefore, the coastal state has full property rights to the fishery resource within the EEZ[7].

The coastal state is subject to certain obligations, but these are less than demanding. Thus, the coastal state is admonished to utilize the fishery resources within its zone 'optimally.' The coastal state is, however, given very wide latitude in defining the term 'optimal.'

The apparently most demanding obligation is contained within Article 62 in the form of the so-called 'surplus principle.' The coastal state is called upon to set Total Allowable Catches (TAC's) for all fisheries within its EEZ. If, for a particular fishery, the coastal state finds that it is incapable of taking the entire TAC because of limits to its harvesting capacity, then a 'surplus' is deemed to exist. The coastal state is obliged to grant other states, for example, distant water fishing nations, access to these surpluses.

The obligation is largely empty in economic terms. First, Article 61 grants the coastal state full power in setting the TAC's. Of perhaps greater significance is the fact that Article 62 goes on to grant the coastal state very broad powers in drawing up terms and conditions of access to be imposed upon distant water fishing nations seeking to harvest the 'surpluses.' Certainly, there is no question that the coastal state can demand remuneration from distant water fishing nations harvesting the 'surpluses.' Indeed, it can be argued that an imaginative coastal state could readily design a set of terms and conditions of access that would bar all distant water fishing nations from its EEZ.[8]

The convention (Article 63) admonishes coastal states with transboundary resources to co-operate where necessary with other coastal states and/or distant water nations for the conservation of the resources but provides no specific suggestions as to the form such co-operation might take. Article 63 also makes it clear, however, that when the relevant resources are present in the coastal state EEZ, the coastal state retains full Article 56 powers over the resources.

Finally, in reviewing Part 5 of the convention, reference should be made to the anadromous species article, Article 66. The term anadromous species refers to those fish which breed in fresh water rivers and lakes but spend most of their adult life in salt water.

To Canada, anadromous species meant salmon in general, and Pacific salmon in particular. Canada pressed hard in the conference, in alliance with the United States, for protection against high seas fishing. In this they were moderately successful, thanks to the incorporation in Article 66 of what has become known as the State of Origin Principle. The principle maintains that the state in whose fresh water the fish are produced shall have 'primary interest in and responsibility' for the fish. The principle was to play a major role in Canada's negotiations with the U.S. on the joint management of Pacific salmon.

The fisheries issues of interest to Canada were effectively settled in the Third Law of the Sea Conference by the spring of 1975. That the conference continued until the end of 1982 was due largely to disputes over the issue of deep sea mining. The early settlement of the fisheries issues, combined with the protracted nature of the conference, resulted in coastal states being increasingly tempted to introduce EFJ unilaterally. In Canada, the state of the Atlantic fisheries made the temptation particularly difficult to resist.

By the spring of 1976, it was clear that both the United States and Mexico were preparing to declare their intention to implement EFJ unilaterally. Canada formally declared its intention in June of that year, and by 1 January 1977 Canadian EFJ was an accomplished fact. In so doing, Canada made it apparent that it would adhere strictly to the Law of the Sea Convention.[9]

As we have indicated, the major gains to Canada from the EFJ were to be found in the Atlantic region. Of the transfer of renewable resource wealth that Canada enjoyed off her Atlantic coast as a consequence of EFJ, the greatest was unquestionably northern cod. According to the scientists, all but 5 percent of the northern cod stock complex was encompassed by the Canadian EEZ.[10]

The transfers of renewable resource wealth promised substantial economic benefits to Canada in general and to the beleaguered Atlantic coast fishing industry in particular. The promised benefits were, however, accompanied by a set of resource management problems – problems which all coastal states implementing EFJ had to face. If the promised benefits were to be realized, the resource management problems would have to be addressed effectively. The problems were and are: (1) the intra-EEZ common property problem; (2) the management of 'shared' stocks; (3) the management of 'straddling' stocks; and (4) the establishment of economic relations with distant water fishing nations.

While we list the problems separately, it must not be thought that they are mutually exclusive. On the contrary, it will become evident in the discussion to follow that the problems are intertwined, and that the problems interact upon one another.

INTRA-EEZ MANAGEMENT ISSUES

Since this chapter is to address itself to the international dimensions of Canadian fisheries management issues, we shall do no more than offer a very brief summary of the intra-EEZ management issues. The economic case for EFJ was that it would reduce the common property problem associated with fisheries management. The lessons of the Canadian experience is that EFJ can at best mitigate the common property problem; it cannot eliminate the problem. The problem can easily emerge within the EEZ.

The Canadian resource management plan for Atlantic Canada was to rebuild the fishery resources now within her control by reducing foreign harvesting. The Canadian fishing industry would be the ultimate beneficiary from the restored resources.

At first the plan appeared to work well. Then, in 1982, the Atlantic coast fishing industry found itself in yet another crisis. The root cause of the problem lay in a serious overexpansion of both the domestic harvesting sector and processing sector.[11] The common property problem had re-emerged.

The more recent difficulties in Atlantic Canada, involving draconian reduction of harvest quotas (when EFJ should have promised steadily increasing quotas) can be attributed to scientific error. The scientists responsible for fishery resource stock assessments had systematically overestimated the resource sizes, particularly northern cod, since the advent of EFJ.[12] This led to excessively generous TAC's. The industry is now paying for these earlier estimation errors.

The one international aspect of this problem is the assertion that the resource stock problem was due to foreign overexploitation in the segments of the Grand Banks lying outside the 200 mile zone. We shall comment on this further. Now we could only remark that, while the foreign overharvesting was certainly an irritant, it was not the root cause of the problem.

We now turn to the EFJ management issues having true international dimensions. The first such issue is the problem of managing shared stocks.

THE MANAGEMENT OF SHARED STOCKS

As we noted in our discussion of the Law of the Sea Convention, it was inevitable that when coastal states established EEZ's, they would find that some of the fishery stocks encompassed thereby were transboundary in nature. A distinction is now being made between those transboundary stocks which are shared with neighbouring coastal states and those which cross the EEZ boundary into the high seas. The latter are now referred to as 'straddling' stocks. The distinction proves, for our purposes, to be a useful one. We consider the shared stock problem first.

Canada shares fishery stocks with the United States on both her Atlantic and Pacific coasts. On the Atlantic coast, the shared stocks are centred in the Gulf of Maine area and consist of a mixture of pelagic species (surface swimming), groundfish, and shellfish. In economic terms, by far the most important shared stock is a scallop resource on the Georges Bank.

Our earlier discussion of the Law of the Sea Convention made it evident that, while the convention urged coastal states to co-operate in the management of shared stocks, it said nothing about the nature of such co-operation. It is worth our while to enquire whether the economics of fisheries management can provide any insight.

What the economics of the management of shared stocks does indicate is the following. First, with a few exceptions, the economic consequences of non-co-operation are likely to be severe. Even if both sets of resource managers are entirely rational, the outcome is likely to be comparable to that of an uncontrolled common property problem, resulting in overexploitation of the resource. The economic analysis relies on the theory of games, in this particular instance the theory of competitive, or non-co-operative, games. The most famous of non-co-operative games, the Prisoner's Dilemma, proves to have great predictive power in this case.[13] The Prisoner's Dilemma states that without communication, and, hence, co-operation, the two 'players' are driven inexorably to adopt strategies that each recognizes as harmful.[14]

If the joint owners can communicate and do succeed in co-operating, it proves not to be sufficient for the two joint owners to agree on a division of allowable harvests. They must also be prepared to deal with the possibility that they will have different management goals. Means must be found to assign weights to the management preferences of the two (or more) resource owners.[15]

When Canada and the United States implemented EFJ in 1977, the two countries promptly recognized their shared stock problem on the Atlantic coast. They acted as if they recognized fully the consequences of non-co-operation and began negotiating a complex arrangement for joint management of the resources. In March 1979 the two countries signed an agreement – the East Coast Fisheries Agreement. The agreement would cover the management of the shared species, even though the two had not agreed on the boundary between the two 200 mile zones. The boundary issue was to be submitted to the World Court.[16]

The agreement was elaborate. Harvest shares were allocated for the relevant species. A seemingly sensible scheme was established for weighting the management preferences of the two countries for different groups of stocks.

The apparently exemplary agreement was sent to the Canadian Parliament and the U.S. Senate for ratification. The agreement was warmly received in the Canadian Parliament but died in the U.S. Senate. The most convincing reason suggested for the demise of the agreement is that it was vigorously opposed by the New England fishing industry.[17] The New England industry apparently concluded that the American negotiators had been thoroughly outbargained.

While the outcome was unfortunate, it was not disastrous, which is probably a major reason that serious attempts have not been made to revive the agreement. The boundary issue, which was submitted to the World Court, was eventually settled. Once the boundary issue had been dealt with, the most important of the shared resources, scallops, proved to be one of the exceptions in which co-operative management was not required. Heavy exploitation of the resources by Americans (Canadians) on their side of the boundary will have a negligible impact on the harvests of Canadian (American) fishermen on the other side of the boundary.[18] Truly effective management of the relatively minor Atlantic coast shared stocks, on the other hand, does required proper co-operation. What co-operation there is appears to be informal at best.

In contrast to the disappointing experience with the attempt at co-operative management of Atlantic coast shared stocks, a considerable degree of success was achieved on the Pacific coast. Of the species shared by Canada and the United States off their Pacific coasts, Pacific salmon is of almost overwhelming importance. Salmon is important to the fishing industries of Oregon, Washington, and Alaska and is the single most important species for the fishing industry of British Columbia.

Salmon, as an anadromous species, is normally harvested as it is about to go up river to spawn. Pacific salmon is shared by virtue of the fact that some Canadian (American) produced salmon are 'inter-cepted,' that is, caught, by American (Canadian) fishermen as they make their way back to their home rivers.

Canada and the United States have been engaged in the joint man-agement of at least some Pacific salmon since the late 1930s. The original focus for co-operation was the salmon produced in the Fraser River system. The Fraser River has been described as the most import-ant salmon river in the Western Hemisphere. Many of the Fraser River salmon, upon returning to spawn, pass through the Strait of Juan de Fuca and, thus, are particularly vulnerable to American exploitation.

In the 1930s, the two countries implemented a treaty for the joint management of Fraser River sockeye salmon, known as the Convention for the Protection, Preservation, and Extension of the Sockeye Salmon Fisheries in the Fraser River System.[19] The treaty worked well as a conservative device. By the early 1960s, however, the Canadian fishing industry had become convinced that Canada was not receiving an equitable share of the net economic benefits from the fisheries. Pressure mounted on the Canadian government to reopen negotiations.[20]

Before serious attention was given to reopening negotiations, how-ever, both Canada and the u.s. extended their fishing zones from three to twelve miles. Complications which arose therefrom led the two countries to enter into a bilateral fishing agreement. Contained within the agreement was a commitment to consult on all matters pertaining to Pacific salmon. This, in turn, led the two countries in 1970 to commence negotiations on the interception of Pacific salmon. The negotiations were ultimately to result in the Canada-u.s. Pacific Salmon Treaty.

Now up for negotiation was not just Fraser River salmon but all salmon subject to interception in the Northeast Pacific. Included were salmon produced in several rivers other than the Fraser in British Columbia, plus salmon produced in the Yukon and in the states of Oregon, Idaho, Washington, and Alaska.

The negotiating difficulties seemed overwhelming. The first prob-lem to be faced was that of measuring how much each side was gaining and losing through salmon interceptions. The problem proved to be intractable and has not been resolved to this day.

The negotiations were complicated by the fact that the Americans negotiated not as a unit but, rather, as a coalition. The coalition proved to be highly unstable.[21] Negotiations continued throughout the decade. At the turn of the decade, the prospects for a final settlement seemed unpromising at best. Nonetheless, the negotiators were encouraged to continue because the Prisoner's Dilemma was proving to have consid-erable predictive powers. While the Fraser River stocks continued to be protected, more or less, by the Fraser River Convention, which was still in force, there was growing evidence of a 'fish war' centred on other stocks. The high priced chinook salmon was a case in point. Moreover, both the u.s. and Canada had opportunities for salmon enhancement projects. These were held in abeyance as each state feared losing salmon produced, thereby, to interception.[22]

The impasse was eventually broken as a result of an initiative introduced by the Canadian negotiating team. In our examination of the relevant part of the Law of the Sea Convention, reference was made to the anadromous species article, Article 66. This contained the State of Origin Principle.

While Canada was attempting to gain acceptance of the principle in UNCLOS III, she was, at the same time, attempting to have this principle adopted in the Canada-u.s. Pacific salmon negotiations. In this latter context, where it was more commonly referred to as the Equity Principle, the principle states that each state of origin should receive economic benefits equal to those arising from the salmon produced in its waters. Thus, while Canadians might not harvest all of the Fraser River salmon, they could be compensated in some form for Fraser River salmon taken by Americans. Conversely, Americans could expect compensation for, say, Columbia River salmon harvested by Canadians.

While the Americans were much less enthusiastic about the principle in the salmon negotiations with Canada than they were in UNCLOS III, the principle did finally gain acceptance. In consequence, a system was established for a division of the economic benefits from the package of salmon fisheries, even though it was not yet possible to measure the benefits in their entirety. In particular, it meant that, if Canada (u.s.) were to enter into a salmon enhancement program after the treaty was signed, all of the economic benefits arising therefrom would flow to Canada (u.s.).

The finessing of the interception measurement problem, plus the fact that both sets of negotiators were becoming alarmed about the state of chinook salmon stocks, resulted in the treaty negotiations being successfully concluded in 1983.[23] The treaty was then sent to Ottawa and Washington for ratification. Upon reaching the u.s. Senate, the treaty died. It was the East Coast Fisheries Agreement all over again – or so it appeared.

The problem lay within the American coalition. While, generally speaking, Oregon and Washington were satisfied with the treaty, Alaska was not. Opposition from Alaska was sufficient to block the treaty in the u.s. Senate.

In contrast to the East Coast Fisheries Agreement case, there was no tame acceptance in Canada of the u.s. Senate's decision. Canada developed a two part response. On the one hand, Canada let it be known that it was prepared to accept the treaty as it stood. On the other hand,

Canada reverted to competitive behaviour and re-ignited the 'fish war.' The Canadians, in particular, brought pressure to bear on the already threatened chinook stocks. Those Americans who stood to suffer most from the renewed 'fish war' were the co-operative Washingtonians and Oregonians, not the recalcitrant Alaskans.[24]

Nonetheless, the pressure had the desired effect. Further negotiations took place within the American coalition. With a judicious mixture of bribes and threats, the Alaskans were persuaded to view the treaty with greater favour. U.S.-Canada salmon negotiations recommenced. A revised treaty was signed and the consent of the U.S. Senate was promptly given. Prime Minister Mulroney and President Reagan exchanged the instruments of ratification in March 1985.

No attempt will be made to review the details of the treaty or the mechanism of implementation.[25] Rather, we will only remark that in the few years in which the treaty has been in operation there have been numerous expressions of irritation and many complaints to the effect that the treaty is not working as it should.[26]

Having said this, however, it is also true that both sides recognize that they are far better off with a treaty than without. In light of the immense difficulties confronting the negotiators, what is surprising is not that the treaty works imperfectly but, rather, that the mechanism for co-operative resource management was ever established.

Indeed, one can go so far as to say that although the treaty was not related directly to UNCLOS III, the Canada-U.S. Pacific Salmon Treaty and its operations will be studied intensely by the many coastal states confronting the problem of managing shared fishery resources under EFJ. The signing and implementing of the treaty must be seen as one of the major successes of post EFJ Canadian fisheries management policy.

DISTANT WATER FISHING NATIONS AND STRADDLING STOCKS

In the previous section we discussed the management of stocks shared with neighbouring coastal areas. We now turn to the more difficult problem of managing stocks that cross the EEZ boundary into the high seas – the so-called 'straddling stocks.' This issue is so closely linked to that of economic relations with distant water fishing nations that we treat the issues as one.

With respect to distant water fishing nations, for example, the Soviet Union, Spain, and Portugal, it will be recalled that the federal government had been strongly encouraged in the mid-1970s to implement EFJ unilaterally because of the apparently uncontrollable depletion of fishery resources off Atlantic Canada by these same distant water fishing nations. It seemed obvious that once Canada had implemented EFJ it would seek to minimize distant water fishing operations in its EEZ to the extent allowed by the Law of the Sea Convention. Indeed, during the crisis year of 1974, the federal minister responsible for fisheries, Jack Davis, minister of the environment, said just that in looking forward to EFJ: 'The long term is for Canadians. Canada is not only going to reach out and encompass all of the living resources off its continental shelf and slope, we are going to make sure that they are harvested by Canadians, in Canadian-owned vessels, and processed in Canada as well.'[27]

What may appear to be an obvious policy is not necessarily a sensible policy in economic terms. If we return to the Law of the Sea Convention, we are reminded of the fact the fishery resources within the EEZ constitute coastal state property. While the coastal state is called upon to grant distant water fishing nations access to segments of the TAC's 'surplus' to coastal state harvesting capacity, in no sense is the coastal state required to grant such access free of charge. We argued that in fact an imaginative coastal state could establish access conditions so onerous that distant water fishing nations would be effectively barred from the EEZ.

If distant water fishing nations are to be invited over the long term to participate in fisheries in the coastal state EEZ, it will be because it is in the selfish interest of the coastal state for this participation to take place. This, then, raises the following question: under what circumstances, if any, would distant fishing nation participation in EEZ fisheries be to the economic advantage of the coastal state?

One approach to analyzing this question, which this author has found useful in the past and which is now being adopted by others,[28] is to think of a coastal state permitting distant water fishing nation activity in its zone as 'importing' harvesting and/or processing services.[29] To take but one example, suppose that the coastal state authorities agree to the establishment of a joint venture between a domestic fishing company and a distant water entity in which foreign vessels harvest a fishery resource within the EEZ and then deliver the harvested fish for onshore processing by the domestic fishing company. One could, in this case, think of the coastal state as 'importing' foreign harvesting services.

Seen in this light, the argument for considering granting distant water fleets access to the EEZ is a variant of the argument for free trade. Distant water fleets in a particular fishery may have a comparative advantage in harvesting or processing or both. If the objective is to maximize the economic returns from the relevant fishery for the coastal state as a whole, it, consequently, may be sensible in economic terms to draw upon the distant water fishing nation services. If for a particular fishery the comparative advantage in harvesting and processing lies with the coastal state, then distant water fishing nation participation should not be given serious consideration.

There are numerous reasons why a distant water nation might possess a comparative advantage in harvesting and/or processing in a given fishery. These have been discussed at length elsewhere; we shall not repeat them here.[30] We would only comment that the pattern of comparative advantage is not static – it may shift through time. Thus, a coastal state's comparative disadvantage in a particular fishery could be transformed into a comparative advantage over time.[31]

Arguments against permitting distant water fishing nation participation in coastal state fisheries, even when the distant water fishing nation possesses a clear comparative advantage, can be seen as arguments for the protection of the domestic fishing industry. This can become complex, since there are, of course, two segments to the domestic industry: harvesting and processing. Protection of one segment may come at the expense of the other.[32]

Arguments for protection cannot be rejected out of hand. The argument for free trade is essentially an argument for maximizing efficiency in the world economy. Individual countries may benefit from protection, albeit at the expense of the rest of the world economy. Our concern is with the individual coastal state.

Economists have, as a consequence, made a distinction between what they term 'legitimate' and 'illegitimate' arguments for protection. 'Legitimate' arguments are those which, if implemented, would benefit the country as a whole; illegitimate arguments are those which, if implemented, might benefit certain domestic industries but at the expense of the rest of the country. What is perhaps the most famous of the 'legitimate' arguments for protection is the infant industry argument. The argument has direct relevance to coastal states – distant water fishing nation relations under EFJ.

The argument states that a country may have a latent comparative advantage in a particular economic activity. A domestic industry based on the activity cannot become successfully established in the face of entrenched foreign rivals. Therefore, the 'infant' should be protected until it has gone through the necessary learning process. The country's comparative advantage in the activity will then be revealed, and the protection can be safely removed.

In the case of EFJ, we are faced with a situation in which domestic fishing industries are attempting to become established in fisheries that hitherto had been international common property. As 'infants' in these activities, the domestic fishing industries appear to be uncompetitive in comparison with entrenched distant water fishing rivals. If the domestic industries are given protection while they pass through their infancy, the country's true comparative advantage will become revealed.[33]

While the infant industry argument, however applied, has legitimacy, there are several caveats which accompany it. The most important one is that it is very difficult to determine beforehand which 'infants' do in fact have genuine prospects for achieving maturity. If protection is given to an infant industry which in fact has no such prospects, the economy may be burdened permanently.

There is another argument for protection which has great relevance for Canada's Atlantic coast fisheries. This is the employment argument, which we might describe as 'semi-legitimate.' The argument states that if unemployment is a chronic problem, domestic industries should be protected in order to maintain, and hopefully expand, employment. Hence in the case of fisheries, domestic harvesting and processing should be protected in the face of lower cost distant water harvesting/processing in order to maintain employment opportunities.

The argument has legitimacy to the following extent. In assessing domestic versus foreign comparative advantage, one should look at the true costs to society of the domestic operation. In the case of labour, this is the opportunity cost of labour – what the labour could produce elsewhere in the economy. If the only alternative for labour engaged in a fishery operation is unemployment, then the opportunity cost of labour will be low – almost certainly below what the labour is being paid by private industry. Hence, it is quite possible that the economics would dictate using the domestic operations, even though on the basis of private costs the advantage would appear to lie with distant water nations.

Beyond this the employment argument is questionable. If unemployment is a chronic problem, one must ask if there are not less damaging ways, in economic terms, of dealing with the problem. Indeed, acceptance of the employment argument may simply excuse the authorities from dealing with the true causes of the unemployment.

This author has reviewed, in some considerable detail, the policy of the Canadian government with regard to distant water participation in the Canadian EEZ up to the mid-1980s.[34] The evolution of the policy was described as a reluctant retreat from marine autarky. There have been certain specific instances in which the authorities countenanced long-term arrangements with distant water fishing nations. One involved a hake fishery off British Columbia. Prior to EFJ, the domestic industry took no interest whatsoever in the resource. Following EFJ, the industry had no interest in processing the harvested fish. An arrangement was allowed to develop in which Canadian trawlers harvested the resource for delivery to foreign vessels with onboard processing capacity. Most of the vessels were from Eastern Europe. The arrangement has continued to the present day and can be expected to continue for the foreseeable future.

Off the Atlantic coast, the authorities followed the policy of permitting foreign harvesting of stocks in which the Canadian industry had shown little or no interest. Fees were charged, but the fees were designed to do no more than defray part of the management costs. The authorities also permitted, from time to time, joint venture type arrangements, in which Canadian harvesters would deliver fish to foreign processing vessels, or the reverse, in which foreign harvesters would deliver fish to Canadian onshore plants. The authorities made it clear, however, that these arrangements were to be seen as temporary and were to be phased out with all possible speed.

The authorities also allowed some distant water nations – Western Europeans in particular – small amounts of 'non-surplus' fish in exchange for 'commensurate benefits,' such as improved market access.[35] An important example of such non-surplus fish was northern cod. In June 1986 it was announced that allocations of 'non-surplus' fish to foreigners would cease as of 1987.[36]

In following what was essentially an autarkic approach, the government was given strong support by the 1982 Task Force on Atlantic Fisheries, more popularly known as the Kirby Commission. The Kirby Commission brought to bear both the infant industry and employment arguments for protection we described earlier. The commission argued vociferously that, within the Canadian EEZ, Canadians should both harvest the resource and process the catch wherever feasible.[37]

Since the mid-1980s, the adherence to what is essentially autarkic policy has not weakened. If anything, it has become more determined. The extent to which the authorities have been prepared on occasion to carry out the process of 'Canadianization' was exemplified by an announcement made in 1987 concerning an Atlantic offshore resource – silver hake. Silver hake was a resource in which the Canadian industry had shown little interest in the past and which had been made available to foreign harvesters. The then minister of fisheries and oceans announced a 30,000 tonne allocation to the Canadian industry to provide more throughput for Atlantic coast processing plants.

There was, however, one condition. The fish had to be harvested by Canadian vessels. Foreign harvesting was not to be countenanced. If a Canadian fishing company wishing to participate in the scheme lacked adequate harvesting capacity, it would have to lease additional capacity from another Canadian company. The implication was that, if the aforementioned company was unable to lease the capacity from a Canadian source, it would forego the fish.[38]

The argument for such a policy would presumably be that it would create employment opportunities at sea. It is trivially easy to demonstrate, however, that the policy could readily lead to the loss of employment opportunities. The processing and sale of silver hake is, for the Canadian industry, marginal at best on economic grounds. Consider a situation in which foreign harvesting costs are significantly below Canadian harvesting costs. Then suppose that onshore plants would find it economically feasible to process the fish if delivered by low cost foreign vessels but infeasible if delivered by high cost Canadian vessels. Given the policy described, the fish would not be processed by the plants, and employment opportunities would be lost.[39]

The argument has been made that, whatever the economics of allowing distant water activity within the EEZ may be, Canadian companies were opposed to granting distant water fleets access and that, in any event, all other developed coastal states, at least, were following a similar policy.[40] What is true is that Canada's immediate neighbour, the United States, is following a similar policy.[41] It is not true, however, that every developed coastal state is autarkic. There is one important counter example, namely, New Zealand.

New Zealand has the fourth largest EEZ in the world. When New Zealand introduced EFJ, it came to realize that it had valuable offshore groundfish resources in which the New Zealand industry had heretofore shown little interest. With the advent of EFJ, the domestic industry's interest in the resources increased substantially.

New Zealand fishing companies were allocated tradeable harvest quotas for the exploitation of the resources. Outside of the restriction that a minimum percentage of the harvest must be landed in New Zealand for processing, the companies are effectively able to utilize the quotas as they see fit. If a New Zealand company wishes to use its own vessels to harvest its share of the TAC, it may do so; if it wishes to charter foreign vessels to do the harvesting, and possibly processing, it may also do so.[42]

The nature of the scheme is such that New Zealand industry objections to the presence of foreign vessels is removed. Indeed, the New Zealand companies make the initial decision as to whether or not foreign vessels are to be employed. Secondly, the question of comparative advantage ceases to be one of simply academic interest. Those companies which choose to ignore the dictates of comparative advantage are subject to swift and certain financial punishment. The scheme has now been in place for several years. Foreign vessels continue to play a significant role in New Zealand's offshore fisheries.[43]

When commentators, such as this author, discussed in the past the advantages and disadvantages of a distant water fishing nation presence in the EEZ, we either ignored or treated lightly one advantage which can be summarized in one word – leverage. This leads us to a consideration of 'straddling' stocks.

We referred earlier to the Nose and Tail of the Grand Banks, those segments of the eastern and southern parts of the Grand Banks, respectively, lying outside Canada's EEZ. There existed, as well, fishing ground off Atlantic Canada, wholly outside the EEZ, in which Canada had an interest, known as the Flemish Cap. With the implementation of EFJ, Canada adopted the seemingly very sensible policy of establishing an international organization to manage the resources on the Nose and Tail of the Bank and on the Flemish Cap. The international organization, essentially a successor to ICNAF, was the Northwest Atlantic Fisheries Organization (NAFO). Distant water fishing nations operating in the area were strongly encouraged by Canada to join. NAFO commenced operation on 1 January 1979.[44]

The Nose and Tail of the Bank plus the Flemish Cap constituted the NAFO regulatory area to be governed by a NAFO commission. The commission was to ensure that its policies were compatible with those of Canada. Canada was to have preferential harvesting rights in the regulatory area (NAFO Convention, Article 11). In other words, Canada had, within NAFO, the whiphand – or so it would have seemed.

The stocks, subject to NAFO management, which would meet our definition of 'straddling' stocks, were cod in the Tail of the Bank, flounder in both the Nose and Tail, redfish in the Nose of the Bank, plus capelin and squid. Notable for its absence was northern cod. While the resource extends into the Nose of the Bank, the relevant scientists had maintained at the onset of EFJ, it will be recalled, that 95 percent of the resource was encompassed by the Canadian EEZ. The resource was, therefore, declared to be an exclusively Canadian stock, subject to Canadian management alone.[45]

One distant water fishing nation, which had a history of fishing in the region dating back to the sixteenth century, was Spain. Canada had difficulties with this distant water fishing nation from the earliest days of EFJ. As Canada moved towards EFJ, Canadian-Spanish fisheries relations deteriorated severely. Spain was effectively excluded from the Canadian EEZ and refused to join NAFO. Spain did, however, continue to operate in the Tail of the Bank as a non-member. Moreover, other non-member vessels began appearing, flying flags of countries such as Panama and Venezuela. Several of these vessels bore a striking resemblance to Spanish trawlers. Spain was eventually persuaded to join NAFO. Its behaviour, however, continued to be less than exemplary.[46]

The single most important member in NAFO, outside Canada, is the European Community (EC). During the first several years of NAFO's existence, the EC was co-operative. Canada argued for the same type of management regime it was following within its EEZ. That policy was conservationist in nature, calling for resource stock levels considerably above those prevalent in the ICNAF regime. The EC concurred with Canadian resource management policy.[47]

The West Europeans had a particular interest in northern cod. Until the mid-1980s, the Canadian authorities granted modest allocations to Europeans, in the order of 20,000 tonnes per annum. To put this amount in perspective, the total northern cod TAC at this time was in the order of 270,000 tonnes per annum.

In 1985 EC negotiations with Spain and Portugal were completed. The two countries were scheduled to become EC members at the beginning of 1986. Canada's problems with Spain now seemed to be at an end.

In fact, Canada's problems in the NAFO zone were about to become much worse. Canada's hitherto satisfactory relations with the EC deteriorated. The EC announced in 1985 that it had had a change of mind about the resource management policies followed up to that time. The policies had, the EC contended, been excessively conservationist. The EC refused to accept NAFO established quotas and began to set its own unilaterally. The EC catches began exceeding the quotas assigned to the EC by NAFO by a wide margin (Table 1).

TABLE 1
EC NAFO quotas and catches in NAFO regulatory areas,
1986-8 ('000s of tonnes)

Year	Quota	Catch
1986	23.3	110.2
1987	23.2	105.4
1988	19.0	46.4

SOURCE: Department of Fisheries and Oceans

To what extent the EC's actions were motivated by Canada's decision to phase out all foreign allocations of northern cod is not known. What is known is that the EC began openly defying Canada and started exploiting northern cod extensively on the Nose of the Bank, as is indicated in Table 2. While the reference in the table is to 'foreign harvests,' the foreign harvests were accounted for almost exclusively by EC members, or soon-to-become members, that is, Spain and Portugal.

TABLE 2

Canadian allocated quotas to foreigners and foreign harvests
(northern cod), 1984-9 ('000s of tonnes)

Year	Quota	Harvest
1984	20.0	29.6
1985	16.3	44.2
1986	16.3	65.8
1987	9.5	35.7
1988	0.0	20.0

SOURCE: Department of Fisheries and Oceans

Let us digress for a moment and return to the issue of the management of northern cod in general and the reduction of northern cod quotas. There can be no question that the EC defiance over northern cod exacerbated the problem. The EC harvest level in 1986 appears to be particularly outrageous.

Yet these figures must be kept in perspective. The Kirby Commission had predicted confidently that the northern cod TAC would be 400,000 tonnes by the late 1980s. It proved in fact to be only 266,000 tonnes. Then the government announced that the TAC would have to be reduced to less than 200,000 tonnes. Some scientists called for a TAC of only 125,000 tonnes.[48] Also let us recall further that the scientists' overestimates of the stock levels had dated back to the advent of the EFJ and had persisted throughout a period of exemplary behaviour on the part of the EC.

To return to Canada's problem with distant water fishing nations, in addition to the EC's defiant stance in the Nose and Tail of the Bank, there was a significant increase in the number of vessels in the NAFO regulatory area flying non-NAFO flags.[49] There is reason to believe that many of the vessels are NAFO member country vessels carrying new names and flying new flags.

In reviewing the data and other evidence, one is forced to say that recent NAFO developments bear all the signs of a moderately effective co-operative game having been transformed into a destructive, competitive game. Interestingly, there is a current parallel in the American EEZ off Alaska.

The American bonanza from EFJ consists of a set of groundfish stocks in the Gulf of Alaska and the Bering Sea. A portion of the resource extends beyond the EEZ into a high seas area of the Bering Sea referred to as the 'doughnut.' Prior to EFJ, the resource (excluding halibut) was exploited largely by distant water fishing nations, for example, Japan and South Korea. Little harvesting occurred in the 'doughnut.'

As we have noted, the U.S. has followed an autarkic fisheries policy very similar to that of Canada. The distant water fishing nations have been steadily pressured out of the American EEZ off Alaska. A recent study by Edward Miles of the University of Washington[50] shows that the exclusion of foreigners from the EEZ has been accompanied by an alarming increase in foreign exploitation of the 'straddling' stock extending into the 'doughnut.' Miles observes that in driving the distant water fishing nation from its EEZ, the U.S. now finds that it has lost all leverage over the foreign harvesters.[51]

It will take a future historian sifting through evidence not yet in the public domain to determine fully the reasons for the collapse in Canada-EC fisheries relations. What is apparent, however, is that Canada, like the U.S., has, by reducing distant water fishing nation activity in its EEZ to the minimum, sharply reduced its leverage over these nations.

What can now be done to address the situation is unclear. The apparently obvious solution is to extend Canada's EEZ to the edge of the continental shelf. Yet the 200 mile boundary of the EEZ, unsatisfactory though it may be, represented a carefully balanced compromise in UNCLOS III. An attempt by Canada to violate that compromise unilaterally could have serious international legal implications. Canada may find itself being forced to rely on the not encouraging option of moral suasion.

In reviewing the problem of the management of transboundary fishery resources, it is reasonable to ask why the problem appears to be tractable when it appears in the form of 'shared' resources but intractable when it appears in the form of 'straddling' stocks. This author would maintain that the answer lies in part in the nature of the relevant property rights. When a fishery resource is shared by two (or more) coastal states, the Law of the Sea Convention gives reasonably clear guidance as to the nature of the shared property rights. This issue is discussed at some length in McRae and Munro in a 1989 paper.[52]

On the other hand, the nature of property rights to fishery resources in the high seas adjacent to EEZ's is opaque at best. The interested reader is directed to a recent article by Edward Miles and William Burke,[53] which makes the unsatisfactory nature of property rights transparently obvious. With the rights and duties of coastal states and distant water fishing nations regarding the 'straddling' stocks unclear and subject to dispute, it should come as no surprise to find that establishing effective co-operative management regimes has proven to be difficult in the extreme.

CONCLUSION

The United Nations Third Conference on the Law of the Sea has led to a revolution in the management of world fisheries. Fishery resources, which hitherto had been international common property, were transferred to coastal states. Canada gave strong support to Extended Fisheries Jurisdiction and enjoyed large transfers of renewable resource wealth off its Atlantic coast. These resources had, before EFJ, been heavily exploited by distant water fishing nations, to the detriment of the Canadian fishing industry and of the Atlantic coast economies supported by the industry. EFJ held out considerable promise for Atlantic Canada.

Transfers of renewable resource wealth were, however, accompanied by resource management problems, several of which had international dimensions. At the time of writing, the benefits of EFJ appear to be disappointing, as the Atlantic coast fishing industry finds itself in yet another serious crisis. We have identified the crisis as due in part to past stock estimation error on the part of the scientists and to a deterioration of relations with distant water fishing nations exploiting the so-called 'straddling' stocks extending beyond Canada's EEZ.

Dealing with the stock estimation problem necessitates a painful, but hopefully temporary, reduction in harvest quotas. The difficulties with the distant water fishing nations appear to be longer term. We express doubts as to whether the frequently suggested solution of extending the boundaries of Canada's EEZ's to eliminate 'straddling' stocks is in fact feasible.

While there have been disappointments, most of them highly visible, there have also been successes, which have enjoyed much less publicity. A prominent example is provided by the management of 'shared' fishery resources. The most important of Canada's 'shared' fishery resources is Pacific salmon, which is shared with the United States. While salmon negotiations with the United States preceded UNCLOS III, a link was established between these negotiations and UNCLOS III.

The salmon negotiations ultimately resulted in the Canada-U.S. Pacific Salmon Treaty, which came into force in 1985. Although there are complaints that the treaty is not working as effectively as hoped, the treaty must, nonetheless, be regarded as one of the successes of post-EFJ

Canadian fisheries management policy.

EFJ has been in effect for over a decade in Canada. Given the revolutionary impact it has had upon world fisheries management, one must expect that post-EFJ Canadian fisheries management policy will necessarily continue to evolve for some time. One can hope that, as the evolution continues, Canada will, in spite of earlier disappointments, come to enjoy the full economic benefits of EFJ.

CHAPTER TWELVE

Air, Water, and Political Fire: Building a North American Environmental Regime

Don Munton and
Geoffrey Castle

Flowing across the world's longest undefended border is not only an unparalleled level of trade in goods and services but also what one Canadian environment minister has called 'a massive international exchange of...pollutants.'[1] The concerns these transboundary flows arouse have, in turn, prompted efforts to develop norms that would govern the production and control of the pollutants and hence reduce their transboundary movement. What are needed, in the words of the same minister, are 'new rules which could allow one nation to tell the other to turn off the pollution at the source.' It is the purpose of this chapter to trace the slow and somewhat unsteady growth over the twentieth century of these rules and norms, or of what are increasingly called environmental 'regimes,' between Canada and the United States and to evaluate and understand Canadian interests and policies in this regime-building exercise.

ENVIRONMENTAL REGIMES

There is much scholarly disagreement over what constitutes an international 'regime' and what does not.[2] Where most who use the term will agree, however, is that a regime is a set of rules and norms applied by countries to some aspect of their international activity. We assume that these rules, as they are mutually accepted, are usually incorporated and evident in treaties or agreements, such as the Canada-U.S. 1972 Great Lakes Water Quality Agreement or the 1991 Air Quality Agreement. There is more to an international regime than just formal agreements, however, as judicial and quasi-judicial decisions, customary norms, and political practice all contribute to declared and observed rules and norms.

The focus of our discussion will be on the efforts undertaken to create the Great Lakes regime and the policies pursued in the ongoing attempts to construct a similar regime for the air and, specifically, the control of the long range transport of air pollution and acid rain. In both cases, the history of Canada-U.S. co-operation and conflict goes back several decades. In both cases, as well, there has been a history of governments ignoring in practice the rules they have committed themselves to in principle. On both sides of the border, governments have refused to follow up rhetoric with action, to set and implement pollution control laws, to provide the funding often required by abatement programs, and to take action if necessary against polluters.

In 1909, Great Britain, on behalf of the then semi-sovereign Canada, and the United States signed the Boundary Waters Treaty.[3] Although it dealt mainly with the 'levels and flows' of the boundary waters, this treaty provided the keystone of what has become the emerging bilateral regime for water quality.[4] Its provisions included nothing less than a general prohibition on the pollution of the boundary waters. The second paragraph of Article 4 states that 'the waters herein defined as boundary waters and waters flowing across the boundary shall not be polluted on either side to the injury of health or property on the other.'[5] Arguably, the sweeping, absolute nature of this provision was, in fact, its Achilles heel. Given the common environment, water currents, and wind patterns, it was virtually impossible to prevent all injurious pollution from crossing the boundary. Article 4 was thus too broad and absolute a prohibition to prevent misuse of the waters or to provide a guide for day by day policy decisions. It was thus ignored. When faced, only a few years after the Boundary Waters Treaty was signed, with serious typhoid epidemics in cities on the Great Lakes due to waterborne bacteria from human sewage, governments on both sides responded, not by eliminating raw sewage outflows (as 'required' by Article 4) or by treating them but by continuing to pollute and adopting the less expensive measure of chlorinating drinking water supplies.

In the case of air pollution, the ultimate resolution of the Trail Smelter case of the 1930s and 1940s upheld the responsibility of good neighbours not to pollute each other's territory. The International Joint Commission, in ultimately awarding damages to American farmers affected by 'fumes' from the large Cominco smelter located but a few miles north of the 49th parallel, declared that:

[U]nder the principles of international law, as well as the law of the United States, no state has the right to use or permit the use of its territory in such a manner as to cause damages to another state or to the properties or persons therein, when the case is of serious consequence and the injury is established by clear and convincing evidence.[6]

This statement of principle, in the view of one of Canada's most eminent international lawyers and jurists, 'anticipated modern transboundary air pollution rules by two generations.'[7]

Despite the Boundary Waters Treaty and the Trail Smelter case, the principles stated therein had little effect on well established practices. They had little effect, that is, in preventing the serious pollution problems which emerged over the coming decades. By the mid-1960s it was clear that pollution in the Great Lakes had become steadily and dangerously worse. It was also clear, at least to the scientists involved, that the pollution problems of the lakes, and their causes, had become much more complex.

By the late 1970s it was also widely accepted within the scientific community that transboundary air pollution, in the form of acid rain, had also become a serious environmental problem. In distinct contrast to the Trail smelter situation, the scientific evidence on acid rain pointed, not to a single major source, but to a large number of diverse sources. Coal-fired electrical generating plants, other industries, and American urban centres were the major sources of the transboundary flows of air pollutants. In the case of Great Lakes water quality, the other most prominent environmental issue on the bilateral agenda, the shared lakes receive more pollution from the United States than they do from Canadian sources. In fact, the transboundary flows of pollution from the United States are so much greater than what is produced 'domestically' that Canada can be described as being 'environmentally dependent' on the U.S. – at least in these two cases. Due to the relatively smaller loads it receives back across the frontier the same cannot be said of the United States. Given this situation of environmental dependence, it is by no means surprising that the government of Canada has, within limits, sought to prod Washington into the creation and strengthening of bilateral international environmental regimes. Canada has been the demandeur, in other words, in recent major environmental negotiations with the U.S.

A GREAT LAKES REGIME

If the Boundary Waters Treaty provides, in a single principle, the foundation of the emerging Canada-United States regime in international environmental issues, the 1972 Great Lakes Water Quality Agreement, renegotiated and broadened in 1978 and modestly revised in 1987, provides much of the framing. A thorough history of the development and negotiation of this agreement would be a lengthy one.[8] Suffice it to say here that it emerged in part out of scientific work pointing to new and alarming pollution threats. Principal among these, the scientists said, was the problem of eutrophication, or the accelerated aging, of the lower lakes due to excessive nutrients. The agreement and various other environmental laws at the time were also greatly facilitated by mounting public concern over water pollution in the late 1960s – early 1970s, which, in the United States, was partly focused on the 'death of Lake Erie.'

The Canadian policy objective, originally, was to secure such an accord and, laterally, has been to maintain its integrity. Canadian governments developed the concept of this accord, pursued it doggedly through bilateral discussions and then formal negotiations over the period 1970-2, celebrated its signing in April 1972, and then pressed for its full implementation in the following years. The motivations on the Canadian side stemmed more or less directly from the basic underlying realities of transboundary water pollution in the lakes. As the IJC technical report, which first called for bilateral co-operation had shown, the vast bulk of pollutants came from American sources.[9]

Once the pioneering 1972 accord was put into place, however, some Canadian reticence emerged about certain ways in which the accord, and hence the regime, might be broadened and strengthened. The essence of the 1972 accord, maintained in the 1978 and 1987 versions, was agreement on some common general water quality objectives and specific regulatory standards, and on a collaborative monitoring of subsequent progress, along with mutual commitments to implement national programs to achieve these objectives.[10] The accord itself specified water quality objectives and standards in terms of maximum levels of particular pollutants allowed in the open waters. In one sense, then, the 1972 agreement represented an elaboration and definition of that key clause (Article 4) of the Boundary Waters Treaty. As an attempt to translate this article into practical goals, it was an important, indeed essential, refinement of the bilateral environmental regime.

A key point, often misunderstood, is that while the objectives and standards are joint, and the monitoring of progress is a collaborative effort under the aegis of a binational organization (the International Joint Commission), the pollution control programs are national. Though intended to be complementary, the regulatory programs of the various jurisdictions – federal, state, provincial, and municipal – are designed to meet their own differing needs and are implemented more or less autonomously within each country and jurisdiction. The Great Lakes agreements, therefore, effected no significant devolution of sovereign authority for pollution control actions. This aspect of the ongoing accord is central to an understanding of both the principles and the implementation process of environmental regimes for North America not only for water quality problems but also, as we will show, with respect to air quality problems. In fact, the Great Lakes Water Quality Accord was used by both governments as the model, both in terms of process and of substance, for the effort to fashion the first ever bilateral air quality accord.

The Water Quality Agreement of 1972 (and, later, of 1978) gave the International Joint Commission new responsibilities – for the collection and analysis of information on water quality objectives and pollution control programs, for the independent verification of data, and for the publication of reports, on at least a biennial basis, assessing progress towards these objectives. In addition, these agreements gave the IJC responsibility for providing 'assistance in the co-ordination of the joint activities.' Both accords further directed the IJC to establish a Water Quality Board to assist the commission on pollution control issues, a Research (later termed, Science) Advisory Board to advise specifically on scientific issues, and empowered the commission to establish a Great Lakes regional office, within which much of its staff work would be carried out, in addition to the offices it maintains in Ottawa and Washington. The result of this new and broader mandate was a rather rapid expansion of the staff, expertise, responsibilities, and budgets of the IJC – changes which were not well received by some of the officials responsible for pollution control programs on both sides of the border.

The bilateral co-ordinating process for the national pollution control policies for the Great Lakes that evolved in the years following the first agreement was complex, perhaps even cumbersome. Each of the two federal, eight state, and two provincial governments (Ontario and Quebec) pursue their respective policies to a greater or lesser extent in the context of the international agreement. The water quality and science advisory boards meet regularly and, every two years or so, draw up a substantial report evaluating the progress achieved. These reports are then formally presented to the commission at a public meeting (though in fact the practice now is for the board members and commissioners to meet and discuss the reports beforehand). The commissioners and their staff, in turn, prepare and debate, behind closed doors, an official IJC report to the governments. Officials then prepare and politicians approve for each government a formal response to those points in the IJC report to which they choose to respond. Thus, the various governments may or may not eventually be stimulated to improve or otherwise change national programs.

One of the purposes of this elaborate superstructure and process, for the agreement's Canadian negotiators, had been to make more difficult the kind of benign neglect by governments which had often followed other technical reports and verbal commitments. These officials, perhaps because they were Canadian, were always particularly concerned about the depth of the American resolve to tackle the pollution problems of the Great Lakes. Their fears were not long in being realized. In November 1972, barely seven months after the agreement was signed, President Nixon, in the name of fiscal restraint, impounded federal funds authorized by Congress for building municipal sewage treatment plants, including ones around the Great Lakes. A few years later the IJC observed solemnly that progress so far had been 'generally slow, uneven and in certain cases, disappointing.'[11] Despite frequent claims by administration officials at the time that the impoundment action had not significantly slowed U.S. control programs, there is little question it did precisely that.[12] It would be early in the next decade before the American municipal reductions originally anticipated for 1975 would come into effect. Neither its own formal commitments nor bilateral pressures from Canada moved Washington to proceed more quickly.

To reiterate: as both the provisions of the accord and its history evince, the agreement presented no significant threat to sovereign national control over relevant public policies. At most one could argue that it begins to confer very modest independent powers on the IJC in the above-described provisions. The dominance of the boards by government officials, however, as well as the tight reign to which the IJC is often subjected by governments, constrained any supranational aspirations that might have emerged from within the IJC structure proper and stymied any such hopes on the part of the IJC's proponents.

Although the commission is often mistaken for a supranational authority by individuals and some environmental experts alike, its role remains more akin to that of a standing royal commission than that of, say, the Canadian Radio-Television and Telecommunications Commission or the Canadian Transport Commission. It is in no sense a transboundary binational environmental regulatory agency. Effective control of ongoing environmental policy lies not with the IJC or even with governmental officials meeting under the aegis of the commission; control remains firmly based in the national, state, and provincial capitals. The bilateral co-ordinating process did, however, offer opportunities for embarrassing governments which remained reluctant to regulate firmly against major polluters in their own jurisdictions. The extent of concerns of this sort, however, and fears about supranational activity beyond what Ottawa and Washington are willing to countenance, is demonstrated well in the 1977-8 renegotiation of the 1972 accord.

When originally negotiated, the 1972 Great Lakes Agreement focused largely on the problem of eutrophication due to excessive nutrients, especially phosphates, in the lakes. As a result of improved detection instrumentation (making possible the identification of trace pollutants) and more research into the consequences of other substances through the 1970s, two new, related foci – those of industrial effluents and toxic chemicals – pushed their way onto the Great Lakes agenda. These put the spotlight on non-municipal sources – agricultural runoff and, in particular, industrial effluents. This shift, in turn, caused the political focus to move and to highlight not only American sources but also Canadian sources. Ontario's industrial pollution control programs, which lagged far behind its own municipal ones, became a target for U.S. officials now tired of being on the defensive.

During the renegotiation of the agreement in 1977-8, U.S. officials pressed particularly hard on two fronts. One was for the revised agreement to commit both sides to the industrial effluent standards now enshrined into American law by the tough 1972 Clean Water Act and for these standards to apply to tributaries. This negotiating position, as the American side well knew, put Ontario in a difficult position. The second offensive was launched against the increasingly active IJC regional office, which some American officials had come to regard as no less than a threat to the sovereignty of the United States.[13] Ottawa held firm with Ontario on the former point, and the province got off that hook. On the latter, agreement was eventually reached to restructure the IJC office and reassign authority over its more sensitive functions to government bureaucrats.

While the basic structure of the accord, in terms of authority and commitments, was maintained, its substantive focus in terms of pollution problems shifted considerably. The negotiators drew up a list of hundreds of hazardous chemicals that were to be eliminated from the lakes, and the revised agreement heralded a new attack against toxic substances. The parties committed themselves, as well, to adopting an 'ecosystem approach' rather than trying to attack each pollutant or problem-area individually, although what this approach would involve practically was less than clear.

As had happened in 1972, U.S. inter-agency approval of the revised agreement was delayed by the Office of Management and Budget, which scrutinized it closely for any provisions that might involve expenditures not already authorized by Congress and accepted by the administration – that is, for any hidden attacks on the sovereign authority – and budget – of the government of the U.S. But eventually, in late

1978, the new pact was signed.

Implementation continued, albeit not apace. The IJC reports during the 1980s tended to focus on what the Water Quality Board had come to call 'areas of concern' – particularly polluted and degraded areas of the lakes where remedial action was most needed. One perennial area of concern, for example, is Hamilton harbour. Another is the complex of chemical industry dumps near Niagara Falls, New York. The infamous Love Canal area, which was largely evacuated, its homes bulldozed, and its toxic ground water still being collected for disposal, is one of the smallest of these dump sites. The highly contaminated waters of the Niagara River – into which more than 3,000 pounds of pollutants are discharged daily, 90 per cent of them from the U.S. side – are appalling evidence of the scope and severity of the toxin problem. The cleanup of these dump sites has long been stalled by the high costs and uncertainties surrounding the optimal set of remedial actions, including who should pay for it. Under a new and separate accord concluded in early 1987, both federal governments, New York, and Ontario agreed to cut these emissions in half by 1996, thus recommiting themselves to commitments already implied under the 1978 agreement.

The Niagara problem has long been of particular concern to Canada because of the 'downstream' effects. The river and its pollution load flow over the famous falls and into Lake Ontario. Metropolitan Toronto, the largest single urban concentration in Canada and the largest by far on the lake, receives its drinking water from those same waters. Indeed, two out of every three Canadians obtain their drinking water from the Great Lakes - St. Lawrence system. The impact on the Canadian side is actually exacerbated by the fact that, as recent scientific research has shown, the physical dynamics of Lake Ontario are less those of a giant sink than that of a river – a river of pollutants – which run in a counter-clockwise direction around the circumference of the lake, thus carrying much of the pollutant loading past major urban centres. Despite cutbacks of nutrients and despite considerable progress in sewage treatment, Canada's situation of environmental dependence thus continues.

REVIEWING THE GREAT LAKES AGREEMENT

A comprehensive, non-governmental review of progress under the Great Lakes Agreement by the Royal Society of Canada (RSC) and the National Research Council of the U.S. National Academy of Sciences (NRC) in 1984-5 concluded, in essence, that there had been significant progress but that implementation was still lagging far behind declared principles and official commitments.[14] The IJC itself urged that the governments should maintain the 1978 agreement but undertake measures 'to clarify, strengthen and support' the existing provisions.[15] They were clearly concerned that the agreement, if opened for renegotiation, might be weakened by pressures from the U.S. side, that is, from the anti-regulatory Reagan administration. But such pressure was never mounted. The discussions between the two sides during the fall of 1987 were low key, congenial, and conducted largely at the technical level. And they were brief. No substantial gutting of the agreement's provisions occurred; nor, for that matter, did Canada or the U.S. propose any major substantive improvements. The emphasis was less on the substance of programs than on their implementation or 'delivery.' But there were no major new initiatives, no significant new spending programs, and no substantial institutional reforms – such as a strengthening of the IJC's independence.

The emerging regime for the Great Lakes has had a mixed record with respect to improving the quality of the waters concerned. On the one hand, the nutrient reduction objectives of the original agreement have largely been met, and the eutrophication problem is under control. On the other hand, scientific evidence of the seriousness and complexity of the toxic waste problem in the lakes has grown since 1972, and the government programs in this area have not yet begun to show substantial results. The most recent review of the state of the Great Lakes suggests that the pattern of failure to implement commitments to abstract principles remains unfortunately strong. The U.S.-based Conservation Foundation and the Canadian-based Institute for Research on Public Policy concluded in 1990 that 'neither country is spending enough, or doing enough, to check the insidious long-term decline of the Great Lakes ecosystem. On the remedial front, it is painfully clear that only the easiest problems have been tackled and the cheapest remedies ... applied.'[16]

AN EMERGING AIR QUALITY REGIME

Compared with the water quality regime, and despite the decades-old Trail Smelter case, the development of a North American air quality regime has only just begun. 'Acid rain' was first brought publicly to the agenda of Canadian-American relations in June 1977 by then federal environment minister Romeo LeBlanc. It was, he warned, 'an environmental time bomb,' indeed, 'the worst environmental problem [Canada has] ever had to face.' LeBlanc also suggested that '[we] do not have time to wait for final research before beginning political action.' Formal negotiations towards an international air quality agreement, he said, would begin 'within weeks.'[17] The minister was optimistic – indeed, decidedly so.[17] It would be not weeks but years before serious negotiations began and a decade and a half before any co-ordinated political action was taken.

The popular term 'acid rain' has come to stand for a complex set of physical and chemical phenomena by which gases, especially sulphur and nitrogen oxides, are emitted as a result of combustion and other processes and then transformed chemically into acidic compounds while being transported through the atmosphere. They are then deposited by rain, snow, and dry particles onto land and water surfaces.[18] A bilateral Canada-U.S. report in 1979, which offered the first compilation of existing scientific information on the origins, transport, and deleterious effects of acid precipitation in North America, warned of 'irreversible' damage being caused to lakes, rivers, and fish.[19] Subsequent research and reports also examined more fully the evidence for impacts on forests, human-made structures, and human health.[20]

There are some striking parallels between acid rain and water pollution in the Great Lakes in terms of the locations of their sources and their respective transboundary flows and, as a result, in terms of their politics. The 1979 bilateral scientific report estimated that American emissions of sulphur dioxide were five times greater than were Canadian emissions and American emissions of nitrous oxides were ten times greater. While both countries polluted their own and the others' territory to some extent, given the prevailing southwesterly winds on the eastern half of the continent, the U.S. produced, overall, about 70-80 per cent of transboundary air pollution. Subsequent scientific studies into the atmospheric chemistry and meteorology of acidic precipitation show that the bulk of southern Ontario and Quebec, where the most serious damage has occurred, are more affected by pollution from U.S. than from Canadian sources. Given this structural reality, acid rain, like water pollution in the Great Lakes, creates for Canada a condition of environmental dependence.

For these reasons, policymakers and publics in Canada have consistently perceived and addressed acid rain as a problem largely originating with their giant neighbour to the south and, therefore, requiring international collaboration.[21] Americans, on the other hand, have tended, once they became aware of the problem, to see acid rain as a national or, more correctly, as a domestic and regional issue. The reasons for this rather different American perspective also lie, to a very considerable extent, in the structural conditions of the acid rain issue, that is, in the asymmetries of its origins and impacts.

First, relatively little acid rain falling in the u.s. results from trans-boundary flows into the country, from Canada or anywhere else. There is thus no culpable foreign entity and little incentive to see acid rain as an international issue. Second, the serious impacts of acid rain in the u.s. are felt most in the northeast, especially upstate New York and New England, while the major pollution sources, especially coal-burning electric generating plants, are heavily concentrated in the u.s. Midwest states. Moreover, because their bedrock and soils are generally alkaline and, thus, well 'buffered' against acidification, these states suffer little from acidic deposition. In contrast, New York and the New England states have low bicarbonate soils with little or no buffering capability. (Much of Ontario, Quebec and the Atlantic provinces is in the same predicament.) The political problem for American federal authorities vis-à-vis domestic polluters, therefore, as well as the political problem for Canada vis-à-vis the u.s., is compounded because the major source areas are not the major recipient areas. The former therefore stand to benefit little from costly reductions in their own emissions. These differing circumstances lead to political divisions. The northeast states, concerned about environmental damage, long pressured the EPA for more stringent control of acid rain-causing pollutants; the midwest states, concerned about economic costs, tended to argue strongly against such controls. As a former governor of Ohio, James Rhodes, once said: 'You're talking about some fish in the northeast, while in Ohio we've got 22,000 unemployed coal miners' (*Cleveland Plain Dealer* [7 August 1991], 1).

The perspective of successive Canadian governments regarding the need for u.s. co-operation on the acid rain problem has been consistent. From Romeo LeBlanc's first acid rain speech, in which he called for bilateral negotiations to 'draw up new rules,' every environment min-ister has taken up the task. John Fraser, the minister in the short-lived Conservative government of Joe Clark, further explained Canada's dilemma: 'even if we closed down every emission source in Canada we would still have a problem,' he said, 'because of the prevailing winds from the u.s. It's not just a question of Canadian standards.' It is, rather, 'really a question of working out a legal regime in conjunction with the Americans that will result in control methods having the desired results on both sides of the border.'[22] John Roberts, who held the environment portfolio during the last Trudeau government, similarly observed, in 1982, that: 'It is time for both countries to look at laws and regulations. It is time to revise our legislation in a manner conducive not only to maintaining and improving local air quality but to reducing long range transport of air pollutants.'[23] More recent ministers have similarly defined the problem as a bilateral issue, first and foremost.

Tom McMillan, one of a succession of environment ministers in the Mulroney government, came to follow the examples of his predecessors and spent much of his time after 1986 on speaking tours in the U.S., pleading for American co-operation on acid rain.[24]

The essential Canadian policy objective, then, has been to seek U.S. reductions in emissions and, therefore, in transboundary flows of the pollutants which cause acid rain and to secure these commitments through the mechanism of a bilateral accord. The target became quantified as a 50 per cent reduction in the key sulphur dioxide emissions in both countries. The 50 per cent figure was calculated, using both sophisticated long-range transport computer models and acidic deposition data, to be the level of reductions required to prevent the most sensitive lakes from becoming acidified.

The foreign policy instrument initially adopted by Ottawa to pursue this Canadian objective was the traditional diplomatic one. The arguments to be marshalled for taking action, though, were primarily scientific rather than political. The need to act together was substantiated by scientific evidence of the transboundary character and deleterious effects of acid rain for both countries. Taking up issues of concern to one side or the other through formal diplomatic channels rather than pursuing them through public, less co-operative avenues is one of the unwritten norms of Canadian-American relations. It is also a consistent theme, historically, of Canadian foreign policy.[25] Moreover, this route had proven successful in securing the 1972 Great Lakes Water Quality Agreement. The concept of an acid rain accord and its pursuit were modelled, to a significant extent, on the Great Lakes Agreement and the process by which it came about.[26] The process that actually unfolded, however, did not follow the 1970-2 script.

QUIET ACID RAIN DIPLOMACY

No progress occurred on the diplomatic front in the months following Leblanc's 1977 proposal of bilateral talks. Some friendly, informal meetings were held, but the Americans were not ready to negotiate. While the Canadian side continued to envision negotiation of an air quality treaty, the U.S. aim was but 'to get a picture of the present state of air pollution across the border.'[27] Some pressure for bilateral talks was created within the U.S. in the fall of 1978 when the U.S. Congress passed a resolution requiring the State Department to enter into negotiations with Canada towards an air quality agreement. The key figures behind this unexpected move were a small group of border state congressmen, whose constituents were concerned, not about long-range acid rain, but about possible short-range air pollution from sources in Canada. In particular, the concern was focused on two coal-fired power plants being planned for sites just across the international boundary in southern Saskatchewan (Poplar River project) and northwestern Ontario (Atikokan project). Two meetings were subsequently held, but they did not progress beyond the exploratory discussion stage. The initiative soon died, without fanfare, in quiet diplomatic fashion. The State Department well understood, even if Congress did not, that a new bilateral air quality agreement which dealt with acid rain would cost the U.S. much more than Canada and would benefit Canada more than the U.S..

The immediate problem facing Ottawa was that acid rain was not even on the American political agenda. Chief among the directly conflicting priorities was reducing U.S. dependence on foreign oil in the aftermath of the oil crisis of the 1970s. Making the U.S. less dependent on imported oil meant increasing the use of domestic coal, which, in turn, would likely bring increases in acid rain.[28] Increased coal usage, however, was not the basic problem. Nor was it that acid rain remained largely unknown. The underlying policy problem was that the United States lacked the necessary legislation to deal with the acid rain problem and lacked the necessary political consensus on the need to pass any such legislation. While the 1972 and 1977 clean air acts mandated significant improvements in local urban ('ambient') air quality, these otherwise tough statutes contained no provisions specifically designed to combat the problem of long-range transport of air pollutants. In order to obtain reductions in these acid-forming pollutants, significant amendments would have to be made to the Clean Air Act. That was not to prove an easy task.

The core opponents to new controls on the emission of acid pollutants were industrial interests, including coal-mining companies and electric power utility companies,[29] and the coal-producing, coal-using states of the American Midwest. This area, roughly centred on the Ohio River Valley, is responsible for the bulk of U.S. sulphur dioxide emissions due to a large number of old, unregulated electric power plants burning locally-mined, high-sulphur coal. The economic interests of these 'coal states' dictated opposition to sulphur dioxide emission controls. Not only would there be serious impacts on the coal industry and the regional economy if less local coal were to be burned, there would also be economic costs in the form of higher electricity rates if expensive pollution controls were mandatory. The politics of acid rain, as politics often do, reflected the economics. And the political pressures from the U.S. Midwest against sulphur dioxide controls were fierce.

The Carter administration may have been unable to deliver what

Canada was asking for, but it was not deaf. After more informal talks, it signed with the Trudeau government in August 1980 a joint 'Memorandum of Intent' (MOI), committing the two countries to negotiate an acid rain agreement. The MOI not only detailed a technical working group structure, procedures, and a schedule but outlined the major features of the prospective agreement and committed both governments, albeit only rhetorically, to pursue vigorous enforcement actions under existing statutes. But even as the document was being signed, in the midst of the 1980 presidential election campaign, the U.S. commitment was being put in doubt. As a senior American official noted quietly, 'This all goes to hell if Ronald Reagan gets in.'[30]

And, of course, he did. Even after Carter's defeat at the polls, the lame-duck Democratic administration still attempted to bind the incoming Republican president to reducing acid rain emissions through the use of a little-known section of the existing Clean Air Act. Section 115 of the 1977 act authorized the EPA administrator to order cuts in pollution emissions causing damage in another country, provided reciprocal treatment was offered by the other country. As part of this strategy, the Canadian government moved quickly in December 1980 to amend the Canadian Clean Air Act, adding a reciprocal treatment clause. But the attempt came to naught. A long involved battle in U.S. courts ultimately brought the Section 115 process to an end. Avoiding the merits of the case, the Reagan administration successfully argued that former administration's finding – that U.S. pollution was adversely affecting Canada – was arrived at without following the necessary rule-making procedures.[31]

GOING PUBLIC WITH ACID RAIN

The impact of the Reagan White House on relations, environmental and other, with its northern neighbour was felt soon after the election.[32] Its list of Canada-U.S. priority 'irritants,' beginning with the Foreign Investment Review Agency and the National Energy Program, was as long as, if not longer than, that drawn up by the Nixon administration in 1971. Bilateral environmental issues were conspicuously absent from this list. The officials Reagan put in charge of U.S. environmental policy were a crop of pro-industry figures committed, along with their new colleagues in other agencies, to regenerating America's flagging economy, withdrawing government from the marketplace, and deregulating American industry, especially through the loosening of 'excessive' pollution controls. Canada's acid rain concerns were listened to, for the most part politely, but not heard. 'The administration's real position,' said a senatorial aide at the time, 'is to do nothing about acid rain.'[33] This proved an accurate forecast.

A few Canada-u.s. negotiation sessions were subsequently held, following on from the Memorandum of Intent, but there was no progress. The Washington refrain became 'more research has to be done.' But on at least one occasion, when that research looked a mite too definitive, senior Reagan political appointees set about rendering it less so. The conclusions in the scientific report of a bilateral group established during the Carter period were rewritten before Washington would allow its release.[34] Unwilling to pursue the MOI, the Reagan administration was even less interested in new emission controls.

Scientific arguments, evidently, were not enough to sway the Reaganites. Canada's political tactics had already begun to change somewhat, and the process was now accelerated by the stalemate in the official diplomatic negotiations. Officials in Ottawa and at the Canadian Embassy on Washington's Massachusetts Avenue began to carry their arguments more often and more directly to the u.s. Congress and to the American public. This 'interventionist' public diplomacy was a distinct contrast to the old sacred cows of Canadian-American 'quiet diplomacy.' The diplomats often operated in alliance with the Canadian Coalition on Acid Rain, an umbrella organization supported by a wide range of environmental interest groups in Canada and richly funded by Ottawa. While it is easy to exaggerate the impact of this public and political lobbying effort, it is perhaps fair to say, as one EPA official did, that 'the Canadian campaign helped to keep the issue alive.'[35]

DOMESTIC AND MULTILATERAL DIPLOMACY AND ACID RAIN

In addition to traditional diplomacy and public relations, Ottawa also pursued two other strategies – one domestic and the other international. Domestically, federal environment officials sought the agreement of the seven eastern provinces to reduce their emissions by half. The first step towards this objective was taken in March 1984, when federal Environment Minister Charles Caccia talked his provincial counterparts into accepting the overall target in principle. A second, and vital, step was the decision of the new Ontario Liberal cabinet in December 1985 to require reductions from that province's four largest sources of sulphur dioxide (Inco, Ontario Hydro, Falconbridge, and Algoma Steel). The last government to sign on to the federal-provincial agreement – that of coal-producing and coal-burning Nova Scotia – finally did so in late 1987.

This federal-provincial agreement was only in part intended to solve Canada's acid rain problem, since it could not do that unilaterally; it was also designed to fulfil what would be the Canadian commitments in an eventual Canada-u.s. acid rain agreement and to make a symbolic statement. Reductions of emissions in Canada had come to be recognized not only as the necessary quid pro quo in any such agreement but also as a politically essential a priori step by Canada. It was the Canadian response to the charge, frequently made by Americans, that Canada was telling the u.s. to reduce acid rain but was doing nothing itself. It was also quite clear that the Canadian commitments were of symbolic importance rather than practical value to the u.s. acid rain problem. The contribution of Canadian sources to acidic deposition in the United States is so slight that even more stringent controls in Canada would make little difference to the severity of environmental damage in the u.s..

Internationally, Canada encouraged and signed two multilateral agreements dealing with acid rain. On 13 November 1979, Canada and the u.s. had joined thirty-two European countries in signing an agreement calling for the reduction of air pollution and, especially, the reduction of long-range transboundary transport of acidic pollutants. This resolution represented a modest result of long-standing but largely unsuccessful pressure by the Scandinavian countries on their neighbours. It also reflected the political resistance put up by the major polluting states, as it did not actually commit its signatories to undertake specific reductions.

In the spring of 1984, Ottawa was instrumental in calling and organizing the inaugural meeting of what became known as the '30 per cent club' – a group of developed states committed to reducing sulphur dioxide emissions by at least 30 per cent within their own national territories.[36] The club, needless to say, did not include the United States, although the embarrassed Americans insisted they be invited to the meeting as observers. The Ottawa meeting was described later by Fitzhugh Green, an associate administrator of the Reagan EPA, as 'a hanging in effigy of the American policy.'[37]

PERSONAL DIPLOMACY AND ACID RAIN

The Conservative victory in the Canadian federal election of September 1984 led not only to the dismantling of the Trudeau government's Foreign Investment Review Agency and its National Energy Policy but also to a decline in Ottawa's 'public diplomacy' approach on acid rain. All were out of keeping with Prime Minister Brian Mulroney's vision of, and rhetoric about, a new co-operative era in Canadian-American relations. The Mulroney government also pursued a softer line than the 1979 Conservative government, whose environment minister, John Fraser, had worked hard and enthusiastically at raising the public profile of acid rain in the u.s.. For awhile, ministers' speechwriters avoided phrases referring to u.s. garbage being thrown into the Canadian backyard.

The co-operative bilateral rhetoric of this new era was enshrined in the Shamrock Summit of 1985. When even this personal diplomacy failed to make any breakthrough, the two leaders' salvage teams came up with what appeared to many observers as a mere face-saving action – they appointed two 'special envoys' to investigate the problem and report back in a year.

The envoys concluded that acid rain was, indeed, a problem, not a myth, but did not recommend immediate emission reductions. Instead, they proposed a major and long-term $5 billion investment by industry and government into research, development, and demonstration of so-called 'clean coal' technologies. 'Clean coal,' however, was more promise than prospect. First, the Reagan administration was slow to put its share of the promised money into its development. Despite summit promises, only after forceful Canadian representations during a visit by Vice-President George Bush to Ottawa the following year did the White House finally seek funding for the 'clean coal' technology demonstration program recommended by the envoys. It soon became clear, however, that decades would pass before such technologies could be adopted and begin to reduce emissions from the major sources of acid rain.[38]

The third annual Reagan-Mulroney summit of April 1987 found the prime minister once again going one-on-one with the president over acid rain. His efforts succeeded only in extracting a meaningless Ronald Reagan pledge that he 'agreed *to consider* the prime minister's proposal for a bilateral accord on acid rain' (italics added). After three face-to-face meetings, it was not much. As one sympathetic EPA official noted, 'Canada got snookered again.'[39]

CLEAN AIR AND BUSH COUNTRY

The American presidential election of November 1988 was remarkable in a number of respects, but certainly for the extent to which the heir of the Reagan legacy, George Bush, sought to outflank his Democratic opponent, Michael Dukakis, in pledging an attack on pollution. As political initiatives go, this was not excessively bold, let alone dangerous. It was clear to all that in late 1988 the country's mounting environmental ills were firmly and squarely back on the political agenda. The victorious Bush then symbolically broke with eight years of Reaganism in appointing a well-known environmentalist as administrator of the EPA and by committing his administration to formulating a new Clean Air Act, including, most importantly for Canada, provisions to reduce the sulphur and nitrogen oxide emissions that produce acid rain. The new administration's proposals were forwarded to Congress in the fall of 1989.

Another important political development was the replacement as Senate majority leader of Senator Robert Byrd of coal-dependent West Virginia, an arch opponent of acid rain controls, with George Mitchell of Maine, long a strong proponent of such controls. After a careful weighing of the balance of forces, Mitchell and his supporters made a pact with the White House on a sweeping set of improvements to the act, with which both sides could live, and proceeded through the early months of 1990 to gain Senate approval for them. Included in the set were requirements to reduce the precursors of acid rain by approximately 50 per cent from 1980 levels – a figure which had become accepted by most of the players on all sides of this issue. Major electrical generating plants in the Midwest states were specifically targeted for reductions. The costs of the war on acid rain, which had once appeared so formidable, were actually dwarfed by other costs to clean up America's air. In May 1990 the House of Representatives passed a similar bill, and in the fall both the Senate and House approved a common version of the much strengthened Clean Air Act. The U.S. administration now had, at last, the necessary statutory basis for dealing with the acid rain problem and, thus, for proceeding to negotiate the kind of international agreement which Canada had long sought.

Bilateral consultations between Washington and Ottawa were actually initiated during the summer months, even before the new U.S. act was enacted. Formal negotiations commenced shortly after Congress finalized it and did not take long. Nor did they add much to what was already in place. Given that both countries had initiated domestic emission control policies, there were few substantive issues to discuss, much less ones requiring negotiation. The text of the Air Quality Agreement was initialled by officials before the end of the year. The long-awaited accord then waited a little longer, until the hostilities of the Gulf War had ended, but was finally signed by the prime minister and the president during a short visit by Bush to Ottawa in March 1991. The first-ever Canada-U.S. Air Quality Agreement features sulphur dioxide and nitrogen oxide emission reduction commitments by both sides, establishes a research and monitoring network, and creates a bilateral co-ordinating group. It also provides a framework within which other emerging transboundary air pollution problems might be addressed. In contrast to the Great Lakes Water Quality Agreement, after which it was modelled, however, the new accord does not mandate the International Joint Commission to act as a watchdog over the implementation process. The governments themselves will decide whether or not they are meeting their commitments.

With passage of the new U.S. Clean Air Act the *Globe and Mail* was prematurely announcing that 'Canada will have finally won its fight.'[40] While in one sense the congressional action had made the bilateral accord inevitable, the experience with Great Lakes water quality would suggest sober second thoughts are in order. That experience has shown policy implementation does not always follow neatly along in the wake of lawmaking in matters of bilateral pollution control. Although the Canadian acid rain program is 'ahead of schedule'[41] in meeting emissions reduction targets, several factors could stall efforts on both sides of the border. Economic recession, in combination with the ongoing budgetary difficulties of both countries, may undermine implementation. The 1990 U.S. Clean Air Act amendments, which have been estimated at costing Americans around $35 billion, could well run afoul of continuing industry reluctance or of governmental restraint, much as the Nixon impoundment of sewage treatment plant construction funds stalled U.S. water pollution programs in the early 1970s. The possibility of another period of rising world crude oil prices means that there may well be pressures for increased, or less-regulated, coal burning and, thus, for less than expected decreases in transboundary acid rain, unless Washington is especially vigilant in enforcing the new Clean Air Act.[42]

There are also questions that quickly emerge about the adequacy of the new regime for air pollution, even assuming that present commitments to reduce by 50 per cent are met. Was the threshold for acid deposition set low enough to halt further acidification of the terrestrial and aquatic systems in eastern North America? Was it set low enough for previously acidified ecosystems to recover? If not, when and to what extent should there be further reductions? In addition, there are several other pollutants, such as volatile organic compounds and airborne toxics, which need to be addressed in a continental context. These concerns will require, in addition to domestic action, periodic review and renegotiation of the bilateral air quality agreement. Though important steps have been made, the regime for air is still in a nascent stage.

CONCLUSION: EVALUATING THE REGIMES AND CANADIAN POLICY

We are witnessing the development, albeit a painfully slow and unsteady development, of an international environmental regime in North America regulating transboundary pollution The process is as old as the Boundary Waters Treaty of 1909 and the Trail Smelter case of the 1930s.[43] It has by no means come to completion with the signing of the Canada-U.S. air quality accord. That agreement, like the 1972 Great Lakes Water Quality Agreement, will only begin to define the substance of the bilateral regime with respect to air. Just as subsequent efforts have broadened the Great Lakes Agreement substantively, incorporating commitments on toxic chemicals, for example, and have modified its implementation processes, future scientific and political work on transboundary air quality will certainly take the new accord beyond its initial focus on acid rain.

The driving factor forging these evolving regimes has been the interplay of science and politics. To an important degree, often underestimated by scientists themselves as well as by nonscientists, the findings of scientific research have set the agenda in the sense of providing the needed evidence of environmental degradation and of potential new threats. Widespread public concern, in part mobilized by the scientific community and the media and in part by political élites, has then provided the essential political push for the statements and actions of governments. The growth of the air and water quality regimes is, therefore, well characterized by E.B. Haas's description of regime change as 'the interactions of homo politicus with nature and culture.'[44]

Canadian governmental officials, along with some observers, have long maintained that the Canadian government has been a good deal more enthusiastic than has the American in the pursuit of these emerging regimes. Critics of Canadian policy claim, on the other hand, that the end result of Canada-U.S. environmental negotiations almost always represents an outcome closer to American than to Canadian objectives. Both arguments are true. Canada has, in both the cases examined here, been the demandeur. It is also true that the Canadian objective of the creation of effective, independent regulatory regimes embodying stringent pollution control guidelines has been only partially realized. The Great Lakes regime and the emerging air quality regime are, in substantive regulatory terms, no more than ratifications of predetermined American policies. The reasons why both these claims are valid lies to a considerable extent in the set of factors we call 'environmental dependence.'

The now abundant literature on dependence and dependencia emphasizes the extent to which a country's economy is tied to foreign purchasers of goods and suppliers of capital.[45] The crucial factor, though, is neither mere linkage nor even the concentration on a particular purchaser or supplier but, rather, the extent of alternative opportunities and the costs of shifting to such new arrangements. Through most of its history, Canada has been dependent economically and strategically on a major power, first Britain and then the United States, for its markets and capital and for its military defence. In a similar sense, Canada has become increasingly dependent on the United States with respect to the quality of its environment.

Most, but not all, of the pollutants dumped into the Great Lakes originate on the u.s. side. The sulphur and nitrogen oxides that lead to most of the acid rain in North America as well as to most of that in Canada originate in the United States. The transboundary flow of acid rain means in both cases that unilateral Canadian action to deal with the problem would be ineffective. Even drastic controls on the sources of acidic pollution in Canada, for example, would not sufficiently protect the Canadian environment. Thus arise the Canadian initiatives to strengthen the bilateral regime. The only feasible option is for Canada to seek American co-operation in the form of programs to reduce emissions in the United States. And, therefore, on issues such as acid rain and water pollution in the Great Lakes, Canada pursues international agreements as a way of securing an American commitment to deal with the sources of what are necessarily common problems. The sine qua non for conclusion of these agreements, as long as they are not treaties approved by the u.s. Senate, is a basis in existing u.s. legislation. And thus arise the domestic constraints on the strength of those regimes.

The other side of this relationship has its logic too. Given the large u.s. population and industrial base, the sheer amounts of both air and water pollutants produced in the United States are enormous. Thus, in both cases, the costs of any potential cleanup on the u.s. side are considerable. Second, at least some, and perhaps much, of the benefit of reduced u.s. emissions accrues not to the American environment but to the Canadian environment. Moreover, the extent of transboundary pollution from Canada into the United States is generally so small, comparatively, that there is little potential benefit to be derived in the u.s. from any reductions undertaken on the Canadian side. Thus, for both reasons – high costs and limited benefits – the u.s. political system finds bilateral agreements less attractive and is relatively slower to act on many transboundary pollution issues. But it is not always so.

The Reagan administration moved extremely quickly in late 1986 and early 1987 to conclude an international air quality agreement with

Mexico.[46] Why the contrast? The fundamental difference between the Canada-U.S. and Mexico-U.S. cases is that in the latter it is the United States which is the major recipient of transboundary pollution. The major air pollution problem along the Mexican-American border was a new, very large, Mexican smelter: it is thus a problem of long-range transport of air pollution *into* the United States. And it was therefore a problem on which the Reagan administration, not surprisingly, found little research was needed and on which action was taken immediately.

The Canadian bargaining position on environmental issues is not strong.[47] When the Great Lakes Water Quality Agreement was first being negotiated, the Canadian side was trying to extract greater American commitments on the nutrient problem; as the demandeur it had little to offer in return. In the end it had to settle for the limited reductions that the Americans were willing to carry out. The dynamic with respect to the negotiation of an air quality accord has been, essentially, the same. The main difference is that an informed and aroused Canadian public made it clear to Ottawa that a weak compromise on acid rain with the United States would not be tolerated.

Why, then, has the negotiation of an acid rain agreement taken so long while the Great Lakes Agreement took only a few years? Even taking into account the six year long IJC investigation which preceded the 1972 agreement, the acid rain issue was more laboured. The delays have rather little to do with differences in the underlying structures of the two issues, for these are remarkably similar. Nor does it have much to do with differences in Canadian or American strategies. It does have something to do with the novelty of the acid rain problem. Pollution of the Great Lakes circa 1970 was easily categorized as part of the broader, well-recognized problem of water pollution; the long-range transport of acid rain did not fit into existing conceptions of the 1970s and 1980s, especially American conceptions, of air pollution as a local, ambient air quality problem. The delays in dealing with acid rain also have much to do with timing. The Great Lakes issue rose to prominence and was pursued during an upsurge of environmental concerns in the U.S. and Canada during the early 1970s. The acid rain issue, however, was raised by Canada during a period when environmental concerns, especially in the United States, had been overwhelmed by economic and energy issues, and was initially pursued at a time when an environmentally atheistic political faction controlled the White House.

If we are to reflect on these cases for the broader question of regime change, there are three implications. One is that stronger, more comprehensive environmental regimes are pursued most zealously not by the dominant or hegemonic power, as is often the case with economic regimes, for example, but rather by the smaller or politically weaker state or states. That is, environmental regime building is the goal of the environmentally dependent.

A second implication is that the development of environmental regimes is a slow, evolutionary process. It is slowed, in particular, by the political constraints felt most acutely and naturally in the state which is the major source of pollutants. But it is slowed as well, in all states that are part of the developing regime, by the scientific uncertainties which can initially confound prescriptive action, by the reluctance and political clout of polluters, and by the often substantial financial and economic costs of pollution abatement. Environmental regime building at best proceeds slowly from principle to practice. It likely proceeds even more hesitantly under conditions of environmental dependence than under those of symmetrical transborder flows.

A third observation is that however broad a regime may be in substantive terms, there is substantial resistance, even on the part of the state that is environmentally dependent, to broaden it in terms of supranational authority. The example of the limited devolution of national sovereignty to the International Joint Commission provided by the 1909 Boundary Waters Treaty with respect to transboundary levels and flows has not been followed with respect to transboundary pollution. Environmental issues are today much too close to the political bone, fraught with too many serious implications for jobs and economic growth, let alone human health, for any government to countenance such a loss of control. But sovereignty is not what it used to be. Though both Canada and the United States still enjoy both legal sovereignty and substantial political autonomy in formulating their environmental policies, the problems with which they grapple are increasingly transboundary in nature, and the structures within which they operate are, increasingly, artifices of the emerging bilateral regimes.

Closing Perspective

CHAPTER THIRTEEN

Changing Multilateral Institutions: A Role for Canada

Sylvia Ostry

INTRODUCTION

It has become almost platitudinous that we are witnessing the unfolding of the most momentous political and economic transformation of the century. In a period of accelerating change, inertial political and institutional mechanisms cannot adapt with appropriate speed. The malady of systemic myopia, or making policy in a rearview mirror, escalates the risk of policy error. This risk is further heightened in today's multipolar world. In the absence of a dominant hegemony, who will provide the leadership essential to counteract the systemic myopia with what President Bush has disparagingly termed 'the vision thing?'

There is an argument to be made that a multipolar world offers an opportunity for coalitions of middle-sized powers to exert more influence than is possible in conditions of undisputed hegemonic governance. Coalitions are a means of leveraging power. Indeed, such coalitions have operated with surprising effectiveness during the Uruguay Round of the GATT negotiations. The glue that binds the coalitions (whatever the specific objective of their activity) is the strong preference for a world trading system governed by rules rather than power, since, by definition, they have the most to lose from the latter.

Canada is in some sense unique among the middle-sized powers who are the true stakeholders of multilateralism. The description 'the smallest of the large and the north of the south' reflects our membership in the G7 and mixed north-south forums such as the Commonwealth and la Francophone, which enhances the potential for coalition activit in the more global multilateral institutions. In other words, Canad in a position to exert a leadership role, via the power-leveraging of coalitions, in policy issues linked to systemic strengthening.

Let me, then, describe a real-world example of such an issue today – the Canadian initiative to build a World Trade Organization, or WTO. I will also argue that Canada could play a lead role in proposing a new role for the OECD, which I believe is also an essential element in strengthening multilateralism.

THE GATT AND THE WTO

The multilateral institutions – the International Monetary Fund, the World Bank, and the GATT – were established after the Second World War in a world far less interdependent than is today's. The trade, financial, and technology links that now draw countries more closely together have dramatically changed the policy context for governments, international institutions, and multinational corporations. Another dramatic change over the next several years will be the accession of the Soviet bloc countries to the multilateral institutions. The GATT, for many reasons, has found it increasingly difficult to adapt to change. Alternatives to multilateralism, including regional blocks, sectoral managed trade arrangements, and more active and aggressive unilateralism are likely to figure as more prominent forces in the international trading system should the Uruguay Round fail. It is by no means clear, however, that all negotiators understand that what is really on the table in Geneva is multilateralism itself.

The GATT was designed to deal primarily with border protection in the form of tariffs, and it did so with enormous success. Confronted in the 1970s with the rise of non-tariff barriers, both domestic and border, the Tokyo Round of the 1970s was less successful. The credibility of the GATT steadily eroded as the co-called new protectionism (domestic non-tariff measures and distorted use of the trade remedy laws) steadily increased. The Uruguay Round, launched in September 1986, must deal with this heritage of failure as well as with the extension of the GATT model to the new issues of services, trade-related intellectual property and investment measures, and the neglected old issue of agriculture. Is it too much too late? I will argue that the answer to that question will, in the long run, depend on whether the round includes a significant institutional strengthening as part of a successful Brussels package this December. In the absence of such strengthening, GATT will, over time, become essentially a forum for trivial disputes, lacking, as it has over the past several decades, any real capacity for adapting to change in the international economy. It is no accident that of the three postwar institutions, the weakening of the GATT is the most marked. A significant difference between the GATT and the Bretton Woods institutions is not only their vastly greater institutional capacity but also their greater influence in national capital, reflecting the power of finance ministries. Trade ministers are pretty low on the power totem pole in most capitals. An elevation of the status of the GATT would also feed back into the power configuration in national capitals and, thus, improve the prospects for institutional adaptation.

Let me briefly elaborate on the reasoning behind my emphasis on the urgent need for institution-building before detailing some proposals in that sphere. First, and probably most important, there has been a fundamental change in U.S. trade policy in the 1980s, which significantly dilutes the historic and unequivocal American commitment to the GATT. Since neither the EC nor Japan is likely to accept the role of guardian of the system, a change in U.S. policy has systemic implications. Thus, it is essential to seize the opportunity of the Uruguay Round to build a new trade institution, for such an opportunity may not again present itself. Second, even as the Uruguay Round draws to a close, new sources of international friction are apparent which are not covered by the round negotiations, ambitious as they are. A new initiative in the OECD provides the only multilateral option to deal with these issues. The OECD initiative should be developed as a complement to and not a substitute for the strengthening of the GATT.

As to American trade policy, the roots of change go back several decades, but the announcement of a new multi-track policy – multilateralism, bilateralism, and unilateralism – dates from President Reagan's speech of September 1985 following the Plaza Accord on exchange rates.[1] The timing was not an accident.

In the first half of the 1980s, a rising trade deficit and overvalued dollar (the product of Reaganomics) as well as growing concern about Japanese competitiveness in sector after sector, had created the powerful political pressures which forced the 1985 change in both exchange rate and in trade policy. In trade, the change was profound, marking a move from the postwar norm of a single overriding concern with multilateralism to the present mix, which includes the Uruguay Round; the FTA with Canada, plus negotiation of a free trade agreement with Mexico and perhaps others; and the use of Section 301 of the Omnibus Trade Act of 1988 and other types of unilateral initiatives, such as the Structural Impediments Initiative (SII) negotiations with Japan.

The SII negotiations are also an example of the new type of international discord which is not likely to be easily settled and which goes well beyond the agenda of the Uruguay Round and the mandate of even a greatly strengthened GATT. I shall come back to this issue at the end in connection with the OECD. But now, let me turn to the question of institutional reform of the trading system.

As has been mentioned, the GATT suffered a steady decline in credibility from the early 1970s. There were many reasons for this, which have been detailed in a number of studies, and it is not my purpose here to delve into the issue. Suffice it to say that efforts by the Americans to launch a new round in the early 1980s, which would have probably had some beneficial effect in at least stemming the rise in protectionism, were blocked by both the EC and a number of developing countries until September 1986. In the Punta declaration there was recognition of the problem of systemic weakening in the establishment of the FOGS (functioning of the GATT system) negotiating group and the priority accorded the improvement of the GATT dispute settlement process.

At the Montreal mid-term ministerial meeting in December 1988, some progress was achieved in the FOGS group, by instituting a trade policy review mechanism on a provisional basis and agreeing to more regular ministerial meetings to raise the political profile of GATT, and in dispute settlement, by establishing the right to a panel to hear disputes and by tightening up the process through the establishment of tighter deadlines. So far so good. But there is still much work to be done before the Brussels meeting in December that concludes the round. In point of fact, developments since the launch of the round have raised the stakes for systemic strengthening. An effective disputes settlement process and, in the words of the Punta declaration, 'an improvement in the overall effectiveness and decision making of the GATT,' will require the creation of a genuine world trade organization.

Let us start with dispute settlement. A detailed analysis of the GATT process in the latter half of the 1980s shows that it has been more heavily utilized and is operating more effectively than at any time in the past. The verdict among experts would probably accord a B-grade for recent performance. One might conclude that some modest further reforms by the end of the round could be both achievable and adequate. Alas, that is simply not the case. Because the real issue now at the heart of the negotiations on dispute settlement is to curb the unilateralism of U.S. trade policy in Section 301 of the 1988 Trade Act, the requirements for strengthening the GATT mechanism are far more demanding than they appeared to be in the 1986 context of the Punta launch.

Section 301 was, among other things, a reflection of the view of the U.S. Congress that the GATT legal system was not working. If all or some 301 powers are to be exchanged for an improved GATT mechanism, the parameter of reform will have to be carefully spelled out. At a minimum three key rights have to be established: (1) the right to convene a tribunal or panel (agreed at Montreal); (2) the right to have the panel's ruling adopted unless it is overturned by a competent authority; and

(3) the right to retaliate if a ruling is not complied with in a reasonable time.

The main objective for the Brussels meeting is to establish steps (2) and (3). The main obstacle to each of these is the GATT practice of consensus, which means, in effect, that a defendant can block adoption and authorization to retaliate for non-compliance.

There are now several proposals circulated in Geneva which seek to deal with the rights of adoption and compliance. But there is also another problem, which is the inadequacy of the GATT legal apparatus per se. Thus a government might be reluctant to give up its veto over a ruling if the panel's reasoning is weak or erroneous in legal terms. Hence, some way of improving the legal quality of panel reports must also be established, which may be difficult. Current proposals for an appeal tribunal to ensure the right of adoptions of a panel's findings raise a host of questions, such as staffing, mandate, panel membership, and so on. In other words, essentially institutional questions.

If a more fundamental institutional reform of the GATT is necessary for achieving a genuine and durable improvement of dispute settlement, it may also be a condition for the effective implementation of key parts of the Uruguay package, those which are essential for U.S. congressional acceptance of the negotiation outcome. Let me explain the reasoning for this assertion.

The GATT, as is well known, lacks an institutional base. This did not seem to be a serious handicap during the 1950s and 1960s, the golden age of trade liberalization through tariff reduction. However, as a result of the Tokyo Round, a process of fragmentation of the system began. The Tokyo Codes are legally separate from the GATT and apply only among the signatories, who vary from code to code. A fragmentation of dispute settlement procedures developed as a consequence, creating legal and political difficulties and the opportunity for 'forum shopping' to evade discipline.

This fragmentation will be greatly exacerbated by the Uruguay Round. It is difficult to imagine how the contemplated General Agreement on Trade in Services (GATS) or obligations on the level of intellectual property rights or even new disciplines in agriculture can be effectively integrated with the GATT. The legal and political complexities may prove so formidable that, over time, the results of the negotiations could well be negated. If this issue is not confronted well before the Brussels meeting, it could well jeopardize the entire outcome. Indeed, the powerful U.S. business sector services coalition has already signalled that it would prefer to retain 301 if the problem of legal fragmentation is not settled.[2]

But because the GATT has been judged virtually impossible to amend, the Tokyo Round 'solution' of side codes may tempt a number of contracting parties. However, this minimalist – and highly risky – approach has now been challenged by a Canadian proposal, in April, to establish a world trade organization. As the press release announcing the proposal stated: 'Developments in the substantive negotiations are now demonstrating that the Uruguay Round results cannot be effectively housed in a provisional shelter. It is also becoming clear that the post-Uruguay trade policy agenda will be complex and may not be adequately managed within the confines of the GATT system as it now exists.' While the detailed negotiating proposal will not be tabled until July, when the first outline of the overall substantive MTN package is due, the idea is to create an institutional framework and formal legal status for a world trade organization, which could be approved by national legislatures as part of the implementation of the Uruguay Round agreement. Clearly the creation of a WTO depends on a successful overall package. But, as I have argued, the reverse is also true, though less widely appreciated.

The WTO would not change the substantive obligations of the GATT, its side codes, or the Uruguay Round agreements. It would, however, provide for the basic attributes of an international organization, including provisions on membership, governing body or bodies, secretariat, director general, unified settlement procedures, provision for new agreements of future negotiations, privileges and immunities of staff, relations with other organizations, and so on.

The WTO treaty would also have to provide for the legal establishment of the Trade Policy Review mechanism, which was instituted on a provisional basis in 1988, and for a policy forum for regular review of developments in the international trading system. The substantive terms of international surveillance and, as a number of countries have suggested, improved domestic transparency mechanisms,[3] would have to be spelled out in the final agreement of the FOGS group. These surveillance procedures are a vital component of a strengthened GATT, since they provide the only means for continuing assessment of the economy-wide and systemic impact of trade-related policies. It is only through an effective surveillance mechanism which monitors changes in country policies and in the international economy, that a process of institutional adaptation can be developed through more frequent negotiations. If the traditional rules-based orientation of the GATT is not buttressed by a broader and more flexible policy focus, a new crisis of credibility will inevitably emerge as multilateral disciplines become less and less relevant to the real pressures of the changing international economy.

There seems little likelihood of genuine co-ordination with the

Bretton Woods institutions in the absence of a political upgrading of the GATT, a stronger secretariat, and a genuine micro-surveillance mechanism. A WTO would thus complement the macro surveillance mandate of the IMF and add, for developed countries, the structural adjustment focus which the World Bank now applies to the LDC's.

Finally, another compelling reason today for institutional reform of the GATT is the accession of the centrally planned economies (CPE's), who are engaged in a lengthy and difficult transformation process to market-based systems. In the past, the GATT has treated each new accession of a CPE on a case-by-case basis. But the cases were limited and so was the impact of membership. I would argue that we should seize the opportunity now, in the creation of a WTO, to consider a special 'generic' arrangement for integrating these countries to govern the period of transition to market economies and, indeed, to provide an external discipline to enhance domestic reform. The main reason for this proposal relates to the role of prices in the CPE's and the GATT-sanctioned use of the trade remedy laws of antidumping and countervailing duties. As long as it remains difficult to evaluate internal costs and prices in these countries, it seems likely that allegations of dumping and subsidization will mount as east-west trade flows are expanded. This would lend not only to a proliferation of disputes, likely to increase east-west friction, but also (judging from experience among market economies) to an increase in bilateral managed trade restricting the volume of exports. An increase in bilateral quantitative restraints is not likely to enhance the credibility or viability of a liberal multilateral trading system!

THE OECD: CONVERGENCY INITIATIVE

As mentioned at the outset, new sources of international friction have become increasingly visible since the launch of the Uruguay Round. Largely directed at Japan, the discord centres on the high profile issue of competitiveness and the role of government policy in influencing the competitive advantage of the private sector. As I have argued elsewhere,[4] the pressure for managed trade generated by this high-tech neo-mercantilism, as it has been christened, will become increasingly powerful unless a concerted effort is made to reduce the divergence in key domestic policies which strongly influence innovation and competitive performance.

The key policies to target for harmonization would include:

– *trade policies* – especially standards, government procurement, subsidies, intellectual property, and antidumping rules

- *competition policy* – different rules or different enforcement of rules create markedly different market structures and business behaviour within the OECD
- *technology policy* – for example, government-led consortiums, such as Joint European Submicron Silicon (Jessi) in Europe, Sematech in the United States, and a range of MITI-inspired networks in Japan, should be open to foreign access on a reciprocal basis; subsidies should be made transparent and harmonized, and so forth
- *investment policy* – both explicit and more complex barriers to access arising from securities regulation, etc.
- *capital market regulation* – differences in the cost of capital depend on macro-forces, such as savings behaviour, fiscal policy, and inflation, but also on capital market structure (for example, the role of banks, and regulation on linkages between banks and commercial firms), which affects the cost and time horizon of investment.

Convergence in these policies within the OECD, and especially in the triad of the three major trading blocs – the United States, Europe, and Japan – would reduce international friction and lessen asymmetry of access in trade, investment, and technology. Competition among transnational corporations would still be fierce, but at least with similar rules the game would be, and would be perceived to be, 'fairer.'

In launching such an initiative at the OECD it would be important to establish a continuing relationship with the more advanced developing economies. This is, in fact, a process which has already been launched in the so-called dialogue with the DAE's (the dynamic Asian economies), which Canada actively promoted. Over time, it might be possible to develop a set of codes which could then be transferred to the WTO. In any case, stronger linkages between the OECD and the WTO would be required, since there is a risk that the developed countries might come to regard the OECD as a substitute rather than a complement to the global trading institution. And that would negate much of the purpose of striving for the WTO, that is, a more effective integration of a truly multilateral trading system.

Machiavelli has written: 'There is nothing more difficult to plan, more doubtful of success, nor more dangerous to manage than the creation of a new system. For the initiators have the enmity of all who would profit by the preservation of the old system and merely lukewarm defenders in those who would gain from the new one.'

Let us hope he is proven wrong in Brussels this December. And let us hope that the success of the Canadian WTO initiative provides that proof.

Notes

INTRODUCTION

1 'Canada in the World: Foreign Policy in the New Era,' delivered on the occasion of the 66th Meeting of the Canadian-American Committee of the C.D. Howe Institute, 13 September 1990, Ottawa, Ontario. Reproduced in *Statements and Speeches*, Foreign Policy Communications Division, External Affairs and International Trade Canada, 90/11, 3.

2 Friedrich Kratochwil and John G. Ruggie, 'International Organization: A State of the Art on the Art of the State,' *International Organization* 40 (Autumn 1986):759.

3 This is the definition adopted in Stephen D. Krasner, ed., *International Regimes* (Ithaca and London: Cornell University Press 1983), 2. The selections in this volume provide a good introduction to regimes analysis. For a useful review of the literature on international regimes, see Stephan Haggard and Beth A. Simmons, 'Theories of International Regimes,' *International Organization* 41 (Summer 1987):491-517.

4 See Robert O. Keohane, *After Hegemony: Cooperation and Discord in the world Political Economy* (Princeton: Princeton University Press 1984) for the theoretical foundations of functional analysis. For a review and criticism of functional theories of regimes see Haggard and Simmons, 'Theories of International Regimes,' 506-9.

5 Mark W. Zacher, 'Toward a Theory of International Regimes,' *Journal of International Affairs* 44 (1990):139-57.

6 See Haggard and Simmons, 'Theories of International Regimes,' 500-6, for a review and criticism of hegemonic stability theory.

CHAPTER 1: POSTWAR INTERNATIONAL TRADE POLICY

1 Richard Gardner, *Sterling-Dollar Diplomacy in Current Perspective* (New

York: Columbia University Press 1980).

2 Michael M. Hart, *Canadian Economic Development and the International Trading System* (Toronto: University of Toronto Press 1985), 10.

3 More in-depth analyses of the basic principles and rules of the GATT can be found in Kenneth Dam, *The GATT: Law and International Economic Organization* (Chicago: University of Chicago Press 1970); John H. Jackson, *World Trade and the Law of GATT* (Indianapolis: Bobbs-Merrill 1969); Jock A. Finlayson and Mark W. Zacher, 'GATT and the Regulation of Trade Barriers: Regime Dynamics and Functions,' in Stephen D. Krasner, ed., *International Regimes* (Ithaca: Cornell University Press 1983); and Frank Stone, *Canada, the GATT and the International Trade System* (Montreal: Institute for Research on Public Policy 1984).

4 Michael M. Hart, *A North American Free Trade Agreement: The Strategic Implications for Canada* (Ottawa: Centre for Trade Policy and Law 1990), 15.

5 Jackson, *World Trade and the Law of GATT*, 124.

6 J.L. Granatstein, 'Free Trade Between Canada and the United States: The Issue That Will Not Go Away,' in Denis Stairs and Gilbert R. Winham, eds., *The Politics of Canada's Economic Relationship with the United States* (Toronto: University of Toronto Press 1985), 36-40; and R.B. Byers, 'Canadian Defence and Defence Procurement: Implications for Economic Policy,' in Denis Stairs and Gilbert R. Winham, eds., *Selected Problems in Formulating Foreign Economic Policy* (Toronto: University of Toronto Press 1985), 181-3.

7 Economic Council of Canada, *Looking Outward: A New Trade Strategy for Canada* (Ottawa: Supply and Services Canada 1975), 4.

8 Granatstein, 'Free Trade Between Canada and the United States,' 43.

9 Another series of GATT negotiations was held over the period 1960-2 (the so-called 'Dillon Round'), but this multilateral bargaining session produced meagre results. Useful reviews of the Kennedy Round are John Evans, *The Kennedy Round and American Trade Policy* (Cambridge: Harvard University Press 1971) and Ernest Preeg, *Traders and Diplomats: An Analysis of the Kennedy Round of Negotiations* (Washington: Brookings Institution 1970).

10 Preeg, *Traders and Diplomats*, 208-11, 251.

11 Tariff escalation refers to the well-documented fact that, under the tariff schedules maintained by most countries, higher rates of duty are charged on processed than on unprocessed raw materials products. For a resource-rich country such as Canada, an important policy goal is to upgrade resource-based products prior to export in order to encourage forward integration of manufacturing industries and generate spin-off demands for industrial products and various services. However, the tariff escalation characterizing the tariff structures of Canada's trading partners creates a disincentive to 'add value' to resource-based products through

processing activity within Canada.

12 By the end of the 1970s, merchandise exports accounted for more than 25 per cent of gross domestic product. Department of External Affairs, *A Review of Canadian Trade Policy: A Background Document to Canadian Trade Policy for the 1980s* (Ottawa: Supply and Services Canada 1983), 20.

13 For an analysis of the politics and economics of the Auto Pact through the first decade of its life, consult Jim Keely, 'Cast in Concrete for All Time? The Negotiation of the Auto Pact,' *Canadian Journal of Political Science* 16 (June 1983). The impact of the Auto Pact on the Canadian automobile assembly and parts industries is examined in Ross Perry, *The Future of Canada's Auto Industry* (Ottawa: Canadian Institute for Economic Policy 1982).

14 Lorraine Eden, 'Multinational Responses to Trade and Technology Changes: Implications for Canada,' paper presented at the conference on Foreign Investment, Technology and Economic Growth (Ottawa: Investment Canada, September 1990). Good general discussions of intra-industry and intra-firm trade can be found in David Greenaway and Chris Milner, *The Economics of Intra-Industry Trade* (Oxford: Basil Blackwell 1986) and Nigel Grimwade, *International Trade: New Patterns of Trade, Production and Investment* (London: Routledge 1989).

15 Department of External Affairs, *Foreign Policy for Canadians* (Ottawa: Supply and Services Canada 1970), 23-4.

16 Initially, U.S. Treasury Secretary John Connally's package of measures to address the deteriorating American balance-of-payments situation also included a proposal to unilaterally abrogate the Canada-U.S. Auto Pact. Fortunately, this idea was abandoned at the last minute, following interventions by senior U.S. Department of State officials. J.L. Granatstein and Robert Bothwell, *Pirouette: Pierre Trudeau and Canadian Foreign Policy* (Toronto: University of Toronto Press 1990), 65-71.

17 Mitchell Sharp, 'Canada-U.S. Relations: Options for the Future,' *International Perspectives* (Autumn 1972, Special Issue):1-21.

18 For a critical analysis of the origin and impact of the 'Third Option,' see Granatstein and Bothwell, *Pirouette*, 162-72 and Harald Von Riekhoff, 'The Third Option in Canadian Foreign Policy,' in Brian Tomlin, ed., *Canadian Foreign Policy: Analysis and Trends* (Toronto: Methuen 1978).

19 Hart, *Canadian Economic Development and the International Trading System*, 114-21. The GATT Multifibre Arrangement (MFA) entered into force in January 1974 and has been renewed several times since then. It replaced an earlier GATT accord known as the Long-Term Arrangement Regarding International Trade in Cotton Textiles. Under the MFA, importing and exporting countries negotiate bilateral restraint agreements covering trade in textile and clothing products, subject to a limited number of multilateral disciplines. The MFA's acceptance of bilateral trade controls

constitutes a major derogation from the GATT non-discrimination principle. The negotiation of bilateral trade restraints under the MFA provides a
classic example of 'managed trade'; however, the existence of certain
disciplines and multilateral surveillance through the GATT distinguishes
managed trade in textiles/clothing from that characterizing most other
products. For an extended discussion of the MFA, consult Vinod Aggarwal,
Liberal Protectionism: The International Politics of Organized Textile Trade
(Berkeley: University of California Press 1985). The evolution of Canadian
policy with respect to the textile and clothing sector is assessed by Rianne
Mahon, *The Politics of Industrial Restructuring: Canadian Textiles* (Toronto:
University of Toronto Press 1984).

20 Bela Balassa, 'The "New Protectionism" and the International Economy,'
    The Journal of World Trade Law 12 (September- October 1978):409-36. Other
    useful reviews of rising protectionism since the early 1970s can be found
    in Susan Strange, 'Protectionism in World Politics,' *International Organiza-
    tion* 39 (Spring 1985):233-40 and Sheila Page, 'The Rise in Protection Since
    1974,' *Oxford Review of Economic Policy* 3 (Spring 1987):37-51.

21 John H. Jackson, 'The Crumbling Institutions of the Liberal Trade System,'
    The Journal of World Trade Law 12 (March- April 1978):93-106.

22 Department of External Affairs, *A Review of Canadian Trade Policy*, 133.

23 The six NTM agreements negotiated in the Tokyo Round were: The Anti-
    dumping Code, the Subsidies/Countervail Code, the Code on Customs
    Valuation, the Government Procurement Agreement, the Agreement on
    Import Licensing, and the Agreement on Technical Barriers to Trade. In
    the case of anti-dumping, a previous code that expanded on existing GATT
    rules relating to dumping was negotiated during the Kennedy Round.

24 G.E. Salembier, Andrew R. Moroz, and Frank Stone, *The Canadian Import
    File: Trade, Protection and Adjustment* (Montreal: Institute for Research on
    Public Policy 1987), 111-15.

25 Ibid., 127-33, for a review of SIMA.

26 Under 'conditional MFN,' the signatories to various GATT sub-agreements
    and codes extend the benefits resulting from these arrangements (e.g.,
    improved access to markets) only to those states which are also signato-
    ries, not to the entire GATT membership. Many GATT members, notably LDC's,
    have not signed the codes negotiated during the Tokyo Round.

27 One leading text in the field of Canadian foreign policy in the early 1980s
    scarcely mentioned trade and commercial policy issues. Michael Tucker,
    Canadian Foreign Policy: Contemporary Issues and Themes (Toronto:
    McGraw-Hill 1980).

28 'World Trade Growth Slows Down,' FOCUS: GATT *Newsletter* 80 (April
    1991):5.

29 In 1989, Canada ranked as the seventh largest importer and seventh
    largest exporter in the world. Ibid., 5. The dramatic economic slowdown

in Canada in 1990, and the appreciation of the Canadian dollar, may partially explain the slippage in Canada's ranking between 1989 and 1990.

30 Statistics Canada, *Preliminary Statement of Canadian International Trade* (December 1989).

31 Ibid.

32 For a discussion of Canadian trade in advanced technology products, see Andrew Sharp, 'Measuring Canada's International Competitiveness,' *Perspectives on Labour and Income* 2 (Summer 1990):13-16.

33 Glenn Williams, *Not For Export: The Political Economy of Canada's Arrested Industrialization* (Toronto: McClelland and Stewart 1983), stresses the role of foreign-owned branch plants in limiting the scope for manufactured exports. Liberal economists have pointed to small size and insufficient scale as the culprits. See D.J. Daly and D.C. MacCharles, *Canadian Manufactured Exports: Constraints and Opportunities* (Montreal: Institute for Research on Public Policy 1986). A more recent study by the Corporate Higher Education Forum criticizes corporate managers for paying too little attention to international business opportunities and imperatives. *Going Global: Meeting the Need for International Business Expertise in Canada* (Montreal: The Corporate Higher Education Forum 1988).

34 These and other developments which are currently reshaping the global environment for Canadian business are reviewed in a lengthy study published by Investment Canada, *The Business Implications of Globalization* (Ottawa: Investment Canada Working Paper Number 1,990-V).

35 The FTA appears to be fully compatible with the GATT, including Article 24 of the General Agreement, which outlines the conditions which customs unions and free trade areas must meet in order to qualify under GATT rules. See Michael Hart, 'GATT Article 24 and Canada-United States Trade Negotiations,' *Review of International Business Law* 1 (December 1987):317-55.

36 Useful reviews of the economics and politics of the FTA include Peter Morici, ed., *Making Free Trade Work* (New York: Council on Foreign Relations 1990); Economic Council of Canada, *Venturing Forth: An Assessment of the Canada-U.S. Free Trade Agreement* (Ottawa: Supply and Services 1988); and Jeffrey Schott and Murray Smith, eds., *The Canada-United States Free Trade Agreement: The Global Impact* (Ottawa: IRPP 1988). A more critical perspective can be found in Duncan Cameron, ed., *The Free Trade Deal* (Toronto: Lorimer 1988).

37 Paul and R.J. Wonnacott, *Free Trade Between the United States and Canada: The Potential Economic Effects* (Cambridge: Harvard University Press 1967).

38 Standing Senate Committee on Foreign Affairs, *Canada-United States Relations, Volume 3*: Canada's Trade Relations with the United States (Ottawa: Senate of Canada 1982).

39	Royal Commission on the Economic Union and Development Prospects for Canada, *Final Report* (Ottawa: Supply and Services 1985).

40	Twelve separate volumes of research published for the Commission focused wholly or mainly on bilateral trade and economic relations. Several other volumes dealt with broader trade policy issues.

41	Peter Morici, 'The Environment for Free Trade,' in Morici, ed., *Making Free Trade Work*, 1-26; Jock A. Finlayson, 'Canadian Business and Free Trade,' *International Perspectives* (March-April 1985).

42	Paolo Cecchini, et al., *The European Challenge 1992* (Brookfield, VT: Gower Publishing 1988); Dennis Swann, *The Economics of a Common Market* (London: Penguin Books 1990).

43	I.M. Destler, *U.S. Trade Politics: System Under Stress* (Washington: Brookings Institution 1986). The figures on antidumping and countervail petitions are from 'A Survey of World Trade,' *The Economist* (22 September 1990), 11.

44	Richard Lipsey and Robert York, *Evaluating the Free Trade Deal* (Toronto: C.D. Howe Institute 1988); Murray Smith, 'The Free Trade Agreement in Context,' in Schott and Smith, eds., *The Canada-United States Free Trade Agreement*; Economic Council of Canada, *Venturing Forth*.

45	Useful reviews of the Uruguay Round are Sidney Golt, *The GATT Negotiations 1986-1990: Issues and Prospects* (British North American Committee, November 1988) and Jeffrey Schott, ed., *Completing the Uruguay Round* (Washington: Institute for International Economics 1990).

46	Individual negotiating groups exist for each of the following issues: tariffs; non-tariff measures; natural resource-based products; textiles and clothing; agriculture; tropical products; GATT articles; multilateral agreements and arrangements; safeguards; subsidies and countervailing measures; trade-related aspects of intellectual property rights; trade-related investment measures; dispute settlement; functioning of the GATT system; and trade in services. In some cases, various sub-groups have been established to tackle specific issues falling under these headings. In the case of the group on negotiations on services, for example, separate working groups were created for telecommunications, construction, transportation, tourism, financial services, and professional services.

47	As reported in 'A Survey of World Trade,' *The Economist* (22 September 1990), 8.

48	The Cairns Group and Canada's role in it are discussed in greater detail in Jock A. Finlayson and Ann Weston, *The GATT, Middle Powers, and the Uruguay Round* (Ottawa: North-South Institute 1990).

49	'John Crosbie: My Plan for a World Trade Organization,' *The International Economy* (June/July 1990):40-3; 'Crosbie Presents Detailed Proposal for Strengthening the GATT System,' *Canadian Trade Law Reports* 7 (31 May 1990):1-5.

50	Susan Strange, *States and Markets: An Introduction to International Political*

Economy (London: Pinter 1988).

51 Sylvia Ostry, *Governments and Corporations in a Shrinking World* (New York: Council on Foreign Relations 1990).

52 Ibid., 3-4.

53 For a critique of regional trade blocs, see Michael Aho, 'More Bilateral Trade Agreements Would be a Blunder: What the New President Should Do,' *Cornell International Law Journal* 22 (Winter 1989):25-38.

54 Hart, *A North American Free Trade Agreement;* Sidney Weintraub, *Marriage of Convenience: Relations Between Mexico and the United States* (New York: Oxford University Press 1990); Steven Globerman, ed., *Continental Accord: North American Economic Integration* (Vancouver: Fraser Institute 1991).

55 Gary Clyde Hufbauer, 'Beyond GATT,' *Foreign Policy* (Winter 1989-90). A similar proposal was advanced by the Atlantic Council of the United States in 1974.

56 Examples include the Lomé Convention between a group of more than 50 LDC's and the European Community; arrangements between several North African states and the EC; and the U.S. Caribbean Basin Initiative.

CHAPTER 2: FTA AND THE MULTILATERAL TRADING SYSTEM

1 The author served as senior policy advisor to the federal minister for international trade during the FTA negotiations.

2 Robert E. Hudec, *The GATT Legal System and World Trade Diplomacy*, 2nd ed. (Salem, NH: Butterworth Legal Publishers 1990), 59-61. See also William Diebold, *The End of the ITO* (Princeton University: Essays in International Finance 1952).

3 Michael Aho, 'What Changes are Needed at the International Level for Improving Trade Relations?' in *Canada and the Multilateral Trading System* (Toronto: University of Toronto Press 1985; published in co-operation with the Royal Commission on the Economic Union and Development Prospects for Canada and the Canadian Government Publishing Centre), 151-4.

4 Colleen Hamilton and John Walley, 'Canada and the Future of the Global Trading System,' in *Canada and the Multilateral Trading System*, 132-3. Aho, 'What Changes are Needed . . . ,' 151-2.

5 *Trade Policies for a Better Future* (GATT 1986).

6 The director general's worry was borne out by subsequent events. The negotiations were to be completed in Brussels in December 1990. They foundered over the crucial issue of agricultural reform. As a result, the ministerial meeting failed, and it took the director general months to forge a consensus to restart the negotiations. At the time of publishing, it is expected that the round will be completed by March of 1992.

7 Gilbert R. Winham, *Trading with Canada: The Canada-u.s. Free Trade Agreement* (New York: Priority Press Publications 1988), 5. It is also fair to say that both parties recognized the potential sensitivity that free trade negotiations would have in the smaller country. It was thought that were the United States to seek negotiations, the political reaction in Canada would be such that it would be difficult for the Canadian government to proceed.

8 Jock A. Finlayson, 'Canada, Congress and u.s. Foreign Economic Policy,' in *The Politics of Canada's Economic Relationship with the United States* (Toronto: University of Toronto Press 1985; published in co-operation with the Royal Commission on the Economic Union and Development Prospectus for Canada and the Canadian Government Publishing Centre), 140-2.

9 Brian Tomlin, 'The States of Prenegotiations: The Desire to Negotiate North American Free Trade,' *International Journal* 44 (Spring 1989):266; Finlayson, 'Canada Congress and . . . ,' 140-2, 152-6.

10 Winham, *Trading with Canada*, 20.

11 D.L. McLachlan, A. Apuzzo, and W. Kerr, 'The Canada-u.s. Free Trade Agreement: A Canadian Perspective,' *Journal of World Trade* 22 (August 1988).

12 Tomlin, 'The State of Prenegotiation 1s . . . ,' 266; Winham, *Trading with Canada*, 20-2.

13 Winham, *Trading with Canada*, 20.

14 Interviews with federal officials.

15 John Whalley and Roderick Hill, 'Introduction: Canada-u.s. Free Trade,' in *Canada-u.s. Free Trade* (Toronto: University of Toronto Press 1985; Published in co-operation with the Royal Commission on the Economic Union and Development Prospects for Canada and the Canadian Government Publishing Centre), 3.

16 Ibid., 3-5.

17 Gerard Curzon, *Multilateral Commercial Diplomacy: The GATT and Its Impact on National Commercial Policies and Techniques* (London: Michael Joseph 1965), 57- 70, 260-90. See also D.M. McRae and J.C. Thomas, 'The Development of the Most Favoured Nation Principle: Treaties of Friendship, Navigation and Commerce and the GATT,' in Maureen Irish and Emily F. Carasco, eds., *The Legal Framework for Canada-u.s. Free Trade* (Toronto: Carswell 1987), 225-48.

18 Hudec, *The GATT Legal System* . . . , 211-14.

19 McRae and Thomas, 'The Development of the North . . . ,' 225-48.

20 Tomlin, 'The State of Prenegotiations . . . ,' 265 and Winham, *Trading with Canada*, 5.

21 Christopher Walton, 'International Trade: United States-Canada Free Trade Agreement,' *Harvard International Law Journal* 29 (Spring 1988):579.

22 Winham, *Trading with Canada*, 19.

23 Whalley and Hill, 'Introduction: Canada-u.s. Free Trade,' 109.

24 David Leyton-Brown, 'The Political Economy of Canada-u.s. Relations,' in *Talking Trade: Canada Among Nations* (Toronto: James Lorimer and Company Publishers 1987), 154.

25 Gordon Ritchie, 'The Negotiating Process,' in John Crispo ed., *Free Trade: The Real Story* (Toronto: Gage Educational Publishing 1988), 18.

26 Ibid., 20.

27 Leyton-Brown, 'The Political Economy . . . ,' 154.

28 Michael Aho, in Crispo, ed., 'What Changes are Needed . . . ,' 182.

29 Madelaine Drohan, 'Simon Reisman's Way,' *Maclean's* (5 October 1987), 22.

30 Mary Jarigan, 'Walkout From the Talks,' *Maclean's* (5 October 1987), 14-17.

31 Jarigan, 'Walkout From the Talks,' 14- 17.

32 Charles Doran, 'Canadian Relations with the u.s.,' *Current History* (March 1988):98.

33 'Talks: What Went Wrong,' *Financial Post* (28 September 1987), 37.

34 Jarigan, 'Walkout From the Talks,' 14- 17.

35 William Diebold Jr., ed. *Bilateralism, Multilateralism and Canada in u.s. Trade Policy* (Cambridge, MA: Ballinger Publishing 1988), viii.

36 Winham, *Trading with Canada*, 33.

37 Winham, Ibid., 34.

38 Gilbert R. Winham, 'GATT and the International Trade Regime,' *International Journal* 45 (Autumn 1990):797-811.

39 Hudec, *The GATT Legal System*, xi-xiii.

40 See *Free Trade Law Reporter* (Don Mills, ON: CCH International, 1988-9) and *Canada Trade and Sales Tax Cases* (Don Mills ON: Richard De Boo Publishers 1988-9).

41 See *Basic Instruments and Selected Documents* (Geneva: Published by GATT 1986-90).

42 Frank Stone, 'Canada-United States Economic and Trade Relations: Institutional Arrangements,' in Irish and Carasco, eds., *The Legal Framework for Canada-United States Trade*, 225-48.

43 'Acceleration of Reduction of Customs Duties: Round Two,' *The Free Trade Observer*, No. 5 (Don Mills ON: CCH International, February 1990), 50; 'Acceleration of Reduction of Customs Duties,' *The Free Trade Observer*, No. 1 (Feb. 1989), 5.

44 L.H. Legault, 'Institution and Dispute Settlement Procedures Under the Canada-u.s. Free Trade Agreement,' in Donald M. McRae and Debra P. Steger, eds., *Understanding the Free Trade Agreement* (Halifax: Institute for Research of Public Policy 1988), 21-9.

45 *Free Trade Law Reporter* (Don Mills, ON: CCH International, 16 October 1989), para. 75- 001.

46 'Ch. 18 Lobster Panel: The U.S. Wins!' *The Free Trade Observer*, No. 8 (May 1990), 90-1.

47 'Binational Panels: Are They Fulfilling Canada's Objectives?' *The Free Trade Observer*, 15 (December 1990), 195-7.

48 *Free Trade Law Reporter* (15 December 1989), para. 75-002.

49 *Free Trade Law Reporter* (2 April 1990), para. 75-008.

50 *Free Trade Law Reporter* (24 August 1990), para. 75-017.

51 'GATT Panel,' *The Free Trade Observer*, No. 11 (August 1990), 131-2.

52 'Synopsis of the Agreement,' *Free Trade Law Reporter* (1980), para. 85-200 – para. 85-231.

CHAPTER 3: AGRICULTURAL PROTECTIONISM

1 Gerard Curzon, *Multilateral Commercial Diplomacy: The GATT and its Impact on National Commercial Policies and Techniques* (London: Michael Joseph 1965), 166-7; T.K. Warley, 'Western Trade in Agricultural Products,' in Andrew Shonfield, ed., *International Economic Relations of the Western World 1959-1971*, VOL. 1: 'Politics and Trade' (London: Oxford University Press 1976), 343.

2 Frank Stone, *Canada, the GATT and the International Trade System* (Montreal: The Institute for Research on Public Policy 1984), 155.

3 Stephen D. Krasner, 'Structural Causes and Regime Consequences: Regimes as Intervening Variables,' *International Organization* 36 (Spring 1982):186.

4 Donald J. Puchala and Raymond F. Hopkins, 'International Regimes: Lessons from Inductive Analysis,' *International Organization* 36 (Spring 1982):248. The 'nesting' terminology was coined by Vinod K. Aggarwal. See Aggarwal, *Liberal Protectionism: The International Politics of Organized Textile Trade* (Berkeley: University of California Press 1985).

5 Mark W. Zacher, 'Trade Gaps, Analytical Gaps: Regime Analysis and International Commodity Trade Regulation,' *International Organization* 41 (Spring 1987):175-6. Some of the definitions in this section are taken from the Zacher article.

6 Alternatively, it is useful to speak of a 'global food regime' when one is examining the linkages between various types of food activities, such as food security, food aid, and food trade. For discussion of a global food regime see the articles in Raymond F. Hopkins and Donald J. Puchala, 'The Global Political Economy of Food,' *International Organization* 32 (Summer 1978). Other relevant writings by these two authors include 'The Failure of Regime Transformation: A Reply,' *International Organization* 34 (Spring 1980):303-5 and 'International Regimes: Lessons from Inductive Analysis.' See also Helge Ole Bergesen, 'A New Food Regime: Necessary

but Impossible,' *International Organization* 34 (Spring 1980):285-302 and Theodore H. Cohn, *The International Politics of Agricultural Trade: Canadian-American Relations in a Global Agricultural Context* (Vancouver: University of British Columbia Press 1990).

7 For a detailed discussion of the major principles of the international trade regime see Jock A. Finlayson and Mark W. Zacher, 'The GATT and the Regulation of Trade Barriers: Regime Dynamics and Functions,' *International Organization* 35 (Autumn 1981). While the Finlayson-Zacher article refers to these as 'norms,' Zacher describes them as 'principles' in a later article. See his 'Trade Gaps, Analytical Gaps,' 176, n. 8.

8 While Finlayson and Zacher focus on a 'safeguard' principle, which is designed to exist on a temporary basis, my 'exemptionalism' principle explicitly includes exceptions that are more permanent in nature.

9 Kenneth W. Dam, *The GATT: Law and International Economic Organization* (Chicago: The University of Chicago Press 1970), 259-60.

10 References to GATT articles are taken from the General Agreement on Tariffs and Trade, *Text of the General Agreement* (Geneva: GATT, July 1986).

11 A concessional sale 'involves price or credit terms that contain substantial ... government subsidies.' See Ronald D. Knutson, J.B. Penn, and William T. Boehm, *Agricultural and Food Policy* (Englewood Cliffs, NJ: Prentice-Hall 1983).

12 Warley, 'Western Trade in Agricultural Products,' 338-9.

13 Food and Agriculture Organization, FAO *Principles of Surplus Disposal and Consultative Obligations of Member Nations* (Rome: FAO, 2nd ed., 1980), 2.

14 Jon McLin, 'Surrogate International Organization and the Case of World Food Security 1949-1969,' *International Organization* 33 (Winter 1979):54-5. See also Theodore Cohn, 'The 1978-9 Negotiations for an International Wheat Agreement: An Opportunity Lost?,' *International Journal* 35 (Winter 1979-80):132-49.

15 Dale E. Hathaway, 'Agricultural Trade Policy for the 1980s,' in William R. Cline, ed., *Trade Policy in the 1980s* (Washington, DC: Institute for International Economics 1983), 453.

16 Ernst Haas, 'Words Can Hurt You; or Who Said What to Whom about Regimes,' *International Organization* 36 (Spring 1982):211.

17 James N. Rosenau identified four 'central features' of interdependence issues, and in each case he cited examples in the food and agricultural areas. See his 'Capabilities and Control in an Interdependent World,' *International Security* 1 (Fall 1976):40-3.

18 Bayless Manning, 'The Congress, The Executive and Intermestic Affairs: Three Proposals,' *Foreign Affairs* 55 (June 1977):309.

19 Warley, 'Western Trade in Agricultural Products,' 293-4.

20 Statement by Oran Young quoted in Ernst Haas, 'Words Can Hurt You,' 210-11.

21 Agriculture Canada, *Canada's Trade in Agricultural Products* (Ottawa: Minister of Supply and Services, various years).

22 Charles W. Gibbings, 'A Canadian Looks at Some Wheat Questions,' *Requested Papers*, 8 (Washington, DC: National Advisory Commission on Food and Fiber 1967), 82. See also T.K. Warley, 'Canadian Agriculture in a Global Context: An Overview,' in Irene Sage Knell and John R. English, eds., *Canadian Agriculture in a Global Context: Opportunities and Obligations* (Waterloo: University of Waterloo Press 1986), 19.

23 In January 1989 the federal grains minister announced that the Wheat Board would no longer export oats starting from 1 August 1989.

24 Aggarwal, *Liberal Protectionism*, 28.

25 GATT Contracting Parties, 9th Session, 'Summary Record of the 44th Meeting,' (Geneva, SR 9/44, 15 March 1955), 10.

26 GATT Negotiating Group on Agriculture, 'Proposal by Canada Regarding the Multilateral Trade Negotiations in Agriculture' (MTN.GNG/NG5/W/19, 20 October 1987), 3.

27 The U.S. was also unwilling to make the necessary concessions required for a breakthrough in agriculture in the Kennedy and Tokyo Rounds. See Robert L. Paarlberg, *Fixing Farm Trade: Policy Options for the United States* (Cambridge, MA: Ballinger Publishing 1988), 48-52.

28 Agriculture Canada, *Canada's Trade in Agricultural Products: 1980 1981 and 1982*, 13; *Canada's Trade in Agricultural Products: 1986 1987, and 1988*, 20.

29 The founding members of the Cairns group were Argentina, Australia, Brazil, Canada, Chile, Colombia, Fiji, Hungary, Indonesia, Malaysia, New Zealand, the Philippines, Thailand, and Uruguay.

30 Barry Wilson, 'Wise Wants Canadian Support for U.S. Subsidy Fight,' *Western Producer* (10 September 1987), 3.

31 GATT, 'Proposal by Canada Regarding the Multilateral Trade Negotiations in Agriculture,' 3.

32 'MTN: Subsidies and Countervailing Measures,' background on Canadian Submission to the General Agreement on Tariffs and Trade, Geneva (28 June 1989), 2.

33 Countervailing duties are imposed to offset subsidies which producers receive in the exporting country, and antidumping duties are assessed against sales of foreign goods at prices below those charged in the home or third-country markets.

34 U.S. General Accounting Office, *International Trade Commission's Agricultural Unfair Trade Investigations* (Washington, DC: NSIAD-88-58BR, December 1987), 10-12. In a countervail case, the ITA determines whether subsidies are provided to foreign producers, and the ITC determines whether these subsidies are a cause of material injury to U.S. producers.

35 In 1859 the Canadian tariff provided for an undervaluation duty, which was removed in 1904 when the antidumping duty was introduced. See

John H. Young, *Canadian Commercial Policy* (Ottawa: Royal Commission on Canada's Economic Prospects 1957), 135; and G.A. Elliott, *Tariff Procedures and Trade Barriers* (Toronto: University of Toronto Press 1955), 180.

36 Debra Steger, 'Recent Canadian Experience with Countervailing Duties: The Case of Agriculture,' in *Canada-U.S. Trade in Agriculture: Managing the Disputes* (Guelph: University of Guelph Department of Agricultural Economics and Business 1987), 16.

37 Rodney de C. Grey, *Trade Policy in the 1980s: An Agenda for Canadian-U.S. Relations* (Montreal: C.D. Howe Institute 1981), 56-7.

38 Karl D. Meilke, 'Overview and Conclusions,' in *Agriculture in the Uruguay Round of GATT Negotiations: The Final Stages,* proceedings of a conference sponsored by the University of Guelph and the Ontario Ministry of Agriculture and Food, Guelph Ontario, May 1990, 72-3.

39 The first two definitions of 'remedy' in *The American Heritage Dictionary* (1975) are 'something, such as medicine or therapy, that relieves pain, cures disease, or corrects a disorder' and 'something that corrects any evil, fault, or error.'

40 The terms 'contingent' and 'contingency protection' are used in Grey, *Trade Policy in the 1980s,* and in Fred Lazar, *The New Protectionism: Non-Tariff Barriers and Their Effects on Canada* (Toronto: James Lorimer and Company 1981). For the use of more neutral terms see Murray G. Smith, 'Negotiating Trade Laws: Possible Approaches,' in Murray G. Smith with C. Michael Aho and Gary N. Horlick, *Bridging the Gap: Trade Laws in the Canadian-U.S. Negotiations* (Toronto: Canadian-American Committee, January 1987), 5.

41 GATT, 'Proposal by Canada Regarding the Multilateral Trade Negotiations in Agriculture,' 3.

42 Minister for International Trade, 'Canada Tables First Comprehensive Proposal for New GATT Subsidy-Countervail Rules,' *News Release* No. 158 (28 June 1989), 1.

43 Ibid., 2. See also K.D. Meilke and T.K. Warley, 'Agriculture in the Uruguay Round: A Canadian Perspective,' paper prepared for the Canadian Agricultural Economics and Farm Management Society's Annual Meeting, Montreal, 9-13 July 1989, 2.

44 GATT/1396, 'Ministerial Declaration on The Uruguay Round,' 25 September 1986, 6.

45 Agriculture Canada, *Growing Together: A Vision for Canada's Agri-Food Industry* (Ottawa: Minister of Supply and Services 1989), 55.

46 Meilke, 'Overview and Conclusions,' 73-4.

47 Richard Blackhurst, 'The Twilight of Domestic Economic Policies,' *The World Economy* 4 (December 1981):358.

48 Organization for Economic Co-operation and Development (OECD), *National Policies and Agricultural Trade: Country Study-Canada* (Paris: OECD

1987), 73.

49 Ibid., 75. It should be mentioned that OECD countries in general tend to provide very high levels of income support to dairy producers.

50 See Grace Skogstad, *The Politics of Agricultural Policy-Making in Canada* (Toronto: University of Toronto Press 1987), chaps. 1, 5; Grace Skogstad, 'The Political Economy of Agriculture in Canada,' paper for presentation at a conference on the political economy of Europe-North American agricultural policy and trade, University of Saskatchewan, Saskatoon, 7-9 March 1990, 41 and Theodore Cohn, 'Canadian Aid and Trade in Skim Milk Powder: Some Recent Issues,' *Canadian Public Policy* 4 (Spring 1978):214.

51 T.K. Warley, 'International Pressures on Supply Management,' n.p., n.d., 6; Agriculture Canada, *Growing Together*, 55; and Skogstad, *The Politics of Agricultural Policy-Making*, 111.

52 Cohn, 'Canadian Aid and Trade in Skim Milk Powder,' 214 and Skogstad, *The Politics of Agricultural Policy-Making*, 48-9, 75. See also J.C. Gilson, *World Agricultural Changes: Implications for Canada* (Toronto: C.D. Howe Institute 1989), 190.

53 Skogstad, *The Politics of Agricultural Policy-Making*, 21; Cohn, *The International Politics of Agricultural Trade*, 172.

54 References to the Free Trade Agreement are taken from Canada, External Affairs, *The Canada-U.S. Free Trade Agreement* (Ottawa: External Affairs, 10 December 1987).

55 Agriculture Canada, 'Notes for an Address by the Honourable John Wise, Minister of Agriculture, at the Annual Meeting of the Dairy Farmers of Canada,' 19 January 1988, 3.

56 Canada, External Affairs, *The Canada-U.S. Free Trade Agreement: Synopsis* (Ottawa: External Affairs 1987), 28.

57 U.S. House of Representatives, 'United-States Canadian Free Trade Agreement,' *Hearing before the Committee on Agriculture*, 100th Cong., 2nd sess., 25 February 1988, 29.

58 OECD, *National Policies and Agricultural Trade: Canada*, 59-69.

59 Agriculture Canada, *Growing Together*, 16, 39.

60 Mr. George Fleischmann, President, Grocery Products Manufacturers of Canada, in House of Commons, *Minutes of Proceedings and Evidence of the Standing Committee on External Affairs and International Trade*, Issue No. 41, 19 November 1987, 24.

61 Barry Wilson, 'Sees Peril of Weakening Supply Management,' *Western Producer* (28 September 1989), 6.

62 Government of Canada, 'Canadian Government Responds to GATT Panel Ruling on Ice Cream and Yoghurt,' *News Release*, No. 298 (4 December 1989), 1.

63 Government of Canada, 'Government Expresses Disappointment over

GATT Ruling on Ice Cream and Yoghurt,' *News Release*, No. 218 (15 September 1989), 1.

64 Agriculture Canada, *Growing Together*, 56-7.

65 Multilateral Trade Negotiations, 'Canadian Proposal on GATT Article XI' and Government of Canada, 'Canada Tables Proposal for Strengthening and Clarifying GATT Article XI in Support of Supply Management Programs,' *News Release* (14 March 1990).

66 Madelaine Droman, 'Canada's Farm Policies an Odd Couple,' *Globe and Mail* (15 March 1990), B1.

67 'Comprehensive Proposal for the Long-Term Reform of Agricultural Trade: Submission by the Cairns Group,' November 1989 and Minister for International Trade, 'Canada Endorses Cairns Group Agreement on a GATT Negotiating Position,' *News Release*, No. 292 (23 November 1989).

68 The EEC has linked partial tariffication with 'rebalancing.' See M.N. Gifford, 'A Status Report: The Comprehensive Proposals,' in *Agriculture in the Uruguay Round of GATT Negotiations: The Final Stages*, Conference Proceedings, University of Guelph, May 1990, 12. See also Barry Wilson, 'Canada Feels Naked at GATT,' *Western Producer* (7 December 1989), 3.

69 T.K. Warley, 'Canada's Food and Agricultural Policies,' paper prepared for American Agricultural Economics Association Food and Agricultural Policy Workshop on 'Sharpening Our Understanding of Food and Agricultural Policies in Industrialized Countries,' Knoxville, Tennessee, 30-1 July 1988, 18-19.

70 Agriculture Canada, 'Notes for an Address by the Honourable Don Mazankowski, Deputy Prime Minister and Minister of Agriculture, to a Supply Management Marketing Seminar,' Ottawa, 14 November 1989, 4.

71 William M. Miner and Dale E. Hathaway, 'World Agriculture in Crisis: Reforming Government Policies,' in William M. Miner and Dale E. Hathaway, eds., *World Agricultural Trade: Building a Consensus* (Washington, DC: Institute for International Economics 1988), 58.

72 Warley, 'International Pressures on Supply Management,' 5.

73 See Cohn, *The International Politics of Agricultural Trade*, for a more detailed discussion of these issues.

74 Aggarwal, *Liberal Protectionism*, 28.

75 Barry Wilson, 'Canada Takes on Two Roles at the Same Time,' *Western Producer* (14 December 1989), 6.

76 David Ramsay, 'An Ontario Perspective,' in *Agriculture in the Uruguay Round: The Final Stages*, 50; Jeffrey Simpson, 'On This Political Farm, Some Subsidies are More Inviolable Than Others,' *The Globe and Mail* (1 August 1990), A18.

77 Robert L. Paarlberg, 'Resolving Agricultural Trade Conflict: Multilateral, Bilateral, and Unilateral Approaches,' paper prepared for delivery at the

annual meeting of the International Studies Association, Washington, DC, 10-14 April 1990, 29.

78 Meilke and Warley, 'Agriculture in the Uruguay Round,' 18-19.

79 See Cohn, *The International Politics of Agricultural Trade*, chap. 4.

80 Paarlberg, 'Resolving Agricultural Trade Conflict,' 19.

81 For a detailed discussion of these provisions, see Cohn, *The International Politics of Agricultural Trade*, chap. 7.

82 Leo V. Mayer, 'U.S.-Canadian Negotiations and the GATT Round: U.S. Perspectives,' in *Canada-U.S. Trade in Agriculture: Managing the Disputes*, 40.

83 T.K. Warley, 'Linkages between Bilateral and Multilateral Negotiations in Agriculture,' in Kristen Allen and Katie Macmillan, eds., *U.S.-Canadian Agricultural Trade Challenges: Developing Common Approaches* (Washington, DC: Resources for the Future 1988), 169-78.

84 Cohn, *The International Politics of Agricultural Trade*, chaps. 3, 5.

85 For a detailed discussion of these issues see Cohn, 'The 1978-9 Negotiations for an International Wheat Agreement: An Opportunity Lost?'; Theodore Cohn, *The Politics of Food Aid: A Comparison of American and Canadian Policies* (Montreal: McGill University Studies in International Development, No. 36 1985); and Cohn, *The International Politics of Agricultural Trade*, chap. 4.

86 'Canada Persuades Key Trading Partners to Agree to Place Agriculture High on World Trade Agenda,' Minister for International Trade, *Communiqué*, No. 078, 27 April 1987. The Group of Seven includes the U.S., Japan, Germany, France, Britain, Italy, and Canada; and the Quadrilateral Group includes the trade ministers of the U.S., the EEC, Japan, and Canada.

87 For examples of those referring to the 'crisis' in agricultural trade, see Dale E. Hathaway, *Agriculture and the GATT: Rewriting the Rules* (Washington, DC: Institute for International Economics 1987); Geoff Miller, *The Political Economy of International Agricultural Policy Reform* (Canberra: Australian Government Publishing Service 1987); Paarlberg, *Fixing Farm Trade*; Miner and Hathaway, eds., *World Agricultural Trade*; Michael Franklin, *Rich Man's Farming: The Crisis in Agriculture* (London: Routledge 1988); Michele M. Veeman and Terrence S. Veeman, 'The Crisis in European and North American Agriculture,' paper prepared for the Conference on the Political Economy of European-North American Agricultural Policy and Trade, Saskatoon, 7-9 March 1990; and Cohn, *The International Politics of Agricultural Trade*.

88 Organization for Economic Co-operation and Development, *National Policies and Agricultural Trade* (Paris: OECD 1987), 68.

89 Meilke and Warley, 'Agriculture in the Uruguay Round,' 19-20.

90 *Reforming World Agricultural Trade* (Washington, DC: Institute for International Economics 1988),10-11. See the articles in Miner and Hathaway, eds., *World Agricultural Trade*, for a detailed discussion of 'decoupling' and

of other policy prescriptions for reducing agricultural trade distortions. See also Warley, 'Canada's Food and Agricultural Policies,' 35-6.

91 Barry Carr et al., 'A North American Perspective on Decoupling,' in Miner and Hathaway, eds., *World Agricultural Trade*, 120-37.

92 William M. Miner and Dale E. Hathaway, 'World Agriculture in Crisis,' 85.

93 See Paarlberg, *Fixing Farm Trade*, 68.

94 GATT, 'Proposal by Canada Regarding the Multilateral Trade Negotiations in Agriculture,' 3.

95 Agriculture Canada, *Growing Together*, 56.

96 C. Ford Runge, 'Prospects for the Uruguay Round in Agriculture,' paper prepared for a conference on the political economy of North American agriculture, Saskatoon, 8-9 March 1990, 17.

97 K.D. Meilke and T.K. Warley, 'Agriculture in the GATT After Montreal: What Now?' Guelph, 16 December 1988, 7. See also Barry Wilson, 'Policies Based on Success, but What if GATT Fails?' *Western Producer* (29 March 1990), 6.

CHAPTER 4: PRIVATE INTERNATIONAL TRADE LAW REGIME

1 Department of External Affairs, *Review of Canadian Trade Policy: A Background Document to Canadian Trade Policy for the 1980s* (Ottawa: Minister of Supply and Services Canada 1983), 200-1. Jock A. Finlayson, 'Canadian International Economic Policy: Context, Issues and a Review of Some Recent Literature' and Michael C. Webb and Mark W. Zacher, 'Canadian Export Trade in a Changing International Environment,' both in *Canada and the International Political/Economic Environment*, 28, The Collected Research Studies, Royal Commission on the Economic Union and Development Prospects for Canada (Ottawa: Minister of Supply and Services Canada 1985).

2 J.-G. Castel, A.L.C. de Mestral, and W.C. Graham, *International Business Transactions and Economic Relations: Cases, Notes, and Materials on the Law as it Applies to Canada* (Toronto: Emond Montgomery Publications 1986), 521. It should be noted that there has been a blurring of the distinction between private and public trade, due to the increasing involvement of the state in trade transactions, for example, countertrade, government procurement, and the like.

3 'Unification of the Law of International Trade: Note by the Secretariat,' *Official Records of the General Assembly, Twentieth Session*, Annexes, agenda item 92, UN Doc. A/C.6/L.572, reprinted in *UNCITRAL Yearbook* 1 (1968-73), 13.

4 Jacob S. Ziegel, 'The Vienna International Sales Convention,' in Jacob S.

Ziegel and William C. Graham, Q.C., eds., *New Dimensions in International Trade Law: A Canadian Perspective* (Toronto: Butterworths 1982), 53.

5 Stephen D. Krasner, 'Structural Causes and Regime Consequences: Regimes as Intervening Variables,' in Stephen D. Krasner, ed., *International Regimes* (Ithaca: Cornell University Press 1982), 2.

6 For a review and criticism of functional theories of international regimes see Stephan Haggard and Beth A. Simmons, 'Theories of International Regimes,' *International Organization* 41 (Summer 1987):506-9.

7 'Unification of the Law of International Trade,' 14.

8 Most legal theorists regard the reduction of transaction and information costs as self-evident and as inevitable consequences of unification and do not take the issue further. See, for example, Rene David, 'The International Unification of Private Law,' in 'The Legal Systems of The World: Their Comparison and Unification', *International Encyclopedia of Comparative Law*, 2 (New York: Oceana Publications 1972) and Leon E. Trakman, *The Law Merchant: The Evolution of Commercial Law* (Littleton, CO: Fred B. Rothman 1983). While there is a body of literature on economics and the law, to my knowledge it has not been applied to the modern unification of the laws governing international commerce. For a good short review of economic theories of the law see E. Donald Elliott, 'The Evolutionary Tradition in Jurisprudence,' *Columbia Law Review* 85 (1985):62-71. For the application of transaction cost analysis to international regimes generally, see Robert O. Keohane, *After Hegemony: Cooperation and Discord in the World Political Economy* (Princeton: Princeton University Press 1985); and see Paul R. Milgrom, Douglas C. North, and Barry R. Weingast, 'The Role of Institutions in the Revival of Trade: The Law Merchant, Private Judges, and the Champagne Fairs,' *Economics and Politics* 1 (March 1990):1-23 for the application of transaction cost analysis to medieval commercial law.

9 See Trakman, *The Law Merchant*, for a discussion of the role of commercial law in facilitating both certainty and efficiency in commercial transactions. And see Milgrom et al., 'The Role of Institutions,' for a discussion of the role played by the system of private adjudication in promoting efficiency in medieval commercial transactions.

10 'Progressive Development of the Law of International Trade: Report of the Secretary-General,' *Official Records of the General Assembly, Twenty-First Session*, Annexes, agenda item 88, Doc. A/6396, reprinted in UNCITRAL *Yearbook* 2 (1968-73), 22, para. 23.

11 'Progressive Development,' 22, para. 23.

12 See Trakman, *The Law Merchant*; Clive M. Schmitthoff, 'The Unification of the Law of International Trade,' *Journal of Business Law* (1968):105-19 and H. J. Berman and C. Kaufman, 'The Law of International Commercial Transactions (Lex Mercatoria),' *Harvard International Law Journal* 19 (1978):221-77 for the historical origins of the regime in the medieval law

merchant (Lex mercatoria) and the emphasis placed throughout the history of the regime on the value of facilitating international transactions by minimizing formalities and procedural requirements.

13 'Progressive Development,' 22, para. 23.

14 For the distinction in international relations between rules that empower or permit and those which enjoin or prohibit see Friedrich Kratochwil, 'Thrasymachos Revisited: On the Relevance of Norms and the Study of Law for International Relations,' *Journal of International Affairs* 37 (Winter 1984):343-56; Kratochwil, 'The Force of Prescriptions,' *International Organization* 38 (Autumn 1984):685-708; and Oran R. Young, *Compliance and Public Authority: A Theory with International Applications* (Baltimore: Johns Hopkins University Press 1979).

15 The results of a survey of legal counsel for multinational oil companies conducted by Trakman, *The Law Merchant*, chap. 4 showed that performance disputes tended to be resolved through settlement negotiations. Arbitration and litigation were used only as 'a very last resort.' Furthermore, the respondents showed a preference for arbitration over litigation in national courts, citing less rigid procedures, impartiality, and lower costs as favourable attributes of arbitration.

16 Full treatment of the international agencies involved in the formulation of private international trade law is beyond the scope of this paper. For a good review of earlier unification efforts see 'Progressive Development.' For a review of the formulating agencies see Rudolf Dolzer, 'International Agencies for the Formulation of Transnational Economic Law,' in Norbert Horn and Clive M. Schmitthoff, eds., *The Transnational Law of International Commercial Transactions* (Deventer, The Netherlands: Kluwer 1982), 61-80.

17 The conference has thirty-six members, including Canada, most European states, the United States, Australia, Japan, China, Argentina, and Venezuela. For a review of the methods, objectives and earlier work of the Hague Conference see J.-G. Castel, 'Canada and the Hague Conference on Private International Law: 1893-1967,' *The Canadian Bar Review* 45 (March 1967):1-34.

18 For a more complete review of the unification efforts of the Hague Conference see 'Progressive Development,' 24-5 and Dolzer, 'International Agencies,' 72-3.

19 Dolzer, 'International Agencies,' 73.

20 In 1967, Castel, in 'Canada and the Hague Conference,' considered but rejected possible reasons for Canadian non-participation in the unification efforts of the Hague Conference. He made the case for joining, arguing at page 1 that 'regionalism is out of place in this area of the law. By remaining in jealous isolation, one encourages aimless and inevitable differentiations of legal rules. This is not conducive to the development of international trade, a development that is so important to Canada's

economic growth.'

21 Paul Lansing, 'The Change in American Attitude to the International Unification of Sales Law Movement and UNCITRAL,' *American Business Law Journal* 18 (Summer 1980):270.

22 Peter H. Pfund and George Taft, 'Congress' Role in the International Unification of Private Law,' *Georgia Journal of International and Comparative Law* 16 (1968):671.

23 *Final Act*, The Hague Conference on Private International Law, Tenth Session, 28 October 1964, reprinted in *ILM* 4 (1965):341-7.

24 Reprinted in *ILM* 8 (1969):37-41.

25 Reprinted in *United Nations Treaty Series* 527 (1965):189-203.

26 Reprinted in *ILM* 3 (1964):854-66.

27 'Progressive Development,' 23, para 30.

28 Pfund and Taft, 'Congress' Role,' 270.

29 For further details on the work of UNIDROIT see Dolzer, 'International Agencies'; M.J. Bonell, 'The UNIDROIT Initiative for the Progressive Codification of International Trade Law,' *International and Comparative Law Quarterly* 27 (1987):423-41; and R. Monaco, 'The Scientific Activity of UNIDROIT,' in *New Directions in International Trade Law, Acts and Proceedings of the Second Congress on Private Law*, held by UNIDROIT in Rome September 9-15 1976, Vol. 1 (New York: Oceana Publications 1977), xxvii.

30 Reprinted in M.J. Bonell, 'The 1983 Geneva Convention on Agency in the International Sale of Goods,' *American Journal of Comparative Law* 32 (1984):717-63.

31 Martin Stanford, 'The Ottawa Conventions on Leasing and Factoring,' in the *Sixth International Trade Law Seminar: Proceedings*, Department of Justice, October 1988 (Ottawa: Supply and Services Canada 1989), 86. And see R.C.C. Cuming, 'Legal Regulation of International Financial Leasing: A Canadian Perspective,' *Banking and Financial Law Review* 2 (1987-8):323-56.

32 Draft Convention on International Financial Leasing with Explanatory Report, UNIDROIT Secretariat, October 1987, Study 59-Doc. 48.

33 See Cumming, 'The Ottawa Conventions.'

34 Czechoslovakia, France, Guinea, Nigeria, Tanzania, Morocco, Ghana, and the Philippines.

35 It appears that upon the Canadian request to review the law in this area, UNIDROIT requested that Professor R.C.C. Cuming, College of Law, University of Saskatchewan, prepare a report on the subject. Professor Cuming reported that existing conflict laws governing security interests in mobile goods are inadequate, and that there is considerable support for developing an international agreement on the subject. See R.C.C. Cuming, ' The UNIDROIT Project on International Regulation of Aspects of Security Interests in Mobile Equipment,' in *Seventh International Trade Law Seminar:*

Proceedings, Department of Justice, October 1989 (Ottawa: Supply and Services Canada 1990), 75-86.

36 The International Law Commission was the main United Nations body established for the purpose of developing international law. However, the commission limited its activities to public international law, thus leaving a gap for matters of private law. UNCITRAL was created to fill this gap with reference to the particular needs of international trade law.

37 General Assembly Resolution 2205 (21), 17 December 1966, *Official Records of the General Assembly*, Twenty-First Session, Annexes, agenda item 88, UN Doc. A/6396 and Add. 1 and 2, reprinted in *UNCITRAL Yearbook*, 1.

38 For further discussion of the origin and work of UNCITRAL, see Gerold Herrmann, 'The Contribution of UNCITRAL to the Development of International Trade Law,' in Horn and Schmitthoff, eds., *The Transnational Law of Commercial Transactions*, 35-50 and Erik Suy, 'Achievements of the United Nations Commission on International Trade Law,' *International Lawyer* (1981):139-47.

39 Herrmann, 'The Contribution of UNCITRAL,' 36.

40 See also Clive M. Schmitthoff, 'The Law of International Trade, its Growth, Formulation and Operation,' in Schmitthoff, ed., *The Sources of the Law of International Trade* (New York: Frederick A. Praeger 1964), 3-40; Schmitthoff, 'The Unification of the Law of International Trade'; and Schmitthoff, 'The Codification of the Law of International Trade,' *Journal of Business Law* (January 1985):34-44.

41 General Assembly Resolution 2205 (21).

42 The scheme is regional and membership is rotational. Initially, UNCITRAL membership included twenty-nine states: seven African states; five Asian states; four East European states; five Latin American states; and eight from Western Europe and 'other states.' See Art. 1, General Assembly Resolution 2205 (21). In 1973 membership was increased to thirty-six states, adding two African states, two Asian states, and one additional Eastern European, Latin American, and Western European (including 'other states'). See 'Working Methods of the Commission: Note by the Secretariat,' UN Doc. A/Conf. 9/299, reprinted in *UNCITRAL Yearbook* 19 (1988)165-6. Canada, Australia, and the United States qualify as 'other states.'

43 Senior Legal Counsel, Federal Department of Justice.

44 'Working Methods,' 166.

45 'Working Methods,' 166.

46 See Christiane Verdon, 'Current Developments in Private International Law,' in *Sixth International Trade Law Seminar*, 14.

47 UN Doc. A/Conf. 63/15, reprinted in *ILM* 13 (1974):952-61.

48 Hans Smit, 'The Convention on the Limitation Period in the International Sale of Goods: UNCITRAL's First-Born,' *American Journal of Comparative Law*

23 (1975):337.

49 John Honnold, 'The United Nations Commission on International Trade Law: Mission and Methods,' *American Journal of Comparative Law* 27 (1979):203.

50 John Honnold, 'Uniform Statute of Limitations for International Sales Claims,' *Review of International Business Law* 3 (July 1989):227.

51 Honnold, 'Uniform Statute of Limitations,' 228.

52 UN Doc. A/Conf. 89/13, Annex I, reprinted in *ILM* 17 (1978):603-31.

53 The Hague-Visby Rules may be found in William Tetley, *Marine Cargo Claims*, 2nd ed. (Toronto: Butterworths 1978), Appendix A. Canada is not a party to the Hague-Visby rules, but the Hague Convention forms the basis of the Carriage of Goods by Water Act.

54 According to the federal Department of Justice, accession to the Hamburg Rules is not a 'dead issue' but remains very much alive in consultations with Canadian industry.

55 *Review of Maritime Transport* (UNCTAD 1988), 67. For a discussion of the application and nature of the Hamburg Rules and their legislative history see 'United Nations Convention on the Carriage of Goods by Sea 1978 (Hamburg): Note by the Secretariat,' UN Doc. A/CN.9/306, reprinted in *UNCITRAL Yearbook* 19 (1988), 103-8.

56 According to the federal Department of Justice the common law proscription of penalty clauses places obstacles to the unification of common and civil laws in this area.

57 Reprinted in *UNCITRAL Yearbook* 19 (1988):75-85.

58 See Jacques Gauthier, 'The UNCITRAL Model Rules on Standby Letters of Credit and Guarantees,' in *Seventh International Trade Law Seminar*, 37-54.

59 Convention on Contracts for the International Sale of Goods, UN Doc. A/Conf. 97/18, Annex I, reprinted in *ILM* 19 (1980):668-95.

60 For commentary on the convention see John Honnold, *Uniform Law for International Sales under the 1980 United Nations Convention* (Deventer, The Netherlands: Kluwer 1982) and Peter Schlechtriem, *Uniform Sales Law: The UN Convention on Contracts for the International Sale of Goods* (Vienna 1986). For a bibliography of writings on the convention see Peter Winship, 'A Bibliography of Commentaries on the United Nations International Sales Convention,' *International Lawyer* 21 (1987):585-6 and see the Special Issue of the *American Journal of Comparative Law* 27 (1979) for a review of the unification process and bibliographical references.

61 Herrmann, 'The Contribution of UNCITRAL,' 38.

62 Argentina, China, Egypt, France, Hungary, Italy, Lesotho, Syria, USA, Yugoslavia, and Zambia. See Peter Winship, 'The New Legal Regime for International Sales Contracts,' *Review of International Business Law* 2 (March 1988):107.

63 The Vienna Sales Convention does not generally apply to goods bought for

personal, family, or household use; sales of goods by auction or execution; sales of securities, negotiable instruments, or money; sales of ships, hovercraft, aircraft, or electricity. See article 2. In addition, the convention does not apply to the validity of the contract, the effect of the contract on property in the goods sold, or liability of the seller for death or personal injury. See articles 4 and 5.

64 Article 1(1)(a) provides that the convention applies to contracts for the sale of goods between parties whose places of business are in different contracting states. In addition, under Article 1(1)(b) the convention applies whenever the rules of private international law lead to the application of the law of a contracting state. However, under Article 95, states are free to exclude the application of Article 1(1)(b).

65 Winship, 'The New Legal Regime,' 107. States, in addition, are permitted five reservations.

66 Winship, 'The New Legal Regime,' 109. This is one of the permitted reservations. It has been invoked by China, Argentina, and Hungary.

67 *An Act to Implement the United Nations Convention on Contracts for the International Sale of Goods*, Bill c-81.

68 British Columbia, Alberta, Ontario, Manitoba, Newfoundland, Nova Scotia, New Brunswick, Prince Edward Island, and the Northwest Territories.

69 Winship, 'The New Legal Regime,' 110.

70 *Report to the Uniform Law Conference of Canada: Convention on Contracts for the International Sale of Goods* (July 1981).

71 Ziegel and Samson, *Report*, 25.

72 Ziegel and Samson, *Report*, 29.

73 Ziegel and Samson, *Report*, 31.

74 Henry Landau, 'Background to u.s. Participation in United Nations Convention on Contracts for the International Sale of Goods,' *International Lawyer* 18 (Winter 1984):29.

75 Elizabeth Hayes Patterson, 'United Nations Convention on Contracts for the International Sale of Goods: Unification and the Tension Between Compromise and Domination,' *Stanford Journal of International Law* 22 (Spring 1986):271, cf. 30.

76 'Uniform Law for International Trade-Progress and Prospects,' *International Lawyer* 20 (Spring 1986):639. See also John Honnold, 'The New Uniform Law for International Sales and the ucc: A Comparison,' *International Lawyer* 18 (Winter 1984):21-8.

77 *Report of the United Nations Commission on International Trade Law on the Work of its Eighteenth Session*, 40 UN GAOR Supp. (No.17), UN Doc. A/40/17 (1985). Note that UNCITRAL Conciliation Rules, UN Doc. A/35/17, para. 106, reprinted in ILM 20 (1981):300-6 are also available as an alternative to adversarial proceedings.

78 Michael F. Hoellering, 'The UNCITRAL Model Law on International Com-

mercial Arbitration,' *International Lawyer* 20 (Winter 1986):327.

79 Hoellering, 'The UNCITRAL Model Law,' 329, here cites a report of the secretary general on the possible features of the model law.

80 For example, the UNCITRAL Arbitration Rules, UN Doc. A/31/17, reprinted in *ILM* 15 (1976):701-17 and the *Rules for the ICC Court of Arbitration*, International Chamber of Commerce, Publication No. 291.

81 For a fuller discussion of the scope of party autonomy see Hoellering, 'The UNCITRAL Model Law.'

82 Hoellering, 'The UNCITRAL Model Law,' 331.

83 UN Doc. A/Conf. 9/22, reprinted in *ILM* 7 (1968):1,042-62.

84 All of the Canadian provinces, the Yukon, and the Northwest Territories have enacted legislation implementing the New York Convention.

85 Albert van den Berg, cited in Donald J. Sorochan, 'Recognition of Foreign Arbitral Awards,' in *Commercial Arbitration* (Vancouver: The Continuing Legal Education Society of BC 1986), 6.1.01.

86 Paul J. Davidson, 'Uniformity in International Trade Law: The Constitutional Obstacle,' *The Dalhousie Law Journal* 11 (1987-8):681.

87 Marc Lalonde, 'The New Environment for Commercial Arbitration in Canada,' *Review of International Business Law* 1 (April 1987):32.

88 For the relevant federal and provincial legislation implementing the New York Convention and the Model Law and for variations among jurisdictions in the laws enacted see Thomas Noecker and Matthias K. Hentzen,' The New Legislation on Arbitration in Canada,' *International Lawyer* 22 (Fall 1988):829-36.

89 Noecker and Hentzen, 'The New Legislation,' 834; and see Lalonde, 'The New Environment,' 38.

90 General Assembly Resolution 43/165, 9 December 1988, reprinted in *UNCITRAL Yearbook* 19 (1988):173-86.

91 Bradley Crawford, 'The United Nations Convention on International Bills of Exchange and Promissory Notes: Its Impact on Canadian Practice,' in *Seventh International Trade Law Seminar*, 25-35.

92 Nor does there appear to be a Canadian position on the Draft Convention on International Cheques, UN Doc. A/Conf. 9/212 (1981) adopted by UNCITRAL.

93 Distributed by the United Nations under Sales No. E 87. V. 10, Doc A/CN. 9/SER. B.2.

94 Reprinted in *UNCITRAL Yearbook* 20:(1989), 103-50.

95 Webb and Zacher, 'Canadian Export Trade,' 116.

96 Verdon, 'Current Developments,' 27.

97 'International countertrade: draft outline of the possible content and structure of a legal guide on drawing up international countertrade contracts: Report of the Secretary General,' UN Doc. A/CN. 9/322, reprinted in *UNCITRAL Yearbook*, 20 (1989), 207-16.

98 Webb and Zacher, 'Canadian Export Trade,' 119. The authors cite a return to discriminatory, barter-type transactions, the increase of risks and transaction costs which function like non-tariff barriers to trade, the conferring of non-economic advantages on state-trading countries, and direct threats to Canadian mineral exports as among the negative influences of countertrade on Canada.

99 Christiane Verdon, General Counsel, Constitutional and International Law, federal Department of Justice, reported on these developments at the Eighth International Trade Law Seminar, Ottawa, October 1990.

100 See, generally, Michael C. Rowe, 'The Contribution of the ICC to the Development of International Trade Law,' in Horn and Schmitthoff, eds., *The Transnational Law of International Commercial Transactions,* 51-60.

101 International Chamber of Commerce, Publication Nos. 290 and 322. See G.G. Sedgwick, 'Aspects of Payment and Financing Mechanisms in the Export Trade,' in Ziegel and Graham, *New Dimensions,* 85.

102 *Incoterms 1980,* International Chamber of Commerce, Publication No. 350. See Jan Ramberg, 'Incoterms 1980,' in Horn and Schmitthoff, *The Transnational Law of International Commercial Transactions,* 137-51.

103 *A.G. Canada v. A.G. Ontario,* [1937] A.C. 326 (P.C.). See Davidson, 'Uniformity in International Trade Law' for further discussion of the constitutional limitations on the federal treatymaking power.

104 Now the Constitution Act, 1867.

105 Jacob S. Ziegel, 'Canada and the Vienna Sales Convention,' *Canadian Business Law Journal* 12 (1986-7):369. And see William C. Graham, 'International Commercial Arbitration: The Developing Canadian Profile,' in Robert B. Paterson and Bonita J. Thompson, eds., UNCITRAL *Arbitration Model in Canada* (Vancouver: Carswell 1987), 77.

106 B.C. Law Reform Commission, *Report on Arbitration* (1982), 58; and see Davidson, 'Uniformity in International Trade Law,' 680-5.

107 For an excellent review of the role played by British Columbia and the nature of the BC regime, see the selections by Gerold Herrmann and Bonita J. Thompson in Paterson and Thompson, eds., UNCITRAL *Arbitration.*

108 Bonita J. Thompson, Q.C., former executive director of the British Columbia International Commercial Arbitration Centre and a drafter of the BC legislation, 'BCICAC and Rules,' in *Commercial Arbitration,* 3.1.01.

109 'Canada and the Vienna Sales Convention,' 369-70.

110 Preface, Paterson and Thompson, UNCITRAL *Arbitration,* vii.

111 'Canada and the Vienna Sales Convention,' 367. Note, however, that this does not apply to contracts with the United States or British Columbia, or other jurisdictions that have declared Article 1(1)(b), which provides for the automatic application of the convention to contracts when the rules of private international law lead to the application of the law of a contracting state, to be non-binding. It would, however, apply to transactions with

other trading partners who are party to the convention and who have not made a similar declaration or reservation.

112 Paterson and Thompson, UNCITRAL *Arbitration*, 15. The number of Pacific Rim countries utilizing the ICC arbitration framework increased from 62 in 1981 to 156 in 1985, reflecting an increase from 11 per cent to 20 per cent of total ICC arbitrations. See Sigvard Jarvin, 'An International Chamber of Commerce Perspective,' in Paterson and Thompson, UNCITRAL *Arbitration*, 56.

113 See the selections on China and Japan, in Paterson and Thompson, UNCITRAL *Arbitration*.

114 E.C. Chiasson, cited in Bonita J. Thompson, 'Building an Arbitration and Mediation Centre: From International Foundations to Domestic Rooftops,' presented to the International Congress of Commercial Arbitration in Tokyo , June 1988, 2.

115 Davidson, 'Uniformity in International Trade Law,' 679-80.

116 Davidson, 'Uniformity in International Trade Law,' 691- 2.

117 Davidson, ' Uniformity in International Trade Law,' makes the case for greater reliance on the federal trade and commerce power.

118 Davidson in 'Uniformity of International Trade Law,' 696, recognizes the problem posed by the creation of a dual system of law, one federal and one provincial, governing the same areas. However, he notes that dual legal systems do exist in the United Kingdom for the sale of goods and for arbitration and in France for arbitration.

119 Lansing, 'The Change in American Attitude,' 279.

120 See Haggard and Simmons, 'Theories of International Regimes,' 500-6, for a good concise review of the theory of hegemonic stability. For the participation of the United States in the regime see Pfund and Taft, 'Congress' Role,' and for U.S. leadership in unifying international sales law see the various selections in the Symposium on International Sale of Goods Convention, *The International Lawyer* 18 (Winter 1984).

121 Robert O. Keohane, 'Economic Dependence and the Self-Directed Small State, *Jerusalem Journal of International Relations* 6 (1982):50.

CHAPTER 5: FOREIGN INVESTMENT POLICY

1 There has been a lot of academic research on foreign investment in Canada over the past twenty-five years. A very useful overview of this research is A.E. Safarian, *Foreign Direct Investment: A Survey of Canadian Research* (Montreal: Institute for Research on Public Policy 1985).

2 See, for example, Dewhirst, 'The Canadian Federal Government's Policy Towards Foreign Investment,' in Fry and Randolph, eds., *Regulation of Foreign Direct Investment in Canada and the United States* (1983) and Bliss,

'Founding FIRA: The Historical Background,' in Spence and Rosenfeld, eds., *Foreign Investment Review Law in Canada* (1984).

3 See Graham and Krugman, *Foreign Direct Investment in the United States* (Washington, DC: Institute for International Economics 1989).

4 Gray, *Foreign Direct Investment in Canada* (1972).

5 It is difficult to make accurate cross-country comparisons of living standards. The normal shortcut of taking GDP in domestic dollars and converting by an international exchange rate is only accurate if the price of non-tradeable goods (such as housing) is the same across countries. The fact that some countries, such as Japan and Switzerland, have very high prices for housing and other non-tradeables means that their comparative incomes tend to be overstated. For a discussion of true purchasing power based real income measures see Summers and Heston, 'A New Set of International Comparisons of Real Product and Price Levels,' *Review of Income and Wealth* 34 (1988):1-25. Depending on exactly what adjustments one makes, Canada might be the highest real income country. The other contenders are the U.S. and Norway.

6 A very valuable review of foreign investment policy in Canada is R.K. Paterson (1986) *Canadian Regulation of International Trade and Investment* (Toronto: Carswell 1986).

7 *Final Report of the Royal Commission on Canada's Economic Prospects* (Ottawa 1958).

8 *Report on Foreign Ownership and the Structure of the Canadian Economy* (1968).

9 See Donald G. McFetridge, *Trade Liberalization and the Multinationals* (Ottawa: Economic Council of Canada, Ministry of Supply and Services 1989) for a discussion of the relationship between trade liberalization and the nature of foreign direct investment.

10 The threshold level was $250,000 in assets or $3 million in revenues.

11 A very good study of the temporal consistency of FIRA, containing these and other numbers, is Steve Globerman's, 'The Consistency of Canada's Foreign Investment Review Process: A Temporal Analysis,' *Journal of International Business Studies* (Spring/Summer 1984):119-29. See also Globerman, 'Canada's Foreign Investment Review Agency and the Direct Investment Process in Canada,' *Canadian Public Administration* 27 (Fall 1984):313-28.

12 See, in particular, the empirical evidence examined in James Brander and Steve Dowrick, 'The Role of Fertility and Population in Comparative Economic Growth,' discussion paper, University of British Columbia, 1991.

CHAPTER 6: INTERNATIONAL LEGAL REGIMES

1 See Robert E. Tindall, Multinational Enterprises (Dobbs Ferry: Oceana
   Publications 1975), 148; Georg Schwarzenberger, Foreign Investment
   and International Law (1969), 16; and International Monetary Fund,
   Balance of Payments Manual, 4th ed. (1977), para. 408.

2 The 1982 Canadian Task Force on Trade in Services attempted to define
   services as 'intangible economic commodities produced for sale or distribution or through established programmes or institutions' (p. 6). For the
   European Commission classification of trade in services see Murray Gibbs
   and Ming Mashayekhi, 'Services: Co-operation for Development,' *Journal
   of World Trade Law* 22 (1988):81, 102.

3 Lassa Oppenheim, International Law, a treatise ed. by H. Lauterpact, 8th
   ed. (London: Longmans 1955), 684-90.

4 See Samuel K.B. Asante, 'International Law and Foreign Investment: A
   Reappraisal,' *International and Comparative Law Quarterly* 37 (1988):588.

5 See Oswaldo de Rivero B., New Economic Order and International Development Law (Oxford, NY: Pergamon Press 1980).

6 Final Act and Related Documents, United Nations Conference on Trade
   and Employment, Havana, Cuba, 21 Nov. 1947 to 24 Mar. 1948. The
   Charter of the ITO did not purport to extend itself to trade in services in
   general. The proposed investment provisions would have extended their
   benefits to the establishment of service industries and Chapter V would
   have brought certain services within the provisions concerning restrictive
   business practices.

7 Canadian Administration of the Foreign Investment Review Act. GATT,
   Basic Instruments and Selected Documents (BISD), 30th Supp. (1984), 140.

8 See D.J. Albrecht, 'Canadian Foreign Investment Policy and the International Politico-Legal Process,' *Canadian Yearbook of International Law* 149
   (1983).

9 GATT, BISD 26 Supp. (1980), Article 1(1)(a) 33.

10 Ibid., 56.

11 *International Legal Materials* 15 (1976):967.

12 See Albrecht, 'Canadian Foreign Investment Policy and the International
   Politico-Legal Process,' 173-4.

13 OECD, Code of Liberalization of Current Invisible Operations (Paris 1973).
   Canada's reservations to the Code regarded maritime and inland water-
   way freights, road transport, and insurance.

14 OECD, Code of Liberalization of Capital Movements (March 1982).

15 *Agreement Between the Government of Canada and the Government of the Union
   of Soviet Socialist Republics for the Promotion and Reciprocal Protection of
   Investment*, Moscow, 20 November 1989. Both accords have been signed
   but are not yet in force. Similar accords have now been signed by Canada

with Hungary, Czechoslovakia, and Uruguay.

16 See Robert K. Paterson, 'The Economic Co-operation Agreement Between Canada and ASEAN: Charting a Foreign Investment Course in South-East Asia,' UBC *Law Review* 19 (1985):389.

17 See Mark S. Bergman, 'Bilateral Investment Protection Treaties: An Examination of the Evolution and Significance of the U.S. Prototype Treaty' NYU, *Journal of International Law and Politics* 16 (1963):1

18 Articles 1 and 3.

19 For the text of the ICSID Convention, see *International Legal Materials* 4 (1965):524.

20 Article 42.

21 Article 54(1).

22 See Robert K. Paterson and Bonita J. Thompson, UNCITRAL *Arbitration Model in Canada* (Toronto: Carswell 1987).

23 Article 1402. Existing non-conforming measures may not be amended so as to increase their original level of non-conformity even further; Article 1402.5(c).

24 Article 1402.3.

25 The separate treatment of financial services in the Free Trade Agreement reflects both the sector-specific nature of the accord and the fact that both parties are federations. Chapter 17 lacks the broad framework of principles characteristic of other parts of the agreement and is, instead, a series of agreements on particular matters (such as foreign bank subsidiaries). Unlike the general service provisions of the agreement, however, the obligations contained in Chapter 17 are not prospective but operate to immediately dismantle certain trade barriers – as part of a general process of deregulation of the financial services sector of both economies. The insurance industry is not covered by Chapter 17 but is, instead, covered by the general services chapter (that is, existing barriers to insurance trade remain but any new barriers are subject to a national treatment obligation).

26 A 'business person' is a citizen of either Canada or the United States who is engaged in the trade of goods or services or in investment activities; Article 1506. Under Annex 1502.1, business persons are divided into business visitors, traders and investors, professionals and intra-company transferees.

27 Negotiations on Trade in Services, Part 2, Punta del Este, September 1986.

28 See Phedon Nicolaides, 'Economic Aspects of Services: Implications for a GATT Agreement,' *Journal of World Trade* 23 (1988):125, 129; Canada-U.S. Free Trade Agreement, Article 1402.3.

29 Ibid., 128.

30 See Deepak Nayyar, 'Some Reflections in the Uruguay Round and Trade in Services,' *Journal of World Trade* 22 (1988):35; Gibbs and Mazhayekhi,

'Services Co-operation for Development,' 81; and Janette Mark and Gerald K. Hellemer, *Trade in Services: The Negotiating Concerns of the Developing Countries* (Ottawa: North-South Institute 1988).

31 See Terence G. Berg, 'Trade in Services: Toward a "Development Round" of GATT Negotiations Benefitting Both Developing and Industrialized States,' *Harvard International Law Journal* 28 (1988):1, who notes that a services agreement would give developing countries the opportunity to obtain high quality services at the lowest prices and allow them to combine these with cheap labour to exploit exporting opportunities.

32 See GATT, *Summary of Issues Raised in Exchange of Information on Services*, GATT, Doc. MDF/W/58, at 9.

33 See Bank Act, RSC 1985, c. B-1, s. 8.

34 Articles 1402.1 and 1602.1.

35 See Harold H. Koh, 'The Legal Markets of International Trade: A Perspective on the Proposed U.S.-Canada Free Trade Agreement,' *Yale Journal of International Law* 12 (1987):193.

36 Canada-United States Free Trade Agreement Implementation Act, SC 1988, c. 65, s. 135.

37 See Christopher J. Maule, 'Trade and Culture in Canada,' *Journal of World Trade Law* 20 (1987):615.

CHAPTER 7: INTERNATIONAL MONETARY REGIME

1 This definition comes from Stephen D. Krasner, 'Structural Causes and Regime Consequences: Regimes as Intervening Variables,' in Krasner, ed., *International Regimes* (Ithaca: Cornell University Press 1983):1.

2 The external consequences of macroeconomic policy choices depend on the particular mix of monetary and fiscal policies; for example, expansionary fiscal policy and restrictive monetary policy can produce trade deficits and capital inflows, as occurred in the United States in the early 1980s.

3 See, for example, John Holmes, *The Better Part of Valour: Essays on Canadian Diplomacy* (Toronto: McClelland and Stewart 1970) and A.F.W. Plumptre, *Three Decades of Decision: Canada and the World Monetary System 1944-75* (Toronto: McClelland and Stewart 1977), especially chap. 1.

4 David B. Dewitt and John J. Kirton, *Canada as a Principal Power: A Study in Foreign Policy and International Relations* (Toronto: John Wiley and Sons 1983).

5 This schema borrows from Richard N. Cooper, *The Economics of Interdependence: Economic Policy in the Atlantic Community* (New York: McGraw-Hill 1968), chap. 1, and is common in the literature.

6 Some of these types of policy can also be used to serve other purposes; this chapter focuses on only those elements of these types of policy that are

intended to help reconcile national macroeconomic objectives with international constraints.

7 John Gerard Ruggie, 'International Regimes, Transactions, and Change: Embedded Liberalism in the Postwar Economic Order,' in Krasner, ed., *International Regimes*.

8 Michael C. Webb, 'International Co-ordination of Macroeconomic Adjustment Policies Since 1945,' (PhD dissertation, Stanford University 1990). See also Michael C. Webb, 'International Economic Structures, Government Interests, and International Co-ordination of Macroeconomic Adjustment Policies,' *International Organization* 45 (Summer 1991):309-42.

9 There have also been changes in the international institutional locus of the regime, from the IMF and the Marshall Plan in the early years to the G7 in the 1980s and 1990s.

10 Plumptre, *Three Decades of Decision*, chaps 1, 2; R.D. Cuff and J.L. Granatstein, *American Dollars–Canadian Prosperity: Canadian-American Economic Relations 1945-1950* (Toronto: Samuel-Stevens 1978), 18-19.

11 Ottawa delayed imposing import restrictions for most of 1947 because it did not want to undermine the trade liberalization talks then underway in Geneva. Canadian diplomats worried that if a strong country like Canada took restrictive action, others with weaker payments positions would be encouraged to demand greater freedom to do so in the rules of the forthcoming trade organization.

12 The Canadian import restrictions were designed to avoid the appearance of formal discrimination, but no one was fooled into believing that the United States was not the target. Plumptre, *Three Decades of Decision*, chap. 4; Cuff and Granatstein, *American Dollars-Canadian Prosperity*, chap. 2.

13 Regarding the American suggestion, see Cuff and Granatstein, *American Dollars-Canadian Prosperity*, 58.

14 Ottawa may have believed that an IMF loan would take too long to arrange, but there was also concern that the IMF would be unsympathetic to Canada's problems because Canada had failed to consult with the Fund before changingits exchange rate in 1946; Plumptre, *Three Decades of Decision*, 99-101. In any case, the IMF probably would not have loaned as much to Canada as did the United States, since a loan of $300 million would have been equivalent to 100 per cent of Canada's IMF quota.

15 Cuff and Granatstein, *American Dollars-Canadian Prosperity*, chap. 2; Plumptre, *Three Decades of Decision*, chap. 4.

16 Paul Wonnacott, *The Canadian Dollar 1948-1958* (Toronto: University of Toronto Press 1960); Plumptre, *Three Decades of Decision*, 142-8; J. Keith Horsefield, *The International Monetary Fund 1945-1965: Twenty Years of International Monetary Cooperation*, vol. 1, *Chronicle* (Washington: International Monetary Fund 1969), 159-62.

17 Plumptre, *Three Decades of Decision*, 149; Margaret Garritsen de Vries and

J. Keith Horsefield, *The International Monetary Fund, 1945-1965: Twenty Years of International Monetary Cooperation*, vol. 2, *Analysis* (Washington: International Monetary Fund 1969), 159-60.

18 Kenneth W. Dam, *The Rules of the Game: Reform and Evolution in the International Monetary System* (Chicago: University of Chicago Press 1982), 128-9; Horsefield, *The International Monetary Fund, 1945-1965*, vol. 1, 273.

19 Horsefield, *The International Monetary Fund, 1945-1965*, vol. 1, 273-4.

20 Vote shares are given in de Vries and Horsefield, *The International Monetary Fund, 1945-1965*, vol. 2, 353.

21 de Vries and Horsefield, *The International Monetary Fund, 1945-1965*, vol. 2, 160-2; Dam, *The Rules of the Game*, 129-30.

22 Michael Michaely, *The Responsiveness of Demand Policies to the Balance of Payments: Postwar Patterns* (New York: National Bureau of Economic Research 1971).

23 For example, a 1988 Group of Thirty report described the Bretton Woods era as '"one of significant policy co-ordination," achieved not by ad hoc action but "through countries adusting their policies in response to the discipline imposed by the rules."' Cited in Jacques J. Polak, 'Comments,' in Ralph C. Bryant et al., eds., *Macroeconomic Policies in an Interdependent World* (Washington: Brookings Institution, International Monetary Fund, and Centre for Economic Policy Research 1989), 373.

24 Robert W. Russell, 'Transgovernmental Interaction in the International Monetary System, 1960-1972,' *International Organization* 27 (Autumn 1973).

25 However, Canada did not become a member of the Bank for International Settlements, in which much exchange rate co-ordination occurred, until 1970.

26 The level chosen by Canada was lower than many in the IMF thought appropriate. Plumptre, *Three Decades of Decision*, 165-70.

27 Most international currency support packages in the 1960s involved much larger loans from the United States than from the IMF.

28 Plumptre, *Three Decades of Decision*, 170-1.

29 Plumptre, *Three Decades of Decision*, 170-2; on quantitative restrictions versus tariff surcharges, see John H. Jackson, *World Trade and the Law of the GATT* (Indianapolis: Bobbs-Merrill 1969), 307, 712-13.

30 The following account is based on Gerald Wright, 'Persuasive Influence: The Case of the Interest Equalization Tax,' in Andrew W. Axline et al., eds., *Continental Community? Independence and Integration in North America* (Toronto: McClelland and Stewart 1974).

31 At this time, the IMF still viewed controls on short-term capital flows as an appropriate device for stabilizing exchange rates and facilitating liberalization of trade-related payments, so there would have been little multilateral support for a Canadian effort to keep American capital markets

open.

32 Wright, 'Persuasive Influence,' 148.

33 The United States agreed to disregard the ceiling in December 1968 because Canada had introduced controls to ensure that overseas borrowers did not gain access to the United States through Canada, because Canada was investing its United States dollar reserves in forms which did not show up as liabilities in the American balance of payments, and because Canadian borrowers were beginning to turn to European capital markets; Plumptre, *Three Decades of Decision*, 218.

34 Gordon R. Sparks, 'The Theory and Practice of Monetary Policy in Canada: 1945-83,' in John Sargent, Research Coordinator, *Fiscal and Monetary Policy*, vol. 21 of the research studies commissioned for the Royal Commission on the Economic Union and Development Prospects for Canada (Toronto: University of Toronto Press 1986), 133.

35 Robert D. Putnam and Nicholas Bayne, *Hanging Together: The Seven-Power Summits* (London: Heinemann for the Royal Institute of International Affairs 1984).

36 Peter C. Dobell, *Canada in World Affairs*, vol. 17, 1971-1973 (Toronto: Canadian Institute of International Affairs 1985), 26-9.

37 Sparks, 'The Theory and Practice of Monetary Policy in Canada,' 136.

38 Thomas J. Courchene, *Money, Inflation, and the Bank of Canada*, vol. 2: An Analysis of Monetary Gradualism 1975-80 (Montreal: C.D. Howe Institute 1981), 13.

39 Depreciation would increase the prices of imported goods (which accounted for roughly one quarter of consumption in Canada) and might encourage workers in export industries that benefitted from depreciation to demand higher wages. The Bank of Canada's rationale is described in Courchene, *Money, Inflation and the Bank of Canada*, vol. 2, and Peter Howitt, *Monetary Policy in Transition: A Study of the Bank of Canada Policy 1982-85*, Policy Study No. 1 (Ottawa: C.D. Howe Institute 1986).

40 Howitt, *Monetary Policy in Transition*, argues that the Bank of Canada followed a 'Group of Ten' exchange rate standard, which assigned a preponderant (and, according to Howitt, excessive) weight to the American dollar.

41 Donald J. Savoie, *The Politics of Public Budgeting in Canada* (Toronto: University of Toronto Press 1990), 149.

42 The use of tax expenditures increased in the late 1970s in part because they could be used to increase government spending in particular areas without the increase showing up as an increase in spending.

43 David Wolfe, 'The Politics of the Deficit,' in G. Bruce Doern, Research Co-ordinator, *The Politics of Economic Policy* vol. 40 of the research studies commissioned for the Royal Commission on the Economic Union and Development Prospects for Canada (Toronto: University of Toronto Press

1985), argues persuasively that the growing structural deficits of the 1970s and the early 1980s were caused mainly by tax cuts, not by unconstrained spending growth. See also Savoie, *The Politics of Public Spending in Canada*, and Douglas G. Hartle, *The Expenditure Budget Process of the Government of Canada: A Public Choice-Rent-Seeking Perspective*, Canadian Tax Paper No. 81 (Toronto: Canadian Tax Foundation 1988).

44	Plumptre, *Three Decades of Decision*, 284-8.

45	Putnam and Bayne, *Hanging Together* (1984 ed.), 28, 38, 60.

46	Dewitt and Kirton, *Canada as a Principal Power*, 5; Allan Gotlieb, 'Canada and the Economic Summits: Power and Responsibility,' Bissell Paper No. 1, Centre for International Studies, University of Toronto, December 1987.

47	Savoie, *The Politics of Public Spending in Canada*, 151-63.

48	Putnam and Bayne, *Hanging Together* (1984 ed.), 182.

49	Robert D. Putnam and Nicholas Bayne, *Hanging Together: Cooperation and Conflict in the Seven-Power Summits*, 2nd ed., rev. and enl. (London: Sage Publications 1987), 189.

50	Howitt, *Monetary Policy in Transition*, argues that monetary policy was more restrictive in Canada than in most other countries in the early 1980s.

51	Data on domestic and foreign borrowing is provided in Canada, Department of Finance, *The Budget*, tabled in the House of Commons by the Honourable Michael H. Wilson, Minister of Finance, 20 February 1990, 25-6.

52	Michael Henderson, 'The OECD as an Instrument of National Policy,' *International Journal* 36 (Autumn 1981):794.

53	Gerald Wright, 'Bureaucratic Politics and Canadian Foreign Economic Policy,' in Denis Stairs and Gilbert R. Winham, Research Co-ordinators, *Selected Problems in Formulating Foreign Economic Policy*, vol. 30 of the research studies commissioned for the Royal Commission on the Economic Union and Development Prospects for Canada (Toronto: University of Toronto Press 1985), 32.

54	Multilateral surveillance procedures are described in detail in Wendy Dobson, *Economic Policy Co-ordination: Requiem or Prologue?* Policy Analyses in International Economics 30 (Washington: Institute for International Economics 1991).

55	Multilateral surveillance had been conducted in various OECD and IMF forums since the 1960s but had not been as frequent, penetrating, and high-level as it became after 1986.

56	For details of policy co-ordination in the 1980s, see Webb, 'International Economic Structures, Government Interests, and International Co-ordination of Macroeconomic Adjustment Policies,' *International Organization* 45 (Summer 1991):309-42.

57	Dobson, *Economic Policy Co-ordination*, 126.

58	Communiqué reprinted in Peter I. Hajnal, ed., *The Seven-Power Summit:*

Documents from the Summits of Industrialized Countries 1975-1989 (Millwood, NY: Kraus International Publications 1989), 312-13.

59 Dobson, *Economic Policy Coordination*, 67-70. See Yoichi Funabashi, *Managing the Dollar: From the Plaza to the Louvre* (Washington: Institute for International Economics 1988), for a blow-by-blow account of exchange rate co-ordination in 1985-7; see I.M. Destler and C. Randall Henning, *Dollar Politics: Exchange Rate Policymaking in the United States* (Washington: Institute for International Economics 1989) for a brief account of co-ordination in the 1987-9 period.

60 *Maclean's* (19 May 1986) 21.

61 Dobson, *Economic Policy Coordination*, 40.

62 Dobson, *Economic Policy Coordination*, 62. The United States supported both approaches at different times.

63 Putnam and Bayne, *Hanging Together* (1987 ed.), 208; *Maclean's*, 19 May 1986, 21.

64 Funabashi, *Managing the Dollar*, 140.

65 Sylvia Ostry, Prime Minister Mulroney's 1985-8 sherpa, cited in Stevie Cameron, 'Scaling Summits,' *Report on Business Magazine* (June 1988), 63.

66 Dobson, *Economic Policy Coordination*, 43.

67 This is clear from the detailed account of debates contained in Funabashi, *Managing the Dollar*.

68 Dobson, *Economic Policy Coordination*, 43.

69 Polak, 'Comments,' 376.

70 For example, Canadian officials joined in criticizing the United States at a G7 meeting in September 1990, at a time when Canada's own deficit was still larger than the American deficit (relative to GNP) and when the Conservative government was under attack at home for its failure to reduce its own deficit; *Globe and Mail* (24 September 1990), B1, B4.

71 *Maclean's* (22 June 1987), 35.

72 Statements made in 1987 are cited in Dobson, *Economic Policy Co-ordination*, 83-4. In the economic declaration from the 1989 Paris G7 summit, Canada (along with the United States and Italy, the other two worst deficit countries) committed itself to unspecified action to bring down the budget and current account deficits. The economic declaration is reproduced in Hajnal, ed., *The Seven Power Summits*, 391.

73 Dobson, *Economic Policy Coordination*, 127.

74 See, for example, *Globe and Mail* (17 September 1988), A5; and 30 May 1989, B1, B4, regarding OECD reports.

75 It was rumoured that Department of Finance officials leaked the IMF report 'to pave the way for a harsh deficit-cutting budget'; *Globe and Mail* (8 March 1989), B3.

76 Cited in *Globe and Mail* (13 September 1990), B2.

77 See, for example, the contributions of Douglas Peters, Pierre Fortin, and

Thomas J. Courchene, in Robert C. York, ed., *Taking Aim: The Debate on Zero Inflation*, Policy Study 10 (Toronto: C.D. Howe Institute 1990).

78 Canada, Department of Finance, *The Budget*, tabled in the House of Commons by the Honourable Michael Wilson, 20 February 1990, 41-5.

79 Ottawa's annual budget deficit as a proportion of GDP averaged 4.7 per cent in 1980-4 and 4.5 per cent in 1985-9; comparable figures for Washington were 4.2 and 3.8 per cent. The 1980-4 averages calculated from International Monetary Fund, *International Financial Statistics Yearbook, 1989*, 156; the 1985-9 averages calculated from OECD, *Economic Outlook* 47 (June 1990), 15.

80 See Savoie, *The Politics of Public Spending in Canada*, chap. 4, for a discussion of the Department of Finance's role in budgetmaking.

81 Cited in Savoie, *The Politics of Public Spending in Canada*, 83.

82 Howitt, *Monetary Policy in Transition*.

83 Dobson, *Economic Policy Coordination*, 126.

84 Canada's reserve holdings of yen apparently increased by a few hundred million dollars in March 1990; *Globe and Mail* (5 April 1990), B6.

85 *Globe and Mail* (9 April 1990), B4. The United States and West Germany had also rejected Japan's request, ostensibly for the same reason; they argued that they needed to maintain high interest rates to contain inflationary pressures at home.

86 It also contradicted Canada's efforts in 1986 to persuade foreign countries to reduce high interest rates that were making it difficult for Ottawa to relax monetary policy without triggering a collapse in the value of the Canadian dollar, *Maclean's* (5 May 1986), 45.

87 For Governor Crow's view that a depreciation of the dollar below the 85 cent US range would be inflationary because it would raise returns from exports and, therefore, offset monetary restraint, see 'Minutes of Bank of Canada Board of Directors' Meeting,' 16 February 1990, *Bank of Canada Review* (April 1990), 41.

88 For Governor Crow's views, see 'Minutes of Bank of Canada Board of Directors' Meeting,' 11 May 1990, *Bank of Canada Review* (July 1990), 22; regarding Finance Minister Wilson's views, see *Globe and Mail* (14 July 1989), B1, B2.

89 Batten et al., *The Conduct of Monetary Policy in the Major Industrial Countries*, 1.

90 Bank of Canada, *Annual Report* (1990, 43; and 1989, 43).

91 Funabashi, *Managing the Dollar*, 186-7.

92 *Globe and Mail* (3 December 1990), A7.

93 Paul Wonnacott, *The United States and Canada: The Quest for Free Trade*, Policy Analyses in International Economics 16 (Washington: Institute for International Economics 1987), 10, 164; *Financial Post* (20 September 1986), 1-2.

94 *Globe and Mail* (3 December 1990), A7.

95 Dallas S. Batten, Michael Blackwell, In-Su Kim, Simon E. Nocera, and Yuzuru Ozeki, *The Conduct of Monetary Policy in the Major Industrial Countries: Instruments and Operating Procedures*, Occasional Paper No. 70 (Washington: International Monetary Fund 1990), 1.

96 Although, in February 1989, it was rumoured that the Bank of Canada was trying to keep the dollar within a Group of Seven-approved target range of plus or minus 1.5 cents around 83 cents U.S., and the dollar did trade in that range for some time; *Globe and Mail* (13 February 1989), B1.

97 Cited in *Globe and Mail* (16 May 1989), A4. What Crow neglected to mention was that it was relaxed Canadian monetary policies that drove the dollar down to the low levels from which it appreciated in 1988-9.

98 'Minutes of Bank of Canada Board of Directors' Meeting,' 16 February 1990, *Bank of Canada Review* (April 1990), 40.

99 Ibid., 41.

100 *Globe and Mail* (19 October 1990), B1, B2. Market participants also speculate that the Bank of Canada targets the dollar, based on the record of currency intervention and interest rate changes; *Globe and Mail* (18 February 1991), B1, B2.

101 The minutes of Bank of Canada Board of Directors' meetings reveal detailed consideration of trends in the American economy and American policy, with occasional references to developments in the rest of the international economy.

102 Another reason was that the change in the bank rate was sudden and unusually large; *Globe and Mail* (30 March 1990), B4.

CHAPTER 8: INTERNATIONAL AIR TRANSPORT

1 Services in Canada's far north remained regulated.

2 Bilateral agreements are required because states have sovereignty over the air space above their countries (established by the 1919 Paris treaty), and because there is not a widely ratified multilateral agreement allowing airlines of one country to transport passengers or cargo to a second country without permission of the second country. For an account of the failed attempt to achieve such an agreement at the Chicago Conference in 1944, see William E. O'Connor, *Economic Regulation of the World's Airlines* (New York: Praeger Publishers 1971).

3 Named routes would be Toronto-London or, at best, anywhere in Canada to London for Canadian carriers and anywhere in the UK to Toronto for British carriers, as opposed to the general authority to serve any point in Canada to any point in the UK.

4 A Fifth freedom is the right for an airline of country A to enplane traffic in

country B and carry it to/from country C.

5 For a bilateral agreement negotiated between Canada and the UK, third freedom routes for Canadian carriers would be routes from Canada to the UK, while fourth freedom routes would be from the UK to Canada.

6 International charter rates were not set by IATA but were generally established by individual charter carriers, subject to governmental approval.

7 ICAO, *Civil Aviation Statistics of the World* (various issues, 1977-88).

8 For a discussion of the deliberate actions by the U.S. to undermine IATA's fare-setting role, see Martin E. Dresner, 'Pricing on International Air Routes,' unpublished manuscript, University of British Columbia, (1988). For a discussion of the structural changes to the industry and the environment, see Martin E. Dresner and Michael W. Tretheway, 'The Changing Role of IATA: Prospects for the Future,' *Annals of Air and Space Law* 13 (1988):3-22.

9 'Illegal' discounting refers to the practice of IATA carriers setting fares at less than the amount specified in the appropriate IATA agreement. A common way for carriers to do this is by offering travel agents 'overrides' or extra commissions on the sale of tickets. Travel agents can then remit a percentage of the commission overrides to travellers, thereby effectively offering discounted tickets. For a discussion of how discounting has worked in Australia, see Alex McWhirter, 'The Alex McWhirter Report,' *Business Traveller* (June 1985):10-12.

10 Major examples of these works would be William A. Jordan, *Airline Regulation in America: Effects and Imperfections* (Baltimore: Johns Hopkins University Press 1970) and George W. Douglas and James C. Miller III, *Economic Regulation of Domestic Air Transport: Theory and Policy* (Washington, DC: The Brookings Institution 1974).

11 Although Carter received credit for deregulating the U.S. air transport industry, the first moves towards deregulation were undertaken by his predecessor, President Ford.

12 The four major methods the U.S. used to promote competition on international routes were: Allowing Laker Airways to fly into the United States; the signing of liberal bilateral agreements; the threatening of anti-trust proceedings against IATA; and, the passing of pro-competitive legislation for international air transport.

13 The inability of IATA to co-ordinate fares is illustrated by the increase in the number of carrier-specific fares that were offered on the North Atlantic. In a survey of 37 North Atlantic air routes, Martin E. Dresner, 'Liberal Bilaterals and the Regulation of International Air Transport,' in Paul Beamish, ed., *International Business*, Proceedings of Administrative Sciences Association of Canada (1989):30-9, found that in 1977 there were no carrier-specific fare offerings but by 1981, 30 of the 37 routes had carrier-specific discount fares and 24 routes had carrier-specific regular fares.

14 Stanley B. Rosenfield, 'International Aviation: A United States Govern-ment-Industry Partnership,' *The International Lawyer* 16 (Summer 1982):71-9.

15 See, for example, Klaus Knorr, *The Power of Nations* (New York: Basic Books 1975), 8; John Spanier, *Games Nations Play* 5th ed. (New York: Holt, Rinehart and Winston 1984), 251; James A. Nathan and James K. Oliver, 'The Growing Importance of Economics: Can the United States Manage This Phenomenon?' in Franklin D. Margiotta, ed., *Evolving Strategic Real-ities: Implications for u.s. Policymakers* (Washington, DC: National Defense University Press 1980), 82-3 and Knorr, 'International Economic Leverage and its Uses,' in Klaus Knorr and Frank N. Trager, eds., *Economic Issues and National Security* (Kansas: Regents Press 1977), 110.

16 B. Boyd Hight, 'A Hard Look at Hard Rights,' paper presented at the Lloyd's of London International Aviation Law Seminar, Tobago, WI (16-19 March 1981).

17 For a listing of these agreements, see Peter P.C. Haanappel, *Pricing and Capacity Determination in International Air Transport* (Deventer, The Neth-erlands: Kluwer 1984), Appendix 3.

18 That is, unrestricted fares, 7 day advance purchase fares, 21 day advance purchase fares, and so on.

19 The u.s.-European Civil Aviation Conference (ECAC) Memorandum of Un-derstanding on North Atlantic Air Tariffs was entered into force on 1 August 1982. It is reprinted in Haanappel, *Pricing and Capacity Determina-tion in International Air Transport*, 191-9 and Stanley B. Rosenfield, 'Inter-national Aviation: A United States Government-Industry Partnership,' *The International Lawyer* 16 (Summer 1982):71-9. The original 12 ECAC signatories were Belgium, France, West Germany, Greece, Ireland, Italy, the Netherlands, Portugal, Spain, Switzerland, the United Kingdom, and Yugoslavia. Subsequent agreements included four additional European countries: Denmark, Finland, Norway, and Sweden.

20 Regional organizations which may engage in price-setting include the Association of African Airlines, the Arab Air Carriers Organization, the Association des Transporteurs Aeriens de la Zone Franc, the International Association of Latin American Air Transport, and the Orient Airlines Association.

21 As J. Feldman, 'Regionalism Facing Many Challenges as Replacement for Bilateral System,' *Air Transport World* 48 (August 1983):52, stated: 'For years there has been discontent among Third World countries that IATA and most worldwide fare policies are controlled by the developed coun-tries and their big airlines. The recently independent Third World nations and their airlines are trying to assert their will in international air policy.'

22 See IATA, *International Air Fares in Europe* (Geneva: IATA 1984).

23 ECAC is affiliated with ICAO and has a larger membership than does the

European Community. Decisions of the EC are binding on its members, while those of the ECAC have voluntary participation.

24 The EC proposal was expanded in 1990.

25 Unlimited direct London-Rome flights for a third country airline like Air France have not been agreed upon as yet.

26 Norway, Sweden, and Denmark jointly own a single carrier, SAS. Only Denmark is a member of the EC, thus posing problems for what rules will apply to SAS. The EC negotiations with Norway and Sweden were intended to clarify this problem. Essentially, they determined that the EC rules would apply.

27 Cabotage is the right for a carrier of Country A to enplane passengers in Country B for travel to a second destination in Country B.

28 These are United ($8.8), American ($8.6), Texas Air ($8.4), Delta ($7.4), Northwest ($5.6), Federal Express($5.6), U.S. Air ($5.2) and TWA ($4.4). Pan Am ($3.6) might also be included. Figures in parenthesis are 1988 revenues in billions of U.S. dollars.

29 Michael W. Tretheway, 'Globalization of the Airline Industry and Implications for Canada,' *Proceedings* (Canadian Transportation Research Forum, University of Saskatchewan Printing Services 1990).

30 Each country also has its own domestic carrier.

31 For a description of airline seat management, see Dennis J.H. Kraft, Tae H. Oum, and Michael W. Tretheway, 'Airline Seat Management,' *Proceedings* of the Canadian Transportation Research Forum 21st Annual Meeting, Vancouver, May (Saskatoon: University of Saskatchewan Press 1986), 232-45.

32 The major North American systems are American Airlines' Sabre system, United Airlines Covia CRS, Texas Air's SystemOne, and the proposed amalgamation of the TWA/Northwest PARS CRS with Delta's Soda system.

33 Wayne Lilley and James Bagnell, 'The Trouble With Freedom,' *Financial Times of Canada* (7 January 1991), 10-11.

34 In some cases only one carrier will actually operate between the two countries, but the other carrier will be able to book seats on the operating airline, or there will be a revenue pooling agreement between the carriers.

35 Jeffrey Simpson, 'A Web of Air Rights,' *Globe and Mail* national edition, Toronto (23 May 1986), A6.

36 Canada, 'Statement on Air Policy,' Transport Canada Ministerial Statement (Ottawa: 23 November 1973).

37 In 1990, the ministers of transport and external affairs convened a task force to recommend a new international air policy for Canada.

38 During the same period, several existing agreements were amended through exchanges of diplomatic notes.

39 An eighth agreement, Barbados, calls for prior governmental approval of airline schedules. Although the New Zealand bilateral does not require a

capacity agreement, an exchange of diplomatic notes between Canada and New Zealand set initial capacity levels and required either an airline agreement or government consultations on subsequent levels.

40 For example, Canadian Airlines International, the Canadian designated airline for operations to Israel, has a right to obtain a share of revenues derived from Canadian-Israeli air routes, even though CAI does not operate on these routes.

41 U.S. carriers have not been able to achieve the 25 per cent of the sun charter market that they were allocated.

42 See Joseph R. Chesen, *Canadian American Air Service Negotiations: Ending the Gridlock* (Washington, DC: J.R. Chesen Associates 1989) for a fuller discussion of the Canada-U.S. bilateral stalemate.

43 Philip DeMont, 'Airlines in Holding Pattern Over New Open-Skies Deal,' *Toronto Star* (9 January 1991): F1, F7 reports, for example, that Canadian carriers have access to only 30 per cent of the U.S. market compared to the 90 per cent access U.S. carriers have to the Canadian market.

44 Linda Diebel, 'Open Skies No Benefit to Canada, Letter Says,' *Toronto Star* (13 February 1991): B1-B2 reports that an organization called the United States Airports for Better International Air Service has been formed to lobby for better international air links.

45 See, for example, the following: Martha M. Hamilton, 'U.S., Canada Seek To Forge "Open Skies" Pact,' *Washington Post* (8 March 1991), F1, F4; Wayne Lilley and James Bagnell, 'The Trouble With Freedom,' *Financial Times of Canada* (7 January 1991), 10-11; and, Zuhair Kashmeri, 'Open Skies Mean Open War: Pilots,' *Globe and Mail* (8 December 1990), B3.

46 The province of Alberta's PWA Act further requires that no single individual or entity may control more than 4 per cent of PWA Corp's shares. (PWA Corp. is the parent company of Canadian Airlines International Ltd.) The Air Canada Participation Act requires that no individual may control more than 10 per cent of Air Canada's common shares. Revision to the PWA Act to increase the individual ownership stake to 10 per cent have been tabled in the legislative assembly.

CHAPTER 9: INTERNATIONAL SHIPPING

1 Canada, National Transportation Agency, *Annual Review* 1989 (Ottawa: Supply and Services Canada 1990), 91.

2 For example, in 1988, services from the U.S. to the Far East North Pacific area were provided by 30 companies, the largest 18 accounting for 90 per cent of the container capacity. On the route from the U.S. Atlantic and Gulf Coast to North Europe, there were 28 companies, of which the largest 15 accounted for 90 per cent of the container capacity. United States, Federal

Maritime Commission, *Section 18 Report on the Shipping Act of 1984* (1989) 276, 289.

3 Trevor D. Heaver, 'Container Vessel Size and Service Patterns: Implications for North American Inland Carrier and Shippers,' in Chris Stevens, ed., *Logistics: International Issues* (Cleveland: Leaseway 1985), 241-9.

4 For a history of conferences see Brian M. Deakin, *Shipping Conferences: A Study of Their Origin, Development and Economic Practices* (Cambridge: University of Cambridge 1973), 261 and Daniel Marx, Jr., *International Shipping Cartels: A Study of Industrial Self-Regulation by Shipping Conferences* (Princeton: Princeton University Press 1953), 323.

5 *Annual Review* 1989, 91.

6 H.S. Seidenfus, 'Revenue Pooling in Theory and Practice,' *Proceedings of the International Conference on Transportation Research*, 1973 (Chicago: Transportation Research Forum 1974), 169-75.

7 United Kingdom, *Report of the Royal Commission on Shipping Rings*, Cd. 4668 (1909).

8 United Kingdom, *Report of the Inquiry into Shipping*. Cmnd. 4337 (1970).

9 United Kingdom, *Report of the Inquiry into Shipping*, 133.

10 United Kingdom, *Report of the Inquiry into Shipping*, 128.

11 For a summary of the development of European shipping policy see Jurgen Erdmenger, *The European Community Transport Policy* (Addershot: Gower Publishing 1983), 155.

12 Erdmenger, *The European Community Transport Policy*, 88.

13 Erdmenger, *The European Community Transport Policy*, 89.

14 Erdmenger, *The European Community Transport Policy*, 92.

15 The Consultative Shipping Group is an informal gathering of European OECD members and Japan. The EEC Commission is admitted as an observer.

16 United States, Federal Maritime Commission, *Section 18 Report on the Shipping Act of 1984* (September 1989), 90.

17 United States, Federal Maritime Commission, *Section 18 Report on the Shipping Act of 1984*, 92-3.

18 For a treatment of the role of distance and of shipping in Australian development see Geoffrey Blainey, *The Tyranny of Distance* (South Melbourne: Sun Books 1966), 365.

19 United States, Federal Maritime Commission, *Section 18 Report on the Shipping Act of 1984* (September 1989), 26.

20 United States Committee on the Judiciary, *Report of the Antitrust Subcommittee on the Ocean Freight Industry*, House of Representatives, No. 1,419, 87th Long, 2nd Sess. (1962), 386.

21 Remarks of FMC Chairman, Alan Green Jr., 1984, quoted in Peter A. Friedmann and John A. Devierno, 'The Shipping Act of 1984: The Shift from Government Regulation to Shipper "Regulation",' *Journal of Mari-*

time Law and Commerce 15 (July 1984):315.

22 United States, *Shipping Act of 1984*, 46 USC, Public Law 98- 237, Sec. 10 (6)(9).

23 Elizabeth Canna, 'Cross Atlantic Stabilization Agreement,' *American Shipper* (April 1990):42-4; Elizabeth Canna, 'Has CASA's Umbrella Sprung a Leak,' *American Shipper* (May 1990):8.

24 Jacob Daniel, 'Transpacific Pact Carriers to Hold Down Capacity,' *Journal of Commerce* (8 March 1990):1B.

25 Shippers' associations may be commodity specific, for example, the Pulp and Paper Association of Canada, or they include a spectrum of industries, for example, the Canadian Exporters' Association. The members of shippers' councils are normally industry associations, so that councils represent a broad range of industries.

26 S.G. Sturmey, 'The Code of Conduct for Liner Conferences: A 1985 View,' *Maritime Policy and Management* 13 (1986):189.

27 Delegation of Canada, Final Statement, at the UNCTAD Conference of Plenipotentiaries (April 1974), 2, published in *The Code of Conduct for Liner Conferences* (Montreal: the Canadian Shippers' Council 1974).

28 Delegation of Canada, Final Statement, at the UNCTAD Conference of Plenipotentiaries (April 1974), 1, published in *The Code of Conduct for Liner Conferences.*

29 Delegation of Canada, Final Statement, at the UNCTAD Conference of Plenipotentiaries (April 1974), 2, published in *The Code of Conduct for Liner Conferences.*

30 Sturmey, 'The Code of Conduct for Liner Conferences,' 185.

31 Sturmey, 'The Code of Conduct for Liner Conferences,' 190.

32 Chris Powell, 'Meeting to Review UN Liner Code Ends in Deadlock,' *Journal of Commerce* (21 November 1988).

33 Canada, Restrictive Trade Practices Commission, *Shipping Conference Arrangement and Practices* (Ottawa: Queen's Printer 1965), 100-1.

34 Canada Transport Commission, *International Liner Shipping and Canadian Trade* (Ottawa: CTC Research Branch 1979), 30.

35 Canada Transport Commission, *International Liner Shipping and Canadian Trade*, 6.

36 I.A. Bryan and Y. Kotowitz, *Shipping Conferences in Canada* (Ottawa: Consumer and Corporate Affairs Canada 1978), 106.

37 Bryan and Kotowitz, *Shipping Conferences in Canada*, 103.

38 Bryan and Kotowitz, *Shipping Conferences in Canada*, 104.

39 Trevor D. Heaver, *The Elements and Operation of Australia Shipping Policy*, a Report for Transport Canada, Marine Policy and Planning (1977), 72.

40 Bunker adjustment factors (bafs) and currency adjustment factors (cafs) are adjustments in liner rates to reflect unexpected changes in bunker (fuel) prices and currency exchange rates. The ability of conferences to

vary rates with these cost elements avoids the necessity of building possible changes in costs into rates. However, since the cost information remains confidential to carriers, whether bafs and cafs are really justified by cost changes is controversial.

41 Canada, Minister of Transport, *Freedom to Move* (Ottawa: Supply and Services Canada, T22-69/1985), 58.

42 Canada, Minister of Transport, *Freedom to Move*, 44.

43 Canada, Minister of Transport, *Freedom to Move*, 2.

44 Canada, National Transportation Agency, *Annual Review 1988* (Ottawa: Supply and Services Canada 1989), 76.

45 For an excellent comparison of the Canadian and U.S. legislation see R.D. Anderson and D. Kholsa, 'Canada's New Shipping Conference Legislation: Provision for Competition within the Cartel System,' *Canadian Competition Policy Record* 9 (March 1988):49-67.

46 See, for example: 'Shippers and NVO's Settle Cases for $1,145,000,' *American Shipper* (April 1990), 12; Bill Mongelluzzo, 'Pacific Rebate Probes will Continue 2 Years,' *Journal of Commerce* (14 March 1990): B8. For a description of FMC tariff enforcement see *Section 18 Report*, chap. 27, 543-53.

47 *Section 18 Report*, 622.

48 See, for example, William Diebenedetto, 'Evergreen Wants Ruling on "Me-Too" Service Contracts,' *Journal of Commerce* (14 March 1990), B8. For a description of FMC tariff enforcement see *Section 18 Report*, chap. 27, 543-53. The problems are described briefly in Anderson and Kholsa, 'Canada's New Shipping Conference Legislation,' 54-5.

49 *Annual Review 1988*, 75, and *Annual Review 1989*, 95-6.

50 *Section 18 Report*, 620.

51 *Section 18 Report*, 662.

52 *Annual Review 1988*, 75.

53 *Annual Review 1988*, 94.

54 *Annual Review 1988*, 92-3.

55 *Section 18 Report*, 328-30.

56 *Annual Review 1989*, 89.

57 *Section 18 Report*, 155.

58 Bill Mongelluzzo, 'Shippers Find Pacific Conferences Vary Widely,' *Journal of Commerce* (26 April 1990), 1A.

59 The inefficiency is explained in William J. Baumol, 'Contestable Markets: An Uprising in the Theory of Industry Structure,' *American Economic Review* 72 (1980):12-4. It is related to the position of shipping in Trevor D. Heaver, *Liner Conferences, Issues with Special Reference to Freight Rates*, a Report to the Interdepartmental Committee or the Shipping Conference Exemption Act, (1982), 30-1.

60 J.E. Davies has suggested that the contestability of liner markets may account for the low profitability of liner shipping in spite of the cartels:

'Competition, Contestability and the Liner Shipping Industry,' *Journal of Transport Economics and Policy* 20 (September 1986):311.

61 The percentage of shippers wishing to prohibit conferences has varied among surveys. FMC surveys revealed fewer (35 per cent) in favour of disallowing conferences in 1988 than in 1986 (42 per cent). However, the numbers are still significant. *Section 18 Report*, 124. The opposition of shippers is a new factor in policy development. See Tony Beargie, 'Very Large Shippers Would Gut 1984 Act,' *American Shipper* (May 1989):14-7. In Canada, Anderson and Khosla, *Canada's New Shipping Conferences Legislation*, footnote 79, indicate that 'a majority of [Canada Shippers'] Council's members would support repeal of the SCEA exemption.' The *Annual Review 1989*, 102, notes that 'the Canadian Shippers Council has called for an immediate overhaul or outright revocation of SCEA.'

62 *Section 18 Report*, 144.

63 *Section 18 Report*, 146.

64 Mr. A.B. Ruhly, president of Maersk Inc., recently suggested that a couple of years of rate war is preferable to the 'slow death' with the conference system and current markets. See Bruce Vail, 'Maersk's Ruhly Prescribes Strong Medicine for Liners,' *Journal of Commerce* (2 August 1990):1A, 10A.

65 This may help to explain the vociferous complaints of shippers through associations, even though many aspects of liner services are competitive. In general, monopolistic structures lead to vocal consumer protests. See Janet Porter, 'P & O Containers' Head Slams Shipper Stance,' *Journal of Commerce* (22 August 1990):1A, 4B.

66 The contrast between the common and contract rate principles in the U.S. regime is noted in Anderson and Kholsa, 'Canada's New Shipping Conference Legislation,' 59. Concerns that might be raised over the interests of 'small shippers' in international trade seem misplaced because of the major role of freight forwarders in providing services designed to provide the expertise and consolidation services needed by many importers and exporters.

CHAPTER 10: INTERNATIONAL TELECOMMUNICATIONS REGIME

1 See, for example, H.N. Janisch and R.J. Schultz, *Exploiting the Information Revolution: Telecommunications Issues and Options for Canada* (Toronto: Royal Bank of Canada, October 1989); Christiano Antonelli, 'Multinational Firms, International Trade and International Telecommunications,' *Information Economics and Policy* 1 (1984):333-43; Bruno Lanvin, ed., *Global Trade: The Revolution Beyond the Communications Revolution* (Montpelier 1989).

2 Francois Bar and Michael Borus, 'From Public Access to Private Connec-

tions II,' OECD-BRIE Telecommunications User Group Project, Paris, 19-20 October 1989.

3 See, for example, Robert R. Bruce, Jeffrey P. Cunard, and Mark D. Director, 'Telecommunications Services and a Multilateral Agreement on Trade in Services: Problems, Issues and Prognosis,' IIC Telecommunications Forum, New York, 14-15 December 1989; Peter Cowhey and J. Aronson, 'Trade in Communications and Data Processing' in Robert Stern, ed., *Trade and Investment Services: Canada/U.S. Perspectives* (Toronto: Ontario Economic Council 1985); Geza Feketekuty, 'The New World Information Economy and the New Trade Dimension in Telecommunications Policy,' in Bruno Lanvin, ed., *Global Trade: The Revolution Beyond the Communications Revolution*; Rod de C. Grey, *The Services Agenda* (Halifax: The Institute for Research on Public Policy 1989); J.V. Langdale, 'International Telecommunications and Trade in Services: Policy Perspectives,' *Telecommunications Policy* 15 (September 1989):203-21; OECD, *Trade in Information, Computer and Communication Services* (Paris: OECD, Information, Computer, Communications Policy Division 1990); Gabriel Warren, 'Telecommunications and Computer Services in the Canada-U.S. Free Trade Agreement,' in *A Legal Mosaic for Global Communications* (ITU Symposium 89, Geneva, 4-6 October 1989); Stephen Zolf, 'International Trade in Telecommunications: Liberalization or Beggar Thy Neighbour?' *Review of International Business Law* 2 (November 1988):331-71.

4 For example, the Royal Bank of Canada states that it spends over $100 million p.a. on telecommunications, and this cost is growing at about 30 per cent p.a. *Globe and Mail* (17 October 1989).

5 See J.D. Aronson and P.F. Cowhey, *When Countries Talk: International Trade in Telecommunications Services* (Cambridge, MA: American Enterprise Institute/Ballinger Publishing 1988).

6 For a useful discussion of many of these issues, see H.G. Intven and L.P. Salzman, *Canada-Overseas Telecommunications in a Global Environment* (study prepared for the CRTC, Toronto: McCarthy Tetrault, March 1991) and Monitor Company, 'Competition in the Canada-Overseas Telecommunications Market: An Industry Structure Analysis,' Attachment I to *Evidence of Teleglobe Canada Inc., Overview and Part A: Issues* (CRTC Telecom Public Notice 90-102, March 1991).

7 See also pro-competition developments in New Zealand and Australia.

8 Generally, see Peter S. Grant, *Canadian Communications Law and Policy* (Toronto: Law Society of Upper Canada, Dept. of Education 1988), 617-747; H.N. Janisch and B.S. Romaniuk, 'The Canadian Telecommunications Industry: A Study in Caution' (revised version of a paper presented at the Conference on Pacific Basin Telecommunications, Hosei University, Tokyo, Japan, October 29-31, 1988, mimeo, 1989); and Steven Globerman with Deborah Carter, *Telecommunications in Canada: An Analysis of Out-*

looks and Trends (Vancouver: Fraser Institute 1988).

9 The big users of long distance services are increasingly becoming infra-marginal, that is, they can economically escape the inefficiency-causing restrictions of the regulatory regime.

10 These were introduced in October 1989 but were not enacted as of the end of December 1991. However, by agreement, in September 1991 Manitoba Tel will come under the CRTC's jurisdiction. Following the partial privatization of its parent in September 1990, AG Tel came under CRTC jurisdiction.

11 'Telus shares firm in heavy trading,' *Financial Post* (4 October 1990), 14.

12 On 20 December 1990 the CRTC issued Public Notice 1990-102 to initiate a public proceeding to address issues related to the regulation of Teleglobe Canada after the transitional period (1 January 1988 to 31 December 1991), during which much of the regulation imposed on Teleglobe came from the Cabinet's 'Direction to the CRTC on...Teleglobe' of 2 April 1987 (PC 1987-705).

13 At the federal level, telephone and telegraph rates are regulated under provisions of the Railway Act which date back to 1903. Rates must be 'just and reasonable' and 'not unjustly discriminatory or unduly preferential,' but the act provides no further guidance as to the goals to be served.

14 These increase with the size of the 'free' local calling area from about $8 to $16/month in 1990.

15 This is often imprecisely referred to as the cross-subsidization of local by long distance services. For example, in 1989 the 'access' costs of Bell Canada ($2,694 million) were recovered as follows: $745 million from local service and $1,892 million from toll calls (Bell Canada's Evidence in the Interexchange Proceeding, 20 November 1990).

16 The three Prairie telcos are heavily dependent upon such settlements revenue – hence they oppose competitive entry and rebalancing of long distance rates. For example, in 1988 some 69.6 per cent (and 66. 4 per cent in 1989) of AG Tel's total revenue came from toll calls – versus 54.4 per cent for all telcos. One-third of its total revenue came from interprovincial toll calls and settlements (from the company's Submission in the Interexchange Proceeding).

17 See, for example, Hon. Marcel Masse, 'Notes for a Speech Concerning Canada's New Policy on Telecommunications' (Ottawa: Department of Communications, October 1989).

18 CNCP Telecommunications' (now Unitel Communications Inc.) application to enter this market was rejected in August 1985. In May 1990, Unitel made another application. See Unitel Communications Inc., *Application to Provide Public Long Distance Service* (Toronto: Unitel, May 1990a) and Unitel Communications Inc., *Evidence: Application to Provide Public Long Distance Service*, 4 vols. (Toronto: Unitel 1990).

19 See H.N. Janisch and B.S. Romaniuk, 'The Quest for Regulatory Forbear-

ance in Telecommunications,' *Ottawa Law Review* 17 (1985):455-89.

20 See Adree Wylie, 'Competition in the Telecommunications Industry and Regulatory Forbearance Under the Railway Act,' *Canadian Competition Policy Record* 9 (December 1988):16-20.

21 The largest fraction was intra-company (57.9 percent) followed by inter-company (22.5 percent). Public long distance revenues in 1986 amounted to 50 per cent of Canadian telcos' total operating revenues – see Federal-Provincial-Territorial Task Force on Telecommunications, *Competition in Public Long Distance Telephone Service in Canada* (Ottawa: Minister of Supply and Services Canada, 1988), 12.

22 Peter A. Stern, 'The Atwater Project on the Impact of Telecommunications and Data Services on Commercial Activity and Economic Development: The International Telecommunications System' (Montreal: Teleglobe Canada, March 1990b), mimeo, n. 17.

23 The changes in the regulation of Teleglobe are described in CRTC Telecom Public Notice 1990-102, 'Teleglobe Canada Inc.: Regulation After the Transition Period,' 1-5.

24 Teleglobe's legal monopoly ends in April 1993, but it is currently under review – see CRTC Public Notice 1990-102 (20 December 1990).

25 In its 1986 *Annual Report*, Teleglobe noted that 'Although international telegraph service reached its peak some years ago and is declining in popularity, the corporation must continue to provide Canadians with telegraph service to over 250 countries and territories.' The facts in the next three paragraphs were obtained from Monitor Company, 'Competition in the Canada-Overseas Telecommunications Market ...'

26 In May 1991 Gordon Capital made an unsuccessful effort to oust the top management of Memotec, Teleglobe's parent (see 'How Gordon Capital was Humiliated,' *Financial Times of Canada* (20 May 1991, 16-18). There were rumours that BCE Inc. was secretly aligned with Gordon. On a fully diluted basis, BCE then held 31 per cent of Memotec.

27 Generally, see Richard J. Schultz, 'Teleglobe Canada,' in Allan Tupper and G. Bruce Doern, eds., *Privatization, Public Policy and Public Corporations in Canada* (Halifax: The Institute for Research on Public Policy 1988); B. Thomas, 'Teleglobe Canada: Outside the (CRTC) Regulatory Camp,' *Canadian Public Administration* 24 (1986); and H.N. Janisch and R.J. Schultz, 'Teleglobe Canada: Cash Cow or White Elephant?' in T.E. Kierans and W.T. Stanbury, eds., *Papers on Privatization* (Montreal: Institute for Research on Public Policy 1985), 185-242.

28 See *Financial Post* (17 November 1989), 15.

29 See *Financial Post* (14 November 1990), 25.

30 The object is to be able to provide voice and data communications for passengers on commercial aircraft. Present communications with aircraft use either high or very high frequencies, which are limited by short

line-of-sight paths and unpredictable atmospheric conditions. Hence, most aircraft cannot use voice communications and radar when flying over most of the major waters, notably the Pacific Ocean. The consortium wants to use the three Inmarsat satellites 35,700 km above the Atlantic, Pacific, and Indian oceans. It will cost about U.S. $500,000 to equip an airliner with the necessary electronics. See Lawrence Surtees, 'Group view to let planes phone home,' *Globe and Mail* (4 September 1989), B1, B4.

31 Monitor Company, 'Competition in the Canada-Overseas Telecommunications Market . . .' (March 1991), 22.

32 See Intven and Salzman, 'Canada-Overseas Telecommunications in a Global Environment,' xiii.

33 From west to east these are BC Tel, Alberta Government Telephones, Saskatchewan Tel, Manitoba Tel, Bell Canada (Quebec and Ontario), New Brunswick Tel, Maritime Tel & Tel (Nova Scotia), Island Tel (PEI), and Newfoundland Tel. The three Prairie telcos are owned by their provincial governments and were acquired from Bell shortly after the turn of the century. (Only 44 per cent of Telus Corp, which owns AG Tel, is owned by the province of Alberta.) Bell Canada accounts for over 60 per cent of all telephone lines in Canada.

34 Telesat Canada (a mixed enterprise formed in 1969) provides satellite-based, private line services directly to business customers (see *Financial Post* [6 March 1989], 47). Generally, see G. Bruce Doern and J.A.R. Brothers, 'Telesat Canada,' in Allan Tupper and G. Bruce Doern, eds., *Public Corporations and Public Policy in Canada* (Montreal: The Institute for Research on Public Policy 1981), 221-49. It provides Message Toll Service essentially as a subcontractor to the terrestrial carriers within Telecom Canada. In 1977 the federal Cabinet overruled the CRTC and permitted Telesat to join Telecom Canada and Telecom members gained effective control of Telesat although in 1990 they own only 41 per cent of the shares. Thus, the terrestrial carriers got control over a potential long distance competitor using satellites. On 21 February 1990, the federal government announced it was selling its 50 per cent interest in Telesat. The *Financial Post* (22 February 1990), 9 estimated this was worth $210 million. In 1989 Telesat earned $21.7 million on $146.5 million in sales (*Globe and Mail* [2 May 1990], B4). It has 850 employees and operates five satellites and 400 earth stations.

35 H.N. Janisch, 'Canadian Telecommunications in a Free Trade Era,' in *Columbia Journal of World Business* 24 (Spring 1989):5-16.

36 In 1985, Unitel (then called CNCP Telecommunications) was not permitted to enter the public and switched its long-distance telephone market pursuant to CRTC Telecom Decision 85-19. See W.T. Stanbury, 'Decision Making in Telecommunications: The Interplay of Distributional and Efficiency Considerations,' in W.T. Stanbury, ed., *Telecommunications Policy*

and Regulation (Montreal: The Institute for Research on Public Policy 1986), 481-516.

37 See Canada, Department of Communications, 'A Policy Framework for Telecommunications in Canada' (Ottawa: DOC, July 1987) mimeo; Canada, Department of Communications (1988) 'Proposed Guidelines for Type I Telecommunications Carriers' (Ottawa: Communications Canada, January 1988a) mimeo; Canada, Department of Communications, *Canadian Telecommunications: An Overview of the Canadian Telecommunications Carriage Industry* (Ottawa: Dept. of Communications, Telecommunications Policy Branch, March 1988). It should be noted that none of these policies has yet been enacted into legislation.

38 GTE is also the controlling shareholder of Quebec Telephone, which operates in part of northern Quebec and is regulated by the province.

39 See Unitel, *Application to Provide Public Long Distance Service*, May 1990 and Unitel, *Evidence*, August 1990.

40 In general, see W.T. Stanbury, 'The Case for Competition in Public Long Distance Telephone Service,' in Jan Fedorowicz, ed., *From Monopoly to Competition: Telecommunications in Transition* (Mississauga, Ont.: Informatics Publishing 1991), 149-98.

41 See Stanbury, 'Decision Making in Telecommunications.'

42 During the period 1984-90, the telcos engaged in what has been called 'passive rate rebalancing.' They sought substantial reductions in long distance rates (about 40 per cent over the period) while requesting only modest increases in local rates (less than the rate of inflation). In November 1990, both Bell Canada and BC Tel, in their *Evidence* re CRTC Telecom Public Notice 1990-83 (i.e., Unitel's application for interexchange competition) proposed that this process continue with a view to having large users of long distance service pay the same rates as exist in the U.S.

43 Bell Canada estimates that the average contribution in 1989 was 19 cents per minute of long-distance traffic (*Evidence*, November 1990). BC Tel estimated the contribution to be 22 cents per minute in 1990. Such contribution amounts to 60 per cent of the price of a long-distance minute (*Evidence*, November 1990).

44 Monitor Company ('Competition in the Canada-Overseas Telecommunications Market . . .' March 1991, fig. 19) indicates that the investment cost for undersea fibre optic cable (per 64K bits half circuit) will fall from almost $24,000 in 1988 (TAT8) to about $5,000 in 1995 (TAT12).

45 For a discussion of recent developments in this area and prospects for the future see 'Airwave Wars,' *Business Week* (23 July 1990), 48-53.

46 See CRTC Telecom Decision 85-19 rejecting CNCP (now Unitel's) application to compete with respect to public voice service.

47 For a survey of the literature on this issue, see Steven Globerman, *The Impacts of Trade Liberalization on Imperfectly Competitive Industries: A Review*

of Theory and Evidence (Ottawa: Economic Council of Canada, Discussion Paper 341, January 1988).

48 See, for example, James R. Melvin, *Trade in Services: A Theoretical Analysis* (Halifax: The Institute for Research on Public Policy 1989) and Robert R. Bruce, 'International Trade in Telecommunications Services: Some Observations about the Current Debate,' paper presented at the McGill University-University of Vermont Conference, Montreal, 15-17 October 1989.

49 To be sure, mobile telecommunications permit some limited degree of geographical mobility to both the sender and receiver. Further, if the communication is a record service (e.g., telex, fax, electronic mail), its transmission can be 'time shifted' and the message can be stored.

50 Because of echo effects, double satellite hops are avoided: Peter A. Stern, 'WATTC-88 and the 1989 ITU Plenipotentiary Conference: How the Multilateral Institutions are Adapting to the Changing Telecommunication Environment,' paper presented at the McGill University-University of Vermont Conference, Montreal, 15-17 October 1989a, 7.

51 See Globerman with Carter, *Telecommunications in Canada*.

52 See Steven Globerman, 'Deregulation of Telecommunications: An Assessment,' in Walter Block and George Lermer, eds., *Breaking the Shackles: Deregulation in Canada* (Vancouver: The Fraser Institute 1991). On the other hand, it appears that Telecom Canada members have been slower to introduce new services than U.S. telephone companies. In his study of the U.S. telephone industry, Tae H. Oum, 'The Effect of Competition in the Public Long-distance Telephone Market on the Productivity of the U.S. Telephone Industry' (study prepared for Unitel Telecommunications Inc., August 1990) finds a robust positive association between competition in the public long-distance market and productivity.

53 Leonard Waverman, 'U.S. Interexchange Competition,' in R.W. Crandall and K. Flamm, eds., *Changing the Rules: Technological Change, International Competition and Regulation in Communications* (Washington, DC: Brookings 1989), 62-113.

54 See, for example, C. Denis Hall, 'A Study of Decreasing Unit Costs in the Public Long Distance Telecommunications Market,' Evidence of Bell Canada, 3, part 6, 30 November 1990.

55 Michael Porter suggests that in the U.S. the cost curve of the new long distance carriers' fibre optic networks lies below that of AT&T. See his *Competition in the Long Distance Telecommunications Market: An Industry Structure Analysis* (Cambridge, MA: Monitor June 1987).

56 Note, however, that when natural monopoly conditions prevail, the cost penalty associated with multiple suppliers may not be great. It depends on the 'steepness' of the cost curve. Moreover, network costs are only part of total costs which include marketing, billing, and other costs. See Porter, *Competition in the Long Distance Telecommunications Market*.

57 This figure includes Canada-Mexico traffic, which is a small component of the overall North American telecommunications market.

58 Intelsat is a co-operative of 119 countries (January 1990) that operates a system of geostationary satellites which allow communications among all areas of the world. Each member of the organization has an investment share generally in proportion to its use of the system, pays for utilization of the Intelsat space segment, and receives compensation for its investment share. Satellite earth stations are generally built, owned and operated by each member country's designated international operator and signatory to the Intelsat agreement. Capacity requirements are established at annual global traffic meetings where the number of satellite circuits is established through bilateral agreements. See Intven and Salzman, *Canada-Overseas Telecommunications in a Gobal Environment*, 12-22. Intelsat in 1986 carried two-thirds of the world's overseas telecommunications traffic (Teleglobe Canada *Annual Report 1986*).

59 We use the term regime loosely, simply to refer to the set of private and public arrangements which govern the flows of telecommunications services between Canada and the u.s. An important aspect of the bilateral and, increasingly, the multilateral regime, which we will not discuss, is the significance of international and national telecommunications policy developments, such as privatization and liberalization, for policies governing foreign ownership – an issue which has particular relevance to Canada. For an early treatment of the issues involved see H.N. Janisch, 'Emerging Issues in Foreign Investment in Telecommunications,' International Business and Trade Law Programme, Working Paper Series, 1988-9(1), 1989.

60 The *Financial Post* (28 May 1991), 4, reports that u.s. Sprint might announce discount transborder service to the u.s. if its application to rent switches at a discount from Unitel is approved. Hence, major customers could use Sprint for all their u.s.-bound traffic. The effect could be 'devastating' for small resellers and Bell Canada. Sprint would lease private lines from Unitel as well. The planned date for service is 3 June 1991.

61 For a discussion of international price comparisons and their implications for incentives to bypass the Canadian telecommunications system, see D.A. Ford and Associates Ltd., *The Impact of International Competition on the Canadian Telecommunications Industry and Its Users* (Ottawa: August 1986) and Intven and Salzman, *Canada-Overseas Telecommunications in a Global Environment*, chap. 3.

62 Indeed, such a restructuring of rates has been taking place over the past few years.

63 See *Financial Post* (28 February 1990), 1. See also *Financial Post* (1 March 1990), 3.

64 AT&T, 'Petition for Expedited Declaratory Ruling,' Federal Communica-

tions Commission cc Docket 86- 494, 5 February 1990.

65 On 28 August 1990, AT&T began marketing 'Megacom' rates in Canada for Canada-UK calling; it is 9 per cent to 30 per cent less expensive than is Teleglobe's service and 3.6 per cent to 19.7 per cent less expensive for Canada-Japan, depending on the volume and whether the calls originated in Toronto or Vancouver. However, the prime attraction of Megacom is on Canada-US. traffic. Once a user subscribes to that service the overseas discounts become available. On 9 July 1990 AT&T filed an amendment to its Megacom tariff to match its competitors by expressly authorizing carriage of Canada-originating traffic and to allow transborder private lines to connect to AT&T's switches in the US. AT&T estimates that 5 per cent to 7 per cent of Canada-US. traffic carried on private lines ultimately terminates overseas. AT&T is seeking to have 25 per cent of its corporate revenues from overseas services and equipment sales in 1995 versus 15 per cent in 1990.

66 See *Financial Post* (10-12 March 1990), 1, 12. More recently, see *Financial Post* (14 November 1990), 25.

67 Globerman with Carter, *Telecommunications in Canada*.

68 These forces are discussed in more detail in Intven and Saltzman, *Canada-Overseas Telecommunications* and in Monitor Co., 'Competition in the Canada-US. . . .'

69 See *Financial Post* (10 April 1990), 3.

70 'AT&T brings global service to Canada,' *Globe and Mail* (11 September 1990), B6.

71 Monitor Company, 'Competition in Canada-Overseas Telecommunications Market,' 16. Monitor estimates that the number of resellers in Canada providing voice services rose from three in 1986 to fourteen in 1989 and to twenty-three in 1991. Their revenues were estimated to be $40 million in 1989 and $170 million in 1991.

72 Mike Urlocker, 'Rate cut sought for overseas calls,' *Financial Post* (29 May 1991), 4.

73 Intven and Salzman, *Canada-Overseas Telecommunications*, x.

74 'Teleglobe in battle over overseas calls,' *Financial Post* (19 November 1990).

75 See, for example, a half page advertisement by the Telecommunications Workers' Union, 'When It Comes to Canada's Phone System . . . There's Nothing Free About Free Trade,' *Globe and Mail* (5 February 1988), 9. In any event, there has not been any genuine deregulation in the US., since all that has happened is that judicial scrutiny on an ongoing basis of divestiture has been added to FCC regulation. See H.N. Janisch, 'Canadian Telecommunications in a Free Trade Era.'

76 Generally, see L.A.W. Hunter and J.F. Blakney, 'Free Trade and Telecommunications: New Developments in the Provision and Regulation of International Services,' paper prepared for Canadian Communications

Law and Policy, Law Society of Upper Canada, 25, 26 March 1988, mimeo; H.N. Janisch, 'Canada/u.s. Telecommunications Interface: Opportunities and Problems Under the FTA,' unpublished paper, University of Toronto, Faculty of Law, mimeo, 1989c; Gabriel Warren, 'Telecommunications and Computer Services'; Steven Globerman and Peter Booth, 'The Canada-u.s. Free Trade Agreement and the Telecommunications Industry,' *Telecommunications Policy* 5 (December 1989):319-28; H.N. Janisch, 'Telecommunications and the Canada-u.s. Free Trade Agreement,' *Telecommunications Policy* 13 (June 1987); Richard J. Schultz, 'New Domestic and International Bedfellows in Telecommunications,' *Media and Communications Law Review* 1 (1991):215-35.

77 Because of space limitations we cannot discuss the provisions of the Free Trade Agreement governing equipment, including tariff changes and, especially, American allegations about Northern Telecom's preferred access to Canadian telecommunications companies.

78 Annex 1408 to Chapter 14 of the Canada- u.s. Free Trade Agreement.

79 Annex 1404C, 'Computer Services and Telecommunications – Network-Based Enhanced Services.'

80 See Federal-Provincial-Territorial Task Force on Telecommunications, *Competition in Public Long Distance.*

81 See J.P. Mongeau, chairman, *Federal-Provincial Examination of Telecommunications Pricing and the Universal Availability of Affordable Telephone Service* (Ottawa: Minister of Supply and Services, October 1986).

82 Hon. Marcel Masse, 'Looking at Telecommunications: The Need for Review' (Ottawa: Department of Communications, 20 June 1985) mimeo.

83 See Janisch and Romaniuk, 'The Canadian Telecommunications Industry.'

84 For a summary of these developments, see Canada, Department of Communications, *Canadian Telecommunications.* The Canadian enhanced service market has received a significant boost with the establishment by Charles Sirois, former chairman of BCE Mobile Communications and builder of the largest radio paging company, National Pagette. See *Globe and Mail* (31 May 1991), B1.

85 For a full discussion of this concern, see Association of Competitive Telecommunications Suppliers, 'Comments on Proposed Guidelines for Type I Telecommunications Carriers,' *Canadian Gazette* (Part I, Notice DGTP-001-99, 29 April 1988).

86 Canada, Department of Communications, 'A Policy Framework'; Canada, Department of Communications, 'Proposed Guidelines.'

87 Richard J. Schultz, 'A Clash of Regimes: A Canadian Perspective on the GATT Uruguay Round,' in Richard Schultz and Peter Stern, eds., *Emerging International Telecommunications Regimes: Their North American Impact* (Montreal: Centre for the Study of Regulated Industries, in press).

88 Canada, Department of Communications, 'A Policy Framework.'

89 See Janisch, 'Emerging Issues.'

90 Annex 1408 to Chapter 14, Article 6(1)(c).

91 Canada, Department of Communications, *Canadian Telecommunications*.

92 In the case of the U.S., this has been done by Richard J. Schultz, *United States Telecommunications Pricing Changes and Social Welfare: Causes, Consequences and Policy Alternatives* (Ottawa: Department of Consumer and Corporate Affairs 1989). For Japan, see Makoto Kojo and H.N. Janisch, 'Japanese Telecommunications After the 1985 Regulatory Reforms,' *Media and Communications Law Review* 1 (1991):307-40.

93 See Federal-Provincial-Territorial Task Force, *Competition in Public Long Distance*.

94 William J. Drake, 'Asymmetric Reregulation and the Transformation of the International Telecommunications Regime,' in Eli N. Noam and Gerard Pogerel, eds., *Asymmetric Deregulation: The Dynamics of Telecommunications Policies in Europe and the United States* (Norwood: Ablex 1990).

95 See Stephen D. Krasner, ed., *International Regimes* (Ithaca: Cornell University Press 1983) and, particularly, the articles by Stephen D. Krasner, 'Structural Causes and Regime Consequences: Regimes as Intervening Variables'; Oran R. Young, 'Regime Dynamics: The Rise and Fall of International Regimes'; and Jock A. Finlayson and Mark Zacher, 'The GATT and the Regulation of Trade Barriers: Regime Dynamics and Functions.'

96 See J.D. Aronson and Peter F. Cowhey, *When Countries Talk: International Trade in Telecommunications Services* (Cambridge, MA: Ballinger Publishing 1988), 45-51.

97 See George A. Codding, *The International Telecommunication Union: An Experiment in International Cooperation* (Leiden: E.J. Bull 1952) and George A. Codding Jr. and Anthony M. Rutkowski, *The International Telecommunication Union in a Changing World* (Dedham, MA: Artech House 1982).

98 Young, 'Regime Dynamics,' 99.

99 Stern, 'WATTC-88 and the 1989 ITU Plenipotentiary Conference,' 10.

100 Krasner, 'Structural Causes and Regime Consequences,' 7.

101 This might be referred to as Orwell's principle.

102 Codding, *The International Telecommunication Union*.

103 Peter A. Stern, 'How the Multilateral Institutions are Adapting to the Changing Telecommunications Environment,' in Richard Schultz and Peter Stern, eds., *Emerging International Telecommunications Regimes: Their North American Impact*.

104 Aronson and Cowhey, 'When Countries Talk'; Drake, 'Asymmetric Reregulation.'

105 Stern, 'WATTC-88 and the 1989 Plenipotentiary Conference,' 17.

106 Ibid., 10.

107 See Eli M. Noam, 'International Telecommunications in Transition' in

Robert W. Crandall and Kenneth Flamm, eds., *Changing the Rules: Technological Change, International Competition and Regulation in Communications*
(Washington: The Brookings Institution 1989).

108 See Noam, 'International Telecommunications in Transition.'
109 Intven and Salzman, *Canada-Overseas Telecommunications*, 85.
110 Stern, 'WATTC- 88 and the 1989 Plenipotentiary Conference,' 30-6.
111 Ibid., 54.
112 Peter A. Stern, 'International Telecommunication Regulation: Issues and
     Tensions,' Centre for the Study of Regulated Industries, McGill University
     Working Paper 89-45, 1989b, 27-8.
113 See Aronson and Cowhey, *When Countries Talk*, chap. 6.
114 Stanbury, 'Decision Making in Telecommunications.'
115 Canada, Department of Communications, 'A Policy Framework.'
116 Generally, see Schultz, 'A Clash of Regimes.'
117 Noam ('International Telecommunications in Transition,' 257) states that
     'a common development is changing all the institutions of international
     telecommunications today: the rent-seeking coalition that provided links
     of shared economic interests across frontiers should be understood as
     nothing more than a normalization – one of the most tightly controlled
     sectors is becoming more like the rest of the economy, not necessarily
     deregulated but more "normal".'
118 Aronson and Cowhey, *When Countries Talk*.
119 Feketekuty, 'The New World Information Economy.'
120 The traditional definitions of these principles is discussed in Finlayson
     and Zacher, 'The GATT and the Regulation of Trade Barriers.' Their content
     or, alternatively, the various contending definitions in the telecommuni-
     cations services context, is explored in a number of sources, such as
     Aronson and Cowhey, *When Countries Talk*; G. Russell Pipe and R. Brian
     Woodrow, *Introducing Trade Rules to Telecommunications Services* (Spring-
     field, VA: Transnational Data Reporting Service 1989); and, particularly,
     Robert R. Bruce, Jeffrey P. Cunard, and Mark D. Director, 'Telecommuni-
     cations Services and a Multilateral Agreement on Trade in Services:
     Problems, Issues and Prognosis,' IIC Telecommunications Forum, New
     York, 14-15 December 1989.
121 Andre Lapointe, Speech to the Law Society of Upper Canada Conference
     'Canadian Communications Law and Policy in the 1990s,' Toronto, April
     1990, mimeo.
122 Lapointe, 'Speech to the Law Society . . . ,' 18.
123 Ibid., 19.
124 Drake, 'Asymmetric Reregulation.'
125 Ibid., 67.
126 Lapointe, 'Speech to the Law Society . . . ,' 6.
127 Feketekuty, 'The New World Information Economy,' 1.

128 Monitor Company, 'Competition in the Canada- Overseas...,' 3.

129 Intven and Salzman, *Canada-Overseas Telecommunications...*, xvi.

130 Noam, 'International Telecommunications in Transition,' 296.

CHAPTER 11: FISHERIES MANAGEMENT POLICY

Funding for this paper was provided by the Donner Canadian Foundation through a grant to the Institute of International Relations research project on 'Canada and the International Regulatory Management Regimes' at the University of British Columbia.

1 Gordon R. Munro, 'Canada and Fisheries Management with Extended Jurisdiction: A Preliminary View,' in Lee. G. Anderson, ed., *Economic Impact of Extended Jurisdiction* (Ann Arbor: Ann Arbor Science 1977), 29-50.

2 Gordon R. Munro, *A Promise of Abundance: Extended Fisheries Jurisdiction and the Newfoundland Economy* (Ottawa: Economic Council of Canada 1980), 15-28.

3 Barbara Johnson, 'Canadian Foreign Policy and Fisheries,' in Barbara Johnson and Mark W Zacher, eds., *Canadian Foreign Policy and the Law of the Sea* (Vancouver: University of British Columbia Press 1977), 52-99.

4 Johnson, 'Canadian Foreign Policy and Fisheries,' 76.

5 Donald McRae and Gordon Munro, 'Coastal State "Rights" Within the 200-Mile Exclusive Economic Zone,' in Philip A. Neher, Ragnar Arnason, and Nina Mollett, eds., *Rights Based Fishing* (Dordrecht: Kluwer Academic Publishers 1989), 97-112.

6 United Nations, Third Conference on the Law of the Sea, *Convention*, Article 56.

7 McRae and Munro, 'Coastal State "Rights",' 110-11.

8 Article 300 of the convention, the Good Faith and Abuse of Rights Article, is supposedly designed to prevent coastal states from doing this sort of thing. What it really does is to call upon a coastal state determined to exclude distant fleets from its zone to use its imagination.

9 The Law of the Sea Convention did not appear in its final form in 1982. There was in 1977, however, a draft convention. The differences between Part 5 of the 1977 draft convention and Part 5 of the convention in its final form are negligible.

10 Applebaum, 'The Straddling Stock Problem: The Northwest Atlantic Situation, International Law, and Options for Coastal State Action,' paper prepared for the 23rd Annual Conference on the Law of the Sea Institute 1989, 5.

11 Canada, The Task Force on Atlantic Fisheries, *Report* (Ottawa: Canadian Government Publishing Centre 1982), 31-5; Gordon Munro and Susan McCorquodale, *The Northern Cod Fishery of Newfoundland* (Ottawa: Eco-

nomic Council of Canada 1981),10.

12 Brian Briffet, 'Fishery Overview: Newfoundland Region 1989,' paper prepared for the Task Force on Northern Cod 1989, 18; Leslie Harris, 'Independent Review of the State of the Northern Cod Stock: Final Report,' paper prepared for the Honourable Thomas Siddon, Minister of Fisheries and Oceans 1990, 73-4.

13 Gordon R. Munro, 'The Management of Transboundary Fishery Resources: A Theoretical Overview,' paper prepared for the Conference on the Economics of Migratory Fish Stocks, Ullensvang, Norway 1990, 10.

14 Munro, 'The Management of Transboundary Fishery Resources,' 10.

15 Ibid., 17-18.

16 David L. VanderZwaag, *The Fish Feud* (Lexington: D.C. Heath and Co. 1983), 89-94.

17 Ibid., 90.

18 Gordon R. Munro, 'The Management of Shared Resources Under Extended Jurisdiction,' *Marine Resource Economics* 2 (1987):270-85. There does, of course, remain the problem of policing. One group may attempt to poach in the other's zone.

19 The treaty came into effect in 1937. Twenty years later, Fraser River pink salmon were brought in under the treaty as well.

20 Gordon Munro and Robert Stokes, 'The Canada-United States Pacific Salmon Treaty,' in Donald McRae and Gordon Munro, eds., *Canadian Oceans Policy: National Strategies and the New Law of the Sea* (Vancouver: University of British Columbia Press 1989), 21.

21 Munro and Stokes, 'The Canada-United States Pacific Salmon Treaty,' 23.

22 Ibid., 23.

23 Ibid., 26.

24 Ibid., 26-8.

25 For a detailed discussion, see Munro and Stokes, 'The Canada-United States Pacific Salmon Treaty,' 28-32.

26 Marilyn Twitchell, 'The Struggle to Move from "Fish Wars" to Cooperative Fishery Management,' *Anadromous Fish Law Memo* 47 (December 1988):2-13.

27 Cited in J.W.C. Tomlinson and I. Vertinsky, 'International Joint Ventures in Fishing and 200 Mile Economic Zones,' *Journal of the Fisheries Research Board of Canada* 32 (1975):2,568-72.

28 See Gordon R. Munro, 'Coastal States and Distant Water Fleets and EFJ: Some Long-Run Considerations,' *Marine Policy* 9 (January 1985):2- 15; Lewis E. Querirola and Richard S. Johnstone, 'Distant Water Fishing Nations and Extended Fisheries Jurisdiction,' *Marine Policy* 13 (January 1989):16-21.

29 Munro, 'Coastal States and Distant Water Fleets and EFJ,' 4-8.

30 Ibid., 6-7.

31 The application of international trade type of analysis to the issue of coastal state-distant water fishing nation relations is useful in determining whether there is any point in considering distant water nation participation in the EEZ fisheries and in estimating the maximum gains to the coastal state from such arrangements. There is no assurance that these gains will in fact be fully realized. This will depend on the design of the terms and conditions of access.

One difficulty which will make it unlikely that the maximum gains will ever be fully achieved is the fact that it will never be possible to monitor the foreign partners perfectly. One attempt to analyze the economic problem of designing optimal terms and conditions of access which focuses directly on the issue of imperfect monitoring is to be found in F.H. Clarke and G.R. Munro, 'Coastal States, Distant Water Fishing Nations and Extended Jurisdiction: A Principal-Agent Analysis,' *Natural Resource Modeling* 2 (Summer 1987):81-107.

32 Gordon Munro, 'Canada, International Trade, and the Economics of Co-operative Fisheries Arrangements,' in *Canada and International Trade* 2 (Ottawa: Institute for Research on Public Policy 1985), 811-52.

33 Munro, 'Coastal States, Distant Water Fleets and EFJ,' 9-10.

34 Munro, 'Canada, International Trade, and the Economics of Co-operative Fisheries Arrangements,' 837-43.

35 Parzival Copes, 'Canadian Fisheries Management Policy: International Dimensions,' in Donald McRae and Gordon Munro, eds., *Canadian Oceans Policy: National Strategies and the New Law of the Sea* (Vancouver: University of British Columbia Press 1989), 3-16.

36 Canada, Department of Fisheries and Oceans, 'News Release,' 13 April 1987.

37 Munro, 'Canada, International Trade, and the Economics of Co-operative Fisheries Arrangements,' 843.

38 Canada, Department of Fisheries and Oceans, 'News Release,' 10 April 1987. It has been suggested to the author that the interpretation is excessively harsh. If presented with an 'emergency' situation, the author has been informed, the Department of Fisheries and Oceans would likely relent and permit foreign vessels to harvest and deliver fish to inshore processing plants, particularly if the plant falls into the 'resource-short' category. The permission would, however, be for strictly temporary use of foreign vessels. M. Moffat, Department of Fisheries and Oceans, personal communication.

39 One might also add that offshore trawling is a highly capital intensive operation, which creates very limited employment opportunities. It was recognized when EFJ was introduced in Canada that the employment opportunities promised by EFJ lay primarily in the processing sector. Munro, *A Promise of Abundance*, 55-8.

40　Copes, 'Canadian Fisheries Management Policy,' 7.

41　Queirola and Johnstone, 'Distant Water Fishing Nations and Extended Fisheries Jurisdiction,' 10.

42　A.J. Duncan, 'Economics of the Deepwater Fishery,' in *New Zealand Finfisheries: The Resources and Their Management* (Aukland: Trade Publications 1983), 94-9.

43　Ian N. Clark, Philip J. Major, and Nina Mollett, 'The Development and Implementation of New Zealand's ITQ Management System,' in Philip A. Neher, Ragnar Arnason, and Nina Mollett, *Rights Based Fishing* (Dordrecht: Kluwer Academic Publishers 1989), 117-45. If one were to attempt to adapt the scheme to Canada, it would, of course, be necessary to take into account the differences between Canada and New Zealand. For example, in light of what we said about legitimate aspects of the employment argument for protection, one might want to insist on most of the harvested fish being processed on shore.

44　There was one distant water fishing nation that was, and is, a special case – France. Canada has had treaty relationships with France pertaining to fisheries dating back to early colonial times in the eighteenth century.

45　Applebaum, 'The Straddling Stock Problem,' 5.

46　Ibid., 11.

47　Ibid., 11.

48　Canada, Task Force on Atlantic Fisheries, *Report*, 241; Harris, 'Independent Review of the State of the Northern Cod Stock: Final Report,' 9-10.

49　North Atlantic Fisheries Organization, 'General Council Document 89/2,' (1989), 3.

50　Edward L. Miles, *The U.S/Japan Fisheries Relationship in the Northeast Pacific: From Conflict to Cooperation?* (Seattle: Fisheries Management Foundation 1989), 10-3.

51　Ibid., 23.

52　McRae and Munro, 'Coastal State "Rights" Within the 200 Mile Exclusive Economic Zone,' 105-7.

53　Edward L. Miles and William T. Burke, 'Pressures on the United Nations Convention on the Law of the Sea of 1982 Arising from New Fisheries Conflicts: The Problem of Straddling Stocks,' *Ocean Development and International Law* 20 (1989):343-57.

CHAPTER 12: AIR, WATER, AND POLITICAL FIRE

1　Ross Howard, 'Industrial Pollutants Time Bomb, LeBlanc Warns,' *Toronto Star* (21 June 1977), B2.

2　For an introduction to the conceptual issues of international regimes in the resource and environmental area, see Oran R. Young, *International Cooperation: Building Regimes for Natural Resources and the Environment* (Ithaca: Cornell University Press 1989).

3 A short history of the Boundary Waters Treaty is provided by N.F. Dreisziger, 'Dreams and Disappointments,' in Robert Spencer, John Kirton, and Kim Richard Nossal, eds., *The International Joint Commission, Seventy Years On* (Centre for International Studies, University of Toronto 1981), 8-23.

4 Maxwell Cohen in *The Regime of Boundary Waters: The Canadian-United States Experience* (Leyden: A.W. Sijthoff 1977) discusses what he sees as a reasonably well-developed regime in international law for the boundary waters covering both water quantity and water quality issues. The focus of the present article does not include the former area.

5 The treaty also established the International Joint Commission (IJC), comprising six commissioners, three appointed by the United States and three by Canada, with significant quasi-judicial authority over 'levels and flows' issues in the boundary waters and a general investigatory function. The IJC quickly became the key inter-governmental body in development of the Canada-U.S. environmental regime. On the commission, see Robert Spencer, John Kirton, and Kim Richard Nossal, eds., *The International Joint Commission* and, especially, the chapter by William Willoughby, 'Expectations and Experience,' 24-32.

6 Decision reported on 11 March 1941 to the government of the United States of America and to the government of the Dominion of Canada by the Trail Smelter Arbitral Tribunal. The Trail case had involved, on the part of the IJC, an earlier report on findings (28 February 1931) and then an initial tribunal decision (16 April 1938). The Trail Smelter principle, it might be noted, qualified the broad principle of Article 4 to the extent that the injury had to be 'of serious consequence' and had to be 'established by clear and convincing evidence.'

7 Maxwell Cohen, *The Regime of Boundary Waters*, 279. Despite the governments' acceptance of this principle, the Trail Smelter case was not without deep political and scientific controversy. The damage claimed by local American farmers was backed up by U.S. studies but disputed by evidence compiled by a Canadian team of scientists. The eventual compensation paid by Canada was a negotiated, 'split-the-difference' figure agreed to by Ottawa only after Washington made clear that this issue was endangering trade relations. See D.H. Dinwoodie, 'The Politics of International Pollution Control: The Trail Smelter Case,' *International Journal* 27 (Spring 1972):219-35.

8 For the background to the negotiation of the 1972 and 1978 agreements see Don Munton, 'Great Lakes Water Quality: A Study in Environmental Politics and Diplomacy,' in O.P. Dwivedi, ed., *Resources and the Environ-*

ment: Policy Perspectives for Canada (Toronto: McClelland and Stewart 1980), 153- 78.

9   International Joint Commission, *Pollution of Lake Erie, Lake Ontario and the International Section of the St. Lawrence River* (Ottawa and Washington 1971). See, especially, Chapter 9. In the case of phosphates, for example, almost two-thirds of the discharge into lakes Erie and Ontario came from the u.s. side. In the case of total solids, the proportion was closer to 90 per cent.

10 For the texts of the 1972 and 1978 agreements see Canada and the United States, *Great Lakes Water Quality Agreement of 1972* (International Joint Commission 1974) and Canada and the United States, *Great Lakes Water Quality Agreement of 1978* (International Joint Commission 1978).

11 International Joint Commission, *Report on Great Lakes Water Quality* (Ottawa and Washington 1975), 1.

12 The argument was that delays in starting many treatment facilities were due not to the lack of funds but rather to the time required to put into place complex administrative regulations and financing arrangements. That the impoundment nevertheless had a significant impact has been confirmed by the head of Nixon's EPA. (Interview with William Ruckelshaus, former EPA administrator, Seattle, December 1979.)

13 For a fuller discussion of this concern and of the general tendency of Ottawa and Washington to 'reign in' the IJC when it appears to be encroaching on the prerogatives of the governments, see Don Munton, 'Paradoxes and Prospects,' in Robert Spencer, John Kirton, and Kim Richard Nossal, eds., *The International Joint Commission*, 60-97.

14 National Research Council, u.s. National Academy of Sciences and Royal Society of Canada, *The Great Lakes Water Quality Agreement: An Evolving Instrument for Ecosystem Management* (Washington, DC: National Academy Press 1985). The RSC-NRC report, the first ever such collaboration of the two countries' leading scientific organizations, was privately funded by grants from the William H. Donner Foundation (New York) and the Donner Canadian Foundation (Toronto).

15 International Joint Commission, *Third Biennial Report Under the Great Lakes Water Quality Agreement of 1978* (Ottawa and Washington 1986).

16 Theodora E. Colborn, et al., *Great Lakes Great Legacy?* (Washington, DC: The Conservation Foundation, and Ottawa: Institute for Research on Public Policy 1990), xxxviii.

17 Ross Howard, 'Industrial Pollutants,' B2. The very first mention by a Canadian politician of acid rain as a problem in Sweden seems to have been by then environment minister Jack Davis during a November 1969 speech at Columbia University.

18 Given that rain, snow, and dry particles can all deposit these acidic compounds, the term 'acidic deposition' is more descriptive. Given that

other substances, particularly toxic chemicals, are also emitted and transported long distances through the atmosphere and pose significant environmental hazards, the term 'long-range transport of air pollution'
(abbreviated LRTAP) is also used. Acidity is conventionally measured on the
PH scale, with low values being highly acidic.

19 Canada-United States Research Consultation Group on the Long-Range
    Transport of Air Pollutants, *The LRTAP Problem in North America: A Prelimi-
    nary Overview* (Ottawa and Washington 1979). This and a second Research
    Consultation Group (RCG) report (see below) were only the bilateral vehi-
    cle for other governmental and non-governmental studies ongoing at this
    time. President Carter had designated $10 million for acid rain research
    and Congress had authorized $68 million for similar purposes. The Clark
    government in Ottawa and the Ontario government both increased Cana-
    dian funding of acid rain research in this period.

20 See Canada-United States Research Consultation Group, *Second Report of
    the Canada-United States Research Consultation Group on the Long-Range
    Transport of Air Pollutants* (Ottawa and Washington 1980).

21 In a 1984 public opinion survey in Canada, carried out for the United
    States Information Agency (USIA), 66 per cent of the respondents agreed or
    strongly agreed with the statement that 'U.S. industries are the main cause
    of acid rain in Canada' (USIA study 18460, 3 October-8 November 1984).
    Although this view is, in fact, an over-simplification of the complex
    reality, it is not basically inaccurate. While Canadian sources of SO_2, such
    as the giant Inco Ltd. nickel ore smelting operation outside Sudbury, are
    by no means inconsiderable, they account overall for less than 50 per cent
    of the acid rain which falls in the Muskoka lakes region of southern
    Ontario, for example.

22 'Interview with John Fraser,' *Nature Canada* 9 (Jan.-Mar. 1980):14.

23 'Acid Rain: A Serious Bilateral Issue,' An Address by the Honourable John
    Roberts, Minister of the Environment, to the Air Pollution Control Asso-
    ciation, New Orleans, 21 June 1982. External Affairs Canada, *Statements
    and Speeches*, No. 82/11.

24 After taking a lower profile in the acid rain battle, McMillan eventually
    advocated a 'massive effort to influence U.S. public opinion.' See John
    Urquhart, 'Taking His Acid-Rain Fight on the Road,' *Wall Street Journal* (16
    October 1987).

25 See K. J. Holsti, 'Canada and the United States' in S. Spiegel and K. Waltz,
    eds., *Conflict in World Politics* (Cambridge, MA: Harvard University Press
    1971), 375-96.

26 The Canadian diplomats who began discussing the acid rain issue with
    their U.S. counterparts in the late 1970s talked with the official who had led
    the Canadian negotiating team on the 1972 Great Lakes Agreement.
    Moreover, the speeches of Canadian leaders advocating an acid rain

agreement often make explicit reference to the 1972 accord.

27 *Winnipeg Free Press* (7 February 1978).

28 During testimony at Congressional hearings on the Carter administration's coal conversion proposal, it was pointed out by witnesses or congressmen that the $400 million provided for pollution control would not be nearly sufficient for all the power plants involved, that many of the plants in urban areas did not have the physical space to install control devices, that the controls were not mandatory, that nitrogen oxides were not covered, and that the utilities were not even required to spend money from the $400 million fund for air pollution control equipment. See United States, House of Representatives, Committee on Inter-State and Foreign Commerce, Subcommittee on Oversight and Investigations, *Hearings on Acid Rain*, Ninety-Sixth Congress, Second Session (Washington: U.S. Government Printing Office, 26 and 27 February 1980), Serial No. 96-150; United States Senate, Committee on Environment and Public Works, Subcommittee on Environmental Pollution, *Hearings on Environmental Effects of the Increased Use of Coal*, Ninety-Sixth Congress, Second Session (Washington: U.S. Government Printing Office, 19 March and 21 and 24 April 1980), Serial No. 96-H45.

29 See William H. Megonnell, 'Atmospheric Sulphur Dioxide in the United States: Can the Standards be Justified or Afforded?' *Journal of Air Pollution Control Association* 25 (1975):9-15. On the economic pressures U.S. utilities are now facing see Sheldon Novick, 'Electric Power Companies: How to Pay More For Less,' *Environment* 18 (1976):7-12. See also the testimony of utility company representatives at the above-noted Congressional hearings.

30 *Globe and Mail* (6 August 1980), 1.

31 Several good analyses of the court battles exist. See Carol Garland, 'Acid Rain over the United States and Canada: The DC Circuit Court Fails to Provide Shelter under Section 115 of the Clean Air Act while State Action Provides a Temporary Umbrella,' *Boston College Environmental Affairs Law Review* 16 (1988):1-37; D.R. Wooley, 'Acid Rain: Canadian Litigation Options in U.S. Court and Agency Proceedings,' *University of Toledo Law Review* 17 (Fall 1985):139-51; John L. Sullivan, 'Beyond the Bargaining Table: Canada's Use of Section 115 of the United States Clean Air Act to Prevent Acid Rain,' *Cornell International Law Journal* 16 (1983):193-227.

32 For a Canadian view of this period see Stephen Clarkson, *The Reagan Challenge* (Toronto: Lorimer 1984).

33 *Cleveland Plain Dealer* (6 February 1982). See also the similar evaluation of a sympathetic congressman, Rep. Toby Moffett, reported in the *Toronto Star* (22 June 1981).

34 Ernest J. Yanarella and Randal H. Ihara, *The Acid Rain Debate: Scientific, Economic and Political Dimensions* (Boulder, CO: Westview Press 1985), 40.

The second bilateral Research Consultation Group report was eventually released in the fall of 1980.

35 Fitzhugh Green, 'Public Diplomacy and Acid Rain,' *University of Toledo Law Review* 17 (Fall 1985):133-9. Green added that: 'In any effective public advocacy effort the theme should be simple and clear-cut. The Canadian strategy was first-rate in this respect. They had oversimplified a complicated issue, and repeated the theme "stop acid rain" until they had received a positive result.'

36 It is worth noting that most of the European countries were willing to reduce emissions by up to 50 per cent. The 30 per cent target was determined by the Canadian government's unwillingness to reduce SO_2 emissions in the three most western provinces and by the Europeans' insistence that the chosen target figure be a national, not a regional, one. They were unsympathetic to a Canadian contention that western Canada's emissions were of little consequence to the North American acid rain problem. 'They just can't conceive of what a large country we have' noted a Canadian official. 'They could only deal with national figures.' Thus, while Canada was committed to reducing the emissions which lead to acid rain by 50 per cent in the region from Manitoba to the Atlantic provinces, it could not agree to any more than a 30 per cent reduction nationally.

37 Fitzhugh Green, 'Public Diplomacy and Acid Rain,' *Toledo Law Review* 17 (Fall 1985): 136.

38 Philip Jessup, *Strategies for Reducing the Cost of Acid Rain Controls: Electricity Demand-Side Management and Clean Coal Technologies* (Washington, DC: Environmental and Energy Study Institute 1988).

39 Confidential interview, Washington, DC, 14 October 1987.

40 Colin MacKenzie, 'Clean Air Act Nearing Deadline on Capitol Hill,' *Globe and Mail* (13 October 1990).

41 Confidential Interview, Environment Canada, October 1990.

42 The U.S. government might even justify inaction on SO_2 on environmental grounds. Recent studies have suggested that atmospheric sulphur dioxides increase the reflectivity of the earth's cloud cover and, thus, may counteract the trend towards global warming.

43 It might be argued that there are always environmental regimes of one sort or another. For instance, it might be argued that a pre-existing North American regime was based on the well-accepted principle of 'freedom to burn.' However, the authors believe that it is conceptually more useful to treat the pre-1909 situation as a 'null regime.' See Oran Young, *International Cooperation*, 21-2.

44 Ernst B. Haas, 'Words Can Hurt You; Or Who Said What to Whom About Regimes,' *International Organization* 36 (Spring 1982):208.

45 For an overview, largely, but not entirely, from an American social science

perspective, of a term and literature developed by Latin American Marxist scholars, see James Caporaso, ed., 'Dependence and Dependency in the Global System,' *International Organization* (special issue) 32 (1978).

46 The 'Agreement of Cooperation between the United States of America and the United Mexican States Regarding Transboundary Air Pollution Caused by Copper Smelters on their Common Border' was negotiated as a result of American concern over a new copper smelter in Nacozari, just south of the Rio Grande. The document is carefully worded so as not to contradict u.s. administration positions on the 'uncertainties' of long-range transport and, instead, focuses on environmental problems 'in the border area.'

47 Given the situation of environmental dependence described earlier, the dependent state has relatively little to offer at the bargaining table. And, unlike the accepted practices of international trade regimes which provide for retaliation in response to unfair trading practices, international environmental law provides no equivalent option. There are, thus, remarkably few avenues for penalizing an offending neighbour, short of attempting to increase transboundary pollution headed into the other state.

CHAPTER 13: MULTILATERAL INSTITUTIONS

1 For a fuller account see Sylvia Ostry, *Governments and Corporations in a Shrinking World* (New York: Council on Foreign Relations 1990), 25-30.

2 *Financial Times* (10 May 1990). The specific issue raised refers to cross-sanctions between GATT and GATS in dispute settlement.

3 See O. Long et al., *Public Scrutiny of Protection: Domestic Policy Transparency and Trade Liberalization*, Special Report No. 7 (London: Trade Policy Research Centre 1989).

4 Ostry, *Governments and Corporations in a Shrinking World*, 79-90.

Contributors

STEFANO BERTASI is a research associate at the Business Council on National Issues, Ottawa. His particular interests are in the areas of Canadian trade policy and European Community agricultural policy.

JAMES A. BRANDER is a professor in the Policy Analysis Division, Faculty of Commerce and Business Administration, University of British Columbia, Vancouver. He has published widely in international trade policy, industrial organization, and related areas. He is co-editor of the *Journal of International Economics*, a research associate of the National Bureau of Economic Research (NBER), and has written a widely used textbook entitled *Government Policy Toward Business*.

GEOFFREY CASTLE received his MA in Environmental Studies from York University, in 1991. He is currently researching policy approaches to hazardous waste management at the University of British Columbia's Sustainable Development Research Institute.

THEODORE H. COHN is a professor in the Department of Political Science, Simon Fraser University, Burnaby, BC. His research and teaching are primarily in the areas of international political economy and Canadian foreign policy. He has written extensively on global food and agricultural issues. His publications include *Canadian Food Aid: Domestic and Foreign Policy Implications* and *The International Politics of Agricultural Trade: Canadian-American Relations in a Global Agricultural Context*.

A. CLAIRE CUTLER is a research associate in the Institute of International Relations, University of British Columbia, Vancouver, and an assistant professor (limited term) in the Department of Political Science at Simon Fraser University, Burnaby, BC. Her interests are in the areas of international law and organization and international political economy.

MARTIN E. DRESNER is an assistant professor of Transportation at the University of Maryland College of Business. His research focuses on air transportation, and he has conducted a number of studies on the effects of competition on carriers and consumers. He has also provided testimony to the U.S. Congress on the economics of aviation safety.

JOCK A. FINLAYSON is vice president, policy and research, at the Business Council on National Issues, an Ottawa-based business association composed of the chief executive officers of 150 of the largest corporations in Canada. He has written extensively on such topics as international primary commodity markets, Canada-U.S. trade relations, and the GATT.

STEVEN GLOBERMAN is a professor in the Department of Economics at Simon Fraser University, Burnaby, BC. He has written extensively on telecommunications economics, including a recent book entitled *Telecommunications in Canada*. He has consulted for the private sector and government agencies, including Alberta Government Telephone, BC Telephone, Bell Canada, the Department of Communications, and the CRTC.

TREVOR D. HEAVER is the UPS Foundation Professor in the Faculty of Commerce and Business Administration at the University of British Columbia, Vancouver. He is also the director of the Centre for Transportation Studies. He has been active in research related to shipping policy and is a past president of the World Conference on Transport Research.

HUDSON N. JANISCH teaches torts, administrative, and communications law at the Faculty of Law, University of Toronto. He has a special interest in the regulation of telecommunications common carriers and has written extensively on regulatory law and policy. Recently, he has visited Japan on several occasions to lecture on Canadian telecommunications policy and to undertake research on the move towards liberalization in Japanese telecommunications.

GORDON R. MUNRO is a professor in the Department of Economics at the University of British Columbia, Vancouver. He has published widely on fisheries management issues, particularly those arising from Extended Jurisdiction, and is co-editor of the recently published volume, *Canadian Oceans Policy: National Strategies and the New Law of the Sea*.

DON MUNTON is an associate professor in the Department of Political

Science at the University of British Columbia. Formerly he was the Director of Research at the Canadian Institute of International Affairs and a member of the Department of Political Science at Dalhousie University, Halifax. He has written extensively on Canada-U.S. environmental issues and on the International Joint Commission. He is currently completing a book (co-authored with Geoffrey Castle) on acid rain and Canada-U.S. relations and is co-editor of *Debating National Security: The Public Dimension* and of *Canadian Foreign Policy: Selected Cases.*

SYLVIA OSTRY is Chairperson, Centre for International Studies, University of Toronto; Chairperson, the National Council of the Canadian Institute of International Affairs; and Western Co-chairperson, the Blue Ribbon Commission for Hungary's Economic Recovery. In 1989 she was Volvo Distinguished Visiting Fellow, Council on Foreign Relations, New York. Her most recent publications include *International Economic Policy Coordination* (with Michael Artis); *Interdependence: Vulnerability and Opportunity*; *The Global Economy: America's Role in the Decade Ahead*; and *Governments and Corporations in a Shrinking World: The Search for Stability.*

ROBERT K. PATERSON is a professor in the Faculty of Law at the University of British Columbia, Vancouver, where he teaches international trade law. He chaired a task force which advised the government of BC on the adoption of the United Nations' Model Law on International Commercial Arbitration and he is the author of *Canadian Regulation of International Trade and Investment* and co-editor (with B. Thompson) of *UNCRITAL Arbitration Model in Canada.*

RICHARD J. SHULTZ is a professor in the Department of Political Science at McGill University, Montreal. From 1982-90, he was director of the McGill Centre for the Study of Regulated Industries. He served on the General Services Sectoral Advisory Group on International Trade for both the Canada-U.S. Free Trade Negotiations and the GATT Uruguay Round. He is co-author of *Economic Regulation and the Federal System.*

W.T. STANBURY is UPS Foundation Professor of Regulation and Competition Policy in the Faculty of Commerce and Business Administration at the University of British Columbia, Vancouver. He is the author or co-author of more than 200 publications, many in the fields of regulation, competition policy, and privatization. In May 1989, Dr. Stanbury was awarded a UBC Killam Research Prize. He was also awarded the Professor Jacob Biely Faculty Research Prize for 1989. His latest books are *Canadian Competition Law and Policy at the Centenary* and *Historical Perspectives on Canadian Competition Policy.*

CHRISTOPHER THOMAS is a partner of the law firm Ladner Downs in Vancouver. He practises in the area of international trade disputes and regulation. He has taught as a professor in the Faculty of Law, University of British Columbia, Vancouver, and at the University of Ottawa.

MICHAEL W. TRETHEWAY is an associate professor of Transportation in the Faculty of Commerce, University of British Columbia, Vancouver. His research focuses primarily on air transportation. He serves as director of research for the Ministerial Task Force on International Air Policy and as a member of the Board of Advisors on Airport Transfers.

MICHAEL C. WEBB is an assistant professor in the Department of Political Science at the University of Victoria. He has published in the areas of Canadian trade policy and international political economy. His current research focuses on the implications of international economic integration for national economic policymaking and international policy coordination.

MARK W. ZACHER is Director of the Institute of International Relations and is a professor in the Department of Political Science at the University of British Columbia, Vancouver.

Index